The Mason County "Hoo Doo" War, 1874–1902

Previous Books in the A. C. Greene Series

The Santa Claus Bank Robbery
    by A. C. Greene

Where I Come From
    by Bryan Woolley

Life of the Marlows: A True Story of Frontier Life of Early Days
    Revised by William Rathmell
    Edited and Annotated by Robert K. DeArment

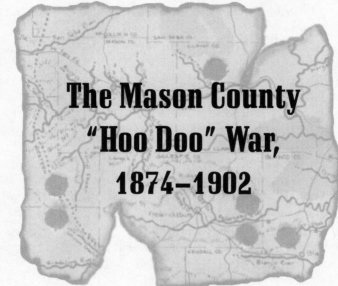

The Mason County "Hoo Doo" War, 1874–1902

by David Johnson

Foreword by Rick Miller

Number 4 in the A. C. Greene Series

University of North Texas Press
Denton, Texas

10 9 8 7 6 5 4 3 2 1

Permissions:
University of North Texas Press
P.O. Box 311336
Denton, TX 76203-1336

The paper used in this book meets the minimum requirements
of the American National Standard for Permanence of Paper for
Printed Library Materials, z39.48.1984. Binding materials have
been chosen for durability.

Library of Congress Cataloging-in-Publication Data

Johnson, David (David D.), 1950–
The Mason County "Hoo Doo" War, 1874–1902 / by David D. Johnson;
foreword by Rick Miller.
p. cm. — (A.C. Greene series ; no. 4)
Includes bibliographical references and index.
ISBN-13: 978-1-57441-204-8 (cloth : alk. paper)
ISBN-10: 1-57441-204-3 (cloth : alk. paper)
1. Texas Hill Country (Tex.)—History—19th century. 2. Vendetta—
Texas—Texas Hill Country—History—19th century. 3. Violence—
Texas—Texas Hill Country—History—19th century. 4. Frontier and
pioneer life—Texas—Texas Hill Country. 5. Texas Hill Country (Tex.)—
Biography. 6. Mason County (Tex.)—History—19th century. 7. San
Saba County (Tex.)—History—19th century. 8. Llano County (Tex.)—
History—19th century. 9. Burnet County (Tex.)—History—19th century.
I. Title. II. Series.
F392.T47J64 2006
976.4'605—dc22
2005026547

The Mason County "Hoo Doo" War, 1874–1902 is
Number 4 in the A. C. Greene Series

DEDICATION

This book is for my father, Charles Mahlon Johnson
May 19, 1918–September 10, 1999
and for my mother
H. Ruth Fergus Johnson.
Thank you for my life.

The Hoodoos

When the sun has set low, then the wind will die down
and darkness will fall across all Mason town.
You'll feel a slight trembling under your feet,
their horses are galloping out in the street.
Bolt your doorway securely, you best stay inside.
It's upon this night surely the Hoodoos will ride.
Coming for all those who have done evil deeds
are the faceless horsemen upon ghostly steeds.

If you have been hateful, if you have done wrong,
and have taken what to you, does not now, belong,
then pity your spirit and God save your soul,
for the Hoodoos are coming and they'll take their toll.
There can be no salvation when the Hoodoos ride
and with the next morning we will witness their wrath
as we survey a most grizzly aftermath.

Now time runs so short, for the light is near gone
and there is not a chance you can make it till dawn.
For the riders are waiting at the edge of the gloom
and there'll be no escaping when the darkness brings doom.
Pray you change your ways now and from trouble stay clear,
your life will be over when the Hoodoos appear.
With black-hearted actions your fate you will seal.
Once the Hoodoos have found you, you can make no appeal.

—Glenn Hadeler

Contents

Foreword by Rick Miller ix

Acknowledgments xiii

Introduction: "A War of Extermination" 1

Chapter 1: "Murderous Passions Unleashed" 7

Chapter 2: "Enough Money to Burn a Wet Dog" 18

Chapter 3: "Stock War!" 33

Chapter 4: "The Fright Hangs Over Us" 51

Chapter 5: "Another Horrible Murder" 64

Chapter 6: "Rance and Co.'s Band of Freebooters" 77

Chapter 7: "A Man of Large Connexions" 91

Chapter 8: "A Most Horrible State of Affairs" 105

Chapter 9: "Intervention Was Necessary" 119

Chapter 10: "Shooting Each Other With Renewed Energy" 133

Chapter 11: "I Think There Is Some Trouble at Hand" 149

Chapter 12: "More Blood" 164

Chapter 13: "The Gladden Trial" 181

Chapter 14: "A Thiefs Paradise" 194

Chapter 15: "Casting Out Devils" 206

Chapter 16: "A Shocking and Lamentable Sequel" 218

Conclusion: "A Bitter Cup of Suffering" 232

Appendix I 240

Appendix II 242

Appendix III 245

Appendix IV 250

Notes 252

Selected Bibliography 306

Index 319

Foreword

Following the Civil War, the citizens of Texas entered unsettling times as Reconstruction turned their routine world upside down. Elected officials were thrown out of office and replaced by political appointees who included a mixture of men ranging from competent to outright inept individuals. Slavery was abolished, but Texas citizen and newly freed slave alike were excruciatingly ill prepared for this new *modus vivendi*, leading to considerable conflict and violence that continued well into the next century. The infrastructure of government no longer provided the stability that had allowed farmers, ranchers, merchants, and professionals to thrive and prosper as they had prior to the war.

Once Reconstruction ended in 1872, communities had to begin from scratch in building a new infrastructure, finding competent public servants to work effectively under a new system and new laws. Add to this that Texas in the mid-1870s was still relatively primitive and communities were somewhat isolated from each other. The train was only now beginning to make inroads to meet statewide transportation needs, and the telegraph was a fragile line stretching from one point to another in order that communities could talk to each other. Further, Texas also had an unsettled frontier on its western fringes, where the Indian was still a very real threat and reports of murder and depredations almost a daily occurrence. Even though Texas was restored to its place in the federal Union, the military presence of the United States in Texas was only now being beefed up to actually contend with not only the Indians, but also Mexican raiders who regularly plundered from across the Rio Grande.

Certainly the mid-1870s were an uncertain time as the state grappled with getting back on its feet, and the strongest quality available to local communities to insure survival in the interim was that of self-sufficiency. There was no effective law enforcement capacity at the local level that could cope with much more than handling the local drunks, collecting taxes, and attending the courts when in session. Thus, when an outrageous crime occurred, or depredations in a community were at a level that severely taxed or overwhelmed the resources available to the local sheriff, there was seldom any other recourse except to resurrect a vigilante movement. News reports in Texas throughout the 1870s are replete with accounts of mobs stepping in to administer summary justice in place of the established system. Accused prisoners were forcefully taken from jail cells, sometimes with the connivance of local officials, and hanged, shot, beaten, and burned. Most of the time they were probably guilty—sometimes they weren't.

With such a fragile hold on civilization in these communities, it is not difficult to understand how "blood feuds" could occur—and occur they did. Although sometimes the origins of a feud are hard to pin down, often it was the perception by one group of people that it had been wronged by another group of people, and one thing generally led to another until killing was routinely taking place. Texas experienced feuds all over the state, especially in its central part. The late Dr. C. L. Sonnichsen ventured into these areas in the 1930s to dig out first-person accounts of the feuds—a gutsy thing to do since bad feelings stemming from those feuds were still simmering and such details were nothing to discuss with a total stranger—leading to probably the best works on feuds.

The better-known and probably bloodiest feuds were the Sutton-Taylor affair in DeWitt and Gonzales Counties, and the Mason County War, which spilled over into Burnet and Llano Counties. Both feuds accounted for a considerable body count, and occurred about the same time. It took the intercession of the newly reorganized Texas Rangers to confront the violence and to help reestablish some modicum of domestic tranquility. In fact, it might even be said that Ranger involvement in these feuds helped cement the reputation as a tough, unyielding law enforcement agency that it enjoys today.

The end of these feuds also essentially marks that approximate point in time when the social controls of a civilized society once more took hold in Texas, and the gunfighter and mob more likely to be held accountable for their crimes. No longer could lynchings and assassination be committed with as much impunity as before—although they did continue to occur.

In the wake of his successful research into the life of Mason County combatant, John Ringo, Dave Johnson has focused on the Mason County War and all of its bloody details in an attempt to give insight as to the factors and dynamics that caused the ongoing dispute. That conflict was unique in that there was a predominantly ethnic divide involved: German immigrants against "Americans." The accepted view is that the German-supported mob initiated the bloodshed to defend what they believed were encroachments on their property—in this case, cattle—in a manner that was time-honored in its European roots. The response was predictable, and the violence escalated.

In locating information about the Mason County War, Johnson has proven a diligent researcher. He tells the story with the help of contemporary newspaper accounts, letters and diaries, and official reports. The origins of the participants are gleaned, and future researchers will not have to reinvent the wheel in order to continue analyzing the affair. For those who are interested in cutting through myth and legend about these long-ago events, Johnson has documented his sources to establish this book as the definitive work on the Mason County War, as well as a case study in frontier violence of the bloodiest kind.

Rick Miller

Harker Heights, Texas

Acknowledgments

Many people helped in the preparation of this book. Among those who deserve thanks, for this effort as well as others, are a triumvirate of historians whom the author values both as friends and colleagues. Both Rick Miller and Chuck Parsons are well-established historians and friends whose knowledge of Texas has proven invaluable time and again. A very special thanks is also due to the guru of archivists and researchers, Donaly E. Brice, who shared his extensive knowledge of Texas and the Texas State Archives without stint. An extra special thanks must go to Claire Brice who not only opened her home to the author but tolerated a horde of researchers descending on her with their minds fixed firmly on nineteenth-century Texas. Also to Ieva Johnson, my wife, who so often recognized the far off look in my eyes. Special thanks also to Jane Hoerster and Johnie Lee Reeves, who gave unfailing support for the project. Beatrice Langehennig, Diane Pence, Joy Kitchens, and Linda Phillips helped far more than they can imagine tracking down ancient records in the Mason County Courthouse, and Karylon Russell was a godsend in Llano County. Nina Olney helped greatly in fleshing out both Olneys and Tanners. Glenn Hadeler shared not only his research but the poem he wrote years ago on the feud.

In compiling this book for publication a number of interviews and significant correspondence has taken place. Those of particular help include, but are not limited to, Bob Alexander, Francis Blake, Vickie Bonner, Joyce Capps, Foster Casner, Tommy Clark, Ina Davis, Joan Buck de Korte, Karen DeVinney, Julius DeVos, Thomas and Susan Doell, Marvin Doyal, R. L. Faith, H. V. "Todd" Faris, Gary Fitterer, Paralee (Mrs. J. C.) Foster, Jo Ann F. Hatch, Clay Lake, Betty Marglon Henning, Era Fay Huff, Jeff Jackson, Norma Karter, Nina Legge, Sarah Lockwood, Dennis McCown, Milton McWilliams, Mrs. Lou Metcalfe, Paula Oates, Jerry Ponder, Michael Redding, David Leer Ringo, Pete Rose, Karylon Russell, George Mack Taff, LaVoy Taylor, Don Watson, Iru Zeller, and Scott Zesch.

Last, but hardly least, is Ronald Chrisman, director of the University of North Texas Press who asked the type of questions that have made this a better book. Without all of you this book would not have been possible.

Introduction

"A War of Extermination"

Lying north and west of Austin, the Texas Hill Country is a rugged, hilly area encompassing roughly thirty-six counties. The area features high plateaus and deep gorges cut by streams and rivers. Much of it is semiarid. One early settler described a part of the Hill Country as having "vast cedar brakes, the abode of wild animals innumerable. . . ."[1] It was a harsh land, and it bred hard men. During the late nineteenth century it was the scene of the most bitter feud in Texas history.

The Hoo Doo War occupies a unique place in feud history. It began in the early 1870s with the intention of protecting the families, property, and livelihood of the largely agrarian settlers in Mason and Llano Counties. These ideals quickly degenerated into a bloody vendetta of personal vengeance. The feud grew and spread like a cancer, and as it spread it evolved taking on new forms and causes long after the original warriors had withdrawn from the field. The final cases were not dismissed until the early 1900s. By then many of the fighters were either dead or too old to maintain the violence, but the prejudice and ethnic hatred that it spawned in the region lingered long after the feud had burned itself out.

On the national stage, the feud itself had no significant impact. Unlike the vicious Lincoln County War in New Mexico, no federal investigator was dispatched to investigate the wrongs, real and imagined, that fueled the violence.[2] It did not have the international ramifications that Leander H. McNelly's invasion of Mexico in the 1870s brought with it.[3] Nor was it rife with partisan politics like the infamous Sutton-Taylor War.[4] There were little, if any, undercurrents of Reconstruction animosities. Both Mason and Burnet Counties had voted to remain in the Union, and Llano voted to secede by only a narrow margin. Most

1

of the men involved were too young to have fought in the Civil War. Those who had had all fought for the Confederacy. Yet the feud remains unique in Texas history, one characterized by the reluctance of the "law and order" forces to discuss their role in the feud while the so-called "outlaws" made no claims to secrecy in their identities or actions.

During the 1870s vigilante groups were common throughout Texas. In this, Mason and Llano Counties were no exception. Following the Civil War, cattle represented money to a cash-poor South, but the industry far outpaced the laws governing it. The law was inadequate to deal with cattle thieves, particularly on the frontier, and Mason County was the frontier. When the feud began Anglo outlaws were not the only problem. Indian raiders struck the area along with Mexican bandits from south of the border. When the mob formed, the intention was to protect their livelihood. Had it remained so the feud might well have burned itself out and provided only an interesting footnote to Texas history. That it did not was due to the underlying ethnic prejudice that existed among the German settlers of eastern Mason County and those ranchers whom they dealt with.

At the outbreak of the feud the Mason mob was comprised almost exclusively of German settlers, commonly referred to at the time as the "Dutch," a corruption of *Deutsch,* German, that made up the bulk of the "mob" or "law and order" faction.[5] On the other side were the "Americans," or "outlaws" as they are still referred to in Mason County.[6] While anti-German sentiment flourished following the Civil War, this ethnic prejudice separated Mason County from other counties with a large German population. No other Texas county having a large German population was involved in a feud along ethnic lines. Only the El Paso Salt War of 1877 involved ethnic hatreds as intense. The conflict was the most bitter feud in Texas history, and the animosity in the area persisted until well after World War II.

Dr. C. L. Sonnichsen, the first historian to seriously study and record Texas feuds, understood clearly that they are complex, living things that evolve over time. They are, as Sonnichsen states, "really a return to the oldest code known to man—the law of private vengeance." It is a concept as old as man summed up in Mosaic law as "an eye for an eye, and a tooth for a tooth." Feuds do not suddenly flare up. "When two people quarrel bitterly on Monday, the chances are that they were not any too fond of each other on Sunday. . . . No man undertakes a war of extermination just because he hasn't anything else to do."[7]

The feud was an outgrowth of complex and varied factors that have been oversimplified by historians and writers. C. L. Douglas ascribed its origins to cattle theft and the murder of Tim Williamson in 1875.[8] Sonnichsen also noted these causes, but pointed out the significant ethnic aspects of the feud.[9] These were exasperated to a small degree by personal vendettas and Civil War animosities. Incompetent and corrupt legal officials and poor laws provided cause as well. Ultimately the feud itself began as a pursuit of money and power. In the end the fighters were left with only their hatred. The fact that most of those involved were basically decent and honest did not save them.

There were ample opportunities to turn from the path of destruction, but the opportunities were squandered. Had the well-intended *Adelsverein* been better informed and listened to prudent council rather than thinking that their station made them experts in colonization, the immigration of German settlers to Texas would not have left an underlying resentment against Meusebach and the Texans who had preceded them to the Hill Country. Had Karl of Solms-Braunfels been more concerned with the safety and wellbeing of the German colonists and less concerned with maintaining ethnic purity, the German settlers would never have been left to die in disease-ridden Karlshafn. Had Governor Richard Coke acted decisively when the first pleas for help came from Mason the feud could have been largely averted. He did not, and contemporary evidence suggests that he was more concerned with maintaining votes and power than with justice.[10] Had both sides tried to understand the other, the feud could have been avoided.

All of it was avoidable. Even as the feud began there were voices of peace, voices that were drowned in the rising tide of hatred and violence. The forces that move men had led them to this moment of history, and they seized it with both hands. Between 1874 and 1893 violence and fear ruled the Hill Country. The pain and grief that accompanied the violence are incalculable and marred their lives forever. In its wake was left a legacy of shattered families, hatred, and bitterness evident to this day. During a visit to Texas in 1984 a grandson of one feudist told the author that he would still ride with the boys if the feud were going on. Others expressed their resentment on behalf of men who had been dead for over a century. One man felt that it would still be a good idea to "burn out the Dutch." In Mason many still refer to the opposing faction as outlaws, and historical markers note this throughout the town. During World War I the German citizens of Mason were forced to renounce the German language in favor of English due to the national prejudice, some of which evolved from the feud. At times they were accused of disloyalty to the United States, an accusation far from the truth.

Unlike other feuds, the Hoo Doo War was not simply a breakdown in law and order. Both sides believed themselves in the right, and descendants of men on both sides of the conflict still believe they were in the right. At the outset of the feud there was much law and little justice. By the end of the feud there was neither law nor justice. Mobs, no matter how well intended, deteriorate over time. Mobs such as those in Mason and Llano, contaminated from the outset by the criminal element, were corrupt from the beginning. In time they believed they were above the law and felt that any threat to them justified violence. The attacks on Tom Gamel and Al Baird are examples. By the time the German ranchers renounced mob activity the feud had gone beyond their ability to control it. Violence bred violence, and for every man who fell, more were drawn into the conflict.

The feud began as violent forces converged in the Hill Country. The resulting maelstrom spread, engulfing whole families and drawing them into the abyss of destruction. Families were destroyed, women widowed, children orphaned. Some families abandoned their homes and fled for safer climates. In the end there were no winners, only losers to various degrees.

The feud's evolution is marked by key events. Following the election of Sheriff John Clark in December 1873, things began to change in Mason. While the records for 1874 are fragmentary, it appears that open hostility not only to cattle thieves but nonresident stockmen as well was on the rise. At least one man was killed and another wounded, but the key event was the arrest of M. B. Thomas and his men in August 1874 while they were gathering their cattle. Angered, the ranchers brought charges of robbery and false imprisonment against Clark and the entire posse, most of whom were German stockmen. This escalated hostilities, and over the months that followed more men were killed and local ranchers who renounced mob action were threatened.

The murder of Tim Williamson in 1875 and the lack of action in bringing his killers to justice brought Scott Cooley into the feud for the first time. Cooley, no stranger to violence and personal vendetta, changed the feud into a bloody quest for revenge. Even then the feud might have played itself out, but Sheriff John Clark, failing to find Cooley, retaliated against the cattlemen who had charged him with robbery the previous year. The intended target was probably George Gladden, the man whose testimony could have proved that Thomas and his men were not stealing cattle. Gladden survived the ambush, but his companion Moses Baird did not. Baird, a well connected and popular man, brought others into the war and until the death of Peter Bader in January 1876, Mason County lived in terror.

Bader's death and the subsequent withdrawal of Baird and his allies should have ended the feud. It did not. To the east, in neighboring Llano County, the mob continued the violence against both cattle thieves and Baird's allies. It was not until the Llano battle of 1882 that the citizenry, tired of the continual bloodshed, brought the Llano mob to an end. Organized mob activity ended at that time although it is possible, but not certain, that the war in neighboring San Saba County was an offshoot of this feud. It was another decade before the last killing was committed, and another decade after that before the final charges were dismissed.

There are lessons that should be learned from the Mason County War, but the lessons are ancient ones that should have been learned centuries ago. The philosopher George Santayana wrote that those who do not learn from the past are doomed to repeat it. In this sense there was no difference between the feud and the bloody conflicts of Scotland, Ireland, and the Balkans. It is a prime example of how good men make bad decisions and how ethnic hatred is ultimately self-destructive.

The feud was heralded as the Mason County War or Mason County Disturbances to the general public although it was never confined to Mason County. Locally it has always been known as the Hoo Doo War, a more appropriate appellation in many respects. While the feud had its origins in Mason County, it remains unclear if the mob in Mason was organized first or if the one in Llano holds that distinction. What is certain is that long after the fighting ceased in Mason, the feud continued in neighboring Llano County.

The origin of the term Hoo Doo has been lost in history. One common account is that following one of the killings a freedman questioned "Who do it?" and the name stuck. There is some merit to this story, for Sonnichsen notes that the term Hoo Doo was applied to "members of a vigilance committee" and that in other parts of Texas the name was applied by freedmen to the infamous Ku Klux Klan.[11] In the early phases of the feud the mob wore masks as did the Klan. The name was also applied in a more positive manner to Lee Hall's company of Texas Rangers.

> The bad were united by a proneness to violence, while the good were so intimidated that each sought immunity for himself by condoning or apparently applauding the wrongful acts of the dominant element, thus in effect adding to its strength.
>
> But the "Hoodoos," as the gallant Hall and his rangers were called, came. They came several times, and placed themselves before the public by acts, entitling them to the gratitude of Texas. . . .[12]

Alternatively the term Hoo Doo may have derived from voodoo, a practice introduced into Texas by slaves.

> VOODOOISM —Austin has a colored doctor named J. M. Donalson, who, for many months, has suffered the pangs of voodooism. He says that the influence of Christine Thomas, a yellow woman, and a white woman who calls herself Lea, has been visited upon him, and though he has doctored faithfully, he is still afflicted, though he expects to get much better at the next change of the moon. Doc says these woman poisoned some water from which he took a drink, and he warns all people against them. The Legislature ought to pass a bill making it a penitentiary offense for any woman to visit upon citizens the horrors of voodooism. This thing of poisoning people with the ashes of dead people is worse than stage robbery or horse stealing.[13]

The term itself has connotations of trouble or bad luck. The Texas Hill Country during the late nineteenth century had an abundance of both.

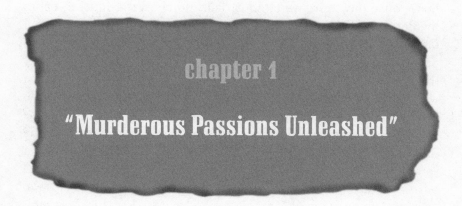

chapter 1

"Murderous Passions Unleashed"

Arriving in Texas during the 1840s, German immigrants left behind them a land composed of a patchwork of kingdoms, duchies, and principalities steeped in feudal tradition and dominated by Austria and Prussia. Following Napoleon's defeat of the German states, social reform had come with the abolition of hereditary serfdom and the establishment of municipal rights for cities for the first time. A system of elementary and secondary education was created, and citizens could now stand for civil offices.[1] The impact of these reforms was apparent to the German colonists. Older members of the families could recall serfdom or knew of it from their parents. Most were the first generation to receive a public education. All of them knew how disunity in Germany had led to defeat and humiliation by the French.

Social reforms notwithstanding, the living conditions in Germany were harsh. Lich writes that "Jobs were scarce, and laborers were poorly paid. Taxes were oppressive, and few people had more money than was required to buy the most essential necessities." Compulsory military service prevailed at that time providing fodder for seemingly endless wars.[2] In overpopulated areas, farms were fragmented to a critical level. Inheritance laws in northeastern Germany prohibited division of farms, and younger sons had to find what work they could in a job-poor market that paid only minimum wages. Farmers were poorly paid for their produce, and barter became an accepted practice due to the general lack of money. Women could only marry, but there was nowhere for them to start a home once they were wed. Industrialization posed a direct threat to the cottage industries that provided farmers with their supplementary income.[3] Moreover, with Napoleon's defeat, the German rulers began a program of vigorous repression to stamp out the sparks of freedom and reform.

Against this backdrop of misery a group of nobles organized the *Verein zum Schutze deutscher Einwanderer in Texas* (the Society for the Protection of German Immigrants in Texas) commonly known as the *Adelsverein* (League of the Nobility) in April 1842 with the view of settling Germans in Texas.[4] After considering the 4000-acre Nassau farm as a colony, the site was rejected because it was "too close to existing American towns for the Germans to be able to preserve their identity."[5] In its place the *Adelsverein* chose the Fisher-Miller Grant for colonization.[6] It was a poor decision that cost dozens of lives. Testifying in 1893, John O. Meusebach[7] stated:

> With the buying of that grant the doom of the company was sealed. They did not know what they bought. They undertook to fulfill what was impossible to fulfill. They did not have the means nor the time to fulfill it. Neither of the contracting parties nor their agents had ever seen a particle of the land in question. The territory set aside for settlement was more than three hundred miles from the coast, more than one hundred and fifty miles outside of all settlements, and in the undisturbed possession of hostile Indians.[8]

The group's first commissioner, Prince Karl von Solms-Braunfels arrived in Texas in 1844. Concerned with maintaining ethnic purity, he decided against using Galveston to disembark the settlers. Instead, he purchased a tract on Matagorda Bay initially christened Karlshafn (Karl's Bay) and later renamed Indianola. Aside from its isolation there was little to recommend it. German colonist Carl Blumberg wrote that the area, infested by mosquitoes and rattlesnakes, was the "cemetery of the poor German" where families rested "under the open sky, subjected to the bad influences of an unhealthy climate, putrid drinking water, and frequent rain showers." Summers were particularly bad "when dysentery, typhus, chills [malaria?], dropsy and other serious illnesses" plagued the area taking "such a heavy toll that often families of eight to ten persons are wiped out in a few days."[9]

Frederick Law Olmsted, following a trip through Texas in 1856, also noted the deplorable conditions at Karlshafn. "The country had been stripped of provisions, and the means of transportation, by the army. Neither food nor shelter had been provided by the association. The consequences may be imagined. The detail is too horrible. The mass remained for months encamped in sand-holes, huts or tents: the only food procurable was beef. The summer heat bred pestilences."[10] Into this gulag poured the families that would form the Mason County mob.

Believed by some to be one of the mob's organizers, Ernst Jordan arrived in Texas shortly before Christmas 1845 with his wife Wilhelmine (Minchen) and daughter Johanne Ernestine Wilhelmine. Accompanying them were Jordan's half-sister, Hannchen, her husband Johann Heinrich Kuchuck and their daughter Johanne.[11] The abnormally rainy winter of 1845–1846 proved a bitter one. Dirt roads were impassable in areas, trapping the colonists in the pest hold that was Karlshafn. During the first months Jordan's wife and sister died. In despair, Kuchuck gave his daughter to a family named Olkers that he had known in Germany and left.[12] Spring brought better conditions, but with the outbreak of the Mexican War in May 1846, transportation became unavailable as teamsters were pressed into government service. Writing in 1931, Gilbert Jordan reflected his grandfather's bitterness. "The United States Government hired all available teamsters to haul supplies for the soldiers, paying such high wages that the Society could not afford to hire teamsters to transport the immigrants." Jordan added further that the teamsters hired by the Adelsverein to transport them to New Braunfels "repudiated their contract."[13] The Kothmann family also recalled that the army requisitioned wagons noting that later in the year the "Torry" [sic: Torrey] brothers were hired to perform the transport but soon entered government service.[14]

Heinrich Conrad Kothmann arrived in Texas during the winter of 1845–1846 with his wife and five children.[15] Like Jordan, the Kothmann family had good reason for bitterness over the "betrayal" by the American teamsters due to the death of their daughter Caroline. As with Jordan, there are reasons to believe that the family had links to the Mason mob. When Jordan purchased a wagon and oxen with his limited funds and headed for the grant lands, it appears probable that he was accompanied by the Kothmanns.[16] By 1847 both families had reached Fredericksburg, the final staging area for departure to the Fisher-Miller grant. Here they became acquainted with another man who has been linked to the mob, Prussian-born Johann Heinrich Hoerster.[17]

Conditions at Fredericksburg proved little better than at Karlshafn. Food was in short supply, and when the U. S. Army established Fort Martin Scott in 1849, impoverished German children often went there for food. Fritz Kothmann recalled that he and his brother, Dietrich, would walk eleven miles from Fredericksburg to the fort where they gathered "corn that was wasted in feeding the army horses" that they took home to make bread.[18] This is confirmed by Heinrich Julius Behrens. Interviewed around 1920, Behrens stated, "Some days [we] didn't have anything to eat and very little to wear." He and other boys would each take a stocking and walk to the fort where they picked up grains of corn that the oxen and horses had scattered while they were eating. The kindly soldiers "would finish filling our pockets and stockings with corn."[19] The situation was so bad that seven men, including Ernst Jordan, Gottfried Bader, and Ernst Dannheim, once walked from Fredericksburg to New Braunfels armed with clubs and demanded supplies.[20] Fritz Kothmann never forgot his childhood poverty and spent the rest of his life in pursuit of wealth.

Famine was not the only unwelcome companion that accompanied the German settlers to Fredericksburg. With it came Karlshafn's epidemics. At New Braunfels one of the first public buildings erected was an orphanage to house children who had lost their parents. It was here that Jordan's daughter Mina died on November 5, 1846.[21] During the winter of 1846–1847 a mob led by Rudolph Iwonski demanded Meusebach's removal and a replacement named to head the colony.[22] The revolt failed, as did a similar mob action at Fredericksburg.[23] At Fredericksburg, Meusebach was presented with a petition dated January 17, 1847, urging him not to resign for the good of the colony. It was signed by ninety-five settlers including some whose families are known to have been involved in the Hoo Doo War such as Gottfried Bader,[24] Johann Adam Keller, Johann Keller, and Conrad Pluenneke. Notably absent are the signatures of Ernst Jordan, Heinrich Hoerster, and Heinrich Kothmann.[25] Meusebach did resign on July 20, 1847.

His efforts had saved the colony, but resentment against him lingered. In time the mob moved against him, and only his stature in the community saved his life.

It was not until the 1850s that the German colonists began moving into the Fisher-Miller grant due to the protection offered by Fort Mason in what is now Mason County.[26] Jordan, Kothmann, and Hoerster arrived at *Oberwillow* (Upper Willow) Creek in 1856. They were soon joined by Ernst Dannheim, Heinrich Hasse, Otto von Donop, Fritz and Christoph Leifeste, Julius Lehmberg, Melchoir Bauer, and Conrad Pluenneke. Across the Llano-Mason line to the east Gottfried Bader settled near what is now Castell. By this time the *Adelsverein* had collapsed in financial ruin.[27] The venture had failed to settle a single colonist in the grant lands and left its promises unfulfilled. The Germans were not ignored, however. The state provided a land grant to each settler.[28]

From the beginning, neither Mason nor Llano was a purely German settlement. American settlers, lured by the opportunity to provide a better life for themselves and their children, had preceded them into the area. William S. "Uncle Billy" Cox is credited with being the first settler in the Mason area, arriving around 1846.[29] When Fort Mason was established he worked as a blacksmith during the construction. Another early settler was a bachelor named Blaylock who had settled along Willow Creek prior to the arrival of the Germans. Soon after their arrival in the area he moved on due to "crowded conditions."[30] Other settlers in the area included Isaac Jones, who had family ties to combatant John Ringo, William Gamel,[31] Matthew Doyal,[32] Jim Bolt and members of the extensive Caveness clan: Jerry, Ed, and Bob.[33]

The presence of Americans on lands promised them by the *Adelsverein* was a sore point for some of the German settlers. The "betrayal" by American teamsters and the subsequent settlement of them in lands promised to the colonists created resentment and bitterness. Many of the Germans were left with a lingering suspicion and animosity toward their American neighbors. This is reflected by several writers who blamed the feud's origins on the jealousy of American latecomers. A. L. Lang reported:

> A shrewd old German, seeing the potentialities of
> this [Mason] county, sent for a number of his relatives

and friends in the Fatherland. They came over and the
Germans established a colony on the fine grasslands
of Mason County. Within a few years most of them
were prosperous stock raisers. There was a native element in Mason County, too, and soon an ill feeling
arose between it and the Teutonic population. As the
county developed many of the natives began to feel
that the Germans had no right there, and that they
should go back to the land from which they came. [34]

Another author adds: "Their [the German's] frugality allowed them
to build bigger and better homes as they prospered, particularly after
the war ended. The Americans scratched out a living on a small dry
land farm, living usually in an undersized house with little prospect of
their life improving."[35]

Neither of these statements is supported by contemporary evidence. What they do reflect is ethnic prejudice between the Germans
and Americans from the German point of view. More visionary men
such as John Meusebach "recognized that the future welfare of the
settlers depended upon their becoming 'Americans'." Many of the
colonists were not as visionary.[36] Lich notes:

> [T]he German newcomers were generally better ed-
> ucated and more widely read than their American
> counterparts; they were tradition-bound and preferred
> their old ways to the new. To them, Americans were
> friendly, but also rambunctious and often vulgar. The
> Germans tended therefore to remain silent and apart
> from their new countrymen, without meaning to give
> offense . . . . [37]

Max Krueger, a peripheral figure in the feud, noted that "The Germans
living in their respective settlements generally confined their intercourse to their own compatriots and did not take part in any except
local politics. They kept true to their native virtues and faults."[38] Emma
Altgelt, another German pioneer, wrote that "The inhabitants intermin-
gle little with Americans," adding "The Germans are not so enterprising as the latter, but they are steady and industrious."[39] Jordan speaks

of "occasional opposition to these 'damn Dutch immigrants'."[40] This clannishness was recognized and resented by the American settlers. George Bernard Erath, an early immigrant from Wurtemberg, alluded to this in his memoirs, recalling that "Americans have been surprised at my association here with Americans alone, and regarding the German not as a fellow-countryman, but simply according to his behavior as a citizen of the United States or of Texas . . . ."[41]

Despite the underlying prejudice, Mason County's organization in 1858 reflected a cross-section of the ethnic community. John McSween was elected chief justice and George W. Todd county clerk.[42] L. Burgdorf was assessor and collector, H. R. Biberstein surveyor, and B. T. Weatherby treasurer. Mason's county commissioners were Heinrich Hoerster, Stephen Peters, H. F. Keyser and J. M. Allen. Thomas R. Cox, W. C. Lewis, and Otto Donop were elected justices of the peace. Thomas S. Milligan was the first elected sheriff, succeeding Fritz Kothmann who had been appointed acting sheriff prior to the election.[43]

Whatever resentment the settlers had for one another was eclipsed by the necessities of maintaining the community and survival itself. The area was the hunting grounds for the Comanches, horse lords of the plains. Calling themselves the Nauni (first alive or alive people), they had conquered this land decades earlier. For a time the land remained firmly in their hands, and from them the Hill Country took its original name: Comancheria. Meusebach had negotiated a peace treaty with them that, combined with the presence of Fort Mason, proved successful in maintaining peace for some time. By 1859 peace ended and attacks on the settlements began in force. The same year Wilhelm Hoerster, Heinrich's fifth son, was captured by Kiowa raiders while herding horses. Hoerster was lucky, for he was ransomed in the infamous Valley of Tears in New Mexico for a mule and returned to his family.[44] The same year, Jonas Dancer was killed in Llano County.[45] Sheriff Thomas W. Milligan was killed within two hundred yards of his house by raiders on February 19, 1860.[46] In August 1860, rancher John Bolt, possibly a brother of William James Bolt, accompanied by five men, went in pursuit of raiders who had stolen some horses. Bolt was killed in the fight. At the same time, another band struck Willow Creek and drove off nearly all of the horses, including those of the Hoersters, Jordans, and Kothmanns.[47]

These raids served to unite the community as evidenced by the *San Antonio Daily Express* of July 14, 1872, when prominent citizens offered $500 in gold "for the first hostile Indian captured within the limits of Mason county, Texas, by any person or persons from any county or place, without regard to age, sex, color or previous condition of servitude, and delivered dead or alive at the Courthouse in Mason." Thirty-six individuals pledged funds including Tom Gamel, Daniel Hoerster and his brothers, Tim Williamson, John Gamel, Franz Kettner, John Meusebach, William Gamel, George W. Todd, and David Doole. Absent from the list were Ernst Jordan and the Kothmanns.

Even as Comanche raids increased in ferocity, war loomed to the east. Following the election of Abraham Lincoln, Texas voted to secede from the Union on February 23, 1861. Mason County was among the minority of counties that voted against secession. The garrison at Fort Mason pulled out in March 1861, taking with it the protection they had provided the community. Herman Biberstein gathered a force of Minute Men to provide some security. Among the recruits were Karl Lehmberg, Dietrich Kothmann, Frederick and Wilhelm Hoerster, Thomas Johnson, and Ernst Jordan. All of these men would later be involved in the feud.[48]

In Austin a paranoid state government viewed the German settlements as a potential threat to the Confederacy. Troops were sent to combat Indian raiders, but in some cases they proved worse than the Indians themselves. The Hill Country became an area of savage guerrilla action. From the Rio Grande Valley Union loyalists raided deep into Texas. Deserters and Unionists banded together for protection, and outlaw gangs added to the chaos. Lily Klasner reported that in 1862, shortly after her birth, a man arrived at their cabin in Mason County. "He was a formidable looking person who wore pistols in open holsters on either side and carried a rifle."[49] The man attempted to rob them but was driven off by Mrs. Casey at gunpoint. Klasner believed that he was a Unionist "outlaw," but he could well have been one of the state troops sent to protect them. William Banta, who served for the Confederacy in the area, was arrested with six other men by Major James Hunter after Hunter took charge of frontier defense. Following the war Banta was one of twenty-five men indicted for mob murders in neighboring Gillespie County. He was not convicted.[50]

1862 saw the controversial Nueces River Massacre in Kinney County when twenty-eight Germans were killed by Confederate troops, nine of them after they had surrendered. German historian Don Biggers called the action "a crime unjustified by even the rules of savage warfare."[51] In June 1864 Mason residents Ludwig "Louis" Martin and Eugene Frandzen were hauling freight to the Rio Grande when they were intercepted near Eagle Pass and lynched with their own ropes.[52] Family tradition recalls that Martin's wife knew the killers were neighbors who had followed him. Fearing retaliation, she refused to identify them.

The war and its aftermath further polarized and hardened men on both sides of the feud. Writing of the South's surrender, Douglas Hale notes that "Considering the murderous passions unleashed by the war, it was a generous peace . . . . "[53] In Texas these murderous passions remained unleashed, and Reconstruction did little to keep them in check. The war left animosities that lasted for decades. Sonnichsen writes of the era that "the post-Civil War Period brought feud troubles in Texas to their climax of blood and hate . . . ."[54] Historian Rick Miller concurs. "The post-Civil War era in Texas spawned a political and social upheaval."[55]

While many, if not most, of the Reconstruction officials in Texas attempted to perform their duties impartially, there were abuses. One such case was an incident in Burnet County involving Brack Thomas, David Epley, Ulysses Howard, and Thomas Johnson who were charged with killing a dog. The men were indicted and bail set at $200 each. On October 23, 1868, Johnson, Thomas, and Epley were brought to trial. Both Johnson and Epley were found not guilty by the jury. Thomas was convicted and sentenced to pay a fine of one cent.[56] Howard did not appear for trial and the case against him was eventually dropped.

Had the citizens along the Texas frontier believed that the war's end would bring a return of the military and protection from Indian raids, they were soon disillusioned. Concerned with protecting freedmen in east Texas, the army had little sympathy for the settlers. Following the military's seizure of the state government under the Reconstruction Act in 1867, the situation further deteriorated.

Even as the government pursued its dog-killing case, Indian raids in the Hill Country continued with relative impunity. One of the hardest hit families was that of Frank Johnson, a friend and ally of the Gamel family. On October 12, 1867, Johnson rode out hunting horses. Normally a cautious man, one grandson later recalled that "He had no gun with him, and grandmother often said she guessed that was the only time my grandfather ever went away from home without his gun." Johnson did not plan to be gone long and must have reasoned that he would not need a weapon. It was a mistake, and on the frontier a single error was sufficient. The evidence suggests that he found both the horses and the Indians who had stolen them. His body was found the following day filled with arrows.[57] His wife Betsy insisted on moving the family back to the relative safety of Llano County where they would be closer to relatives and in a more protected area. On the evening of February 5, 1868, a band of sixteen raiders struck the Johnson home. Five of the family were killed and two children carried into captivity. One woman was left for dead by the raiders. The Legion Valley massacre was the worst raid in Llano's history.[58]

In Mason County animosity over Reconstruction was intense. George W. Todd, who had been elected county attorney, was removed from office by the federal authorities and replaced by James E. Ranck. Adam Keller, elected sheriff the same year, was later replaced by Dietrich Kothmann. Kothmann was in turn replaced by James J. Finney. In 1872 Finney was reelected sheriff on his own. The year also found Francis Kettner[59] Inspector of Hides and Animals, but it would not last. On January 18, 1872, Ben Gooch, James Ranck, and W. P. Lockhart, the county treasurer, wrote to Reconstruction governor E. J. Davis claiming that Kettner was "bold and bitter" against Republicans and requested his removal in order to install Wilson Hey in his place.[60] The move was apparently successful, for on March 4 James M. Hunter, Kettner's deputy, referred to Kettner as "the former Hide and Cattle Inspector." Hunter went on to state that the appointment of Hey was objectionable since he was also serving as Deputy County Clerk and was in the employ of "B. F. Gooch & co. in a large cattle company."[61] Also rallying to Kettner's defense was A. Liemering of San Antonio who stated that Kettner "was a good republican" and controlled the Republican vote in the county.[62]

It was a move that did not sit well with all Mason residents. Writing of the feud in 1875, a correspondent who identified himself as "Dreux" reported:

> The origin of the trouble is this: The control of the finances and offices of the county has for many years been in the hands of two or three shrewd, crafty and dishonest men, who have "got away" with a large amount of the county and State taxes, by which means, as well as by having a very dishonest cattle inspector of the county under their dictation they have become measurably rich. Two years since all this was broken up and changed by the election of Clark as sheriff, and an honest inspector of cattle, Hoesster [*sic*: Hoerster]. . . . [63]

Political extremism was not confined to one party, however. In a letter dated February 9, 1874, George W. Todd stated that Finney was a Radical Republican while Clark was a good man, and a Democrat.[64] Aside from the unfounded accusations of Dreux, no stigma has been attached to either Kettner or Finney. The others accused by Dreux of corruption were James E. Ranck and the Bridges family, all natives of Indiana. Ranck is considered by some as the Father of Mason, hardly a title warranted by a corrupt official.[65]

These charges were a reflection of Civil War animosities, but underlying them was a desire on the part of large ranchers to control the cattle trade in the area. Reconstruction inflamed the situation, creating hostility along political lines. The dormant prejudice budded into open hatred. It would soon blossom into murder.

"Enough Money to Burn a Wet Dog"

Texas is considered by many the original home of large-scale ranching. In part this is confirmed by the 1860 census that reported 3,533,768 domestic cattle.[1] Factoring in wild cattle, the actual total was far greater. Cattleman George W. Saunders recalled: "At the close of the Civil War the soldiers came home broke and our state was in a deplorable condition. The old men, small boys and negroes had taken care of the stock on the ranges and the state was overstocked, but there was no market for their stock . . . ."[2]

While Texas had been left unravaged by the war, the state was impoverished. Money was in short supply, and the cattle trade was largely unprofitable.

> But the year 1866 was, taking all things into consideration, one of great disaster to Southern drovers. All of the great prospects of marketing, profitably, the immense surplus live stock of Texas, faded away, or worse, proved to those who tried branding a serious financial loss. So the last great hope of the Southern cattle man, for an outlet and market for his livestock, proved but bitter disappointment. Never, perhaps in the history of Texas, was the business of cattle ranching at so low estate as about the close of the year 1866 and during the following year. The cattle producing portions of the State were overrun with stock.

> The ranges were becoming depastured, and, as a
> consequence, the unprotected earth became parched
> by the hot sun, and permanent drouth threatened.
> The stocks of cattle would not yield sufficient revenue
> to pay the expense of caring for them -- that is, brand-
> ing, marking, etc. [3]

The trade was saved by Joseph G. McCoy. McCoy envisioned supplying the eastern markets with Texas beef using the railroad and was
successful in establishing a railhead at Abilene, Kansas. On September
5, 1867, the first shipment of cattle headed east. The ready market
brought the dawn of a new era for Texas, and for nearly two decades
herds went up the trail. Fortunes were made and lost during those
years. Mason County cattleman John Gamel was recalled by old tim-
ers in Dodge City as a "flamboyant, forceful Texan" who celebrated
at the end of cattle drives by lighting cigars with ten dollar bills, de-
claring that he had "enough money to burn a wet dog."[4] As early as
1867, Fritz and Karl Kothmann, Fritz and Karl Lehmberg, and Christel
Winkel drove a herd to New Orleans "only to find that the market was
off. The men were forced to sell the hides and tallow. By 1869 they
had recovered from this financial loss. That year Fritz and Dietrich
Kothmann, Karl Keller, Conrad Pluenneke, Daniel Hoerster, Rudolph
Eckert, Otto von Lange and Lace Bridges drove a herd successfully
from Mason to Fort Union, New Mexico."[5]

Mason County, with its abundant grass and natural draws for protection from the cold, was ideal cattle country, and following the war
its principal industry was cattle raising. Early Mason County cattlemen included John W. Gamel, Karl Lehmberg, C. C. Smith, George
Bird, William Wheeler, Fritz and Heinrich Kothmann, Ernst Jordan,
Karl Lehmberg, Heinrich Hoerster, and Conrad Pluenneke. J. Marvin
Hunter noted that "many of the drovers became wealthy during their
operations" adding that "It was during this cattle driving period that a
bloody feud broke out in Mason county between certain factions, during which a number of citizens were killed. This feud is often referred
to as the 'Hoo Doo War,' and is still fresh in the minds of some of the
older citizens."[6] Bierschwale reported that "Except for outside interfer-
ence the business would have been an easy and enjoyable one; Indians
and cattle thieves were the worst menaces of the early days."[7]

Texas was open range during the 1860s and 1870s. Cattle drifted as they pleased with total disregard for either range rights or county boundaries, and it proved difficult, if not impossible, to separate unbranded herds. Brand laws were county-based, and in theory two men could record identical brands in adjoining counties such as Llano and Mason. Range law was looser, and mavericking, a practice where any unbranded cow or maverick older than a year belonged to whoever caught and branded it, was both common and legal. McCoy said of the practice:

> The ownership of the young animal is determined by the brand of its mother. . . . It is . . . a universal practice to capture any unmarked and unbranded animal upon the range and mark and brand the employer's brand, no matter to whom the animal may belong, so be it is over one year old and is unbranded.
>
> It is easy to see that any energetic, enterprising ranchman can greatly increase the number of his stock by this means . . . . [8]

Accommodation marketing made the problem worse. A herder who found a neighbor's cattle in his herd was expected to sell them and reimburse the owner, a practice that depended strictly upon the honor system.[9] Mason County's geography also worked against it. Henry Doell Jr. informed Sonnichsen that the cattle would drift from eastern Mason to the western valleys. "Had there been no rustlers at all, many a cow would have disappeared of her own accord."[10]

Many ambitious men got their start as maverickers, and it was not until the 1880s that the practice was regulated. Karl Lehmberg had a standing offer of five dollars a head for unbranded calves that Sonnichsen felt "was bound to cause trouble."[11] Perhaps, but Lehmberg was neither the originator of the practice nor the only rancher to post such an offer. Dobie notes that the practice was common along the Gulf Coast.[12] Robert Baxter, an early drover, recalled that when he worked in eastern Texas "Some of the stockmen had a standing offer of five dollars a head for any of these wild ones [wild cattle] a cowboy could catch and deliver back to the herd. . . . It was not uncommon for ranchers to offer their drovers five dollars a head for mavericks branded in the outfit's name."[13] In Mason, Daniel Hoerster also paid a drover named Daniel Hester five dollars a head for unbranded calves.[14]

Inevitably the practice led to violence. Practiced by all ranchers, as maverickers established their ranches they began to look askance at enterprising drovers following in their footsteps. Cattle were big money, and the larger ranchers accused smaller ones of stealing their cattle. Small ranchers retorted that their accusers were attempting to dominate the range. Cattle wars such as the Karnes County uprising in 1875 and the Johnson County War in Wyoming during 1892 were common. Lynching abounded, and all too often justice was perverted by powerful men with money. In time the term mavericker became synonymous with cattle thieves or "rustlers."[15] In Mason and Llano Counties the focus of many was on both small ranchers and nonresident stockmen. The nonresident stockmen accused local ranchers of refusing to let them take possession of cattle that they owned. The locals insisted that their counterparts were stealing cattle.

The lure of easy money and lax law enforcement drew professional stock thieves to the region. The Hill Country was the frontier, and stock thieves congregated in the area. Sonnichsen writes that "Organized bands of these human coyotes were at work even before the Indians were neutralized, ranging up and down the frontier and running off small bunches of livestock."[16] Determining who these thieves were is complicated by the burning of the Mason courthouse in 1877 and the Llano courthouse during 1892. Some of the sources survived, and from these and other records a portrait of cattle theft in the region can be constructed.

Among the major players in the area was James M. Riley, better known to the public by the alias Doc Middleton. Riley favored horse stealing over cattle theft, and because of the lack of court records, it cannot be concluded what his role was, if any, in the thefts that plagued the area.[17] In Llano County, colorful Rube Boyce was also considered an outlaw. Although he was never convicted of cattle theft, lawman Dee Harkey recalled his association with Boyce during 1876: "Boyce had a bunch of thieves around him, and they would go out and steal cattle or anything else they could dispose of . . . ."[18] Others considered him "the worst outlaw since Sam Bass."[19] He was certainly one of the most intriguing.[20]

Another well-known family in Llano County was that of Mart Blevins. Well known in the area, Martin J. "Mart" Blevins was one of the men who recaptured Cynthia Ann Parker from the Comanches. Blevins and two of his sons, Hamp and Andy, were indicted in Mason County on charges of horse theft, although the dates of the indictments are unknown. The family eventually moved to Arizona where they are best known for their involvement in the cattle war between the Graham and Tewksbury families.[21]

The most noted gang in the Hill Country during this time was led by Frank Eastwood. Eastwood was living in Kerr County during 1870 at the home of James Johnson, no known kinsman of the Johnsons in Mason County. The census notes he was twenty-eight, born in Texas, and gave his occupation as stock raiser.[22] Both he and Johnson had fought for the Union during the war in the First Regiment, Texas Cavalry Volunteers.[23] Following the war, Eastwood almost immediately began coveting his neighbors' livestock. As early as 1867 Frank Eastwood was indicted for theft of a mare in Williamson County, and during 1870 he was indicted on numerous charges in Kerr County, including theft of a steer, illegally branding and driving cattle, and shooting cattle.[24] Nor was he a stranger to Gillespie County, which wanted him on nine counts of cattle theft during the same year.[25] By 1872 he was actively gathering a gang, and hard cases flocked to the area.[26] Rancher Tom Gamel recalled that the gang employed a "chain raid system" and ranged from Junction to Austin. The gang was targeted by state police and "it was discovered that there were nineteen members of this outlaw gang who had become suspicious and upon their hunch moved on to Kendall County." In 1872, a squad under the command of Nimrod J. Miller located gang member Bill Bell who had killed a man in another county. Bell discovered their presence and was shot by Miller when he attempted to escape. He died later.[27] His death did not deter others from attempting to join Eastwood. Among them were Bill Longley and the Ake brothers, Jeff and Bill.

> Last Friday [*sic*: Wednesday, July 14, 1873] a party of suspicious looking characters (four men and two women) passed through Kerrville traveling in the direction of the "Headquarters." A few hours after, the Sheriff of Mason county accompanied by several

deputies arrived at this place. He had been following them for some time. With the information gained at this place and with the assistance of the Sheriff of Kerr county and the parties who had been successful in arresting other members of the gang, proceeded to a place about 13 miles above this, where they found them encamped for the night. After surrounding them they rested until nearly day-break, when they were quietly informed that they were prisoners. They evidently had not heard of the trouble that their "pals" had met with and were proceeding as they supposed safely and with[out] suspicion to their den.

The names of those arrested and held were Jeff and Bill Ake (brothers) and a man named Longley . . . . [28]

The trouble referred to proved Eastwood's last. On June 29, 1873, following his arrest for murder, a mob took him from jail during the early hours. His body was not found until the following day. He had been shot seven times, and in the violence that followed a number of the gang were killed. The Ake brothers and Longley were freed. The Akes played a minor role in the Hoo Doo War. One paper reported at the time "that the notorious horse thief, Ake" had been arrested in Mason County, concluding that "This scoundrel should have been in the penitentiary years ago."[29] Longley remained at large until he was captured and hung for murder on October 11, 1878.

The largest haven for thieves was in Kimble County west of Mason. Historian Peter Rose notes "West of the Hill Country the Edwards Plateau in the 1870s was a wilderness savanna, uninhabited precisely because there was no permanent water, no reliable streams—and no law."[30] Relatively unknown today, these outlaws plundered the area with relative impunity. Some disguised themselves as Indians during these raids. One posse from Burnet County pursued a band of Indians into Llano County where they killed one and captured half a dozen others who "were recognized when the Indian color was removed by the application of soap and water."[31] It is small wonder that local citizens rose in righteous indignation.

Another of those accused of cattle theft in the area was noted in an interview conducted by C. L. Sonnichsen with Henry Doell Jr.

on July 12, 1944. Speaking of the cattle problems, Doell related that "The cattle didn't want to stay on the east side of the county but alwa[y]s drifted back up into the valleys to the west. Creed Taylor and his crowd were living up there just waiting for the cows to come to them."[32]

Notably, Sonnichsen made no reference to either Creed Taylor or his "crowd" in his work on the Mason troubles although he did in the context of the Sutton-Taylor War. Writing of Taylor, Sonnichsen reported that during the late 1860s Taylor had begun ranching "on the edge of the Indian country near Fort Mason. . . . They did not have the reputation of being interested in other people's cattle when such distinction was rare."[33] This directly contradicts Doell despite the fact that Sonnichsen's interviews for his study of the Sutton-Taylor War extended into 1949, five years after Doell's interview. The reason lies with Creed Taylor himself. Taylor was one of Texas' early heroes, and Dr. Sonnichsen may well have questioned his involvement in cattle theft, particularly since it was the only such accusation made against him.[34]

Just who Doell meant by Creed Taylor's "crowd" is uncertain. Certainly the charge would have included his two oldest sons, John Hays and Phillip DuBois Taylor. The evidence concerning the brothers suggests that Sonnichsen was correct in his assertion that they took no interest in their neighbors' cattle, but they were far from angelic. The Taylors first came to prominence following the Civil War when Hays killed Major John A. Thompson in Mason on November 14, 1867.[35] Both of the brothers were killed before the feud began in earnest. Doell's accusation is significant however, reflecting the bias that existed against nonresident stockmen during the 1870s in Mason County.

Outlaws were not the only threat to ranchers. Among the boldest thieves were Indian raiders. On November 17, 1869, a party struck the area, brazenly riding into the town of Llano and stealing three horses "within forty feet of Captain Gid Cowan's door." The raiders rode off in the direction of Fredericksburg even as another band struck Burnet County, killing a man named Marion Smith.[36] The following year they hit the ranch of Rance Moore in late November. A man named Harris was returning to the house and ran for the safety of the cabin but was shot in the head and killed. The situation was saved when "Mrs. Moore, having put on a man's hat and coat came out with a shotgun, firing at the Indians and driving them away."[37]

The raiders returned in 1871, stealing horses from J. D. Bridges, John Gamel, and Thomas Murray, among others.[38] The following year was worse still when the Indians killed James Sewell and James Bradberry in April.[39] The primary targets of these raids were horses, and it is understandable that most accounts of the time dealt with horse theft. The raiders also killed and drove off cattle. Hermann Lehmann, captured by the Apaches in 1870, soon joined them on raids in the Hill Country. In his memoirs he recalled one raid, this one west of Fort Sill, where a herd of cattle estimated at 1,000 head was stolen. The men drove the cattle back to their village where they traded them to the Comancheros.[40]

Reports of outlaw and Indian activity in the Hill Country during the early 1870s were common. One paper reported that "The white outlaws from Lampasas, in connection with Indians, are thought to be plundering in San Saba county." The same issue reported that Ramon Rios had organized eighty men to raid into Texas from Mexico.[41] Mexican bandits such as Rios' men raided as far north as the Hill Country. This is evidenced by a letter from Mason to the *San Antonio Daily Herald* dated May 25, 1875. The writer reported that "Indians and Mexicans are making a fearful raid in our part of the country just at this time, stealing our property and killing our citizens. . . . Two-thirds of the stealing from this country is done by Mexicans direct from Mexico." The author stated that "The year the war closed three hundred Mexicans drove 15,000 head of cattle from San Saba river and they have been driving each and every year since."[42]

These conditions created the "tidal wave of rustling" noted by Sonnichsen.[43] All of this was well known at the time. With the exception of the Ake brothers, by Jeff Ake's own admission, none of these men has ever been linked to the Hoo Doo War. Not a single memoir located to date dealing with the feud makes any mention of these outlaws or others of their ilk. On the contrary, from the beginning of the feud, ranchers in Mason accused cattlemen in all of the counties surrounding them of cattle theft. In short, the mobs' focus was not on cattle thieves but on nonresident stockmen who did not live in the county but who owned livestock there. Cattle that remained within the county had calves that the local ranchers could acquire.

The Hoo Doo War pitted a predominantly German population, at least in Mason, against their American neighbors. Historian Glenn

Hadeler advanced the theory that an element of religion was involved that created a profound difference between the Mason residents and other Germanic groups.[44] This is confirmed by the residents themselves. Jordan writes, "The Fredericksburg German element was and still is more fun-loving, more easy-going than the Mason County Methodists. The Fredericksburgers love their *Gemutlich Keit*, their easy-going disposition and geniality, as much as the Mason County Methodists love their piety."[45] This pious clannishness was noted by Max Krueger who remarked critically that he found them "very clannish, and a newcomer was not welcomed."[46]

This hostility separated the Mason Germans from both their Anglo neighbors and from neighboring Germans. The conditions in neighboring Gillespie County were virtually identical to those in Mason. Gillespie County, predominantly German from its beginning, never engaged in organized mob activity during the feud despite the outrages that occurred there during the Civil War years. Given these factors, it appears that the conflict never involved cattle theft. Rather, it began as a power struggle for control of the range and illicit use of the nonresident cattlemen's herds.

Unlike their Llano County counterparts, the Germans who made up the "mob" element in Mason remained largely silent about their involvement in the feud. One local historian expressed his belief to researcher Pete Rose that the mob leaders in Mason were Ernst Jordan, Heinrich Hoerster, Fritz, Dietrich, and Wilhelm Kothmann, the Bader brothers, Pete and Karl, and Karl Lehmberg.[47] Historian Glenn Hadeler independently reached similar conclusions.[48] This theory is supported by Brown in his classic study of vigilantes and violence: "Today, among educated men of standing, vigilantism is viewed with disapproval, but it was not always so in the nineteenth century. In those days, the leaders of the community were often prominent members of vigilante movements and proud of it."[49]

These theories have a great deal of merit. Vigilantes in the 1870s were organized generally to protect home and property by the good men of the community, men who emerge as leaders, not the dregs of society. Certainly this is true of many of the men noted. Ernst Jordan was a natural leader, having served ably in both public office and positions of responsibility.[50] His leadership is demonstrated by the speed with which he was able to raise men in 1874 to ride to

Mason. The family recorded that "During all the trying times he stood and fought for right and justice and the establishment of an honest and lawful government in the new country."[51] This phrase is as close to an admission of involvement with the mob as most of the German participants provided.[52]

Fritz Kothmann was also a leader in the community. The most dominant of the brothers, Kothmann served in a number of public offices. Prior to Thomas Milligan's election on August 2, 1858, he served as interim sheriff when Mason County was created. Six years later he was elected sheriff in his own right in August 1864, but resigned after only two months. In June 1866 he was elected county commissioner. He did not hold public office again until late 1875 when he was elected Justice of the Peace for Precinct 3, the Willow Creek area.[53] Unlike his brothers, he never admitted to any role in the feud, but it is highly unlikely that the leader of the brothers remained aloof from the fighting while, by their own admission, both Dietrich and Wilhelm Kothmann were involved.

Dietrich Kothmann also served a brief term as sheriff of Mason County. He was appointed on June 9, 1869, by General J. J. Reynolds' Special Order 136 during Reconstruction. He served only until October 1869 when James J. Finney was appointed in his place. Of Dietrich Kothmann, family members wrote: "All peace-loving citizens were called to arms, and a war followed in which several men were killed. Fortunately, Dietrich Kothmann escaped. Rangers were finally sent out by the Governor, and these soon rid the country of the desperadoes and put an end to the disturbances.[54]

Wilhelm Kothmann also admitted his involvement in the feud: "When in 1874 the Hoodoo War broke out, . . .William Kothmann joined the side which stood for law and order."[55]

Unlike his brothers, Wilhelm had not held public office. The Hoersters had, however. Heinrich Hoerster was elected one of the first county commissioners in 1858 and was reelected in 1860, 1862, and 1864. His son Fritz was appointed sheriff on October 6, 1864, to fill Fritz Kothmann's term and served until August 28, 1865. Daniel Hoerster was elected brand inspector in 1873. The Hoerster family, unlike other Germans in the area, did not distance themselves from their American neighbors. Heinrich Hoerster worked closely with all his neighbors, and the family was respected by both communities. An early cattlemen, he routinely shared information with his contemporaries.

> We learn from Mr. H. Hester [*sic*: Hoerster], a citizen of Fort Mason, who is on his return from Kansas, that there is now 200,000 head of Texas cattle in the neighborhood of Ell[s]worth, Kansas. The highest price now paid is from $17 to $18, and, as a consequence, there are very few sales. This is bad news for Texas stock owners. Should the c[h]olera reach Kansas, it will result disastrously to the stock interest.[56]

Heinrich Hoerster was charged by Henry Doell Jr. as being a member of the mob that lynched the Backuses in 1875.[57] Doell was not the only person to level the accusation. German author, Christopher Hagen, published a novel on the feud called *Gebrandmarkt* following his interviews with several residents of German descent. While admittedly a work of fiction, Hagen intimated that the Hoersters were involved with the mob: "The sheriff related to Betty [Hoerster] what had taken place the previous night [and] although the sheriff was sure that the Hoerster brothers had been implicated in the lynching, he had no positive proof and did not make any arrests.[58] Heinrich Hoerster was one of the farsighted men of his time, and there are indications that his family was one of the first to break with the "law and order" faction.

Unlike the Hoersters, Jordan, and the Kothmanns, the Bader brothers were never leaders in the community. Karl Bader married Hoerster's daughter Katherine after the death of her first husband, Karl Kothmann, in 1870. His involvement in the feud was mainly in a supportive role. His older brother Peter, reportedly a killer for the mob, had a more tarnished reputation.

Peter Bader first encountered the wrong side of the law during 1870 in Kerr County when he shot a hog belonging to Charles Ackse. Bader was charged with malicious mischief but was apparently able to convince the jury that he had intended no harm to Mr. Ackse. He was found not guilty on October 22, 1870.[59] This was not Bader's only encounter with the law. In October 1875 he and August Grenwelge were charged with theft of hogs in Llano County.[60] Records available on Bader indicate curious stock transactions. The 1870 census, taken before his marriage to Augusta Wilhelmina Rossberg, indicates that he was working as a blacksmith and living at his father's home. Within two years he declared livestock amounting to fifteen horses and 200 head of cattle.[61]

Another man of the Peter Bader stripe in the area was Fritz Thumm.[62] Characterized as "aggressive and domineering" with "a propensity for emotional violence," Thumm's involvement in the feud is highly probable, though not as a leader since he had no standing as a man of influence in the community.[63] In stark contrast, no hard evidence linking Karl Lehmberg to the mob has been located. On the contrary, Lehmberg, a prominent rancher in western Llano County, was a friend of Tim Williamson and other men opposed to the "law and order faction."

Some of these men still resented Americans from the time of their "betrayal" at Karlshafn. Some of them had already engaged in vigilante activities. American encroachment on what they viewed as their lands was galling, and it took little to convince them that outsiders, particularly Americans, were behind any problems that they might encounter. Mentally they were prepared to believe the worst. The problem with identifying them as mob organizers lies in the fact that the Mason mob largely disbanded early in the feud, abandoning the battleground to their enemies who swarmed over the area for months afterwards. If they had been its organizers, the fight against John Baird and his allies would have continued. That it did not indicates that, while they may have occupied roles of leadership, they were not the driving force behind the mob.

The mob's creator would have been prominent in the community, a man of authority, someone who was persuasive and whom the community trusted and respected. Such a man was Sheriff John Clark, and his entry into Texas at this time proved pivotal in the feud. Without his presence, it is highly unlikely that the Hoo Doo War would have reached the epic proportions that it did.

Sheriff John Clark has proven one of the most elusive major figures in the feud. This is in part due to the presence of at least thirteen other John Clarks living in the area during this time. Until recently, the most likely candidate was John Rufus Clark, born to Isaiah Clark and

Sarah Elizabeth Low on May 24, 1849, in Missouri. This identification, based largely upon the belief of family members, has since proven erroneous.[64] Research by noted historian Jerry Ponder has unravelled the mystery that is Sheriff John Clark.[65]

John E. Clark, a former Confederate officer, was the son of William and Mary Elizabeth Worley Clark, born around 1834 in Callaway County, Kentucky. His mother's maiden name, Worley, is Anglicized from the German Wohrle, and this may indicate a tie to Johann Anton Wohrle who served as a deputy sheriff for Clark.[66] By 1856 or 1857, Clark had moved to Ripley County, Missouri. Here he served as deputy sheriff and deputy county clerk. When the Civil War broke out, Clark enlisted in the state militia. He was wounded in the leg and captured at Pulliam's farm in December 1863. He was then imprisoned at Camp Chase near Columbus, Ohio. Here the military records concerning him are confused with three other John Clarks. Following his release there is a notable gap in his life until 1870 when he arrived in Burnet County, Texas, to visit his old friend Adam R. Johnson. Clark remained until 1871 when Johnson noted simply "Clark gone to Llano."[67] Later he moved to Mason County where he found employment as a deputy sheriff under M. V. Bridges in 1872.

Clark proved a controversial figure. Writing in 1875, a correspondent identifying himself as "Peter" stated that stockmen charged Clark with "using his office to persecute his personal enemies."[68] Texas Ranger Dan Roberts referred to him somewhat contemptuously as one of the "blue hen's chickens": a former Confederate who sided with the Reconstruction government.[69]

Clark enlisted as a private in Company R of the Minute Men from Mason County under C. C. Smith on December 9, 1873, serving until February 24, 1874. With him in the unit was Heinrich Hoerster's son Daniel. There is also some speculation that he is the same John Clark who served in Company N of the Minute Men in San Saba County from September 13, 1872, to October 20, 1872. This remains speculation at present. Clark had twenty-five days of service in Company R. No service was recorded for his brief tenure in Company N if indeed this is the same John Clark.[70]

Clark was elected sheriff of Mason County in December 1873. His term of office was inaugurated by controversy when Sheriff James J. Finney initially refused to yield the office.

Mason, Texas, Feby. 9th 1874

Governor Coke,

Allow me to state a few facts. Our former sheriff J. J. Finney was notified by his securities that they would not stand for him any longer, he was notified by Co Court to give new bonds, failed to do so. Office declared vacant, election ordered, John Clark elected, date of his qualification sent to you. Finney (former sheriff) refuses to turn over to his successor Clark on account of latter not having his commission.

Clark has complied in all respects with the law but feels a delicacy to act without his commission. Finney full Blown Radical, Clark a good man and Democrat. I have resided here for 20 years, refer you to Judge A. S. Walker, Judge David Shuks, Thomas S. Devine & c. Hope you will commission him at once and can only request that you issue to him his commission if compatable [*sic*].

I am Very Respt.
your obt. servt.
G. W. Todd [71]

Todd's support indicates that he had successfully insinuated himself back into the group holding power. When Clark took office is unclear, but it was probably around the end of February of 1874 when he left Company R. It was an inauspicious beginning. His term of office proved even more controversial. Correspondent Peter wrote:

The Germans, who as a class are farmers, and have small gentle stocks of cattle, accused the stock men of stealing their cattle, and complained that the courts afforded them no protection. The stock men on the other hand assert that many of them were maliciously indicted and prosecuted without cause. They also charged that Clark, the sheriff of Mason county, was using his office to persecute his personal enemies. The other side claim that Clark was a good man and an effective officer.[72]

Clark's effectiveness as a lawman is open to question. One source of information is the prison records for Huntsville Penitentiary. Between January 1, 1874, until the end of his term of office, only one man was sent to the penitentiary from Mason County. This was Miguel Escobel who was convicted of theft.[73] Among the responsibilities of a sheriff is to not only make arrests but to provide the evidence to obtain convictions. While the penitentiary records do not include convictions that resulted in fines, the notable lack of convictions certainly calls into question Clark's effectiveness as a lawman, particularly so considering the number of raiders roaming the area. No records have been located indicating that Clark engaged in any fighting against either Mexican bandits or marauding Comanches. Nor have any records been found illustrating a single major arrest of known outlaws. Rather, the entire focus of his term in office revolves around the pursuit of nonresident stockmen and the Hoo Doo War.

Clark had barely taken office when the killing began. Under the banner of STATE NEWS one newspaper reported "Mr. Morrison, in Mason county, was shot to death a few days ago, by a party of unknown men."[74] Nothing further about this murder has been located, and Morrison's death in late April or early May 1874 remains a mystery having marked similarities to the murder of Tim Williamson a year later. It was an omen of things to come.

Like most prophecies, it went unheeded.

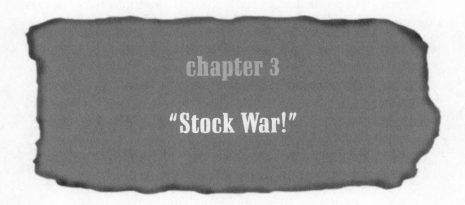

chapter 3

"Stock War!"

Records from the early 1870s illustrate the growing animosity over cattle once the trade became profitable. Mason County's problems began during Reconstruction. The successful removal of Franz Kettner as Hide and Cattle Inspector for Mason County during 1872 was an early attempt to dominate the cattle trade by Ben Gooch, a rancher with widespread cattle interests. In this, Mason County was not unique in either the state or the region. As early as 1871, Llano County stockmen petitioned the government for prohibitions on mavericking, noting in part that "We would further represent that there are many persons Killing Calves in the woods and Marking & Branding calves & yearlings who are known to own no Cattle of any description whatever."[1] In San Saba County, county officers asked Richard Coke "for an organization of some kind of armed force" for protection against "hostile Indians & other marauding parties" who were "continually depredating" on the property and lives of the citizens.[2]

The marauding parties referred to by San Saba officials included both mavericks and nonresident stockmen. The practice of mavericking, entirely legal at the time, posed a threat to established cattlemen, most if not all of whom had gotten their start in the same way. These men generally were looking to start their own ranches, and the increased competition for unbranded cattle and the money they meant. In many cases the mavericks actually worked for nonresident stockmen. Among these, all linked to the Hoo Doo War, were Daniel Hoerster, Karl Lehmberg, and A. G. Roberts.

Roberts was particularly assertive, purchasing small herds in various counties. In Llano County he came under the scrutiny of the mob. Miles Barler, an admitted mob member, reported:

> There was a man by the NAME OF ROBERTS, who came in here and bought up a few little stocks of cattle just to get a claim on the range. He then hired about fifty outlaws and regular desperadoes, and they gathered nearly everything on the range and drove them off to Austin and San Antonio and sold them for what they could get and would divide up the proceeds among themselves and then come right back and get another herd. The people would indict them but they would swear for each other and get out of it every time.[3]

Barler's memoirs are important and provide details about the feud that cannot be found elsewhere. As with those of any feud participant, they reflect a partisan view and must be used with caution. Barler provably falsified, either by omission or commission, some events of the feud and created others out of whole cloth. When he wrote his recollections during the late 1890s he was under the belief that all of the court records pertaining to the feud had been lost. He was mistaken.

Records for both Llano and Mason Counties during this time are fragmented, and a clear picture is difficult to determine. The surviving District Court records for Llano County have numerous charges of cattle theft entered on the docket. In many cases, A. G. Roberts served as surety for the defendant, an indication that the men may have worked for him. One such case was Peter Rainbolt, indicted August 23, 1873, for illegally branding and marking a yearling.[4] Other names linked to the feud were also charged with cattle theft. Among these were Sugar M. Cain,[5] Heinrich Hoerster, Karl Lehmberg, Joe and John Olney, William Murchison, Ike Pryor, Thomas S. and William Z. Redding, and James Williams among others.[6] While the details of the cases are generally lacking, in some instances the circumstances can be determined with clarity.

Mason County cattleman Heinrich Hoerster was indicted in Llano County on August 22, 1872, for purchasing and driving cattle to market without road branding them. The case dragged on into 1873 and was eventually appealed. The court records here are somewhat unclear, but it appears that the Hoerster may have been indicted with others in the German community. "The state by her attorney excepts to the court. Defendant required to enter into recognizance on appeal, and defend. Henry Hoerster & F. Ostrich [sic] and F. A. Grote and Otto Lang in the sum of $500." Hoerster's appeal was disallowed on September 11, 1873.[7] As late as 1875 the case was being continued. The existing documentation remains uncertain if Friedrich Oestreich, Fritz Grote and Otto Lang were codefendants or bondsmen for Hoerster.[8]

In other cases details provided from extant sources prove deceptive. The *1878 Fugitives From Justice* notes that cattleman Joe Olney was indicted for seven cases of "Theft of cattle" committed during the spring of 1874 and assault to murder.[9] A comparison with the Llano court records indicates that this is an error for an aggravated assault charge against his brother John.[10]

If the charges filed lack detail, certain facts can be determined. Most of the charges were filed against nonresident stockmen, but local ranchers, large and small, were also being dragged into court on cattle theft charges in what was a battle for control of the range. Nor was the turmoil limited to Llano and Mason. In Burnet County, another source of friction involved "Daniel Herster" in a lawsuit against A. T. Taylor, an Olney brother-in-law. The names have proven a source of some confusion. Despite their similarity, this was not Daniel Hoerster but one Dan Hester, a farm laborer and drover living in Burnet during 1870. To further complicate matters, Hester was employed by Daniel Hoerster to gather mavericks. Hoerster paid him five dollars per head, the going rate at the time.[11] Burnet County Sheriff J. C. Johnson received the citation on June 25. Deputy J. S. Atchison executed it on July 6 when he delivered it to Taylor. Hester charged that Taylor had promised to "pay to Daniel Herster the sum of One Hundred and fifteen dollars coin, for value received" on October 4, 1873. On August 4 the plaintiff dismissed the suit after Taylor agreed to pay all of the costs.[12]

The rising tension over cattle galvanized politicians in Austin. On March 23, 1874, a new stock law was enacted for the protection of stockmen. It was a well-intended effort that proved confusing. Within days of its passage newspapers across the state published warnings concerning it. On April 17 the San Marcos *West Texas Free Press* cautioned that the law placed "severe restrictions on the promiscuous selling of cattle by men not owning them" and required power of attorney from the owner that had been recorded in the District Clerk's office. The penalty was a minimum of five years in the penitentiary.

Under the new law every county in the state was made an "Inspection District for the inspection of hides and animals." The law also provided that the Inspector of Hides and Animals was to "inspect all hides or animals, known or reported to him as sold, or as leaving or going out of the county for sale or shipment." Two sections of the law were central to the feud and contributed further to animosity between ranchers.

> Sec. 36. Any person who shall drive any cattle out of any county with the intention of driving the same beyond the limits of the State, to a market, without first having road branded the same in accordance with the fourteenth section of this act, shall be deemed guilty of a misdemeanor, and on conviction shall be fined not less than twenty dollars nor more than one hundred dollars for each animal.
>
> Sec. 37. Any person who shall drive any cattle or horses out of any county without written authority and without first having them inspected, shall be guilty of a misdemeanor, and on conviction shall be fined in any sum not less than twenty dollars nor more than one hundred dollars per head for each animal so driven.[13]

Problems were evident almost immediately. Within days of its passage, the *San Antonio Daily Herald* reported that several herds of cattle being driven to Kansas had been stopped at Fredericksburg because the drovers, "either through ignorance of the law or for some other cause" did not have the authority as prescribed by the law. The drovers were jailed and the cattle turned loose. The paper heralded the law as a "practical effort" in stopping "the irresponsible system of driving other people's cattle to Kansas."[14] In an era of nonresident cattlemen and open range, with county-based brands, it also provided the means to control all of the livestock in a given county and ample opportunity for local abuse.

As noted, the law was well intended. The cattle industry was growing and needed controls to protect honest ranchers. The results were neither what the government anticipated or desired. During the summer of 1874 animosity between Mason County ranchers and nonresident stockmen escalated. The confusion that prevailed over the new stock law throughout Texas was exacerbated by the open range that dominated the state. Ranchers could and did have cattle in many counties. Many of these men adopted a practical view of the situation. If a good holding area for a herd was across a county line, the stockmen felt no particular qualms in gathering there. Many ranchers reasoned that if there was no intention to violate the law then no crime had been committed, particularly when they owned the cattle in question. Ranching was, then as now, a business, and time meant money. Most certainly in a county that herders felt was hostile to nonresident stockmen such inspections could cause innumerable delays, and the strong possibility that the herd would be severely cut. Every cow that was not driven from the county meant a potential unbranded calf in the spring, and residents of the county would benefit from the unbranded mavericks, particularly when the brand inspector was also a rancher paying a bounty such as Daniel Hoerster.

Not unnaturally, local stockmen held different views. Livestock driven out of the county could, potentially, contain stolen cattle. Some doubtless wanted to prevent the cattle's removal so that they could benefit from the mavericks. Not unnaturally, losses to herds were viewed as the work of rustlers. As 1874 drew on, anger and tension mounted, and by June it became apparent that trouble was at hand. In a letter to Governor Richard Coke dated June 24, 1874, Wilson Hey, presiding justice of Mason County, reported:

> At the request of the Citizens of this County, I would respectfully represent to you that parties from Llano & other Counties are continualy [sic] depredating upon the cattle of said Citizens; that during the last month parties from Llano Co. (in the Employ of one Roberts) in open violation of law have been

> gathering and driving Cattle from Mason Co. without having them inspected as the laws direct, and it is a positive fact that some of our citizens have had to go to Llano a distance of 25 miles & take from herds the very same milk cows . . . .

Hey went on to note that warrants were issued for the arrest of the "depredators" who in turn "made open threats that if they came after them with the Sheriff that they would mix it with them or in other words fight." According to Hey, Roberts had hired a man named W. Z. Redding who was either a "Deputy-Inspector or Deputy Sheriff" in Llano County. "This Agent (W. Z. Redding) inspects the cattle, signs Roberts name to the bill of sale then certifies that Roberts is the owner or has authority to use such cattle and then certifies that he had inspected them."[15] Hey denied that Redding was an officer, presumably based on testimony of the ranchers who had petitioned him, and requested that a company of Rangers be stationed in Mason County to deal with the situation. Within a year he would retract these accusations.[16]

A. G. Roberts was the most noted man on whom Mason and Llano County ranchers focused their attention. That there was cattle theft in the region is undisputed, and the law was either unable or unwilling to control it. Yet, notwithstanding the claims of Mason concerning nonresident stockmen and Barler's allegations, the available evidence suggests that Roberts was not involved in routine cattle theft operations. Roberts had widespread cattle holdings in a number of counties, but this was not uncommon. Roberts certainly had no more opportunity to steal cattle than any other rancher in the area. What separated him from his contemporaries was his aggressive insistence on maintaining his rights, an insistence that antagonized mob members. It was an ideal situation for others far less scrupulous to gain a strategic foothold. They seized the opportunity with both hands.

Contemporary documents refer to A. G. Roberts as both Allen and Albert G. Roberts. Born around 1843 in Illinois, Roberts had arrived in Texas by the early 1860s. On July 2, 1863, he enlisted for three years or until the end of the war in Captain William G. O'Brien's Company K, Mounted Volunteers, of the Frontier Regiment.[17] The 1870 census shows him living in Burnet County with his wife Louisa and two young children, William and Kate. Roberts' occupation was "driving stock" with personal property valued at $1,000, a significant amount for the times.[18] Roberts also served a brief stint as a State Policeman from September 8 to October 31, 1871.[19]

Contemporary cattle records confirm Roberts' ownership of cattle in both Llano and Mason Counties. A drive log of M. L. Hayes, a drover living in northeastern Mason County, lists both Roberts and W. Z. Redding as owning part of a cattle herd he took up the trail to market.[20] Other records include stock notices appearing in the *Burnet Bulletin*:

> STOCK NOTICE
>
> All parties are hereby notified not to use, drive, or remove from the range either in Burnet or Lampasas counties, any STOCK owned by Roberts & Cavin excepting parties legally authorized by us as agents. And for references to the stock owned by the above firm, parties are hereby referred to the records of Marks and Brands recorded in each county named.
>
> Parties are hereby notified, that the law will be enforced in regard to posting cattle in the county where the mark and brand is recorded.
>
> A. H. CAVIN
> A. G. ROBERTS
> L. W. CAVIN[21]

In addition to the Cavins, Roberts was also a partner of the Baird brothers. Another stock notice warned that J. B. and M. B. Baird had sold cattle to Roberts "in the counties of Burnet, Lampasas, Llano, Mason, San Saba and Brown" but still held a mortgage on them. "All persons are hereby warned against using, driving, or counterbranding any of the said stocks of cattle without my authority." Baird promised that anyone caught doing so would be prosecuted to the full extent of the law.[22] It was a promise that he would keep.

Docket books for Burnet County show no charges filed against Roberts in that county through 1874. He was regarded there simply as a cattleman and later held a position as deputy sheriff. Nor is there evidence that Roberts had a particularly bad reputation in the area aside from Barler's memoir and Hey's statement, which he later retracted. Roberts was not a man prone to violence. His business associates were a harder group, hot-tempered men who, like Roberts, would vigorously fight to defend their rights through the courts. Unlike Roberts, many of them had been involved in violent altercations.

From the beginning, both mobs were infiltrated by stock thieves. Among the known outlaws allied with the "law and order" faction were Caleb Hall, best known for his role in the Lincoln County War of New Mexico Territory, and the Dublin brothers, Dick, Dell, and Roll. Aware of any planned raids, these men were in a key position to tip off their cohorts and direct suspicion elsewhere. Any advantage the mob felt it had due to its clandestine activities was negated. Anglo outlaws in the region knew both their plans and members. How the Dublin brothers became involved with the mob is unknown, but Caleb Hall was a crony of Sheriff John Clark.

Major John B. Jones, commander of the newly reorganized Texas Rangers, did not receive Hey's petition until August 16.[23] By that time a major event in the feud had already taken center stage. The *San Antonio Daily Express* prophetically heralded it under the headline STOCK WAR! In the months that followed, animosity arising from this single event gave way to violence and a brutality unparalleled in Texas feud history.

This article is of great importance in understanding the feud. From the evidence, it is known that the *San Antonio Herald* of August 14 published a letter written by David Doole, a Mason County merchant, purporting to be a factual account of a raid and subsequent arrests in Mason County.[24] While this issue of the *Herald* has not been located, it appears that the *Express* article was drawn from the same source. The *Express* letter was dated August 18, 1874, from Mason and bore the notation of "Correspondence Fredericksburg Sentinel." Doole's letter was inflammatory and stirred up controversy concerning its accuracy, not only with the ranchers whom Doole claimed were cattle thieves but with the Texas Rangers.

According to Doole, on August 9 Sheriff John Clark and a posse of eighteen men went in pursuit of "cow hands of Al. Roberts, who had made a raid into Mason county and driven off 200 head of cattle." Clark overtook the men near Castell in Llano County. When Clark informed them that they were under arrest "they showed fight" but surrendered when they realized that the posse was too big for them. Clark brought eleven of the men back and jailed them in Mason. The cattle in question were allegedly penned at "Mr. Bower's [*sic*: Bauer's]."[25] Doole further stated that "During the night a party of the said Roberts commenced to shoot into the pen, and stampeded the cattle, thereby, as they thought, destroying the proof of their guilt."[26]

What Doole based his accusation upon is unknown. According to the letter, none of the men who allegedly stampeded the cattle were ever apprehended. Nor does he identify any of them beyond the unsupported accusation that they worked for Roberts. Moreover, when witnesses were eventually summoned for the trial, Bauer was not named although he would have been a key witness. In contrast, Roberts stated that Clark "illegally and unlawfully took the cattle from their possession and drove them back into Mason county, turned them loose and scattered them."[27] The evidence indicates that this is far more likely. Certainly it is consistent with similar accounts of the times, such as the description already quoted of the incident in Fredericksburg. The *San Antonio Daily Herald* reported on April 18, 1874, that several herds of cattle were stopped at Fredericksburg and turned loose. By turning the cattle loose, Clark would have been following in the footsteps of other sheriffs in the area although he made a major error in judgment in doing so.

On August 13 two of the drovers were brought to court "upon the charge of driving out of Mason 200 head of cattle without having them inspected. The evidence not sustaining the charges, they were discharged . . . ." [28] The hearing for the remaining nine men was set for the following morning. According to Doole, as court adjourned, a party of "forty armed hands" in the employ of Roberts from Llano and Burnet Counties led by John Baird arrived and informed Wilson Hey, the presiding justice, that they wanted to bail the men out of jail, and "if they could not bail them out they intended to take them out." Hey reportedly agreed that he would fix bail at $5000 and would "approve the bond if the sureties were worth the amount required."[29]

Doole's account lacks internal consistency. By his own admission, two of the men had already been exonerated in court and were at liberty because the evidence did not sustain the charges. Hey knew this, and certainly John Baird did shortly after his arrival in Mason.

Yet the bond appears excessive for nine men likely to be released the following day. Not surprisingly, the account provided by John Baird and Al Roberts differs significantly regarding the event. "There were about forty men from Llano and Burnet counties present at the trial, but they did not create any disturbance or attempt the release of the prisoners. They were not desperadoes but were among the most peaceable and law abiding citizens of Burnet and Llano counties. They had not come for the purpose of liberating the prisoners, but for the purpose of protecting them from being mobbed, as some of the sheriff's gang had made indiscriminate threats against Roberts and his men."[30] Considering the events of 1875, Baird's concerns were not unfounded.

Doole further claimed that in the thirty minutes that Hey required to get ready to approve the bond Clark "rushed around summoning a *posse*" and gathered "fifty well-armed men to see that the prisoners were not turned loose."[31] This statement is in direct contrast to the account of Ernst Jordan. As Baird and his men crossed into Mason County, Jordan observed that "forty men, confederates of the thieves, passed the Jordan house on the way to Mason. Ernst Jordan knew what it meant; they were coming to release the prisoners or to make trouble."

How Jordan came to this revelation is irrelevant. According to the family, Ernst Jordan sent word to his neighbors to meet him in Mason. This is far more likely than Doole's account.[32] Doole claimed Baird and his men were driven out of Mason and concluded that as Baird's men returned to Llano County they "killed cows and shot into the schoolhouse."[33] Not unnaturally Roberts denied that any of this had happened.[34]

According to the *Express*:

> At 9 o'clock the defendants were brought into court for trial, Mr. Todd representing the State, and Mr. J. C. Mathews the defendant. Mr. Todd moved to dismiss as to three of the defendants for the purpose of making witnesses of them. The other parties announced themselves ready for the trial, and plead not guilty, and after a trial of six hours, the jury brought in a verdict of guilty of driving 100 head of cattle out

of Mason county, and assessed a fine of $25 for each
head, against all of the defendants, making the sum
of $2500, whereupon Mr. Mathews moved for a new
trial, which being over-ruled by the court took an appeal to the District Court. On Saturday the prisoners
gave the required bond and were turned loose.[35]

It is worthy of note that Roberts and Baird made no mention of
five of their men having been released. Contemporary evidence demonstrates that none of them had been. According to them there were
"only two head of cattle in the herd" when the men were taken by
Clark "that belonged in Mason county" and "it was shown that these
two head got into the herd in Llano county."[36]

Smarting from the $2500, fine the herders immediately filed an
appeal. Citing the stock law of 1871, section 37, they stated that they
should have been fined, at most, $200 for two head of cattle that were
shown to have "got into the herd in Llano county." Section 37 of the
new livestock law remained much the same, stating that "Any person
who shall drive any cattle or horses out of any county without written authority and without first having them inspected" could be fined
between twenty and one hundred dollars a head, so M. B. Thomas
and his men were clearly in violation of the law. The cattlemen apparently feared that they would not be able to remove their cattle from
Mason without considerable difficulty from Daniel Hoerster and willingly moved the cattle to prevent the loss.

The incident did not rest there, however. Clark had made the arrests in Llano County where he had no authority. Had he wished, he
could have held the men in Llano with the herd until officials from
that county could be summoned. Instead, he drove the herd back into
Mason and scattered it without having it inspected as required by the
same law that he charged Roberts and his men with.

Evidence of Roberts' truthfulness can be found in the court records. In 1877 the appeal was called to trial in Mason County. Both
Roberts and Thomas were charged in three separate counts, two for
theft of a cow, and one for theft of a steer in Mason County—not
for numerous counts as stated by Doole. On November 14, 1877,
Thomas was tried on the theft of steer charge and found not guilty.
The remaining charges were dismissed the same day.[37]

The precision of the cattle count is explained by the card published by Roberts in the *Burnet Bulletin*. While both sources agree that eleven men were arrested, the count does not include two additional men employed by Roberts from Mason County. Neither man was charged in the incident. It is a significant detail not mentioned in Doole's account.

> Knowing the animosity that some of the people of that county have toward non-resident stock men, and wishing to have no misunderstanding or trouble, Thomas hired two men of Mason Co. to stay continually with the herd that he was collecting and cut-out every animal that might get into the herd belonging to anyone in that county.[38]

While the identities of the two men have not been determined with certainty, existing evidence suggests that one of them was Tim Williamson.[39] Williamson had lived in Burnet County for some time but moved to Loyal Valley in southern Mason County between 1870 and 1874. Williamson was an obvious choice since Roberts knew him. Williamson enjoyed a good reputation in Burnet County where his brother Frederick had served as sheriff between 1866 and 1869. He was also a friend of both Daniel Hoerster, Mason's brand inspector, and cattleman Karl Lehmberg.

The second man appears to have been George W. Gladden.[40] Unlike Williamson, Gladden had once been arrested in Llano County by L. J. Parker and N. J. Miller, members of the State Police, and charged with theft of a horse in 1872. He was not convicted.[41] Like Williamson, Gladden can be linked to Karl Lehmberg.[42]

That none of the men were exonerated is confirmed by a document prepared for the state government entitled a *List of Criminals By County* from Mason. In this the herders were identified as Albert G. Roberts et als charged with theft of cow in August 1874 in Mason County. Roberts was indicted again on November 12, 1874. Charged with the same crime were V. P. Hamilton, G. L. Gardner, Newberry H. Holton, A. F. Hanson, G. (George) C. Arnett, B. K. Hamilton, S. M. Sharer, Joe Gardner, and F. J. West, all of whom were indicted on March 12, 1875. Not mentioned by name was M. B. Thomas who was tried on the charge in Mason with Roberts.[43]

Doole's letter prompted an angry response in the form of an insulting card published in the *Burnet Bulletin* signed by Roberts and five other men. Such cards were not uncommon, but in general the authors "took the precaution of removing themselves to other parts." None of them had any intention of "removing themselves to other parts."[44]

Not unnaturally, one of the signatories was M. B. Thomas who had charge of the herd when the men were arrested. Marshal Brackston Thomas was the same Brack Thomas charged by Reconstruction authorities for shooting a dog during 1868. The son of John Preston Thomas and Amanda Melvina Payne, he was born December 2, 1850, in Wayne County, Kentucky, the second of nine children.[45] By 1863 he was working as a drover and was present on a cattle hunt when his cousin John Magill was killed by Indians. The 1870 census notes him as a drover along with his brothers James and Oliver.[46] Aside from the dog-killing incident, Thomas had had no trouble in Burnet.

In addition to Roberts and Thomas, the other signatories on the rebuttal were John and Moses Baird, A. T. Taylor and W. Z. "Bill" Redding. Both Taylor and the Bairds were related by marriage to the Olney family in Burnet County. All of these men would later be involved in the Hoo Doo War.

Roberts was not a man willing to chalk up the experience to bad luck. Once the drovers were safely out of Llano County Roberts moved quickly against Sheriff Clark and his posse. Enraged over the treatment of his men, Roberts and the others rode to Llano where they filed charges against Clark and the entire posse for robbery and false imprisonment. [47] On the same day that these indictments were handed down, Roberts and Wiley Cavin were also indicted in Llano County for theft of cattle in Llano County.[48] Details of this case have not been determined with certainty, but the timing indicates that the events occurred around the same time as those in Mason and may well have been filed by members of the Llano mob.

From the records available the identities of the men involved with Clark in the arrests can be determined. According to both of the available accounts there were eighteen men in addition to Clark. On May 15, 1877, Causes 1, 2, and 3 were reentered on the docket books of Mason County charging "Albert G. Roberts Et Al" with theft of a steer and two counts of theft of a cow. Witnesses for the state included

Sheriff John Clark, Jacob Durst,[49] Barnard Durst,[50] Peter Jordan, Henry Doell, Leo Zesch,[51] Fritz Kothmann, Frederick Schmidt,[52] J. G. Durst,[53] August Leifeste,[54] Daniel Hoerster, August Leifeste Sr.,[55] and August Leifeste Jr.[56] Conspicuously absent is the name of Johann Bauer who, if Doole's version of events is to be believed, had held the herd at his ranch. Mrs. C. Meckel[57] was also noted as a witness although Deputy Sheriff James A. Baird, also indicted for his role in the arrests, was not.[58] Llano records confirm the presence of Frederick Schmidt as a posseman and add the additional presence of Christian Oestreich.[59]

From these fifteen names, the locale where most of them lived and subsequent events, an attempt to discern the identities of the remaining four men can be made. Although one obvious candidate would appear to be Deputy Sheriff Johann A. Wohrle, the evidence suggests that Wohrle acted primarily as the jailer and process server and was probably in Mason at the time. The presence of Oestreich, a Llano County resident, indicates that Clark drew his men from the Germans in the immediate area. That being the case, the group probably included Peter and Carl Bader, both of whom were living near Castell. Other likely candidates are Dietrich and Wilhelm Kothmann. Most of these men lived in the Willow Creek community or its proximity, the very area later charged with being the center of Mason's mob.[60]

Doole also charged that John W. Gamel and Henry W. Morris received "threatening letters" from Roberts, noting that Roberts had a party of twenty men in the country again driving cattle. According to the *Express*, Major John B. Jones, his men, and a posse of citizens were then in pursuit of the drovers.[61] This is confirmed in part by Texas Ranger Samuel P. Elkins who recalled in his memoirs:

> I was detailed to go with Major John B. Jones' escort to Fredericksburg, and when we reached Fort Mason we found a big crowd of men gathered there. The sheriff came to Major Jones and told him that Roberts, an outlaw, was camped two miles from Fort Mason and was stealing all the cattle that he and his gang could find, and they had sent the sheriff a challenge to come to a certain place. The sheriff and his large party fell in front of our little bunch and we went

about six miles out on the Fredericksburg road, when they sidetracked. Major Jones called for thirty volunteers and they promptly stepped out. Twelve men were left with the pack mules, and we went on for two or three miles when the sheriff made the proposition that the rangers, when they came up to the outlaws, demand their surrender, and if they refused, we were to open the fight and the citizens would reinforce us. We were about three hundred yards from the outlaws' camp and Major Jones sent a man to demand their surrender. When the man reached the camp he found it had been vacated, and no outlaws were there, so the citizens returned to Mason.[62]

That Doole's letter was inflammatory is evidenced by the response not only of Roberts and his men but of Major John B. Jones as well. In an angry, terse letter to Doole, Jones wrote that "Your communication of the 14th inst. to the 'San Antonio Herald' concludes as follows: 'The prisoners released by our Presiding Justice are depredating extensively in the settlements. I think Major Jones will bring them to trim; he has ordered Capt. Perry's Company to this place. I am sorry to say that they look upon cattle stealing as a two-handed game.' Some friends of Capt. Perry's Company here think the last sentence refers to that company."[63]

Doole wasted no time responding to Jones' irate letter. On September 4 he apologized for the article claiming that he had written to the editor of the *Herald* after he had read the article himself. "I seen the mistake & wrote to the Editor in regard to the matter. The language made use of by me was that I was sorry to see that the principal stock men of this county took so little intrest [*sic*] in this matter that the[y] seemed to look upon cattle stealing as a two handed game having always looked upon Capt. Perry as a gentleman and knowing that neather [*sic*] him or his men knew what was going on in this county at the time."[64]

Doole's letter underscores the clear division between the German and American stockmen of the county. While the apology may have been sincere, no retraction or correction appeared in the *Herald*. In Burnet County, Roberts and others involved with the "big raid" characterized Doole's letter as "deliberate misrepresentations, and un-called for malicious slander" that was "unparalleled by any vilifying article that ever crept into a newspaper."[65] The enraged authors further charged that the herders had been treated poorly by the authorities. Roberts charged that his eleven men were

> thrown into a foul dungeon, which was reeking with filth and stench, where they sweltered four days and nights, with nothing to eat but bread and water. The sheriff refused to allow them to purchase other provisions although they were anxious to do so and had the money. Several of the men fainted from the terrible heat and suffocation in this close but nauceous [*sic*: nauseous] jail, but were still detained there, which was unnecessary except to gratify the malignant spite of those who took the lead in the matter, as all of the witnesses were present and Thomas and his men demanded their trial forthwith.[66]

Clearly, considering the events of 1875, this statement indicates the belief that mob activity was already a reality in Mason and that Clark was involved as the leader. The "gang" referred to can have been nothing other than the mob itself.

The incident had far reaching impact. One paper reported a garbled account of the affair, confusing Quihi in Medina County with Mason County.

> A letter from Mason, dated on the 14th inst., states that, "great excitement exists at Quihi, on account of the Sheriff of Mason County arresting 11 of the Llano cow boys. Some 40 of their friends came in and attempted a rescue but failed in the attempt."
>
> This disturbance like many others is attributable to the confusion caused by the stock law.
>
> We understand that since the above mentioned letter was written several men have been killed at Quihi in the quarrel.[67]

48

Some perspective on what was happening in Mason County during the time Sheriff Clark was busy pursuing nonresident stockmen adds further insight to the feud. Quoting the *Fredericksburg Sentinel*, the *San Antonio Daily Herald* reported that Indians attacked a pack train "a couple of miles from Mason." On August 10 another party raided a ranch "and even were so bold as to shoot a dog in the yard, and kill chickens."[68] The same raiders, or a part of them, struck Gillespie County on August 21. Attempting to drive off twenty horses they were pursued and the animals abandoned.[69] A week later Indians killed a man named Shelburn while he was working as a contractor building a fence in the Blue Mountains near Mason. He had been killed with a single shot through the body.[70]

The presence of Indian raiders in 1874 indicates that stock was being driven off by men who neither knew or cared about the stock law. While it is well known that the Comanches would steal horses, one of the little known facts about their raids is that they also stole cattle frequently enough that it was not questioned. One such report, under the banner "CATTLE STEALING" was filed by First Sergeant Gustave Valois of the Ninth Cavalry on June 27, 1874. Valois, then stationed at Fort Concho, reported that his scout located a large herd of cattle northwest of his camp six miles from Phantom Hill. The herders had abandoned it upon sighting the cavalry approaching. The cattle were stolen, and Valois reported that the local citizens "all agree that said herd was stolen by either white men or Indians."[71]

The Texas Rangers were also concerned about the Indian raids. Writing from Mason on August 17, Jones issued instructions to C. R. Perry, Captain of Company D of the Frontier Battalion, to move his camp when his scouts returned.[72] Jones also noted that the people of Mason were "a good deal excited in regard to the cow thieves and rumors coming in now of more depredations of the same kind. Will look into it and go after them if I find there is anything in it."[73]

Perry responded on August 25 advising Jones that a band of "Indians or Mexicans" had crossed the San Saba River on August 19. Perry had sent men in pursuit, but they had lost the trail. Others had seen the raiders and confirmed they were Mexicans, noting in part that the "Dutch had a fight on Honey Creek with a party of Mexicans instead of Indians."[74] Clearly these depredations in Mason and the surrounding counties were being committed by Mexican bandits and

Indian raiders, a far more serious threat to cattlemen in the area than Anglo outlaws. Yet the German ranchers in eastern Mason County ignored their presence, and nothing touching on the feud makes any mention of them. Nor has John Clark's name ever surfaced in connection with their activities. The reason is found in the angry rebuttal signed by Roberts, Thomas, and the others: "It is true the sheriff and his whole posse have each of them been indicted by the grand jury of Llano county, for robbing us of our cattle in this manner, but this will not afford us protection in the future . . . ." The rebuttal concluded by denouncing David Doole as "an unqualified, shameless and wanton liar" having "a low meddlesome disposition."[75] The insult could not have been worse. Following the release of the herders, they began to fight back through the legal system. Clark and his posse now found themselves in serious trouble. When Roberts was finally brought to trial in 1877, he had enough evidence to acquit him of all charges. This same evidence worked against Clark and his posse, as the grand jury of Llano County issued indictments on August 24, 1874. A conviction could send some, or all, of the posse to prison. Small wonder that by October the situation had deteriorated in Mason. On October 13 Perry reported that Wilson Hey had come to their camp soliciting aid "stating that a Vigilant Committee were to be organized in a few days." Sergeant N. O. Reynolds and five men left the following day "to quell the intended Riot." Reynolds returned on October 22, reporting all quiet in Mason. "The Sheriff also thought that there would be no trouble in that county."[76] The Rangers' belief in Clark proved a grievous error. In November the *San Antonio Daily Herald* reported that James Trainer had been shot in the leg by "some unknown parties at Mason."[77] Trainer had no links to Roberts and the other herders other than the fact that he was a nonresident cattleman.[78] The reasons for the shooting are unknown, but there appears to have been little investigation into the matter. It was a pattern that would become very familiar as the feud progressed.

chapter 4

"The Fright Hangs Over Us"

1875 dawned with deceptive calm in Mason County. Even then ample opportunity remained for matters to be resolved peacefully, but no one stepped forward as a peacemaker. In later years Ranger Daniel Webster Roberts would recall that "the men supporting civil authority, needed no arrest, and those opposing it, urged equal claims of being right, but would not submit their grievances to law."[1] This is not true. During 1874, both sides had submitted their grievances to the law. The law had failed them. In Mason County, nonresident cattlemen such as Jim Trainer were met with hostility. The German element controlled the law, as represented by John Clark, who did nothing to curb the cattle theft going on in the county by Mexican bandits, Indians, and Anglo outlaws. Likewise the law failed to protect the interests of nonresident cattlemen. A. G. Roberts had submitted his grievances to the Llano courts, and the resulting indictments and arrests served to intensify the animosities between the factions.

Although Dan Roberts does not mention the events of 1874 that propelled the Hoo Doo War into open violence, he cannot have been unaware of them. Unlike Roberts and Thomas, both of whom were exonerated by a Mason County jury, John Clark remained on the Texas Ranger wanted lists until 1878 for the charges brought against him in Llano County.[2] In his recollections of the feud, Roberts put the best light he could on both his role and that of his company. It was his first test in a feud situation, and both he and Company D would prove wanting.

In Llano County the law moved against Clark's posse as the indictments were served. Both Frederick Schmidt and Christian Oestreich were arrested, and it seems likely that the law aggressively hunted the others. Christian Oestreich had been arrested on December 2, 1874. The sheriff was also actively hunting Sheriff Clark whom he could not locate.[3] It appears probable that the balance of the posse had already been charged in Llano County and made bond or were evading the sheriff. Clark remained on the dodge, and as late as August 1875 attorney Henry M. Holmes would write: "His statement that the Sheriff was out of town 10 or 15 miles is true, and generally is, as his usefulness has lately been sadly interfered with by a visit from the Sheriff of Llano who wants him for over zealously discharging his duty, his friends say, the indictments call it 'Robbery and False Imprisonment.'"[4]

Using the court system and the law, A. G. Roberts had fought back effectively against Clark. Clark's actions had backfired, and the posse now viewed the possibility of hefty fines or prison terms on their collective horizons. Moreover, cattle were still being raided and non-resident stockmen were still operating in the county. Clark's big arrest had done nothing to resolve the problems.

In February 12, 1875, Clark arrested nine men and a boy. While one modern writer describes the leaders as the "notorious Backus [sic] brothers," evidence indicates that they were neither notorious nor brothers.[5] Elijah Baccus was born c. 1850, apparently in Lamar County, Texas, to Joseph and Lucinda Brown Baccus. While records of his early life are scarce, by 1860 he and an older brother, Charles, were living with an uncle, Thomas Baccus, in Collin County.[6] The reason for their relocation is unclear, but it may have been due to the death of their mother. Their father Joseph married Rachel Cook on March 1, 1866, in Denton County, Texas.[7] Elijah Baccus has not been located on the 1870 federal census. Sometime prior to 1875 he married Josie Bigelow. L. P. "Pete" Baccus was born c. 1856, apparently in Collin County, Texas, to Benjamin Baccus, a cousin of Joseph Baccus, and his wife Roxanne Stovall.[8] By 1870 the Benjamin Baccus family had moved to Denton County.[9]

By 1874 both of the Baccuses had left north Texas. Although the exact time period has not been determined, local sources state that they and a number of other residents had fled the area due to the

Lee-Peacock feud. Elijah's aunt, Louisa Baccus, was married to Henry Boren, an ardent supporter of Peacock.[10] The men left the region to avoid being drawn into the conflict.[11]

According to Tom Gamel, the people arrested consisted of nine men and a boy. The leader of the group was stockman Elijah Baccus. The others identified were Pete Baccus, Abraham Wiggins, Tom Turley, and Charley Johnson.[12] Nothing has been determined regarding Abraham Wiggins. Tom Turley was described as about twenty years old, light haired with blue eyes and a heavy build.[13] Henry M. Holmes, who was retained to prosecute the case, identified the boy as John Martin, a resident of Mason County. Martin was the son of William W. and Nancy Yoakum Martin and was born around 1864 in Texas. Martin's father is listed as a farmer in the census, born in Missouri, and homesteaded one hundred and sixty acres of land.[14] Charles Walker Johnson was related to the Bolts and Tim Williamson through marriage.[15] The remaining four men have defied positive identification.

Folklore concerning the arrests has arisen. In an interview with C. L. Sonnichsen, Henry Doell Jr. recalled that the "Backer" brothers "were caught west of town with a herd—only 3 head in their brand, and those 3 fresh branded."[16] This same story was used by German author Christopher Hagen when he published his novel on the feud called *Gebrandmarkt,* which translates as "Branded." According to Hagen, Clark ordered a surprise brand inspection of all herds. The Backus herd was found to have only "three head out of twenty-five hundred cattle" with their own brand.[17]

While some historians and writers have presumed the guilt of the Baccuses, contemporary documentation indicates the strong probability that the men were driving cattle that belonged to them. Elijah Baccus is identified in the 1875 tax rolls for Mason County as "Elija Backus" owning 600 head of cattle valued at $3,000 and 47 head of horses and mules valued at $1,175. The rolls had been approved in August 1874. The absence of land holdings indicates the probability that Baccus was a nonresident stockman.[18] Nor were the Baccuses considered outlaws. Naomi Cox Miller, an early resident of Mason, recalled Elijah and Pete Baccus in a positive light, as she "knew the Backus [sic] boys quite well and often danced with them."[19]

The incident has remarkable similarities to the events of the previous year in Llano County. Once again nonresident stockmen had been arrested, this time on Brady Creek in McCulloch County north of Mason. Henry M. Holmes was retained to prosecute the case, and from his carefully kept records facts about the incident can be determined.

Holmes noted in his files that the Baccus "herders" began the drive "on or about 9th of February." The men were seen by "E. Villareal and Eusrbio Villareal" who spent the night with them. The following day the herd moved on. Holmes confirmed that the men were captured in McCulloch County, and witnesses for the state were listed as John Wohrle, _____ Crosby, Alf Baird, the father of James A. Baird, John Clark, Dave Clark (no known kinsman of John Clark), "E. Billareal" [*sic*: Villareal], Anton Hoerster, John Lindsay, Tom Gamel, David Doole, and B. F. Stewart. Charley Johnson was noted as the driver of the provision wagon.[20] John Martin had apparently been retained to handle chores on the drive.

Once again Clark had crossed into a county where he had no authority. This time, rather than drive the herd back to Mason, he had left it unattended while conveying the herders back to Mason. What is not clear from the records is what evidence these men would have presented in their own defense. As with the previous arrests, these too created a sensation in Mason. Lucia Holmes noted in her diary, "Everybody full of the cattle stealing case. Hal not employed this morning. The examination comes off today. . . . Hal retained for the prosecution for 100 dollars and Todd for 50. . . . Hal and Todd talking law all the evening."[21]

The facts of the case were quickly apparent to everyone, and if the men had been brought to trial they would probably have been exonerated. Clark had not scattered the cattle or driven them back to Mason, but his lack of discretion in failing to get a local officer to assist in the arrest could prove disastrous. The herd had been left unattended, and any evidence of cattle theft would have been compromised. It is possible that the Backuses could have brought charges against this posse as well, particularly if the cattle involved all sported the Backus brand. The ranchers had trusted Clark, and once again he had led them into a potential disaster. Moreover, the assertions of Doell and Hagen notwithstanding, it is apparent from the records that the men were charged with driving an uninspected herd across the county line, not theft of cattle. Gamel recalled:

A few days before this occurrence, Lige Backess [sic], Pete Backess [sic], Charley Johnson, Tom Terley [sic: Turley], Abe Wiggins, a young boy and four others were overtaken with a herd of cattle on Brady creek and were arrested by Clark and his men and brought to Mason. They were charged with illegally driving a herd of cattle.[22]

Historian Ed Bartholomew postulated that "these men may have innocently met death from the loose talk of a desperado-informer named Caleb Hall."[23] Considering Hall's subsequent criminal career and vindictiveness, it appears possible that Hall harbored animosity against Baccus for the legal action against him in 1874.

Events now unfolded at a breakneck pace. The leaders of the mob had resolved on radical action, not against the thieves plaguing the area, but against the nonresident stockmen who insisted on gathering their cattle. Lieutenant Daniel W. Roberts reported to John B. Jones, on February 14, that:

Nick Colston [sic: Coalson], who lives on Copperas Creek, tributary of Llano, was shot at his Rancho when putting his horses in the stable—only slightly wounded in hip—the parties that did it are unknown. There was some moccasin tracks & shoe tracks also found near by—but the sign was rather bogus for Indians. I did not go to see anything about it as it was a week before I knew it. Colston lives 35 miles west here.[24]

The shooting of Nick Coalson occurred sometime around the week of February 6, without apparent reason. A native of Illinois, Coalson had come to Texas prior to the Civil War and settled at Jacksboro. In the war's aftermath he settled six miles from the ranch of Rance Moore in Kimble County west of Mason. Coalson was described as "a fearless sort of man, attended to his own business, and was not a trouble-maker."[25] Coalson moved to Edwards County in 1876. The motive for his shooting remains unknown.

In Mason, Tom Gamel filed lawsuits against Elijah Backus on February 16. The suits were on two promissory notes totaling $270, and attachments were made on two of Backus' horses.[26] The following day Backus and his men were bound over in the amount of $5,000. As in the Roberts case, the bond was excessive under the stock law. Lucia Holmes noted, "The case progressing finely in court. [Backus] bound over for 5 thousand dollars. . . . Case put off until Saturday." [27]

Lucia Holmes also reported the next killing in the feud. "A man found killed on the road with a card on his breast saying he wouldn't stop killing cattle so they killed him."[28] The body was discovered by Adam Bradford on the road between Mason and Menard. According to Gamel the man had a card attached to his back with the inscription "Here lies a noted cow thief."[29] He appears to have been Allen Bolt, aged seventeen. One Mason resident would later recall that several men were killed in the feud, including "a boy named Allen Bolt."[30] It may have been Bolt's killing that prompted four of the Baccus herders to leave town. They were pursued to Honey Creek by a posse led by Daniel Hoerster but escaped without their horses. The remaining six were summarily returned to jail.[31]

On February 18 John Clark was again in pursuit of alleged cattle thieves. With a posse composed of himself, Tom Gamel, Dan Hoerster, George Bird, John Brite, and Caleb Hall, he headed for the James River where another herd was believed to be held. The men found no drovers although a small herd had been abandoned there. The herders, or cattle thieves, had apparently gotten wind of Clark's approach and abandoned the cattle.

If this group were cattle thieves, there is small wonder that they knew Clark was in pursuit. In later years Tom Gamel recalled his suspicions of Caleb Hall, whom he believed had warned the cattle thieves. During the pursuit Hall had decided to turn back, and Gamel told him he would kill him if he did. Hall continued with the posse under Gamel's watchful eye. His distrust of the man was founded on solid fact. What the source of his information is cannot be determined, but if Gamel knew about Hall, then Clark, sheriff of the county for over a year, should have known as well.

Hall's presence as a posseman is startling and may well have been the only time in his life that Hall served as a member of a posse although he certainly had experience with them. The son of Caleb and Lucy Hall, he was born Caleb Hall in Graves County, Kentucky, on June 15 (or 16) 1849.[32] When Hall arrived in Texas is uncertain, but he soon make his presence felt upon the frontier. In March of 1871 he came to the attention of authorities when L. H. McNelly's State Police company arrested "Kaleb Hale" [*sic*: Hall] in Harris County on a charge of gambling.[33] More serious charges were made in May 1871.

> Last Sunday night the residence of Dr. Shelbourne, in the western part of this county, was visited by a party of five men, on horseback, for the purpose, it is supposed of killing a Mr. King, and possibly one of the Shelbournes. Ten or a dozen shots were exchanged, but without effect. Subsequently one Caleb Hall was arrested, charged with being a member of the attacking party, but proving an alibi he was released.[34]

On November 4, 1874, Elijah Backus sued Hall in justice court and won seventeen dollars and costs. Hall appealed the verdict and a new trial was granted. In December the case was dismissed. The same month Hall was charged with assault with attempt to kill. He gave bond in the amount of $500 on November 4, 1874. The following day he was again in court charged as being an accessory to the theft of a stallion.[35] In 1877 Hall was indicted for cattle theft in Kinney County.[36] Small wonder that the *Galveston Daily News* would later report, "The notorious Kale Hall, who escaped from the Menardville jail sometime since, was seen on the Llano river in Mason county, day before yesterday.[37]

That Clark considered Hall a suitable posseman is indicative of either a severe lack of judgment or possible collusion between the men. By 1875 Hall was well known as a stock thief to lawmen in the Hill Country. Hall was also a member of the mob, undoubtedly brought in under the sponsorship of John Clark.

As the men returned to Mason, Clark called Gamel to one side and suggested that they take the law into their own hands. Gamel refused. Gamel also claimed that Dan Hoerster also suggested lynching the prisoners during their return to town. He again refused, and when they reached Mason shortly before sunset Gamel prudently rode on to his father-in-law's home.[38]

Gamel's refusal to join Clark and his knowledge of Clark and Hoerster's involvement in the mob made him a threat. From that point on, as Sonnichsen correctly points out, "his accusations may be taken for whatever they are worth."[39] Contemporary evidence indicates that, while biased, they are worth a lot. Around eight o'clock in the evening Caleb Hall rode up to Bob Cavaness' home in Koockville and called Gamel out, informing him that a mob had taken the six prisoners out of jail and that Gamel was wanted in Mason that night. Gamel refused to go. It proved a wise decision.[40]

Around midnight on the evening of February 18 Deputy Sheriff Johann Wohrle's home was broken into by the mob. The men tied him up and began torturing him by strangling while they demanded the key to the jail. Forced to watch, Helena Wohrle, pregnant at the time, went into hysterics and began screaming. Ernest Lemberg later informed Sonnichsen that "she started screaming—such screaming as he never heard."[41] According to Henry Doell Jr., Heinrich Hoerster snarled "Hit her in the mouth so she'll shut up." Another member of the mob, identified as rancher John Lindsay, "said By God or Goddamn every other word."[42] Wohrle was tortured until he gave up the keys.[43] Ernest Lemburg later told Sonnichsen that some people believed that Wohrle was in on the lynching and that the assault on his home was a put-up job.[44] Subsequent events indicate that this was unlikely.

Lieutenant Dan Roberts was staying at Hunter's hotel when John Clark burst into his room shouting that a mob was storming the jail. Roberts hurriedly dressed and, accompanied by cattleman Jim Trainer, newly recovered from his gunshot wound, headed for the jail where they were warned to stand back. Clark then entered the courthouse, ran upstairs, and thrust his rifle out to cover the mob saying that he would kill the first damned man that touched the door. Ten men detached themselves from the mob and entered the courthouse where they conferred in private with Clark. The sheriff later claimed that they told him they would have the men in the jail even if they had to hurt him to get them. Clark abandoned his position and informed Roberts and Trainer that he was going for help.[45] In the interval the mob entered the jail and released the prisoners.

Lucia Holmes recalled the evening with horror. She and her husband Henry had been at John Gamel's, returning home around ten o'clock and going to bed.

> Was wakened up by J. Gamel who told us that there
> was an armed mob at the jail trying to get the pris-

oners out. Poor Mr. Wordly [*sic*] was choked until he had to give up the key. I dressed and ran over to Mrs. Gamels. We watched on the gallery to see what would happen and saw about forty men leading the prisoners come across the flat and go down the road. A lot of Mason men followed them.[46]

Dan Roberts was one of the men in pursuit of the mob as they herded their five prisoners down the Fredericksburg road. When they came into view of the mob, gunfire erupted. Roberts and the men with him returned fire, believing they were being attacked. Holmes, for one, fired at the mob as long as they were in sight. As the mob fled, the rescuers raced to the scene and found both the Baccuses and Turley hanging. Turley was cut down in time to save his life, but the others were already dead. Abe Wiggins was shot in the right side of his head, mortally wounded but clinging tenaciously to life. Charley Johnson had vanished into the night. The mob had left Martin unmolested behind in the jail.[47] One paper reported:

San Antonio *Herald*, 1st: "We see it stated in an exchange that five men were recently hung at Fort Mason. We are able, thanks to a gentleman who was present, to define the deliberations that took place under the spreading branches of a live oak a little more definitely. Some unknown parties (many citizens probably) seized upon the five men who were suspected of being horse thieves, and succeeded in elevating three of the five, when the sheriff put in an appearance. "Many citizens" thought it best to postpone the obsequies of the rest, and withdrew hastily, after wounding one of the accused, who was waiting for his turn to be an angel. The gentlemen in the tree were cut down, and one of them revived, but the other two were . . . dead . . . . So instead of five men being hung, only two were hung, and one was shot. For the sake of the reputation of Mason as a law abiding community we hope this correction will be made.[48]

It was a grim night in Mason, but for Tom Gamel the signs were very clear. Hall had arrived at the Cavaness home around eight o'clock in the evening, roughly four hours before the jail was stormed, a clear indication that Hall had advance knowledge of the lynching. Had he accompanied Hall to Mason it is probable that he would have joined the Baccuses at the end of a rope. It took no great degree of intelligence to understand that the mob had marked him. Sonnichsen summed up Gamel's reaction tersely: "being a tough Texan, he started looking for the men who were looking for him."[49] He would not go quietly into the night.

The lynching in Mason split the community largely along ethnic lines, an event the mob had not foreseen. Fear ruled the county, and from that point Mason split over Sheriff John Clark. In a letter dated August 17, attorney Henry M. Holmes stated in part that:

> Since the 18th day of February, 1875, there have been two distinct parties in this county, namely, the supporters of the Sheriff, and those who will not support him. . . .
>
> The citizens who have since refused to aid the Sheriff do not believe that he did his duty on that occasion, and feel that he failed in giving the prisoners under his charge the protection he should have done.
>
> For this reason many said that for the future they would not be aiding and abetting in the arrest of any parties, and placing them in a position where their lives were liable to be forfeited whether innocent or guilty, and where no help or protection would be accorded to them.[50]

Lucia Holmes noted that the town was "talking about the horrible murder—everybody full of it."[51] From her diary it is apparent that the sympathy of many was with the Baccus family and the men who had been killed. "Mrs. [John] Gamel here on her way to see poor Mrs. (Baccus). Mr. Backus buried this morning early. The other men buried this evening. . . . the fright hangs over us and I dread the nights."[52]

It is of particular interest that John Gamel's wife was concerned to visit Mrs. Baccus, particularly since her husband had been one of the men who had ridden out to inspect the herd Baccus and his men had been charged with stealing and was a witness in the case.[53] Prominent in the community, had the John Gamel family believed the men guilty they would hardly have associated with the Baccus family. That they did clearly indicates that the Gamels did not believe that Clark had a case. Holmes' letter adds further credence to their probable innocence.

Wiggins died on the morning of February 19 without regaining consciousness.[54] Turley was placed back in jail where he received medical attention. No additional guards were employed at the jail to insure his future security despite either the mob's intent or rumors of retribution that swept the town immediately following the lynching. Henry Holmes reported:

> Of course after this occurrence, the public mind was much excited, and all kinds of false reports were started, and apparently believed by some of the sheriff's supporters, as that the brothers of Backus, one of the murdered men, were going to have a bloody revenge, especially on the sheriff. Those who did not support the sheriff, however, did not believe that there was any foundation in the fact whatever for such stories, but that they were made by the sheriff's friends to gain capital on.[55]

The rumors proved just that, but Lucia Holmes's fear of the night was echoed in every home in Mason. One of the mob's supporters, identifying himself only as Dreux, wrote of the affair:

> There is ample testimony to acquit the Germans of any and all complicity in this matter . . . . It can be established in any court of justice that the above lynching was done by a mob of Americans from another county. There are no "two parties" or factions here, as is so often mistaken abroad. The honest people here are a unit in denouncing the deeds of the outlaws,

> and are on good terms generally with each other, but
> the most of the Americans are afraid to take an active
> hand in putting down the malefactors.

This charge, with its oblique reference to the Llano mob, was typical of those coming out of Mason County at the time. If Clark's partisans are to be believed, every action that took place in Mason County during the feud was committed by outsiders. Dreux himself wrote that the feudists were "a numerous and bloody band of outlaws gathered from all the surrounding frontier counties."[56] This refrain occurred repeatedly throughout the early stages of the feud and demonstrates the underlying truth that nonresident cattlemen were viewed as a threat to local cattlemen's dominance. Dreux's letter, the first veiled reference to the Llano mob, also indicates the common belief at the time that the Germans were behind the killings. Llano County's mob acted in concert with Mason's, and their actions are at times indistinguishable.

The terror for citizens of Mason had begun in earnest. On February 25, Helena Wohrle suffered a miscarriage which Lucia Holmes attributed to "her fright the other night."[57] The baby was the fourth victim of the Hoo Doos' spree in Mason, but even the death of this innocent had no effect on the mob's future activities.

Charley Johnson remained missing, and for some time many believed that he had been killed. To the mob he remained a loose end. When the shooting began in the early morning hours of February 19, Johnson was able to flip the noose from his neck, leap a fence and run to safety as the mob fired after him. The man worked his way west, and around February 20 he surfaced at Tom Gamel's home on Bluff Creek. Johnson had known Tom Gamel his entire life, and it was a natural place to seek refuge. Gamel was absent, but a herder working for Gamel, Wes Johnson (or Johnston), was reading by lamplight when he arrived.

> Charley Johnson, the escaped prisoner, stepped
> upon the porch and looked in the door and saw a gun
> standing in the corner of the room and made a dive
> for it. A struggle ensued between the two Johnsons,
> who were strangers, and when Charley got a chance

he told West what had happened and the struggle
ended.

Wes Johnson hid the fugitive, and when Gamel returned home the
following day he sent him on to Roberts' camp. Roberts recalled that
Johnson arrived at the camp "footsore and wild" although it is unlikely that Gamel sent him on foot.[58] Johnson remained in the area and
proved an embarrassment to the mob. He undoubtedly also provided
information to their enemies.

While Turley, and presumably John Martin, remained behind bars
without anything more than a token guard to protect them, the other
four Baccus riders remained at large. None of them could reasonably
be expected to surrender themselves to the mercies of lynch law. Tom
Gamel related that Turley told him where the men would likely be hiding. Having recovered their horses and saddles, Gamel sent word to
the men to come and get them. They did, and Gamel recalled "That
was the last that was ever heard or seen of them."[59] Gamel's com-
ment has been interpreted as a statement that the men fled the area,
but that may not have been the case. The mob had left a number of
loose ends, and they fully intended to tie them up.

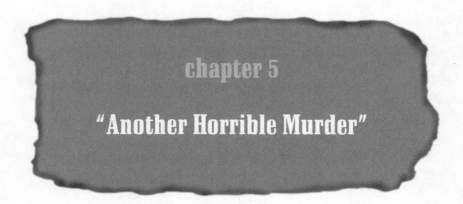

chapter 5

"Another Horrible Murder"

The lynchings in Mason County inaugurated the violence of 1875. Writing from Camp Saline, Lieutenant Dan Roberts reported on March 1, "The mob has been operating some in Llano County lately. Killed one man named Wages—ordered several more to leave the county. As yet they'v[e] harmed no good man."[1]

The man killed in late February was William Wages. Like many others involved in the feud, little is known of Wages' background. In late 1874 he had been charged with killing cattle in Mason County. Ironically, Wages was defended by George W. Todd, who only weeks previously had prosecuted A. G. Roberts and his men. He was convicted and fined twenty dollars, twice the amount of the cows' value.[2] Beyond this, virtually nothing is known of the man.

What criteria Roberts used for determining who was a "good man" is unknown, but from the existing correspondence Roberts appears to have given tacit support to the mob during his involvement in the feud. An eyewitness to the lynching, Roberts made no move to investigate the incident or arrest any of the mob. There is also an ominous silence in the official reports filed by Lieutenant Roberts during this time regarding both the Baccus lynching and the killing of Allen Bolt. Nor was any attempt made to learn the identity of Wages' killers other than the passing reference to the mob. It was a severe error in judgment bordering on dereliction of duty. Had Roberts acted decisively at that time much of the violence that followed might have been avoided. He did not.

In his memoirs, Roberts provides little indication of his thinking at this time. The lone exception was during the hearing for Charley Johnson, where he recalled "we were glad he did not tell any more than he did, as it might frustrate our plans of catching them." What Roberts' plans were remain unknown. None ever evolved, and there is no evidence to show that such plans ever existed. No one was ever charged for these mob killings. Writing nearly forty years after the events, Roberts may well have been second guessing what he should have done, attempting, perhaps, to put the best light on his activities at the time. His memoirs provide no clue. Possibly he believed that Clark and the local authorities would handle the investigation. However, it appears equally possible that he was predisposed to favor the Germans. His father, Alexander "Buck" Roberts, had left Texas rather than fight for the Confederacy during the war. If Roberts believed that the Germans were the victims during the feud and were supporting the law in the form of John Clark, he may have been prone to accept their version of events. Whatever the case, no action was taken by the Rangers. The mob can only have interpreted this as approval of their actions.

But if the Rangers posed no problem for the Hoo Doos, Tom Turley remained a loose end. Turley had survived the attempted lynching and remained in the dubious security of the Mason jail. Wages was scarcely cold in his grave when Lucia Holmes reported a rumor of mob activity in her diary on March 6: "Feel anxious and worried tonight about rumor of a gang of forty men coming up here to take out the prisoners. Hal loaded all his arms."[4]

Turley must have been particularly worried, and the following day he and another prisoner escaped from the jail. There were no guards to stop them as they made their daylight break, a point obvious from Mrs. Holmes next entry, "Tom Gurley [sic] and Caleb Hall escaped out of jail this afternoon by digging through the partition into next cell."[5]

This was the last the feud saw of Tom Turley. How Caleb "Kale" Hall, trusted posseman less than a month previous, came to be in jail is a mystery. Considering the lax security of the jail, Clark's role as an officer again comes into question. Hall and Turley's escape from jail poses unanswered questions. Why was the jail left unguarded when Clark was aware that the mob might attempt another lynching? Was Hall put in the jail simply to assist Turley's escape? No serious attempt was made by Clark to recapture either man, despite the fact that they escaped during the daylight hours. One plausible theory is that the mob had killed the men they really wanted, the Baccuses, and were willing to let Turley go. It is also probable that the mob realized that Turley would not be convicted and were unwilling to risk identification in a court of law. It is a reasonable presumption that Clark would have already questioned him on this point. Given Hall's involvement with the mob and the jail break, it is highly possible that Hall was planted in the jail to assist in the escape so that Turley could be killed in secret. Turley's fate remains unknown. Clark's lack of action against the mob is illuminating.

Suspicion fell on John Clark from the beginning. One indication of the belief that Clark had close ties with the mob is found in the request of Judge I. N. Everett who asked for the Rangers to come and maintain order during district court. Dan Roberts was absent in Austin, and Sergeant Newton H. Murray dispatched nine men to the troubled town.[6] The Rangers returned to camp on March 13, and with their departure the mob was reportedly on the move again the same day. A party of armed men was reported to have headed for the ranch of Al Baird. Henry Holmes and John Gamel approached Clark to see if he wanted them for a posse to intercept the mob. Clark declined. Nothing further of this raid is known except that no one was killed.[7] The following week another man was killed in neighboring Llano County. Reports of the identities of the killers differed: "A man named John Kelley was killed three or four days ago in Llano county. Kelley was supposed to have been killed by some of the friends of the men who were recently taken from the Mason county jail and hung."[8]

The *San Saba News* had a different perspective on the killing, which was picked up by the exchanges.

> San Saba *News*, 20th. "We understand that a man named Kelly was pursued by a party of unknown men and overtaken near Jas. K. Hoy's, on Cole creek, where he was shot and killed. He was charged with being a thief, but of the truth of the man being guilty there has been doubts entertained."

Contemporary evidence points to Kelly's death as a mob killing. A third report of the killing appeared in the *Dallas Weekly Herald* of March 27, 1875. Quoting the *Austin Gazette*, the *Herald* reported that "We learn from Mr. E. Sampson, who is just down from Burnett [*sic*] that news had been received of the hanging of one Keller [*sic*] in Llano county." Kelley had served in Company Q of the Llano County Minute Men under F. C. Stewart.[9] Following so closely upon the Baccus lynching, these killings may indicate the possibility that Kelly and/or Wages may have been Baccus herders. This is speculation, however. What is certain is that within a span of three weeks the mob had killed six men and been responsible for the death of a child without any effort being made to bring any of the killers to justice.

The most serious remaining threat to the mob was Tom Gamel. His testimony could link Clark, Caleb Hall, and Dan Hoerster to the Hoo Doos. More than one jury would want to know how Clark's crony Hall arrived at the Cavaness home four hours before the lynching and announced that it had already taken place. Gamel had eluded their first attempt to kill him, but he was shrewd enough to realize there would be others. His choices were simple: fight or flight. He resolved to carry the war to the mob.

According to Gamel, following the lynching, the mob sent another man to his ranch to inform him that he was wanted in Mason. Gamel, having no intention of placing himself in the mob's hands, informed the messenger that he would be along in a few days. He then gathered his brothers-in-law, Jim and Jap Cavaness, and headed for Camp Saline and the potential safety of the Ranger camp. Roberts was not present, and Gamel told the troops there that he was going to gather as many men as possible who opposed mob law. Roberts makes no mention of Gamel's visit to his camp either in the existing correspondence or his memoirs, and while the truthfulness of this incident may be subject to speculation, Gamel's subsequent actions are not. With the Cavaness brothers in tow, he went to ranchers Dick Roberts and Rufus Winn, both nonresident cattlemen. Together they began gathering forces in Kimble and Menard Counties.[10]

The Cavaness brothers were part of a farflung clan whose life on the frontier had hardened them. Jap Cavaness had the reputation of being a game man. Jeff Ake, who knew Cavaness, recalled that he had once been left on foot by his horse and was walking home armed with a Dragoon pistol and "an old Government sharp-shooter rifle that shot paper cartridges." A man on foot was a perfect target for Indian raiders, and his attackers felt that odds of seven to one were good. It was a fatal error in judgment.

> He killed five of 'em and the other two run. Jap looked 'em over to see if they was dead; scalped 'em, took two of the hosses and come home with the five scalps. We was all surprised when he told us about it . . . . He says: "Hell, I never give them redskins no chance. I killed 'em so fast that all they could do was hit the ground."[11]

Jasper was the elder of the brothers, born March 6, 1848. James N. Cavaness was nine months younger, being born December 22, 1848. Their father Robert Cavaness, also a cattleman, hailed from North Carolina and had come to Texas around 1852 from Arkansas. During the Civil War the older Cavaness had served at Camp San Saba with A. G. Roberts and others involved in the feud. The family had a reputation for standing on their principles, and one of their kinsmen had been killed by federal troops during Reconstruction.[12]

Gamel recalled later that his forces numbered 109 men "opposed to the mob." Significantly, this force was gathered from outside Mason County, undoubtedly from nonresident cattlemen fed up with local attempts to dominate the range. According to Gamel he and the men had met Dan Roberts west of Mason while Roberts was returning to his camp on the Little Saline.[13] Word of his approach preceded him, and when Gamel reached his ranch on March 18 Deputy John Wohrle was waiting for him. Gamel informed Wohrle that the men were strictly against mob law and were on their way to Mason. Wohrle rode back to town "and told the people of Mason of the intentions and purpose of the anti-mob element."[14] That everyone was informed is not correct, for when Gamel's forces entered Mason on March 19, Lucia Holmes wrote, "Mr. Beard [sic: Baird] and Hey came in and Hal made out a paper for men to sign for the preservation of law and order in the county. Tom Gamel and R. Winn brought in ever so many men with him. They camped out tonight. Nobody knows what they are for."[15]

Mrs. Holmes was only partially correct in her conclusion. John Clark knew precisely why they were there, as did the mob. Her husband Henry M. Holmes would later write:

> On the 24th or 25th of March, Mr. Thomas Gamel learned that the mob was about to hang him, what the source of his information was, is unknown to the writer; but evidently it was considered serious by him, as he summoned his friends and came into town to see about it. The sheriff was in town when they arrived, but at once left, though as he never called on any citizen of the place for assistance it is not thought that he considered himself in any danger.[16]

Clark's headlong flight, echoing Ecclesiastes' admonition that "the guilty flee where no man pursueth" confirms his role as the mob's leader, a fact confirmed by his subsequent actions. On March 20 Lucia Holmes recorded that "the town was very much excited. Clark went out to get men."[17] The panicked sheriff headed for his allies in eastern Mason County, gathering forces from the German population, a fact confirmed by Henry M. Holmes: "the sheriff returned to the town, followed by sixty two men, mounted and armed, and it was at once remarked that every one of the gentlemen following him were Germans, not one American amongst them."[18]

Clark had summoned the German settlers, and from this the organization of the Mason Hoo Doos can be surmised. The Germans were traditionalists, and George Bernard Erath recalled military service in the Austrian-German empires: "The latter country [Germany] compelled a man on reaching the age of twenty to serve in the army, but so far behind this was Austria that she exempted no age from conscription, and a boy of fifteen was liable to it. She pressed her subjects at a moment's notice, and rushed them off to some foreign war for, perhaps, a fourteen year's term of service."[19]

Other portions of the empire required military service from all men at age eighteen. This system was now used to raise forces in support of Clark. While there were Americans who supported the mob, men such as David Doole, the Germans provided the nucleus of Clark's power.

By all accounts Gamel and his allies behaved well. Rancher Al Baird and Wilson Hey sincerely wanted an end to mob violence as did rancher Dick Roberts. Roberts hunted unsuccessfully for the absent Clark.[20] On March 22, Clark returned to Mason and sent a dozen men into town to meet with Dan Hoerster. "Clark outside the town with ever so many men about one dozen came in and went to Hester's [*sic*: Hoerster's] house."[21]

The following day Clark entered Mason with his forces. Henry M. Holmes reported that Gamel's party "behaved very well, and left the next day or the day after, which I think was Saturday." Two days later Clark brought in his forces and the "town was held by this party in a kind of semi-military manner for the remainder of the week."[22] Lucia Holmes confirms this, noting that Clark entered Mason on March 23 and stopped at the home of Daniel Hoerster.[23]

The confrontation in Mason was a show of naked force. The Germans had the advantage of official sanction. Gamel had widespread family connections and the support of nonresident cattlemen. No incident in the county's history had the potential for violence that the confrontation in Mason during March 1875 presented. Both sides believed they were in the right, and had the hotter heads among the groups prevailed, Mason would have been turned into a killing ground. Fortunately, cooler heads did prevail.

Dan Roberts arrived in Mason on the 24th to observe the situation.[24] Clark's forces still held the town, but Roberts' intercession brought an end of the confrontation. On March 26 Gamel and thirty men rode into Mason where "they made peace at last and a good many of the Germans went home."[25] The following day Lucia Holmes recorded that nearly all of the Germans had gone and "The rangers came in to protect Clark." This was confirmed by Roberts in his monthly return. "Sergeant [N. O.] Reynolds with 9 men left for Mason the 26th to aid Sheriff if necessary. After arriving at Mason and hearing that the malice that was existing between Sheriff and other parties had been compromised returned to Camp the 29th instant."[26]

Peace lasted exactly nine days after Reynolds left Mason. Confronted by the raw power of the Gamel forces, the mob had compromised and sworn not to engage in violence. It was a promise they had no intention of keeping. On April 8 a "threatening notice" appeared in the courthouse "warning people about driving any cattle but their own."[27] If Dan Roberts was aware of the notice he probably regarded it as an idle threat by a few hot heads. Writing to John B. Jones on the 15th he reported that it was quiet on the frontier.

> The excitement among the stock men of Mason County seems to have subsided. All gone to work & quit quarreling. . . . I think the nest of thieves that had congregated about the mouth of Johnson fork of Llano has left there. There is no considerable band of loafers anywhere on Llano that I can hear of. They were encamped their [sic] during the winter but have left for other quarters.[28]

Roberts was not alone in this belief. A letter from Mason to the *San Antonio Herald* dated the 16th of April noted in part "Nothing very exciting here at present." Lucia Holmes recorded that things were "dull" in Mason.[29]

It would not last. May would see a return to violence.

Within the German community, Sheriff John Clark's support remained strong as an "effective officer" despite the confrontation in Mason. Suspicion, if not outright accusation, of his involvement in the killings of the four men in Mason by the American community remained as well, but aside from the agreement to leave Gamel in peace there were no other ramifications from the violence of February. The death of the Wohrle baby seems to have been regarded in military terms as collateral damage, overlooked and soon forgotten. Certainly no sense of shame for the infant's death attached itself to the mob, and the tragedy has been largely ignored. The mob remained unrepentant and undaunted.

As sheriff, one of Clark's functions was tax collector for Mason County, and in late April or early May he "had a dispute over some taxes" with Tim Williamson.[30] The disagreement appears to have been over a town lot in Loyal Valley valued at $1,200.[31] John O. Meusebach, also a resident of Loyal Valley, owned a store in the town that was assessed at $1,000, $200 less than Williamson's private dwelling. It was a huge amount, far more than other private residences in Loyal Valley were valued at, and Williamson had good reason to believe that the assessment was in error.[32]

Clark rode to Loyal Valley to confer with the rancher on the matter. "Williamson was not at home and Clark proceeded to abuse Williamson's wife," Gamel stated.[33] Why and how Clark abused Mary Williamson is subject to speculation. Certainly she was subjected to some harsh verbal abuse, and Clark might have struck her. Yet any abuse over a simple assessment error appears unlikely, and the intensity of this confrontation points to another, more significant, reason. The most likely explanation involves Williamson's role in the "big raid" of the previous year. If Clark attempted to use the tax issue or threats to have Williamson change or withdraw his testimony and failed, his anger makes far more sense. Whatever the case, when Williamson learned of the incident he rode immediately to Mason intending to fight Clark. Gamel recalled, "A few days later Williamson came to Mason and he and Clark met. Clark was horseback and Williamson followed him around on foot and tried to get a fight out of him, but Clark refused to fight. Shortly afterwards Williamson was charged with stealing a yearling and placed under arrest and gave bond."[34]

Williamson was then under indictment on an old charge of theft of a yearling, a common enough charge in that day and place.[35] Many in Mason did not believe him guilty, including Dan Hoerster who posted bond for his friend. [36] Hoerster was brand inspector and would hardly have posted bond for anyone he believed was a cattle thief. Yet in May 1875 Clark persuaded Hoerster to give up Williamson's bond. The *Statesman* reported that Williamson, "a stock man living in Mason" was under bond for his appearance in court at Mason. "Sometime in May he was met by Mr. Herster, [sic] one of his bondsmen, and Wohrlie [sic], deputy sheriff of Mason county, and was surrendered by Herster to Wohrlie."[37]

How Clark persuaded Hoerster to surrender the bond is unknown, but Clark was a persuasive man. Without bond, Clark was justified in arresting Williamson until a new bond could be secured. Clark then dispatched Johann Wohrle to arrest him at Karl Lehmberg's cattle camp in Llano County.[38] Sending Wohrle after Williamson was an exercise in discretion for Clark. Given the problems between the two men, it is unlikely that Williamson would have greeted Clark with anything short of open hostility. Wohrle, on the other hand, was a well-liked man in the community.

Wohrle executed the warrant for Williamson at Lehmberg's on Thursday, May 13. Karl Lehmberg immediately offered bond for Tim Williamson, but Wohrle refused.[39] Historian Allen Hatley notes that posting bond was "a long-time accepted practice in rural Texas for a man who was not a flight risk."[40] Wohrle's refusal was a direct contradiction to common practice at the time. Lehmberg then saddled up and the men headed for Mason to renew the bond. Near Willow Creek they were met by armed mob members in what can only have been a prearranged ambush. The *Herald* reported that Williamson

> was in the hands of the law in the person of deputy Sheriff John Whorlie [*sic*], disarmed and on the road to Mason to renew a bond for his appearance at the District Court. I have learned that a good bond was offered for him at Lehmberg's, where the re-arrest was made, but was not accepted, for what cause I know not but certain it is that whilst on the road to Mason with his surety Chas. Lehmberg he was set upon by 10 or 15 men with their faces blacked and foully murdered.[41]

DeVos concurs, noting that "According to one account, Charles Lehmberg was accompanying Worley [*sic*] and Williamson to Mason."[42] Lehmberg's presence was further confirmed by newspapers of the time. Under the banner THE OUTRAGE MILL the *San Antonio Daily Express* reported:

> A MAN KILLED IN MASON COUNTY.—The Fredericks-burg *Sentinel* of the 15th states that Tim Williamson, in the custody of Sheriff Clark and accompanied by Carl Lehmberg, of Castell, Llano county, were attacked by a disguised mob, about three miles from Castell, on their way to Fort Mason, and that Tim Williamson was literally riddled with bullets. Sheriff Clark escaped, but Mr. Carl Lehmberg, who is a prominent merchant of Llano county, had not been heard of. — Austin *Statesman.*[43]

Williamson's murder marked a significant benchmark in the feud's progress. As a direct result of this killing, the dynamics and motives that marked the beginning of the Hoo Doo War changed from control of the cattle range to a war of vengeance that raged through Mason County in the months to come. Lucia Holmes recorded the following day that another "horrible murder" had been committed on Willow Creek.[44] At the time she had no concept of how horrible things would become.

Henry Doell Jr. identified the killer as Peter Bader and informed Sonnichsen that "It was all fixed up ahead of time." When Wohrle and Williamson "reached the right place, they were waylaid." According to Doell, Williamson was shot from his horse. Peter Bader then ran up and killed the defenseless man.[45]

Texas Ranger James B. Gillett reported:

> When he saw the pursuing men Williamson divined their purpose and begged the sheriff to let him run in an effort to save his life. Worley refused and, it is said, drew his pistol and deliberately shot Williamson's horse through the loin, causing it to fall. Unarmed and unmounted, Williamson was killed without a chance to protect himself and without any pretense of a trial. After the murder Worley and the mob disappeared.[46]

Gamel confirms this report. "It was reported that at the time Williamson ran, Worley shot Williamson's horse out from under him and the mob killed him. It is said that Williamson asked the mob to remember his wife and children."[47]

Williamson's murder sent shock waves through the Hill Country. In Mason, John Gamel informed Henry Holmes that he intended to run for brand inspector, a declaration complicated by the fact that he made his decision on May 14 and the election was set for the following day. Had the decision been made earlier he may well have won, for Lucia Holmes noted that Gamel was not beaten "very badly."[48] That Gamel and Holmes, both mob opponents, were concerned with Hoerster as brand inspector indicates their belief that Mason's problems lay in the official offices. This was confirmed when no effort was made to discover the identity of Williamson's killers.[49] On May 17 Holmes wrote a petition to the governor for help "to put down the mob."[50] "A petition was sent after remaining two days in the Court house for signatures to the Governor of the State asking his aid, to which no answer whatever was returned."[51] Holmes also began gathering evidence against mob members, and on the 18th he interviewed Charley Johnson concerning the lynching in February.[52] What Johnson told Holmes is unknown. Possibly he was able to identify some members of the mob, but this is speculation.

Scarcely a week later Major John B. Jones passed through Mason. Here he received a detailed account of the problems, but Jones had more pressing problems at the time. Like Adjutant General William Steele and Governor Richard Coke, Jones was later charged with partisanship during the course of the feud. On the frontier Dan Roberts was engaged with Indian raiders who had struck the region. Roberts failed to mention either the Mason troubles or Williamson's murder in his reports despite the fact that he was still camped in Mason County, possibly because he had the opportunity to report them directly to Jones.[53]

Residents of the area can only have interpreted this in one way. During the war and Reconstruction, the government had abandoned them to settle their own problems. The Hoo Doos had killed another man, and this time the law had openly aided them in the murder. Governor Coke, facing serious problems maintaining the Rangers at all in the face of a parsimonious legislature, ignored the citizens' petition. Once again the county was on its own. Williamson's murder would return to haunt them all as others moved to seek justice.

The killings of early 1875 did nothing to suppress cattle theft although the premise that the mob was killing cattle thieves is commonly expressed. Given the upsurge of violence, stock theft in the region should have decreased if the men killed were thieves. A contemporary letter from Mason demonstrates that the premise and the reality of cattle theft in the area are false. Writing on May 25, 1875, cattleman D. S. Willis told of "a fearful raid" happening at the time conducted by Indian and Mexican raiders. Willis went on to say that "Two-thirds of the stealing from this country is done by Mexicans direct from Mexico." The raiders were after cattle, and should have been a primary target for Clark and the ranchers of Mason.[54] Willis' account was confirmed by the *San Antonio Daily Herald* of May 20, 1875.

> MAJ. JAS. TRAINER, from Mason, is in our city. He will be in town for about a week. We learn from him that the Indians are very bad in his section of the country. They killed a woman on Mill Creek 12 miles from Mason, on last Sunday [May 16]. The Indians are said to be Kiowas from the Reservation; but we doubt it, as in that case the Quakers would have teached [*sic*] them to respect the Lords' Day.

William Steele did respond to the Indian threat, penning a letter to John B. Berry, commander of the Mason County Volunteer Company, requesting that he turn over arms to Dan Roberts adding that "The immediate services of Lieut. Roberts' Company are required on the frontier, and it is desired that no delay will result from want of these arms."[55]

Order was breaking down in Mason County. Following the murder of Williamson, Wohrle resigned as Deputy Sheriff. Quite probably it was an open break with the mob.[56] On July 10, Lucia Holmes reported that there were a "Lot of drunken men in town shooting all day and night." No effort was made to stop them by Clark although District Court was to convene only two days later. The summer term of court would prove of extreme importance. Had the cases before it been handled differently it is likely that the Hoo Doo War would have ended with a flock of indictments. It did not.

The feud was about to take a savage new direction.

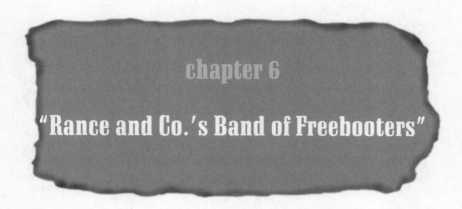

chapter 6

"Rance and Co.'s Band of Freebooters"

On July 12 the summer term of District Court opened in Mason County. Although no one realized it at the time, the summer session was a pivotal moment in the feud. Three separate murder cases and the Baccus cattle theft case were all on the books to be heard. All of these cases were critical to ending mob law, and trouble was anticipated by legal authorities not involved with the mob. Dan Roberts recalled that he received a note from the judge instructing him not to turn Johnson over to any sheriff, undoubtedly to prevent another lynching. When the time came, Roberts brought Johnson into Mason under heavy guard.[1]

From the mob's perspective the charges against Charley Johnson for his role in the Baccus case were clearly important. They anticipated a conviction based upon the very evidence they had used in deciding to lynch the Baccuses. In this they were doomed to disappointment. Both Johnson and John Martin, if the latter were ever brought to trial, were acquitted. It was a clear indication that the charges against Baccus and his men could not have been sustained and served to tarnish the mob's reputation in the minds of some as having lynched innocent men. Johnson was also called before the grand jury in an attempt to identify mob members involved in the February lynching. In his memoirs Roberts recalled that Johnson was sent before the grand jury "to see if he would identify any of the mob." Johnson either could not or would not identify anyone: "He was not prompted by any one to tell, or not tell anything. But we were glad he did not tell any more than he did, as it might frustrate our plans of catching them."[2]

Roberts was also called before the jury and underwent extensive questioning regarding the incident. He stated that he knew nothing at the time that he thought the jury should have and parried them with "semi-truth."[3] In later years Roberts rationalized his actions, stating that some of the mob may have sat on the grand jury, and he did not want to tip the Rangers' hand. While this might well have been a valid plan, the truth remains that Roberts took no action of any kind against the mob as evidenced by the lack of subsequent investigation and arrests by Company D relative to mob activity in the area. Company D proved worse than useless in suppressing the feud.

In the Williamson case, both John Wohrle and Karl Lehmberg would have been called to the stand to testify. Nothing of their testimony has survived. Quite probably Wohrle would have been called upon to explain why he had killed Williamson's mount rather than resisting the killers or fleeing with the prisoner. Both men would have been questioned regarding the killers' identities. Frightened by the near lynching of Tom Gamel, neither was willing to identify any of the killers and place their lives in jeopardy. No indictments resulted. The same was probably true concerning the murder of Allen Bolt. It was a sadly disappointing session, but on the surface things proceeded properly. One contemporary account of the term was reported by an unidentified resident present at the proceedings.

> Our grand jury, composed of a fine and intelligent body of men, seemed to make pretty thorough investigations of offenses against the public peace and good order, but found not more than eight or ten indictments after five days inquest. The new judge impresses every one with confidence in his official ability and integrity, and as it is rare to get such men now a-days, we hope to continue him in the position in case a new election is ordered under a new constitution.[4]

In short, the term accomplished nothing of significance. Attorney Henry Holmes provided a less charitable view. Writing in obvious disgust, Holmes later reported that "No effort whatever so far as is known was made by the authorities to endeavor to discover the perpetrators of this outrage further than to hold a coroner's inquest over the remains."[5] This lack of effort by both local officials and the Rangers to identify the killers was not lost on a young man sitting quietly in the courtroom. The citizens would have done well to note the quiet stranger in their midst. In the months to follow, Scott Cooley's name would become synonymous with terror.

William Scott Cooley was a hard man schooled in Indian warfare, mob violence and blood feud. The earliest mention of the Cooley family located to date is in 1850 when Mathias "Cooly," age thirty-eight, Missouri-born, was enumerated in the census for Izard County, Arkansas, along with his wife Martha, aged twenty-six. Six children ranging in age from nine months to ten years were also noted, including a six-year-old William whose birthplace is also given as Missouri. The two youngest children, John and Thomas, were born in Arkansas, which places the family's arrival there somewhere between 1846 and 1848.[6] William Scott Cooley later stated that he was half Cherokee, probably through his mother. This is confirmed in one contemporary newspaper that described him as "a short solid man, about twenty-eight years old, and looks like he might have some Cherokee blood in him."[7] Another description notes that he had a dark complexion, dark hair and small, black eyes. Cooley was approximately five feet, six inches with "legs rather short in proportion to body, claims to be half Indian."[8]

Sometime after 1856, the family moved to Jack County, Texas, where C. A. Williams enumerated them on the census during 1860. Mathias Cooley was listed as a farmer with a personal estate valued at $400. Absent from the household were sons James, age twenty, and William. There were six more children listed, however, including a five-year-old child named Scott.[9] From Ranger records, it has been determined that Cooley's full name was William Scott Cooley. Apparently the older William had died somewhere between the birth of Frank Cooley in 1854 and that of Scott in 1855. Scott Cooley had been named William in memory of his brother.

Mason County was not Cooley's first brush with mob violence. In 1862, terror had gripped northern Texas when James G. Bourland arrested 150 men on the suspicion of being Unionists. The so-called

Great Hanging at Gainesville had a widespread impact, and the impression left on a child can only have been fear and distrust of mob violence.

Folklore about Scott Cooley has it that his family was massacred by Indians. The basis for this appeared as early as 1875 when a correspondent identifying himself as "Peter" wrote in part that "Cooley is a very young man. When a boy he was cared for by Williamson, to whom he was much attached, and whose death he proposed to avenge with the blood of all those he thinks had a hand in the business."[10] S. P. Elkins, who served in Company D of the Rangers, knew Cooley personally.

> His people were all killed by the Indians several years
> before in Palo Pinto county, in Keechi valley. Scott at
> that time was a small boy and the Indians took him
> captive; he was afterwards recaptured by the whites.
> This gave Cooley a great hatred for the Indians, and
> when he got a chance he fought them hard and close.
> Cooley had no fear and had a blood thirst for the
> Comanches.[11]

Elkins was mistaken, as was Joe Chapman, a resident of Jack County, who recalled that "Some time previous to the killing of my father [July 1860], the Indians had murdered a man named Cooley, our nearest neighbor, three miles away."[12] More reliable information is available in a petition dated June 16, 1871, from Jack County. In it one T. Tooley is noted as having been killed by Indians in November of 1860.[13] None of Cooley's family are known to have been killed by Indians. On the contrary, raiders from the reservation at Fort Sill had good reason to fear these men.

During the 1860s and 1870s Jack County was almost continually under assault by the Comanches. In the midst of this the Cooley brothers emerge as tough, resolute men.

> On Saturday, the 20th, three young men, Cooley
> by name, living on Picket's ranche in White prairie
> came upon four Indians, and killed two of the four,
> one of whom they scalped, while the other dead

Indian was carried away by his companions. The two dead Indians' horses were captured, but the others succeeded in getting away with all the other horses. The fight occurred one and a half miles from the ranche.[14]

Three months later another paper reported: "We learn from the Texas exchanges that the Indians made a raid on Wise county, but the sheriff and the Cool[e]y boys got after them and killed them all."[15]

Men who knew Cooley remembered him as a ruthless and relentless fighter. That he and his brothers carried the fight to the Comanches speaks for itself. Nor were Indians the only targets of their wrath. On May 26, 1870, their father was killed by Joseph Horton in a dispute over cattle. Jim Cooley killed Horton the following day.[16]

According to Gillett, Cooley had worked for Williamson and made two drives up the trail to Kansas with him.[17] This would have been during 1872 and 1873, and evidence of Cooley's presence in Kansas during 1873 exists. On October 16, 1873, Cooley and George Edwards, both of Texas, signed into the Grand Central Hotel in Ellsworth, Kansas.[18] The following year, on May 2, 1874, Cooley enlisted in Company D of the Texas Rangers under C. R. Perry in Blanco County as a corporal.[19] Contemporary records describe him as five feet five inches tall with dark complexion, dark hair and dark eyes, and having the occupation "cowdriver." Cooley gave his age as twenty-two. He was actually nineteen.[20]

By the time Cooley enlisted. he was already a hard man. Service in the Rangers toughened him further, and it was here that he first made his reputation. According to C. R. Perry, Cooley's first commander, he was selected as one of John B. Jones' escort when he made his initial survey of the line that the Frontier Battalion had established. Possibly he was the senior man in the Company D detail.[21] He did not wait long for action. On July 12, 1874, Jones, accompanied by Captain G. W. Stevens, Jones' escort, and other Rangers, went in pursuit of a band of Indian raiders. At Lost Valley they rode into an ambush, and in the resulting fight Rangers D. W. H. Bailey and W. A. Glass were killed. Two other Rangers, Lee Corn and George Moore, were wounded.[22]

For unknown reasons Cooley resigned his rank as corporal on August 15, 1874, choosing to remain on the force as a private.[23] The same month Company D was detailed to accompany Major John B. Jones to Mason County where the early stages of what would become the Hoo Doo War were developing.[24] On November 20, 1874, he again saw action against hostile raiders on Saline Creek in Menard County. One newspaper reported: "The Indians came down Elm [Creek] within a few miles of camp, and, running in on a beef detail of two men, Scott Cooley and Billy Trawick, opened fire upon them, when they fled to camp in hot haste, pursued by the Indians, who fired several shots, Cooley returning the fire."[25]

The Rangers killed five of the enemy and captured another. Cooley's name figured prominently in accounts of the fight. "The boys brought some fresh scalps with them and they report that Scott Cooley, who was fired at and run into camp, not only cut a wounded Indian's throat, but stripped a large piece of skin from his back, saying that he would make a quirt out of it."[26] Nannie Moore Kinser, a resident of Burnet County, recalled of Cooley that "He was a small man but DYNAMITE, and not afraid of anyone."[27] Undeniably the most dangerous man involved in the Hoo Doo War, Cooley was not a man to be trifled with. Saline Creek was the last major action of Cooley's official career. The state of Texas had decided to reduce the level of frontier protection provided to the settlers. Victim of a parsimonious government, Cooley was honorably discharged on December 4, 1874.[28]

At the time of Williamson's death, Cooley was living in Menard County. Texas Ranger James B. Gillett recalled in his memoirs that when Cooley learned of Williamson's murder he was angry and vowed revenge on the killers.[29] The contemporary account provided by Henry Holmes confirms that Cooley was in Company D's camp visiting friends when news of the murder reached him.

> The day the news of Williamson's murder came to the Ranger camp, to which force Cooley at one time belonged, he sat down and cried with grief for the loss of one who he said was his best friend in the world, and declared then that he would have revenge, and this before it was possible he could have had any communication with any of Williamson's friends.[30]

Unlike Sheriff John Clark, Cooley did investigate Williamson's murder. Certain conclusions, drawn from contemporary evidence, are inescapable. The ambush of the men was obviously prearranged as Doell later informed Sonnichsen. Only two men knew when Wohrle would make Williamson's arrest: Clark and Wohrle. It was simplicity itself to inform the mob when Williamson would be brought back to Mason. From this Cooley came to the logical conclusion that one or both of the men had arranged the ambush. Wohrle had no existing grudge against Williamson although he had killed Williamson's horse. Clark did have the rationale to want Williamson out of the way. Reaching the conclusion that Clark had planned the murder it was also logical that Clark not only had connections to the mob but influence as well, probably as its leader. Ultimately, Cooley held both men accountable for Williamson's death.

The killing of Williamson's horse by John Wohrle has never been challenged, and there can be little doubt that Wohrle was involved in the murder. How the story became public can only have been due to Karl Lehmberg, something he would hardly have revealed if he was involved in mob activity. Why Wohrle killed the horse remains open to speculation, but his subsequent resignation as deputy sheriff may indicate that Clark, the mob, or both pressured him to insure that Williamson did not escape. To Clark's mind this no doubt seemed a clever ploy. Unlike the Baccus lynchings in February, no stigma would attach itself to his name. He had not anticipated that Lehmberg would accompany Wohrle and witness the killing. Nor had he anticipated an avenging fury in the form of Scott Cooley.

How Cooley learned the identities of those involved in the killing is also speculation, but the most likely source of information was Karl Lehmberg, the only eyewitness to the crime not connected to the mob. Living in western Llano County, Lehmberg was too close to the mob to insure his safety. He was naturally reluctant to identify the men in court for fear of retaliation. Confiding in Cooley, whom he may have believed was still a member of Company D, presented a way for an investigation that would keep Lehmberg from being involved at least until the men were brought to trial for murder. Lehmberg may have met Cooley in 1874, and if so had every reason for this belief. When Cooley began killing the Hoo Doos involved, Lehmberg had equal reason to remain silent about his role in the affair.

Cooley's entry into the Hoo Doo War marks a major turning point of the feud. The summer term of court was the high water mark for John Clark and the mob. They had killed with impunity, considering themselves above the law. Having dealt in death and terror, they were about to be repaid in kind. The time for the peacemakers had run out for Mason County. It was the worst possible time.

Hampered by financial problems in keeping the Rangers at full strength, Governor Coke and Adjutant General Steele had ignored repeated pleas for help in putting down mob activity. Jones, with limited men, placed them along the frontier to help stem Indian raids. Roberts' plan to investigate the mob, if it ever existed, proved fruitless. With Williamson's death seven men and an infant had died in 1875 without anyone lifting a hand. It is small wonder that the *Austin Daily Statesman* quipped "In Mason county bloodthirsty gangs of murderers ride triumphantly over the rights of law abiding citizens."[31]

Mason County did not wait long for the next killing. The first news arrived in Mason on July 21, according to a correspondent who signed himself Otho.

> This morning Henry Dill [*sic*: Heinrich Doell], a cattle man of considerable wealth, August Keller and three other men, and three boys, were lying asleep in their camp, some ten miles west of this town, when at about two o'clock a. m., the camp was fired into and both Dell and Keller were wounded. The former was shot through the loins and the latter in the foot. While the wound of Keller, though severe, is not serious, the former will probably die. Tracks were seen near the camp afterwards resembling mocassin [*sic*] tracks, but inasmuch as the horses of the sleeping party were not molested, as I am informed by one of the party fired on, and other circumstances arising to dispel the idea that the attacking force could be Indians, the convictions seems to prevail that the assassins are some of the white desperadoes who infest Northwest Texas, who, doubtless, committed this atrocious deed out of revenge for some past real or imaginary wrong, or from pure deviltry and depravity of heart.

> Mr. Dill is a man much respected here, as an up-
> right citizen of integrity, energy and means, while
> Keller is one of our best young men, of good family.
> A messenger came into town post-haste after a physi-
> cian, about sunrise, since when we have heard noth-
> ing from the wounded or in respect to the pursuit of
> the assassins.[32]

Doell's killing triggered an immediate controversy. DeVos wrote that it "has left historical writers wondering what happened and why."[33] Sonnichsen implied that Doell might well have been shot by the mob because he questioned the murder of Tim Williamson although he reported a different version of the murder as well.[34] Lucia Holmes recorded her belief about the shooting.

> News came this morning that someone fired into
> a camp near Tom Gamel's and killed a Mr. [Doell]
> and wounded a young Mr. Kelly [sic: Keller] in the
> foot—supposed to be Indians. Poor Dal [sic: Doell]
> died at 9 o'clock and was brought to Mason. His wife
> came here too late to see him before he died.[35]

It is apparent from her diary that Lucia Holmes believed Doell's murder had nothing to do with the feud. Tom Gamel echoed this view. Gamel, who attempted to track the killer or killers, set it apart from the feud in his recollections. Unlike Lucia Holmes, he did not believe that Indians were responsible for the killing. According to Gamel, he and John Lindsay followed the trail of the killer as far as Streeter before giving it up. Gamel recalled that while following the trail "several cigarette stubs were found which was conclusive that the cow hunters had not been attacked by Indians."[36]

This same view was also noted by Otho. Continuing his letter on the afternoon of July 21, he reported that Doell had lived five or six hours after being shot. "The German population of this county is large, about one-half, and this atrocious assassination has greatly incensed them. No man believes that the deadly work was done by Indians, in spite of the moccasin tracks seen near camp this morning." He further reported that "six or eight" horses were driven off at the same time.[37]

This was apparently the view published in the Fredericksburg *Sentinel* as well. In a letter to the San Antonio *Herald*, Henry M. Holmes stated: "Further, the Sentinel may know why Mr. Doell should be an object of vengeance, we do not. I have always heard of him as a man of large family, industrious and kind-hearted who would have scorned the idea of taking part in a mob, either to hang Backus [*sic*] or murder Williamson, then why should vengeance fall on him."[38]

In his memoirs Gamel provided further details about the shooting. On July 20, Doell, Fritz Kothmann, Al and John Lindsay, and August Keller were on a cow hunt in western Mason County and stopped at the home of his father, William Gamel. After dinner, the men rode about a mile east and set up camp. Around two o'clock in the morning Doell was shot, the bullet hitting him in the right side.[39] The bullet passed through Doell and hit Keller in the leg, a painful but not serious wound. Doell lingered until morning, dying around nine o'clock on July 21. Only one shot was fired at the herders.[40]

The motive for Doell's murder remains a mystery. Adding to the complexity is a local belief that Fritz Kothmann was the intended target, probably based upon his involvement in the feud. One account that reached Austin agreed with Otho's assessment and was apparently the official view adopted by the sheriff's office: "Hy. Doell and A. Keller, of Mason county, were hunting on Mason Creek and [were] fired upon by men disguised as Indians. Doell was shot, perhaps fatally, through the body, and the other through the foot. These robbers were thought to belong to 'Rance and Co.'s' band of freebooters."[41] This has some basis in fact. On July 1, Major Jones reported from Kerr County that there had been five or six raids by Indians and outlaws since May. Two of the parties had been overtaken, and both an Indian and a white horse thief had been killed by the Rangers. Jones continued:

> I am satisfied there is an extensive organization of thieves on this part of the frontier. . . . The white man who was wounded in the fight died near here. He confessed to being a member of an organized band of horse thieves and robbers. Had been in the clan but a short time and was not fully informed of their plans and operations, but thought there was sixty or seventy of them, that they carried their stolen

stock out to the head of the Llano when it was kept for some time, the brands and other marks by which they could be identified changed, and then sent off to different places.[42]

Jones makes no mention of anyone named Rance in this correspondence. Not surprisingly, but authorities in Mason had, at least on an unofficial basis, charged the murder to another nonresident stockman, Rance Moore.[43] It was by now an all too familiar charge having marked similarities to charges made against Creed Taylor, A. G. Roberts and other nonresident stockmen.

Moore was not alone in being accused of the murder. Doell's son Henry provided C. L. Sonnichsen at least one motive why the shooting may have been done by the mob.

> Mr. Doell & his father [Heinrich Doell] were riding with two of this gang, and Mr. D's father said it was a shame what they did to Tim Williamson—he was no worse than they were. "You've mavericked and sleepered and I've mavericked and sleepered. And besides those weren't Tim's cattle. They were Lehmberg's. Tim was just working for him." The other men changed the subject and asked how many calves he had branded that year.[44]

If the mob believed that Doell might reveal who was involved in Williamson's death, it is possible that they decided to eliminate him to insure his silence. Beyond this, Doell's son also informed Dr. Sonnichsen about another version of his father's killing that he personally believed. According to Doell, his father had been killed over a red cow with white ears and her calf found during Doell's last cow hunt. The cow had

> the V of his brand (V6) changed to an 8—Alf. Gammel's [sic] brand. . . . Alf was the outlaw and did this killing. Henry was never told of it until Alf and Tom were dead. Alf used to come by his home regularly and borrow a chew of tobacco. There were a good many

indictments against Alf Gamel for cattle stealing when the courthouse was burned in '77 or '78. The burning was done to burn up the indictments—others probably had same reason.

Mr. Doell [Heinrich] found the cow with blotted brand and said, "I'm going to keep this cow, but there won't be any trouble." . . . Gamel had the nerve to make Henry swear that Indians did the job.[45]

Brand records do confirm certain details of this story. On June 20, 1876, Hermann Theis recorded the brand VD that notes further "this Brand formerly recorded for Henry Doell." The V6 brand was actually registered by Henry Vasterling of Llano County on June 3, 1878. Alfred Gamel did record an 86 brand, but it was not recorded until October 8, 1877, two years after Doell's murder.[46] Another problem with identifying Gamel as the killer is that Alfred Hunter Gamel was born June 10, 1862, making him just thirteen when Doell was killed. While it is certainly possible that a boy could have fired the killing shot, it is equally inconceivable that Alf Gamel, age thirteen, had "a good many indictments" against him for anything. This story was nothing more than local gossip aimed at discrediting the Gamels.

Confronted by a myriad of suspects, contemporary evidence indicates that none of the men was specifically targeted. Both Otho and Gamel reported that the shooting had occurred around two o'clock in the morning. Even under a bright moon, the shapes of the sleeping men would have been indistinguishable dark forms against a lighter background. Unless the killer had marked his target before dark or had an accomplice in the camp itself, there was no way that a specific individual could have been selected. Henry Holmes clearly believed that this was impossible.

They were camped on high open ground, no cover for any lurking foe, an impossibility for any one to distinguish between forms laying on the ground unless they had followed the party up, and seen where they slept, which it would have been impossible to do undiscovered, and further their horses stolen and driven out of the country and not heard of since and no tracks but those of moccasins.[47]

In 1928 J. Marvin Hunter pointed to the logical conclusion concerning Doell's death:

> For some time, it was thought that this shooting had been done by white men or Mexicans belonging to a band of outlaws then rendezvoursing [*sic*] in Kimble and other sections of the western country, in an effort to terrorize the cattlemen from this country to such an extent that they would keep out of the of the [*sic*] cattle rustler's territory. But as the horses belonging to the outfit were all driven off and some of them were later recovered many miles west, in an exhausted condition, it is now generally beli[e]ved that the killing and stealing was done by a small band of Indians. In later years, a Mexican boy, at one time a captive with the Indians, was reported to have said that he was with the Indians, and that he did the shooting, and was severely punished by the Indians for having fired the shot, as the Indians did not want to create any alarm, only desiring to make a peaceful escape with the stolen horses.[48]

Regardless of who the killer was, the end result was the same. Once again the county was divided over the murder. Clark and his supporters charged it to white "outlaws" in an effort to justify their mob activities despite the evidence pointing to Indian raiders as the likely culprits.

Once again the Rangers were summoned to Mason County. John B. Jones reported that:

> I reached this, Lt. Roberts' camp day before yesterday, find the company in good condition and doing good service, having one scouting party out and another just starting. They are having or anticipating more trouble in Mason and at the request of the

civil authorities I sent Lt. Roberts and a few men to preserve order there during the session of the Court which meets there next week.[49]

On July 23, another shooting occurred. Writing in her diary, Lucia Holmes noted that "Kelly [*sic* Keller] boy shot at in his field on Friday night."[50] No one was ever charged in the case, and no motive is known for the shooting. As July closed Mason remained a community divided over the shootings and the motives for them. The next killing would leave no doubts in anyone's mind.

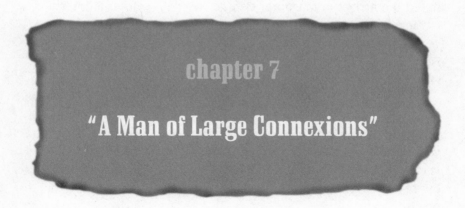

"A Man of Large Connexions"

In later years Tom Gamel recalled Cooley's presence in Mason as the ex-Ranger observed the legal proceedings and began his investigation into Williamson's murder. When the session closed, Cooley left Mason and was gone about a month although no reason for his absence has been determined. When he returned, his first call was on gunsmith Joseph Miller whom he informed that "he wanted his gun fixed" since he was about ready to use it. Cooley then informed John Gamel "that he thought he had found the man that was responsible for Williamson's death."[1] John Gamel immediately informed his brother of Cooley's remarks. The brothers immediately began searching for Wohrle to warn him that Cooley was hunting him. It was a logical conclusion that took little guesswork, particularly if the claim that Wohrle had killed Williamson's horse had come out during court.[2]

Wohrle had resigned as deputy sheriff and was now earning his living as a handyman and carpenter. On August 10 he was working with Charles "Doc" Harcourt and a man identified by Gamel only as "Doc's Little Yankee" either cleaning or digging a well. Possibly Harcourt and Wohrle were old friends, both men having served in Troop B, Third U. S. Cavalry.[3] Unlike the Gamels, Cooley knew exactly where Wohrle was.

For no apparent reason, Lucia Holmes' diary falls silent on August 9, 1875. The killing of Wohrle on Tuesday, August 10, has no contemporary mention. When she resumed writing on August 14, she recorded nothing of her feelings concerning John Wohrle. That day she noted the arrival in Mason of George Paschall, who asked her to go to Menard to visit with his family. Understandably, Lucia Holmes accepted the invitation. In her diary she notes that "Vanty Scott and old Foley drunk tonight and shooting all over the town—horrid times."[4] Order in Mason was dissolving, and her first instinct was to run.

John Wohrle's killing is well documented. Gillett reports that once Cooley completed his investigation into Williamson's murder, he returned to Mason where he found Wohrle "engaged in cleaning out a well." Cooley asked for a drink of water, then engaged Wohrle in conversation. When the unsuspecting Wohrle began to draw his assistant out of the well, Cooley "declared his mission and shot Worley [sic] to death."[5]

Gamel provides further detail. Harcourt was in the well bucket while Wohrle and the third man lowered him down. When Cooley killed Wohrle his companion fled and Harcourt plunged to the well bottom. Harcourt survived the fall, and provided first hand information on the killing.

> When Harkey [sic: Harcourt] came to his senses, he said that Cooley rode up where he and Worley [sic] and the little Yankee were at work on the well and talked with them for a long time. Harkey got up and got in the well bucket and made the remark that he had to go to work and Worley started to let him down. Just as his head got below the top of the well Cooley made the remark "Worley, why did you kill Williamson?" Worley answered, "Because I had too," and Cooley replied "For the same reason I am killing you," and Cooley shot Worley . . . . [6]

A more sensationalized version reached the newspapers, providing what may have been the "official" version.

> Horrible murder at Mason.—From the *Freie Presse* of the 17th inst., we translate the following:
> "On the 10th of August, during the afternoon, Mr. John Wohrly [sic] , a quiet respectable citizen and former Deputy Sheriff, was assisting a man by the name

of Harcutt [*sic*] in digging a well, when a young man of about twenty-four years of age, rode up and began conversing with Wohrly in the most friendly manner, stating among other things that he was looking for two horses. He asked Wohrly for a piece of leather with which to fasten his gun to the saddle, which request was complied with. While the villain was apparently fixing the leather to his saddle, Wohrly and another man who was present, began hauling Harcutt up from the bottom of the well. While they were thus engaged the stranger took advantage of the opportunity to shoot Wohrly through in the back of the head, the ball coming out near his nose. Whorly fell dead, his companion, being without arms, fled, and Harcutt fell to the bottom of the well, a distance of forty feet, where he remained senseless.

The murderer then fired six shots into the dead body of Wohrly, stabbed it in four places with his knife, and finally took his scalp, whereupon the fiend mounted his horse and rode off.

It is probable that the murder[er] will evade all earthly punishment, as he is evidently the paid assassin of men who will back him up."[7]

Wohrle's death made news across Texas. In Galveston it was reported simply that "Worley was shot six times and then scalped."[8] The Jacksboro paper carried a summary of the above article concluding the article "No clue" as to the motives or identity of the killer.[9] Cooley's identity did not remain secret for long. An Austin newspaper soon reported:

The murder of John A. Whorly [*sic*], deputy sheriff of Mason county, of which we gave inaccurate details, some days ago, creates great excitement. Scott Cooly [*sic*] was the murderer. Seven bullets penetrated the head of Whorly, and Harcourt was found at the bottom of the well almost dead. Cooly fled and has not been heard from. It is believed that Cooly was paid to murder Whorly and Harcourt by the citizens of Fredericksburg, and amongst the distributors of bribes one is mentioned distinguished for piety. The Governor has been asked to intervene to repress violence in Mason county. The people are now thoroughly aroused, and if Scott Cooly be captured he will speedily make atonement for his misdeeds.[10]

Again the recurring theme of neighboring citizens preying on Mason, by now an all too familiar theme, was released to the press. This time the accusation was laid at the door of neighboring Gillespie County residents as having hired an assassin without any apparent motive to support the allegation. Clearly evident is the fact that Clark and his faction used Wohrle's murder in an attempt to generate more animosity against outsiders, most particularly since the accusation was made before the killer was identified. Henry M. Holmes, among others, was enraged by the charge. In a letter to the *San Antonio Herald,* Holmes blasted the reports that had come out of Mason, appearing in the *Fredericksburg Sentinel* on August 14. The author, signing himself Justice, stated: "The general belief is that he was paid to perpetrate this hellish crime and that his instigators and accomplices live in this town in part at least, and it is said that they are known." Holmes reported angrily that:

> I deny that it is the general belief that Scott Cooley was paid. The day the news of Williamson's murder came to the Ranger camp, to which force Cooley at one time belonged, he sat down and cried with grief for the loss of one who he said was his best friend in the world, and declared then that he would have revenge, and this before it was possible he could have had any communication with any of Williamson's friends. [11]

The actual letter from "Justice" has not been located, but hints provided by Holmes indicate his belief that the author was David Doole, the same man who had penned the letter regarding Roberts and the "big raid" in 1874.

Cooley fled west from Mason toward Bluff Creek where he en-countered Tom Brite hauling a load of corn to his home. Cooley asked for Brite's hat, as he had lost his. Brite refused because he had just bought it. Cooley then pulled Wohrle's bloody scalp out and present-ed it to Brite who relinquished the hat without further protest.[12]

Cooley's pursuers returned empty handed to Mason. The killing left confusion in its aftermath. That Wohrle had killed Williamson's mount was well known, yet the Hoo Doos, obsessed with their ani-mosity toward their neighbors, completely failed to grasp the motive and remained oblivious to their danger. Cooley was not a man who would accept the killing of his friend with resignation. Nor did he have the restraint that A. G. Roberts, Baird, and Gamel exercised early in the feud. There would be no reprieve or mercy. The next killing left no doubts that vengeance had come for the mob.

On August 19, Carl Bader was killed. Bader's death proved as con-troversial as Doell's, a controversy that persists to this day. Part of this lies in the fact that the date of Bader's death was uncertain among researchers. DeVos initially placed the killing on August 11, the day after Wohrle's death.[13] Based on the *San Antonio Herald* of January 20, 1876, which mentions the killing "about" two months earlier, Sonnichsen placed Bader's death in November of 1875.[14] Church re-cords accurately record Bader's death on August 19, 1875.[15]

In light of later events, Bader's killing is significant in determining when the Bairds entered the conflict. As with Doell's murder, there are a number of accounts dealing with the killing, and confusion over who killed him. Gillett stated that Cooley acted on his own. "Making a quick ride across Mason County to the western edge of Llano County, Cooley waylaid and killed Pete Border [*sic*: Carl Bader], the second on his list of mob members."[16] Others reported different versions. Gamel recalled that John Baird, Scott Cooley, George Gladden, and Charley Johnson raided one of the Bader family homes near Castell. They struck by mistake Carl Bader's home, "killing an innocent man," or at least the wrong brother while he was in the fields hauling top fod-der.[17]

Contemporary newspapers dispute this identification. One noted in part: "Then came the murder of Charley [Carl] Bader, supposed by George Gladden and Moses Beard [*sic*: Baird]."[18] Hagen states on unknown authority that the killers were Cooley, Gladden, and John

Ringo, adding the detail that Bader was scalped.[19] DeVos cites the *San Antonio Freie Presse* of September 25, 1875, in support of Cooley and another unnamed man having committed the killing. According to this account, Bader was waylaid on the road. While one man distracted him, the second shot him. This is the only contemporary account located to date.[20]

The subsequent actions of the accused are important in order to determine the truth of this matter. Scarcely two months after Bader's death, Major John B. Jones wrote, "One Johnson, who escaped from the mob who hung the Baccuses last spring is an applicant for service . . ." in the Rangers.[21] Had Johnson been involved in the shooting it is highly unlikely that he would have boldly ridden into a Ranger camp and applied to become a Ranger. Similarly, Hagen's inclusion of Ringo on the list of suspects is unsupported by any contemporary document.[22] A similar case can be made showing that neither Gladden or the Baird brothers were involved in the fighting at this time. The subsequent actions of these men, particularly Moses Baird and George Gladden, make it obvious they had no reason to believe Carl Bader's death had put them in harm's way. The identity of the second man, if indeed there was one, may never be determined with certainty.

Following Bader's killing, Cooley dropped from sight. The Hoo Doos now realized that they had become targets. Gillett recalled that the killings "struck terror into the heart of nearly every citizen of Mason County."[23] His statement is confirmed by the *Austin Daily Statesman* which wrote:

> No arrests have been made, and every man about Mason is afraid to open his mouth one way or the other. Neighbors are afraid of each other, and will not travel the road in company with any man. Lieutenant Roberts may succeed in restoring quietness, but the apprehension is that the worst has not come.[24]

Posses roamed the county in a pursuit that proved fruitless. One such was recalled by Wilhelm Kothmann. He, Henry Pluenneke, and Sheriff Clark were out on a scout when they saw a campfire. The men approached it carefully but found "the fire to be that of a party of cow hunters—Hans Marschall with a Mexican and a negro hand."[25]

Only one of the two men with Marschall was identified by Kothmann. Booker was described as a powerful man "noted for his size and strength, weighed over three hundred pounds and could pick up a barrel of flour with his teeth and raise it to table height." The posse questioned Booker concerning the whereabouts of outlaws in the area, then warned him not to tell anyone that he had seen them. This man may have been Booker Sweeney born around 1848 in Missouri. Sweeney was working as a farm laborer in Burnet County during 1870 with his twenty-one-year-old wife, Mariah. Booker played a small role in the fighting, siding against the mob.[26]

The posses did not stop the rising violence in Mason. On September 2, 1875, Joseph Miller was killed under circumstances that remain controversial and mysterious. No motive for the killing was ever established, nor was a killer ever identified. The most likely suspect is Scott Cooley, although if suspicion fell on him at the time it remains one of the best kept secrets of the feud.[27]

Sometime after the Bader killing, George Gladden rode into Mason to buy supplies and was met by Dan Hoerster at Ben Stewart's store. Hard words passed between the men and a fist fight broke out. The pair were separated by Anton Hoerster who ran into the store and broke up the fight.[28] The cause of the argument remains unknown, but it probably stemmed from the 1874 arrests of Roberts and his men. No records have survived to indicate if either man was charged in court, but it may have been this incident that determined Clark's move.

Clark's failure to capture Cooley placed him in a precarious position. Action was necessary to maintain the confidence and support of his followers. Clark contacted the governor to request a reward on Cooley for Wohrle's murder. Coke obliged, offering a $300 reward on September 6, 1875.[29] In itself this can have done little to buoy the spirits of his followers, particularly after Christian Oestreich turned state's evidence on August 17 in Llano County for the robbery of Roberts and his men.[30]

Galvanized to action by Oestreich's arrest, Clark now realized that decisive action was necessary to maintain his hold over his followers. What he needed was a target. Clark was about to make his next major mistake. It would bring disaster to both him and his followers.

According to Gamel, Dan Hoerster and John Clark paid a man named Jim Chaney (or Cheyney) fifty dollars to ride to Loyal Valley and inform Moses Baird and George Gladden that they were wanted in Mason for some unknown reason. The evidence suggests that Clark sent him to summon Gladden, a Loyal Valley resident. Clark had no way of knowing that Baird would be present. Chaney arrived in Loyal Valley on September 7 and apparently had little difficulty convincing Gladden to come to Mason. Gladden immediately saddled up and Baird apparently decided to accompany Gladden to keep him company, a confirmation of their innocence in the Bader killing since neither man would have ridden to Mason if they suspected trouble. The men rode for Mason but never succeeded in overtaking Chaney who had ridden on ahead.[31]

At Hedwig's Hill, the natural stopping point on the road from Loyal Valley to Mason, Baird and Gladden stopped to refresh themselves. Dan Roberts, who was not present at the time, reported that:

> They saw two men coming up to the store, and when they got pretty close to the store, Sheriff Clark saw that they were Mose Beard [sic] and George Gladden. Those two men were considered among the fighting men opposing the Sheriff. They rode up and dismounted, and the Sheriff stepped out on the porch, with his rifle in hand, and the firing commenced at about 30 paces. . . . Within perhaps two minutes firing ceased on Beard and Gladden's side.[32]

This account can only have had its source in John Clark himself. More reliably, Gamel reported the ambush for what it was. When Baird and Gladden stopped at Keller's store in Hedwig's Hill, "Clark and Hoerster, with about sixty men, who were awaiting them, opened fire on the two."[33] Henry M. Holmes, confirming Gamel's version of events, wrote that the men were surprised by a "large number of Germans" led by Sheriff John Clark.[34]

In an act of courage as magnificent as it was ultimately futile, Gladden attempted to protect Baird. Gladden managed to get the wounded man onto his own horse then mounted behind him even as bullets continued to slam into their bodies. As the luckless pair fled for their lives Clark's faction was already moving in pursuit. The Germans' horses were concealed in a meadow near Hedwig's Hill, and it took some time to gather the mounts.[35] In the meantime Gladden and Baird were able to reach the Beaver Creek crossing. In close pursuit the posse shot Gladden again, and he fell from the saddle. As part of the men continued to pursue Baird the remainder stopped to finish off Gladden. Carl Keller interceded, leveling his pistol on the posse. "The mob attempted to shoot Glaton [sic] again but at this Charley Keller said, 'I'll kill the first man that shoots him again.'"[36] Keller, a Clark supporter, was only one of those who questioned the attack. Gladden had good reason to thank Keller for his life, and in the violence that followed the Kellers were left in peace.

Baird managed to ride farther down the creek before he too fell from the horse. Hard on his heels came Pete Bader and a portion of the band. As Baird lay bleeding and defenseless Bader killed him with a single shot, then dismounted and cut off a finger to obtain a gold ring Baird was wearing.[37]

The feud's escalation was readily apparent to people in the region. The *San Antonio Daily Herald* reported:

> KILLING AT FREDERICKSBURG.—A letter from Fredericksburg, dated Sept. 8th., has been received in this city, and conveys the following startling news: "H-ll has broke loose up here. Mose Beard was killed yesterday; Geo. Gladden is badly wounded, but there is some hope of his getting well. He is shot through the arm, and in the face. All this happened at Keller's store on the Llano."
>
> We fear this is but the beginning of a bloody solution of the difficulties about stock, that have become so serious of late.[38]

Lucia Holmes summed up her feelings succinctly: "Two more murders on Monday night—Mose Beard and George Gladden—Gladden still alive."[39] Henry Holmes penned yet another letter to the governor in an attempt to draw Coke's attention to the disintegration of order and rising violence in the county. Writing from Mason on September 8, Holmes reported the shooting, noting that "The stories of the killing are dramatically opposite and I certainly can not inform you as to whom the cause most attaches. The men shot were alone and were killed by a large number of Germans" under Clark's command. Holmes continued, "The Germans claim that Beard [*sic*] and Gladden began the fight firing about fifty shots at ten or twelve paces from Mr. Clark. No one was hurt however except the two men Beard and Gladden. Mr. Beard is a man of large connexions [*sic*] in Burnet County and if something is not done a civil war will be inaugurated."

Holmes clearly realized that the situation had gone far beyond Mason's ability to control it. After stating that the local authorities were paralyzed, he reported that in late August or early September a large public meeting had been held where Clark and the other county officials were requested to resign.

> The Sheriff has not done so but still is leader of a band composed exclusively of Germans. He is a fugitive from justice there being five indictments against him in Llano County for Robbery and false imprisonment—he cannot be arrested with the force at the disposal of the justices and now holds the County in awe with some fifty men. The lives of all those who do not belong to the mob are in danger and quiet can hardly be restored until some steps are taken to bring the perpetrators of the late murders (10) to justice and this cannot be done in this county by any jury grand or petit summoned from the vicinity.[40]

In contrast, correspondent Dreux, frequently cited as an unbiased reporter of events in Mason during this time, heatedly denied that such a situation existed. Writing to the *Austin Weekly Statesman* Dreux claimed. "The county of Mason is *not* in reality ruled by 'two factions' as 'Peter' observes. . . . Though in perfect accord with the Germans in opposing the doings of the outlaws, the American population take no open action against them lest they, too, should fall before the bullet of the concealed or midnight assassin. . . ."[41]

Dreux's partisan statements are at variance with the facts. The county had fractured largely along ethnic lines. Order within the county had disintegrated, and the county officers were asked to resign. A contemporary account reported "The people of Mason county have held a public meeting and requested all their present county officers to resign."[42] John O. Meusebach, disgusted with the mob's actions, resigned as justice of the peace for Precinct 3 as did the other three justices of the peace for the county: Robert Zesch, Otto Donop and L. Kuhn.[43] Wilson Hey remained in office to maintain some semblance of order.

Historians have generally claimed that Gladden and Baird were ambushed for their role in the death of Carl Bader. This was not Clark's rationale, however. Within hours of the shooting he claimed that the men had attacked Clark's posse of forty to sixty men, an incredible charge apparently not believed by any except the most diehard Clark supporters. Clark quickly realized this. Sometime after the initial story was released he claimed that Baird and Gladden had killed Bader. The new story appeared in the *Dallas Weekly Herald* on September 25, 1875: "The Fredericksburg Sentinel gives a characteristic letter from the sheriff of Mason county, describing the killing by him of Moses Baird and the wounding of George Gladden by him. They were resisting arrest."

As noted, this claim is patently false. Had the men been wanted on a criminal charge, Clark would have arrested Gladden following the gunfight. Instead he permitted the wounded man to be taken back to Loyal Valley without a guard.

But if neither of the men was wanted by the law, the rationale for the shootings remains obscure. The most logical theory is that Gladden was the intended target. If Gladden was the second man hired by Roberts to cut the herd in 1874, the reasons for the attack become clearer. With Gladden and Williamson dead, the case against Clark and his men would have fallen apart. Oestreich would have been persuaded to recant his testimony. Moses Baird was simply in the wrong place at the wrong time, collateral damage to Clark's mind. The ambush proved a major blunder. Baird was killed and Gladden was not. Nor was he arrested. Holmes entertained little hope that the lethargic government in Austin would respond to his plea after so many petitions had fallen on deaf ears. For Scott Cooley the shooting was an opportunity to gather allies for his private vendetta against the Hoo Doos. Riding to Loyal Valley he met with John Baird. Baird had already sent word to Burnet County concerning his brother's death. Allies were already advancing on Mason County.

Baird's forces, a large number of men drawn from Llano and Burnet Counties, accompanied a wagon as guards on the trip to Hedwig's Hill to recover Moses Baird's body. In later years Bill Faris told his grandchildren that "They were so upset by the news that they did not eat before they left. When they arrived they found Mose so ripe that they could not eat on the way back. Vultures followed the wagon all the way back to Burnet."[44]

Sam Tanner, who drove the wagon, informed his family that he made the entire trip with his rifle across his lap, fully expecting to be shot off the wagon at any moment.[45] In addition to Tanner and Faris, John Olney is known to have accompanied the group. Other likely riders include Al Tanner, Sam's brother, the Erwin, Cavin, Faris, and Olney brothers, John Carson, John Ringo, and Abe Taylor. Reportedly there were between thirty and fifty riders.

The evidence of the ambush was clear. Both of the men were riddled with bullets. Gladden had been hit nine times, and his granddaughter would later recall, "They shot him to rag dolls."[46] Baird was shot fifteen or sixteen times and mutilated.

Unprepared and apprehensive about the armed force that arrived, Clark garrisoned Hedwig's Hill and sent David Doole to inform Tom Gamel that he was needed at Hedwig's Hill. Accompanied by Deputy Sheriff James A. Baird, Gamel left Mason on September 9. The men found Clark and his men waiting at Keller's store in anticipation of an attack from Loyal Valley. At Clark's request, the men went on to Loyal Valley to learn what Baird's intentions were.

Clark's selection of Baird and Gamel as his emissaries is obvious. Gamel had been a mob target earlier in the year, and Baird wanted nothing to do with the mob, particularly since they had threatened his father Alf Baird. Neither of the men were unlikely to draw enemy fire. If they did, Clark may have reasoned that they were expendable.

The pair found Baird, Cooley, John Ringo, and a man identified by Gamel only as Williams, possibly Jim Williams of Llano County, at Gladden's home.[47] Following their arrival, Cooley suggested that they let Gladden rest. The men then went to a saloon and ordered drinks. When they had finished, Cooley answered the unspoken question by pulling Wohrle's bloody scalp from his pocket and laying it on the bar. The bartender refused payment, stating that the drinks were on him.[48] Baird and Gamel then started back to Hedwig's Hill where the mob waited eagerly for news.

> They were anxious to find out how the other side felt. Tom Gamel talked with Dan Hoerster and he asked him what Glaton's [sic] friends and Beard [sic] were going to do. Tom said, "I don't know but Glaton said that he would be in the saddle in eight more days." Dan Hoerster said, "Tom, you tell Scot Cooley that the next time we meet one of us is going to die." Tom said, "I will tell him." Hoerster replied, "I want you too."[49]

Students of the feud have interpreted Hoerster's final remark as a threat against Gamel, but in all likelihood the phrase should have been recorded in Gamel's recollections as "I want you to," which has a far different meaning. Hoerster had no quarrel with Tom Gamel. Still grief-stricken over the killing of his brother-in-law, the threat was obviously intended for Bader's killer. Had he wished to kill Gamel there was no better opportunity than the meeting at Keller's.

The mob's fears of an immediate attack proved unfounded. Baird and his men returned peacefully to Burnet where another tragedy awaited them. Laura Ann Olney, sister of the Bairds and wife of Samuel Olney, apparently went into shock after viewing her brother's mutilated and decaying body. Pregnant at the time, on October 7 Laura gave birth to a child who lived only long enough to be named Samuel Tanner Olney.[50]

For John Baird, who had ample reason to dislike and distrust both John Clark and the Germans, the killing of his brother was a blow that screamed for vengeance. Hearing Gladden's version of the ambush, Baird realized that the law would not deal with the killers. No court in Mason County would indict or convict Clark or any member of the mob, as Holmes had pointed out. If justice was to be had, Baird would have to take matters into his own hands.

Moses Baird's murder had a sobering effect on the German Hoo Doos. Their actions had already opened a rift in Mason County, and the resignation of the justices of the peace left doubts in many of their minds as to exactly what they had gotten into. Cattle were still being stolen, but now the ranchers were so engaged in the feud that they had little time to protect their herds. Loyalty to Clark wavered. Most of the men wanted to return to their homes, perhaps hoping that the whole thing would blow over. As a descendant of one German family later stated, "When the good guys start behaving like outlaws it is time to quit."[51]

The mob entertained a vain hope. Baird's killing would not blow over. Otto Ernest Hofmann later told his children what he had heard from his father Wilhelm about the killing. "It was the most foolish thing that the mob could have done. Men came from as far away as San Antonio to avenge him."[52] By the time the news broke across the state, men were already on their way. In killing Moses Baird, the mob had effectively acquired a host of enemies determined to avenge his death. It was a major turning point in the feud. Left to his own devices Cooley would probably have abandoned the fight. Baird's murder gave him new life in his pursuit of revenge. The mob had had their day. Within days of the killing they found themselves engaged in a bloody war for survival.

chapter 8

"A Most Horrible State of Affairs"

Holmes' contention that Moses Baird was "a man of large connexions [sic]" was an understatement.[1] This succinct phrase underscores the next phase of the feud as it escalated out of control. Baird was very popular in both Burnet and Llano Counties, and the brothers were connected by marriage, friendship, and business to a number of large families in the area who in turn had ties to others. These alliances provided a small army of fighting men, many of whom would have sought vengeance even had John Baird not. Prior to this, the feud had been a private vendetta, but it had now escalated into a full scale war. The opportunities for peace were gone.

The Baird family originated in Ireland, their grandfather William Baird having settled in Missouri. One of his sons, Hartshorn, married "Arminty Eten" there on August 11, 1846.[2] Census data indicates that Hartshorn "Beard" [sic: Baird], age twenty-eight was born in Missouri. Living in the household were his wife, Areminthy, age twenty-four, born in Tennessee, and two sons: John R., age three and Moses B., age one. Both of the brothers are noted as born in Missouri. Hartshorn Baird's occupation is listed as carpenter.[3] Records at this point become unclear. By 1860 the family had relocated to Burleson County, Texas. Hartshorn Baird had apparently died, either in Missouri or enroute to Texas, for A. P. Baird is listed as head of household in the 1860 census. Her age is now given as twenty-nine, a native of Tennessee. There are four children in the household: John R., age thirteen, Moses, eleven, Marietta, eight, and

Laura, six. All of the children had attended school within the previous year. The family was not wealthy, having real estate valued at $300 and personal property at $312.[4]

By 1868 the Bairds had moved to Burnet County. On October 23, Moses Baird was paid four dollars for serving two days as a court bailiff.[5] On September 17, 1869, his brother John purchased four half-acre lots from Hugh Allen for $400.[6] The following year found the family living along the Colorado River in western Burnet County. The head of household was their mother, now listed as Lucy A. Baird, age forty-four, "keeping house." Both Mary and Laura had attended school during the previous year, but John and Moses listed their occupation as "driving stock." The family declared $400 in real estate and personal property valued at $100.[7]

John Baird enlisted in Company Q of the Minute Men under F. C. Stewart in Llano County on September 8, 1872, serving until August 9, 1873. Official reports describing the activities of the company are lacking, but John Baird served as first corporal for the company.[8] On May 1, 1873, John married Nannie Robison.[9] The young couple apparently had a daughter, Edna, born in 1875. The census for 1880 indicates that Lucy Baird and Edna Baird, age five, were living in the household of Samuel Olney.[10] Both brothers were involved in various land deals between 1873 and 1875.[11]

DeVos correctly points out that the Baird brothers had "records of multiple arrest . . . back to 1869."[12] Burnet County's District Court records confirm this although details of most of these indictments lack specifics regarding the incidents. However, from them a pattern emerges that indicates that the pair were hot tempered men given to fighting.[13] From these same records an insight into how the community viewed the family and their standing in Burnet County society can be gleaned. On April 5, 1871, John Baird was charged with two counts of aggravated assault. Baird posted a $250 bond, his bondsmen being W. B. McFarland,[14] M. J. Bolt[15] and B. H. Cavin.[16] All of these men were well respected within the community, and all of them had ties to the cattle trade.

Court records for Burnet County indicate that the Cavins were occasionally in trouble, as were most cattlemen of the day, over livestock.[17] Legal difficulties notwithstanding, the Cavins were generally well regarded in Burnet County. Brief items about them were not uncommon in the local paper. One noted that, "Mr. Rusk Cavin, who lives two miles below town, on Hamilton creek, has just threshed his wheat. The yield is very fine, averaging 20 or 30 bushels per acre."[18] Another related, "A. H. Cavin has raised the champion yield of wheat in Burnet county this year. On six acres of land he averaged 41 bushels to the acre. Who can beat it?"[18]

Two of B. H. Cavin's brothers, John Edward "Ed," born circa 1854 in Mississippi, and William Thomas, born May 18, 1857, can be linked directly to the feud.[19] It appears certain that their kinsmen provided support.

The Bairds were also tied to the Olneys through the marriage of their sister, Laura Ann, to Samuel Olney.[20] It was through the Olney connection that the best known participant in the Hoo Doo War was drawn into the fighting, John Peters Ringo, better known in later years for his activities in Cochise County, Arizona.[21] Commenting on Ringo's character, a contemporary newspaper would later write that he was "a recklessly brave man, who. . . was far from being a desperado." He was regarded as "strictly honorable."[22]

In time Ringo was acknowledged as a leader in the feud. Like the Bairds, Ringo also had trouble in Burnet County. On December 25, 1874, he was celebrating Christmas in Burnet and fired his pistol across the town square. Ringo was charged in Cause 854 with disturbing the peace on April 5, 1875. His bondsmen were M. B. Thomas and John W. Calvert.[23] Calvert, a stock raiser, was involved peripherally in the feud.[24] Other families linked to the Olneys included the Tanners,[25] Taylors,[26] and Farises.[27] Each of these families had extended kinsmen and friends, all of whom allied themselves with the Baird cause.

Contrary to the folklore concerning the feud, the Baird brothers were cattlemen, not outlaws. One livestock notice published in the *Burnet Bulletin* reads:

> NOTICE TO STOCKMEN.
> The public are hereby notified that the undersigned holds a mortgage upon all stock of cattle heretofore sold A. G. Roberts by the undersigned and M. B. Baird in the counties of Burnet, Lampasas, Llano, Mason, San Saba and Brown.

> All persons are hereby warned against using, driving, or counterbranding any of the said stocks of cattle, and any person doing so without my authority, will be prosecuted, to the full extent of the law. J. B. BAIRD[28]

The only charge yet located against either of the Bairds for the theft of cattle was against Moses Baird. On March 30, 1875, he was charged in Burnet County with stealing ten head of cattle from S. W. Covington. Baird appeared for trial on the charge on August 6, 1875, and was found not guilty.[29]

Even as allies flocked to Baird's cause, John Clark's support in Mason County dissolved quickly. In a county divided for months, the German ranchers began to openly question their leadership's activities and motivations. The promised benefits of a reduction in cattle theft and control of the range had not materialized or been reduced by the killings. The accusations against Baird and Gladden were not supported by evidence, but now the stakes had changed. They had participated in what many of them regarded as murder. Several of the mob had been killed, and they had acquired an army of new enemies. The unity of the mob dissolved as men returned to their homes. The Mason County Hoo Doos were effectively broken. It could not have come at a worse time for John Clark.

In Burnet, men gathered, waiting for Gladden to recover enough to join them. Many of them had been pushed by John Clark and the mob until they felt they were backed into a corner. All of them wanted vengeance on Baird's killers. Now they would push back. For the Hoo Doos the unthinkable was about to happen. Within a month the remnants of the mob would be shattered like fragile crystal.

Holmes' letter to Governor Coke finally brought belated action. Coke ordered Adjutant General William Steele to place a lieutenant and "at least thirty men in Mason County to preserve the peace" and to remain there until further notice. Steele forwarded the new orders to Major Jones on September 23.[30] In separate correspondence Coke notified Holmes of the actions that were being taken. Holmes' response reflects his relief.

Mason, Texas
September 24, 1875

His Excellency Richard Coke
Governor of Texas
Dear Sir

I thank you very much for your letter of the [no date] inst. and hope that the good sense, law and advise [*sic*: advice] contained therein will tend to improve the condition of affairs here.

I have given it to a large portion of each party to read and all concur in the views expressed and assert a desire to act up to them.

A few days after I wrote you, a petition to yourself was gotten up for assistance & c. and for consistency's sake I signed it, at that time I supposed it would be forwarded to you by mail, but I have since learned that a Mason man was to hand it to you in person.

In reference to this I would say that though I signed the petition for assistance, erroneously believing that it could be furnished under section x art. 4 Constitution I do not, nor, I will be responsible for saying, do any but a very small minority of the citizens of this county intend to endorse any statements the frame of said petition may make.

An election for various county officials to fill vacancies occasioned by these conditions has been ordered for the 6th prox. and I think a very excellent man for sheriff will be elected Mr. James Baird, at present the only candidate. He has plenty of courage and time to do his work well and a sure intention of keeping within the law and staying with the law, and better than all he will carry with him the support of all classes and shades of opinion in the performance of his duties.

With his election I look for a more orderly and law abiding spirit to spring up and hope, but dare not say however, that peace will be restored.

I am
Very respectfully
Your obedient servant
Henry M. Holmes

Holmes' hopes for peace were shattered before he could post it. In a hurried postscript he added, "I open this letter to say that James Cheney was shot this morning at his home about 1 1/2 miles from town. Verdict of Coroners jury 'Shot by parties unknown.'"[31]

The killers were soon identified. On September 25, 1875, Cooley, Ringo, and six or eight other men rode brazenly into Mason. While Cooley and most of the others waited in town, Ringo and a man identified only as Williams headed north toward Comanche Creek and the home of Jim Cheyney. Expecting no trouble, Cheyney met them on the porch of his home and invited them to breakfast. Cheyney washed and was drying his face when the pair unceremoniously gunned him down. They then returned to Mason, and the group rode to the store of David Doole, demanding that he come out. The terrified Doole prudently refused, and the men moved on to Lace Bridges' hotel where they met Wilson Hey. Hey invited them in to breakfast. Cooley responded that "You go inside and tell Mrs. Bridges there is some fresh meat up the creek." The men ate leisurely, then rode unmolested toward Willow Creek.[32]

Uncertainty exists concerning the identities of those who entered Mason with Cooley but in 1877 Ringo summoned seven men for his defense: William Olney, Bud Faris and Andy Murchison[33] of Llano County, Carl Akard of Bandera County, Mark Hopkins of Gillespie County, and both Wesley Johnson and Sam Monroe of Kimble County.[34] Cooley and possibly Williams were dead at the time. Little is known concerning Akard, Hopkins, and Monroe, but Wesley Johnson was the drover who had helped Charley Johnson months earlier.

Ringo's summons of these seven men as witnesses is not proof of their presence in Mason at the time although they may have been, considering the similarity in the numbers involved. It does serve to illustrate that allies were arriving from all over central Texas. Gamel may have had this in mind when he recalled that following Cheyney's killing Dan Hoerster thought about the fifty dollars that had been paid to lure Gladden and Baird to Hedwig's Hill.[35] Nor was he the only one having second thoughts. In Castell, Peter Bader was preparing to flee the state. In his memoirs Max Krueger recalled that Bader had taken his family to Fredericksburg for safety. Bader planned to sell his holdings and flee to Florida.[36]

Another individual having second thoughts on the feud was rancher Adolph Reichenau. During the fall of 1875 rumors began circulating at Hedwig's Hill that a big raid on the Germans was planned. Reichenau was told that he had been targeted by Cooley, allegedly over something he had said. Taking the threat seriously, Reichenau moved his family up to the hill behind his home and stuffed the bed on the front porch where he slept during the summer. That evening several men rode up to the house and fired a number of shots into the bed. Reichenau believed that the riders were members of the Cooley faction and soon had the opportunity to find out. While on a trip to Mason he encountered Cooley and asked him if Cooley was angry with him. Cooley responded that he was not and considered Reichenau one of his friends. Reichenau was never bothered after that time.[37]

Reichenau's story adds additional mystery to the feud. While the rancher believed that Cooley or his allies had attempted to kill him, there is no obvious motive for the attack. John Baird made it clear from the beginning that he was after the men responsible for the death of his brother. Cooley was after the men who had killed Williamson. There is no evidence to suggest that Reichenau was involved in either group. On the contrary, Reichenau enjoyed cordial relations with the Bolts, Gamels, and Johnsons. A more likely scenario is that the shooters had come from Hedwig's Hill. Clark and a small band who remained loyal to him had garrisoned themselves there anticipating an attack from Loyal Valley that never materialized. Had the Reichenau family been killed, citizens of the county would likely have blamed Baird and rallied to Clark's support. The motive for the attack and the identities of the participants remain a mystery.

Jones received Steele's orders on September 26 as he was starting a scout into west Texas. In his response to Steele, Jones reported:

> Taking away "thirty" men weakened my force so
> much that I abandoned my proposed scout, and
> having no men that could be well spared from the

111

front and thinking it probable that I might be able
to gain more towards restoring peace and quiet to
this distracted community than could be done by a
Lieutenant I started next morning on a forced march
for Mason with twenty men of my escort, Co. A.[38]

Dan Roberts had arrived in Mason ahead of Jones. On September
13, 1875, he married Lou Conway in Columbus, Texas, then stopped
at Mason on the 25th while returning to Menard County. Here he
asked the Holmes family to look after his wife while he continued to
Menard to arrange boarding for her. Lou Roberts ruefully recalled in
her memoirs that "It was when he left me at Mason that my troubles
began."[39]

Jones reached Mason County on September 28 and struck north
for Mason. At Hedwig's Hill he rode into an ambush. About "fifteen or
twenty men, armed with Winchester carbines and six-shooters rose
up from behind a stone wall ready to fight" he reported. Recognizing
that Jones and his men were Texas Rangers, violence was averted.
Jones stopped to interrogate them and found that their leader was
"Mr. Clark, the sheriff of the County." Clark informed Jones that they
had received a report that "the Gladden party of Cold Springs [Loyal
Valley] and the Beard [sic] party from Burnett [sic], some thirty men
in all, were at Cold Springs and intended coming up today or tonight
to 'burn out the Dutch.'" Jones prudently returned to Loyal Valley to
learn the truth of the matter. He found a community prepared for the
worst.

I find the houses closed [with] a deathlike stillness in
the place and an evident suspense if not dread in the
minds of the inhabitants. Every man is armed but so
far as I have been able to ascertain there is no body
of armed men in or near the place, at present. In fact
there are scarcely any men here and as yet I have not
been able to ascertain where they are.

Jones and his men remained for the night hoping to learn the whereabouts of Baird and Gladden so he could meet them and persuade
them to return peacefully to their homes.[40] Clark's intelligence was

wrong, however. Baird and Gladden were already in Mason with Scott Cooley planning an ambush of their own.[41]

One of those who had broken with Clark and refused to remain at Keller's store was Daniel Hoerster. Following the ambush he returned to his legal duties, trying to put the violence behind him. One family story relates that Hoerster was inspecting a herd when an argument broke out over a brand. One of the drovers drew his pistol but was covered by Heinrich Pluenneke from behind. Hoerster was certainly within his rights to have the man arrested. No longer trusting Clark, he told them both to forget the incident and shrugged it off.[42] Accompanied by Pluenneke and his brother-in-law Peter Jordan, Hoerster returned to Mason on the morning of September 29. At Koockville, Wilhelm Koock, the town's founder, warned him that Cooley and Gladden were in Mason. Hoerster responded simply that he did not care and rode on.

In Mason, Cooley, Gladden, and John Baird were waiting for an opportunity to kill John Clark. Following their arrival in town, the men left their mounts in the care of Booker before taking up positions in Tom Gamel's saloon.[43] With them was an employee of John Gamel named Bill Coke.[44] The men were at the saloon when Tom Gamel rode in and told Baird that he had seen his "meat" headed on down the road.

"I told Bill Coke that was Clark and Bill said it wasn't. But I'll get some of them before I leave town," returned Baird. He then walked with Cooley to a barbershop across from the Southern Hotel and took up positions behind it. They did not wait long. Daniel Hoerster and his companions were riding into Mason from the northwest. As they approached the barbershop Baird fired his shotgun at Hoerster. Four of the buckshot caught him in the throat, killing him instantly.[45]

In the shop, the barber was stropping his razor when the blast startled him so badly that he cut the strap in two. Immediately after Baird fired, Cooley and Gladden opened fire on Jordan and Pluenneke. The men leaped from their horses and ran to the rear of the Southern Hotel. Once inside, they seized rifles, then emerged on the porch to return fire. During the exchange a bullet grazed Peter Jordan's head.

At the Holmes house Lou Roberts recalled what she knew of the fight:

Next morning, while at breakfast, we heard the report of a gun uptown. Rushing out into the yard, we saw two men, bareheaded, with guns in their hands, come toward us at full speed. We rushed into the house, locked the doors, and Mrs. Holmes and I went into her room, which had but one window. To our horror the men rode right up to the window. I looked for a place of safety, and the only one I could see was the space under the bed, which I pointed out to my hostess. She refused. . . .[46]

Others in the community were braver, if not wiser. One of these was Karl Hofmann, a local carpenter and relative newcomer to Mason. Hofmann had arrived in Mason with his mother, brother, and sister around 1870. Seizing his rifle when the gunfire broke out, he rushed toward the firing. Fortunately for him the fight was over when he arrived. It was only then that he realized that his weapon was not loaded.[47] In another part of town, Karl's younger brother, Wilhelm Hofmann, heard the gunfire while he was at the home of John Reugner. Wilhelm was reading aloud, and as the gunfire rose in intensity he read louder to drown it out.[48]

One of the bullets shattered a window, the broken glass cutting Laura Hunter's face. Another man who had recently arrived from Camp Colorado to see John Gamel was hit by buckshot in the back, inflicting a painful, but not serious wound. After the shooting he asked if anyone knew John Gamel. Answered in the affirmative, the irate visitor told them, "Well, when you see him tell him if he wants to see me to come to Colorado. I am not going down the road another damn step."[49]

Peter Jordan later related to his family that he saw Gladden make a dash between two buildings carrying a rifle in one hand and a box of cartridges in the other. Jordan fired quickly and saw the cartridges fly into the air as the bullet hit Gladden's hand.[50] After a further exchange of shots Cooley and the others withdrew to Gamel's saloon where Booker had their horses. Gamel recalled in his memoirs that they then forced Bill Coke to accompany them and gave him a buffalo gun since he was unarmed.[51]

The claim that Coke was an innocent bystander forced to accompany Cooley is suspect. Gamel's account of Coke's actions following

114

the shooting indicate an attempt to gloss over Coke's involvement. As the men fled town a second round of gunfire erupted, apparently resulting in no further injuries. Coke seized the opportunity and "left out toward Centennial Springs and lost his gun as he went down the bank of the creek. From there he went to Mill Creek Ranch."[52] Had Coke been innocent he could simply have returned to Gamel's saloon where other witnesses knew that he had been forced to accompany the killers. There was no reason for the men to kidnap and arm Coke, then force him to flee Mason with them. On the contrary, there was every reason not to. Perhaps Coke panicked at being dragged into the Hoerster killing, but the circumstances strongly indicate that he was a willing participant in the attack.[53]

Daniel Hoerster was a popular man, and Lucia Holmes recorded sadly: "Came out on the galery [sic] and heard a lot of shooting uptown— Poor Dan Herster [sic] killed—Two men came riding to the house and we all went in and locked the doors—Antone Herster was with us—they proved to be Germans. We were all fearfully frightened. . . . Town full of Germans and Clark here too. Rangers and Mr. Jones in."[54]

Jones sent three scouts in pursuit of the men. There was little hope of catching them, and Jones was pessimistic about his chances for success.

> I have three parties out after them now and will have the county thoroughly searched for them but have very little hope of catching them at present as they are well mounted, know the country well and have many friends in this, and the adjoining Counties. The National prejudice is so very bitter here. American against German and vice versa, that I find it impossible to get a consistent or reliable account of the troubles and am sorry to have to report that very few of the Americans whom I have met yet manifest any disposition to assist in the arrest of the perpetrators of yesterdays deed, or any particular desire to have them arrested.[55]

In addition to the three Ranger scouts, two German posses, one with Clark as the leader, were in the field.[56] The Rangers had no luck, but the Germans did. Riding directly to John Gamel's Mill Creek ranch, they surrounded it and demanded to know if either Tom Gamel or Bill Coke was there. Ike Beam, Gamel's foreman, informed them that Coke was there, and Coke surrendered without a fight. According to Gamel, Clark arrested both men. Beam and Coke were then seperated. Adolph Reichenau, J. P. Miller, and four others were assigned to escort Bill Coke to Mason. He never arrived. "Miller testified before the grand jury that when they got within about three miles of Nixon Pass, he had occasion to stop, and the other five went on with Coke. They had not gone far until he heard some shooting, and when he overtook the gang they told him Bill Coke had escaped."[57]

The general suspicion was that Coke had been murdered by his guards. Dan Roberts hunted unsuccessfully for Coke and later recorded "William Coke was never heard of, and we think his bones were bleaching in some cavern, so often the receptacle of crime."[58] Henry Doell Jr. expressed his certainty that Coke had been killed.

> Bill Cook [*sic*: Coke] was just putting his six-shooter back in the holster and the bullet hit his gun—cut his hand up. They caught up with Cook at old man [Ischer struck out] below Nixon's Pond and identified him by his damaged hand—they had a hard time to catch him, ran him round and round—finally got him and shot him and buried him on Isher's [*sic*: Ischar's] place. They shot him because he tried to get away, they said. Isher's oldest boy had the job of burying him.[59]

The Isher noted by Doell was Johann Georg Ischar, a German colonist who had come to Texas for "political and military" reasons.[60]

The killing of Dan Hoerster proved as shocking as Baird's death had. The *San Antonio Express* reported under the banner of "Dastardly Murders":

> From the Fredericksburg Sentinel we learn that on last Wednesday morning between seven and eight o'clock, Daniel Horster, one of the best and most favorably known citizens of the county, was shot and killed at Mason; and at the same time Peter Jordon

was shot at, escaping however with but a slight wound.

Mr. Horster [*sic*] was killed in the vicinity of the Post office, in Mason county, and was then scalped. The killing was done in the presence of several witnesses who have made affidavits against the murderers, and Maj. Jones of the Frontier Battalion . . . . [The balance is torn and garbled.][61]

Correspondence from one "Alazan" also noted the Hoerster killing, stating that he "was shot dead by unknown parties in the streets of Mason." Alazan then continued with his opinion of the ethnic problems in Mason County.

From what I can glean from the correspondence of the German *Freie Presse*, of this city, and other sources, it appears that the contest is gradually becoming one of nationalities, the Germans being pitted against the Americans. Which is in the right is "one of those things no fellah can find out." Even the parties themselves are not a unit on that subject.[62]

Members of the Llano mob were vocal in denouncing the killers. In a letter from Llano dated September 30, a writer who signed his initials L. M. P. stated

The troubles in Mason county seem to be progressing rapidly. On the 28th inst. there was another murder committed in the town of Mason in daylight, and without any fear of apprehension on the part of the murdere[r]s. Daniel Hoerster, formerly a cattle agent, was killed, another slightly wounded, and a third thrown from his horse. The murderers remained in town for some time after the killing, then rode off triumphantly to the hills, their place of safety, where they no doubt will plan another raid on the Dutch. The murderers were most likely J. -----, G. ----- and S. -----. They are the worst men on the frontier of Texas, and would not hesitate to do anything to gratify their prejudice and passions.

Pretty soon there will be some of the other party killed, as ----- ----- says he has a list showing the names of the men he intends to kill. I think the sooner they are put out of the way the better it will be for the country. They have always been drawing their revolvers on some quiet citizen. So you see it is good riddance of bad rubbage when one of them is picked off.[63]

None of them would be picked off, however. In the weeks to come the mob would learn hard lessons about terror.

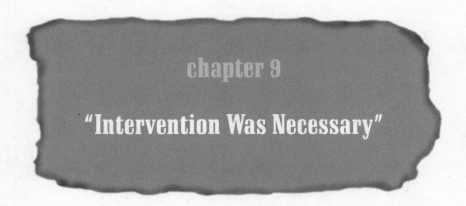

chapter 9

"Intervention Was Necessary"

The terror that gripped Mason in the fall of 1875 is almost impossible to comprehend. On October 4 it was rumored that John Baird was in town. The rumor proved false, but it provides glimpses of rampant tales that spread fear in the community.[1] At the same time, Clark and his men rode to Loyal Valley and proceeded to terrorize the community. One of the citizens harassed was John O. Meusebach. The mob stormed into his store and shots were fired that grazed his legs. "He did not move a muscle but with a withering gaze looked directly into the faces of the attackers. After a moment his molesters dropped their eyes, turned sheepishly, and rode away."[2]

Meusebach's biographer believed that the attack was committed by the Baird faction during the feud. However, the only documented raid on Loyal Valley was perpetrated by John Clark and the Hoo Doos. Additional insight into the incident is found in a petition to Jones.

> Sir:
> The undersigned citizens of Loyal Valley are under the impression that you are in command of the State Troops sent to this county to suppress disturbances and to aid in keeping up peace and good order. Yesterday [October 3] about at dinner time an armed force of 30 to 40 men entered this town and searched nearly every house without our knowing for what pur-

pose. To day just at daybreak we were told that it was a posse of the Sheriff. But as far as we know Sheriff Clark has resigned and the new Sheriff seated has not as yet qualified. We wish to know whether this party searching and disturbing us in our homes is acting under your orders. We are willing cordially to welcome and to cooperate with the Troops under your command and under your orders. We wish you would station a detachment of these State Troops here at this place immediately and we pledge ourselves to aid them all in our power to preserve peace and good order, but we are not willing to submit to the dictates of one party [while] our families [are] being harassed by the repeated searches, and disturbed, and in fear day and night. We have selected a committee of old quiet men, not being implicated in any party strife or feeling to confer with you and respectfully request you to give us notice of a day when we can meet you here and talk with you in reference to this matter. The committe [*sic*] to consist of myself, Mad[ison] Putman, John P. Moseley, R. G. Stone.

Loyal Valley, Mason County, Texas
Octbr. 4th 1875[3]

The petition was signed by a number of men, including John O. Meusebach. Contrary to the view of one local historian who considered it a "side issue," the petition is damning in its implications.[4] The mob was desperate to find the killers. The Loyal Valley raid was an attempt by Clark and the mob to maintain control of the county. Anyone not in the mob was considered to be against them. It proved another ill conceived plan on Clark's part.

Jones was also learning hard lessons concerning the feud. The Rangers he had taken to Mason were composed of Company A and nine men from Company D under the command of Sergeant N. O. Reynolds.[5] Roberts' men proved far from impartial as Jones quickly discovered. Like Roberts, they too had made up their minds as to the right and wrong of the matter. Unlike their commander they came down firmly on the side of Scott Cooley. James B. Gillett, a Company D Ranger, recalled in his memoirs that when he arrived in Mason, Jones sent out a number of scouts to hunt Cooley. The scouts proved fruitless, and after two weeks he "learned that nearly the whole of his command, especially the Company D boys who had ranged with Cooley" were in sympathy with the former Ranger. "It was even charged that some of the Company D rangers met Cooley at night on the outskirts of Mason and told him they did not care if he killed every damned Dutchman in Mason County who formed part of the mob that had murdered Williamson."

It was an intolerable situation. Jones addressed the troops and advised them that, while the murder of Tim Williamson had been horrible, it did not justify Cooley's war against the mob. Jones offered any of the men who felt that they did not want to hunt Cooley an honorable discharge. According to Gillett, "about fifteen men stepped to the front."[6] Contemporary records refute this. Only three men resigned at this time. On October 7, 1875, N. O. Reynolds and James P. Day, both of Company D, were discharged on the grounds that "they cannot conscientiously discharge" their duties.[7] Four days later Paul Durham, also of Company D, received his discharge on the same grounds as Reynolds and Day.[8] Reynolds later reenlisted in the Rangers and served with distinction.

In retrospect, Jones should have been more concerned about those who did not step to the front. The presence of the Rangers served to deter further violence, but over the next few weeks he realized that Company D was worse than useless in hunting Cooley and his allies. Company A proved little better. The momentum had clearly swung against Clark's faction. While Cooley and others were well known and hunted by the mob, local law enforcement did nothing to bring them to justice. John Clark had also run out of time. On October 14 he was bound over to the grand jury on a charge of false imprisonment in Mason County. Mrs. Holmes noted that her husband was prosecuting Clark and "won his case." Clark left Mason that night under bond. The case was called again on November 12 when, to no one's surprise, a no-bill by the grand jury was found against him.[9] Clark had already fled the county, and his ultimate fate remained unknown for decades. James Baird, who succeeded him as sheriff, would later express his belief that Clark had been killed. "In 1875 he was appointed sheriff of Mason county, Texas, the office having been made vacant by the killing of the previous incumbent."[10]

James Baird was mistaken. Clark successfully eluded his enemies, fleeing back to the sanctuary of Ripley County, Missouri. On March 3, 1876, four months after Clark broke bond and fled Texas the Doniphan, Missouri, *Prospect News* reported succinctly that "Captain John Clark has returned from Texas and will take up farming in this county." Clark purchased land in a rugged, remote part of the county and remained in hiding for the rest of his life.

In Mason, Jones continued his systematic sweeps for Baird's faction and the men who had captured Coke, for whom warrants were issued on October 5.[11] Reports that Gladden and Cooley were in Menard prompted Jones to write to Dan Roberts on October 16.[12] Roberts received the order the following day and immediately replied.

> I've just recd the papers—by Corpl Griffin also your letter by morning mail. Cooley nor Gladden— either one has been at Menardville—nor do I think Cooley has been about the old man Jacksons place. They don't like him very well & if he should make an appearance there they would inform on him immediately, but I shall go to find out if he's been there.[13]

As Roberts had predicted, Company D found nothing. In the same letter Roberts advised Jones that the forage around Menard was largely exhausted. On October 18 Jones ordered Roberts to bring the rest of his command to Mason to arrive on the 25th.[14]

Jones' time in Mason provided him a first hand education on the dynamics of blood feuds. On October 14, William Steele wrote to Major Jones informing him that reports had come to the governor accusing Jones of taking sides in the feud. Coke had Steele "instruct" Jones "of the necessity that you do nothing outside of the law and that you give no cause to think you favor one or the others party to the feud."[15] Jones' caustic response to Steele reflects his anger at the accusation.

> In reply to your communication of the 14th inst. I have to say that I am not surprised that reports have

gone to the Governor that I had taken sides with one or the other party to the terrible feud in this county, but am surprised that he should have taken any notice of it. Having had some experience in troubles of this kind before I knew the difficulty of steering clear of imputations of partiality when I came here and consequently was a[s] careful as possible from the first to act in such a manner as to give no cause for such a suspicion even.

With this object in view I avoided any particular personal or social intercourse with either party, fearing that if I was known to be often with one party the other would think I was taking sides. Notwithstanding this I had not been here more than ten days before each party accused me of taking sides with the other and for that reason I am at a loss to form an opinion as to which party, if either, has made the complaint to the Governor. My object at first was to quiet the immediate trouble and stop further blood-shed, and then in due time take the proper course to vindicate the law by arresting all parties who had offended against it. I have been so far successful [*sic*] that there has been no blood shed since I came here. I have arrested some fifteen persons, some of them have been tried and acquitted and others bound over to answer charges before the District Court of this and Llano Counties and the community is more quiet I am told then it has been for several months.

If any complaint has been made to the Governor against me I should like to know the nature of it and by whom it was made, and I think I have a right to know in order that I may be able to vindicate myself.

The same charge, however, has been made against the Governor by one of the parties here and I have had to defend him against the charge on several occasions. The anti-Clark party say they made several applications to the Governor while Clark and the "Dutch" had the advantage of them and no notice was taken of their applications but as soon as they began to "kill the Dutch" and they became alarmed and called on the Governor for help it was sent at once and some of them thought I was sent here expressly to take the "Dutch" side of the question.

Mr. Holmes, a lawyer here, is the chief complainant against the Governor, but rather by innuendo and "they say" than direct charge, and I suspect that he, if any one, has made the complaint against me, from the fact that I have on several occasions declined taking his advise [sic] and told him very plainly that I came here in the interest of no party but in the interest of law and order and that in my management I would not be led by either party to the prejudice of the other.

But it would require a volume to give anything like a detailed account of the troubles here and I will not inflict you with it now.[16]

Replacing Company D with Ira Long and thirty men from Company A was a good plan. Yet ultimately they proved little more effective than Company D in apprehending the feudists. In Austin both Coke and Steele smarted at Jones' report, unable to effectively respond to the charges. Like Marley's ghost, their previous inaction had returned to haunt them.

Clark's flight marked the end of organized mob activity in Mason County. The sheriffs who succeeded him proved capable officers more concerned with law and order than with political power. The Hoo Doos of Mason County never rode *en masse* again, and the single man remaining in the area whom Cooley and Baird both wanted, Peter Bader, was in hiding. An election was held in October to fill the vacant county offices. Deputy James A. Baird was elected sheriff. Not surprisingly, Fritz Kothmann was elected Justice of the Peace for Precinct 3 in eastern Mason County. It was a final attempt by the Hoo Doos to cling to power. By early 1876 this too was swept away.

In Austin, Governor Coke felt the need to defend himself to Jones. At his direction, Steele wrote Major Jones on October 22, 1875.

Considering the unanswered petitions that had reached him earlier in the year, the response to Jones was lame.

> Your letter of the 20th inst is at hand & has been shown to Gov. Coke who says that he has had no communication from anyone on the Subject but that his instruction to me to write to you arose from the desire to remind you of the necessity of avoiding a semblance of taking sides.
>
> The order to send troops to Mason was not made upon the application of any one but that it had become aparent [sic] that intervention was necessary to prevent bloodshed. The information came to me from [several ?] residents of Mason and adjoining Counties. Scott Cooley was home a few days since and I am told talked openly of his actions and said that there was not men enough in Texas to keep him from killing Clark. Beard and Gladden were with him. They are said to be now in Burnet.[17]

At the same time, the discharges of Day, Durham, and Reynolds left gaps that had to be filled. Jones sent Roberts authorization to replace the men on October 11, then noted, "One Johnson who escaped from the mob who hung the Baccuses last spring is an applicant for service, but as I learn he was in the ranks with Gladden, Beard and Cool[e]y, last week I think him disqualified for our service."[18] Johnson's attempted enlistment in the Rangers was a strategic move. Obviously allied to Cooley's faction, his enlistment as a Ranger would have served to provide Baird with a proven informant within the ranks of Company D. Jones' knowledge of the local situation prevented infiltration into the ranks. It was an excellent strategy, one that was not abandoned by the anti-mob forces.

While Roberts looked for capable recruits, Jones learned more bitter truths about the events of 1874 that had helped start the feud. A number of men, including Wilson Hey, had changed their position regarding Roberts and the "big raid." After only two weeks in Mason County, Jones penned an exasperated letter to Steele on October 12.

Please have Mr. [Henry] Orsay to look among my papers in the old desk and send me all the papers he can find from Wilson Hey, presiding Justice of this county. There is one which I want particularly, a petition or memorial to the Governor some time last year signed by Hey and probably other officers in regard to the Al. Roberts gang of Cow thieves and other out laws which was referred by yourself to me in June or July of last year, also one from the same parties to Capt. Perry in August last year, which latter caused me to come to this county at that time.

Some parties here have "changed" sides since that time and I want to show up their former record.[19]

October saw the appearance of many of the feudists in District Court. Jones reported to Steele that he had arrested the posse that had captured Coke after warrants were delivered to him by Wilson Hey. Warrants were issued for the arrests "of Clark, Perryman, Miller and five or six Germans who were at this time scouring the country in search of Beard, Cooley and Gladden, charging them with 'threatening to kill', 'false imprisonment' and 'attempting to kill' a man whom they had arrested as accessory to the murder of Dan Hoerster and who was seen with the murderers just before and rode off with them after the killing." Learning of the warrants, all of the men surrendered to the Rangers. The "charges against them were dismissed except one against Clark in which he was required to give two hundred dollars bail to answer before the District Court."[20]

None of this could have surprised anyone. The conviction of any mob member would only have intensified the resentment between "Dutch" and "Americans" and caused further violence. Possibly a deal was struck insuring that the Mason Hoo Doos were finished in return for a dismissal of the charges. Those supporting John Baird were not so fortunate. As Jones had reported earlier, he had "arrested some fifteen persons, some of them have been tried and acquitted and others bound over to answer charges before the District Court of this and Llano Counties . . . ."[21] One of them was the Williams charged with killing Jim Cheyney. Gamel recalled that Williams had a speedy trial.

When the Rangers came to Mason, William[s] was arrested for killing Chaney. When the case was called for trial Chaney's wife was asked by the council if Williams or either of the men that participated in the killing of her husband, Chaney, were present in the court room. At this time, Williams was standing at the bar. Mrs. Chaney carefully scrutinized him several times—Williams looking her right in the eye with an unconcerned expression on his face. Suddenly Mrs. Chaney said, "No, this is not the man." This incident cleared Williams, and he left the country.[22]

While Williams eluded conviction, his trial was a clear message to Baird and Cooley. Existing documentation shows that there was widespread sympathy for the anti-mob forces in the area. Any trial, however, would be in Mason. None of Baird's men were willing to surrender themselves to the tender mercies of Mason's Hoo Doos. To them, incarceration in Mason was synonymous with a death sentence, either by the courts or the mob.

Jones reported a total of twenty-two arrests, twelve of them for offenses in Mason, one for horse stealing in San Saba County, and the remaining nine for warrants issued in Llano County where Clark's posse, including newly elected sheriff James Baird, were charged with robbery and false imprisonment from the events of 1874. All of the men gave bond and were released.[23]

Even as Jones presided over an uneasy peace in Mason, the cattle trouble continued in both Mason and neighboring Llano Counties. On October 4 Mathew Moss Jr. killed one Blue Foster. Writing to the *San Antonio Herald*, Steve Moss reported that Foster was killed at the ranch of James A. Haynie.

The cause of the trouble was that Foster claimed a mark and brand belonging to Moss and had the same recorded in his own name. The same mark and brand had been recorded by Moss before the records were destroyed by the fire last winter, but he had not re-recorded since the fire. Foster went and recorded the same and claimed it as his own mark and brand.

Moss sent word to him not to handle the cattle as they were his property, but Foster gathered the cattle, sold some of them and had others under herd. Moss came to the pen and talked to the cow-boys a short time and then rode up to Foster and emptied both barrels of his shot-gun at him, the shot taking effect in the left side, nearly under his arm, when Foster fell from his horse. Moss then drew his pistol, walked up to him and shot him in the chest and head, then waved his six-shooter and asked the crowd if they wanted any of it, if so, he was the best man on the place, and then mounted and rode off.[24]

The Moss family was and remains one of the highly regarded families in Llano County. Evidence suggests that they supported John Baird and the Olneys in their war against the mob.[25]

Far from being an isolated event, Foster's killing was symptomatic of the times. Even as the Mason mob abandoned lynch law as a means of resolving disputes, the Llano contingent of the Hoo Doos remained undeterred and unrepentant. Their leaders clearly understood that open support of their allies would broaden the war and bring unwanted Ranger attention to their activities. Nor were there as many mob members in Llano as there were in Mason. Consequently, while the feud reached epic proportions in Mason County, the mob in Llano remained largely quiet, biding their time for a more propitious moment.

Part of the folklore that surrounds the feud is the belief that Scott Cooley was the leader of the "American" faction. Certainly, while it is true that Cooley's quest for revenge on Tim Williamson's murderers generated widespread sympathy among the Rangers, there is no evidence to suggest that his vendetta aroused the community as a whole other than generating passive supporters. It was not until Moses Baird was killed that significant numbers of men rallied against the mob. Moses Baird had been a popular man, and from the time Cooley allied himself with John Baird, he effectively took a secondary role in the feud. Baird had a significant number of allies willing to help him avenge his brother's death. They were his supporters though, not Cooley's. The reality is that John Baird, not Scott Cooley, was the leader of the anti-mob faction.

Most of Baird's allies were drawn from local cattlemen and wranglers, but this small army could not remain indefinitely on enemy soil. They had families and businesses of their own that needed attention, and many of them returned to their homes following Hoerster's killing to attend to business, ready when Baird needed them. Cooley may well have felt the need for a stronger force around him, a fact alluded to by Jeff Ake. Ake claimed that he and six others were out at the head of Devil's River "looking over the country to maverick" when they were ambushed by Comanches. Ake's horse was shot, and in the ensuing fight he escaped on foot but was separated from his companions and forced to walk for the safety of the settlements. On the sixth day without any food he was fortunate enough to steal a horse from the Comanches and eventually reached Table Mountain in Burnet County. "When I come to the gap on the way to the mesa . . . a feller throwed down on me, till he knowed who I was. The Ringo-Gladden crowd was in there, living on beef and roasting ears; they had a war on with the Dutch." Bill Ake and the others had already found the camp. After some time the "Gladden boys" asked them to join them, but the Akes declined since they had had trouble enough for one trip: "The Rangers was out thicker'n hair on a dog's back; stopping and questioning everybody. The Dutch—the Borders gang—was big dogs in Gillespie county then, and they had forced trouble on the Ringo-Gladden-Cooley bunch at first."[26]

This is verified in part by John B. Jones who wrote Neal Coldwell, Commander of Company F of the Frontier Battalion, on October 25 noting in part that

> some fifteen men, very suspicious looking fellows, passed through Loyal Valley en route for the Upper Llano where it is thought they will make a camp and probably take up winter quarters. Several horse thieves of notoriety have lately gone from San Saba, Lampasas and other places in that direction also.
>
> I wish you as soon as practicable to make a scout in that section of country and search thoroughly as far out as the "eight mile water hole." If you do not find them on the Llano, go to the Nueces and wherever you go keep a sharp lookout for Scott Cooley and

129

George Gladden. It is thought by some that they will rendezvous out there with other out-laws.[27]

Ake's reluctance to join Cooley due to the presence of the Rangers is understandable. The *Galveston Daily News* reported in 1877 that "the celebrated outlaws, Bill and Jeff Ake, who for years after the war were the boss thieves of this and adjoining counties" had been arrested. "They are said to have stolen as many horses as any two men in Texas, and have been in jail often and been tried but seldom, having usually broken jail."[28]

The mere rumor that Cooley was hunting allies such as Ake can hardly have been viewed with sympathy. West Texas at the time had a bad reputation.

> One thing, however, is certain, that the region of country west of here [San Antonio] almost swarms with hard cases from other States. There is every reason to believe that there is a perfectly organized band of upwards of 200 horsethieves, whose operations extend from the Rio Grande to St. Louis. Criminals of all descriptions, for whom such large rewards are offered in other States that they can not remain there, find security and booty on our extreme Western frontier. . . .[29]

It was a tactical blunder. While action taken against the killer of a friend or relative was understandable, even expected, bringing in known outlaws as allies was unthinkable. This may well be the basis for Miles Barler's assertion that A. G. Roberts had "hired about fifty outlaws and regular desperadoes."[30]

On October 21, Jones countermanded his orders for Roberts to bring his company to Mason. The official reason was a concern that Indians would come down during November.[31] In separate correspondence Jones revealed his true motives to Steele.

> I brought with me Lt. Longs Co. and eight men of Lt. Roberts Co. the latter for the reason that they had been here before and were well acquainted with

the country, intending to remain here only a few days however and then station Lt. Roberts company here and leave it here for some time to come. Within a few days however I became convinced that it would only aggravate the trouble to leave Lt. Roberts company here for the reason that the sympathies of his men were entirely with one of the parties to the fued [sic], that the notorious murderer Scott Cooley having at one time been a member of the company had many friends among the men who were in sympathy with him and his party and entertained a violent prejudice against the Sheriff Clark and the German population.[32]

Long's selection to command the forces in Mason was logical. Long knew no one in the county and, to Jones' mind, would prove more neutral than Roberts' men had been. Although a good officer, Long was characterized as lacking "the aggressiveness characterizing most men of authority, but was gifted with initiative."[33] Long attempted to keep the peace in Mason, but the company proved as ineffectual as Company D in bringing any of Baird's fighters to heel. Part of the reason was that their ranks had already been compromised by Baird forces. Allen Young Tanner, an uncle of Joe Olney, enlisted in Company A of the Texas Rangers on September 2, 1875, and served through November 30 of that year.[34] Tanner's brother, Sam, had been one of the men who came from Burnet to claim Moses Baird's body. It is probable that Allen Tanner kept the Baird party advised as to Company A's movements.

The dismissal of the charges against Clark's men on October 23 and Williams' acquittal during the same time period were cause for festivity in Mason. On October 25 Lucia Holmes noted that a new barroom had opened and "everybody on a spree."[35] Among those celebrating was Tom Gamel who was "in town shooting and drunk all day. . . . Shooting at 12 o'clock at night."[36] It was a grand time for Mason, as the county basked in a false sense that the feud was over. One correspondent, signing himself NOMAD, wrote on the 22nd that "Since Maj. James [sic] and his company of Rangers made their appearance in our midst, every thing has been in status quo, no one

131

being killed since the death of Houston [*sic*: Hoerster]. How long this will last I cannot say, but it is to be hoped that we will have a duration of it."[37] Long dutifully sent the proceedings of the court term to Steele. Steele correctly understood that the verdicts would not satisfy all of the feudists and responded on November 6 that Long was to remain in Mason.[38] By that time Long already knew that the feud was not over. Peace lasted exactly one week.

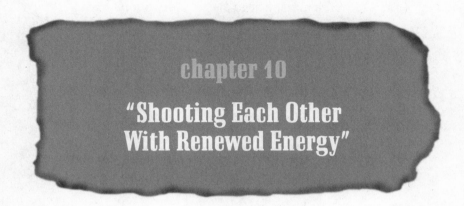

chapter 10

"Shooting Each Other
With Renewed Energy"

On October 29 Lucia Holmes noted in her diary that "Old Man" Miller was shot at dark.[1] Writing from Fredericksburg one correspondent erroneously reported that "reliable information from Mason" told of the killing of a "Mr. Martin."[2] Two days later the same paper corrected itself, stating in part that "The Fredericksburg correspondent of the Freie Presse mentions the killing of a Mr. Mueller in Mason."[3] Gamel also recalled the man as Miller but provides no first name. Contemporary records indicate that the man was J. P. Miller.[4]

Miller had been assigned the task of constructing the coffins for the men lynched in February but was never paid for his work. When Charley Johnson was arrested, he had a "fine pearl handled 45 Colts sixshooter" that was taken from him. How Miller came into possession of the pistol is unknown, but he decided to keep it in payment for his work. When Johnson wanted the weapon back, he asked Tom Gamel to get it for him. Miller refused, claiming that it was his payment for time and materials. Johnson worked for Gamel long enough to earn money for a new pistol, then rode to Miller's and asked him if he had a good pistol available. Miller responded that he had had one but sold it.

"The one I've got is alright [sic]," returned Johnson. He then drew and shot Miller as he turned to run. Only the intervention of Miller's wife prevented Johnson from killing him.[5] Gamel's account is substantially the same as appeared in the *San Antonio Daily Express*.

Last week a man called at the house of one Miller, a gunsmith in Mason and asked for a pair of gun-barrells [*sic*] which had been left with him a number of months previous. As Miller turned to get the gun-barrels, the visitor shot him through the right shoulder, and hastily decamped. This occurred in the town of Mason, about dark one evening last week, but no one seems to know or is willing to venture an opinion, as to why the deed was perpetrated, and from what I could learn this seems also to be the case in all these murders.[6]

Correspondence from Dan Roberts at this time indicates that there may have been a far different motive for the shooting.

Desperadoism has somewhat ceased. The old man— Miller (who had charge of Coke when he escaped) was shot at his house in Mason County a few days after you started up the line, but was not Killed. It was said to be Johnson who shot him. Scott Cooley was in Menardville a few days since—called at the Blacksmiths to get his horse shod early in the morning -- told him to do the job quick and left immediately. Said he was going to Kicapoo . . . .[7]

Another correspondent who signed himself ALIZAN quoted a letter stating that Miller was seventy-two years old, which is hardly likely if he was riding in a posse in pursuit of Scott Cooley, and that Miller "detested these thugs, and had to suffer for it."[8]

November 1875 began with a rumor that the "Germans and Americans" had had a fight near Spring Ranch in Comal County which resulted in one man being killed and several badly wounded.[9] The rumor was apparently false, but it was not promising when District Court opened on November 8. Lucia Holmes noted that her husband was busy all day. Among his cases was one against Benjamin Franklin "Frank" Bolt for forgery. Bolt was indicted on October 2, but details of the case against the eighteen-year-old are lacking.[10]

Among those who visited Mason during November was a correspondent to the *Austin Statesman* who identified himself as Peter. Writing from Fredericksburg on November 12, Peter reported under the headline THE UNCIVIL WAR IN MASON that:

> The condition of affairs in Mason county is truly deplorable. We found the court in session at Mason, Hon. W. W. Martin presiding, but there was nobody in attendance except those who were compelled to be there. The people of the county are so equally divided, actively or in sympathy, between the prominent agitators of the local quarrel, that it is feared a grand jury cannot be formed to indict, or a petit jury to convict, and those who are disposed to do their duty impartially are deterred by fear of personal consequences. Judge Martin delivered a very decided and fearless charge to the grand jury, and while he did not fail to call all the lawless acts that have been committed by their right name, he imputed the principal wrong to those citizens who raised the first mob to kill men who were already in the custody of the law. The war that has since been waged has been one of retaliation, and the Cooley party saw that they will not rest until they have killed two or three other individuals whom they do not hesitate to name. [11]

Dr. C. E. Fisher was also visiting Mason at the time accompanied by G. W. Bartholomew. [12] In a letter dated November 9 from Mason, Fisher reported the most complete account of the court session. Fisher had promised the editor of the *San Antonio Herald* a letter "concerning the cattle feud" in hopes of learning details of the troubles. He was soon dissuaded

> after making numerous inquiries and catching a glimpse of the popular feeling on the subject, I have concluded not to interfere, but to let them fight it out to their heart's content. The fact of the matter really is that you can get no information from any reliable per-

son, as experience has taught them all to keep their own counsel.

Fisher noted that in the case of the feud the residents professed to know nothing and ignorance was bliss because "it is dangerous to be wise." Fisher gave up the attempt after "numerous futile attempts." He was, however, able to provide a description of the court session.

Fisher was impressed by Judge Martin whom he described as "a young man, less than forty years of age, tall and slender, of very dark, tawny complexion, with hair and beard as black as the raven, and a keen quick eye to match. He evinces in every look, word and action a calm, dispassionate determination to do his whole duty, and if the cessation of hostility depended on Judge Martin alone, they would soon be brought to a finis." Martin delivered his charge to the jury in an impassioned speech.

> In his charge to the jury, the Judge explained . . .
> "Men are being shot down in your very streets and murders are of daily occurrence; Mason county is becoming a by-word throughout the State; strangers and travelers are afraid to come within the lines of your county, and lawlessness reigns supreme. Both parties are equally guilty and by taking their revenge by their own hands, are transgressing the law, and it is your duty to put a stop to this state of affairs. It remains with you as Grand Jurymen to urge upon your county authorities and all good citizens the fulfillment of their duties, and if proper measures are taken by you during the present term, much good must result." The Judge cited the case of one man who had surrendered himself to a posse, they pronouncing themselves officers of the law. Neither the posse nor the prisoner has been heard from since, and a few such occurrences, would render the arm of the law powerless. Certainly no man, however good a citizen, will surrender himself under any circumstances to men purporting to be officers of the law, unless personally acquainted with them, when such a state of affairs exists, and as

strangers in the county we could heartily second the
Judge in his every utterance on the subject.[13]

Martin's admonition accomplished nothing. On November 12 a
no bill was found by the grand jury against Clark, and he immediately
fled the area. Gamel reported that his brother John later thought that
he had seen Clark in Nebraska but was not positive.[14] Clark's escape
from justice was not lost on anyone, and the grand jury's failure to
indict a single person raised a furor across Texas. The radical *San
Antonio Express* reported that the grand jury "reported to the Judge
that it is impossible for them to do anything with the matter, and
asked to be discharged." According to the *Express* the "whole population of the country is ranged on the two sides in this war." Continuing,
the paper raged:

> The county and its people should be taken care of
> by the State Government or it will become a bloody
> wilderness. Martial law and military occupation
> should be the first remedies and then have matters
> investigated according to law, the troops serving all
> processes. The State is already disgraced by affairs in
> DeWitt and Mason.[15]

While the newspapers castigated Mason and the feudists, Ira
Long's Company A remained busy. On November 2 six of his men
met Sheriff Baird and captured some cattle thieves on Bluff Creek.[16]
One newspaper reported that there were five men taken when "Long,
of the Rangers, and a squad of his men recently surprised the outlaws
in their camp and captured them. The rangers also captured a party
under Scott Cooley, wounding that noted leader."[17] One of the captured men was rumored to be John Ringo.[18]

From the tone of the story it appeared that Cooley was with the
cattle thieves, but this was not the case. Dr. Fisher's account clarified
the situation. On November 20, Cooley and a number of others rode
into Mason.

> Then again on Saturday night a party supposed to be
> the Cooley party came to town heavily armed, but

were pursued by the Rangers and three of their number captured, and as rumor has it, Cooley himself was wounded. The Rangers are still in pursuit, and the result awaited for.[19]

Cooley may well have been wounded, but nothing in the Record of Scouts for November indicates that anyone was captured during the latter part of the month. Long sent men out on the 21st, 25th, and 28th. The scout Dr. Fisher referred to was probably that of the 23rd when "Sergt. Simmons with 12 men left camp at Mason" to search for outlaws. The men returned empty-handed.[20] Lucia Holmes noted of the matter only that there had been shooting after she had gone to bed.[21]

Rumors that more Rangers had been called in to quell the feud abounded. Fisher reported on November 15 that

> During the morning drive we suddenly ran across a squad of Rangers who emerged from a sharp defile in the mountains much to our surprise, as the approach to their camp seemed so inacessible [sic] that we had no idea of meeting any human being in that locality. There they were, however, and a rougher more uncouth looking set I have never seen. They were twelve or fifteen in number, well mounted and armed to the teeth (not figuratively speaking either); dressed roughly, with hair and head unke[m]pt, they certain[ly] presented an appearance more like guerrilas [sic] than officers of the law, and we were excusable therefore in wishing ourselves well out of the neighborhood, as we did when we first saw them. These men were a portion of Capt. McNelly's brave band, and were on the search for the authors of the Mason county troubles, with whom they have had slight skirmishes of late.[22]

The incident described by Dr. Fisher took place near Kerrville, and the identification of these men was erroneous. The entry of Leander H. McNelly's company into the feud, combined with Coldwell, Long, and Roberts' companies, would have meant that four of the seven companies of Texas Rangers in the state were actively hunting Cooley in the region. In truth, at this time McNelly was camped along the Rio Grande preparing to invade Mexico.[23] The party remains unidentified, but it cannot have been lost on either Coke or Steele. Nor was the fact that none of the Rangers had apprehended any of the feudists. On the contrary, violence continued. In late November, possibly on Sunday, November 21, a man named William Cook was shot down at Loyal Valley. "Alizan," quoting a letter from the *San Antonio Freie Presse*, reported that a man named William Cook, who was visiting Mason on business was reported "murdered by the well known band in the most brutal manner." Cook was staying in Loyal Valley and had left his hotel for Meusebach's store when he was killed. Cook lived three days in agony before dying, having "received thirty bullets in his body." Alizan reported that Cook was believed to be a spy.[24]

Nothing further is known about either Cook or his murder. The Germans were quick to blame the Baird partisans for the killing, but the phrase "well known band" could refer to either Baird's faction or the mob partisans. As December arrived in the Hill Country, terror ruled supreme. Commenting on the affairs in Mason, Reverend Johann Gottloeb Stricker stated:

> A band of murderers persist in the county; they follow their victims and, if need be, shoot them down right on the street. Since I have been here, no less than ten murders have been committed, several of them right near to me. . . .The alienation between Germans and non-Germans has turned into bitter hatred.[25]

Families were fleeing the area. A gunsmith named Diene reported in Fredericksburg that he had been forced to flee the area because of "several attempts having been made to murder him, and his house was frequently fired into." The same paper reported that "A great many families, mostly Germans, have fled from the upper country, as their lives are constantly in danger. They arrive here [Fredericksburg] without means as they have been compelled to abandon everything."[26]

In Llano County, men were also taking precautions. William Siree Kidd, born June 15, 1869, in Loyal Valley to William and Matilda Jane

Stone Kidd, recalled as a boy carrying supplies to a cave on House Mountain for nearly a year to a family relative hiding there. At one time he fell from his mule and cried so loudly that his brother John feared their discovery.[27] As December 1875 dawned the situation was caustically summarized by Alizan.

> Law and order once more prevail in Mason county almost as completely as it does down in DeWitt county—that is to say, that the people are shooting each other with renewed energy. Whenever I meet the driver of the Mason stage and inquire the news from Mason, he smiles in that quiet, pensive way peculiar to stage drivers, and says something about the people being busy killing or burying another fellow just as the stage left.[28]

Alizan was not the only person disgusted with the state of affairs. The *Austin Daily Statesman* quipped: "The Cuero *Star* should proclaim it, and the people of Mason never forget that few people of the better class care to emigrate to a country where they think it necessary to wear a six-shooter at their side, a bowie knife in their boot, and keep an eye over both shoulders to insure safety."[29]

During early December there was a lull in the fighting, though not from any Christmas cheer. Many of the fighters were in Burnet County, appearing unmolested in court on cases unrelated to the feud. On December 5 John Baird and A. T. Taylor entered a plea of guilty on an outstanding case and were fined ten dollars and costs. M. B. Thomas, Joe Olney, and Sam Olney waived juries in their cases and were fined ten dollars each. There was no move on the part of the authorities to detain Baird. Certainly none of the lesser known participants in the feud were arrested. To the contrary, some charges were dropped by the district attorney.[30] In Burnet County, Baird and his allies still enjoyed a high degree of local support even at this late date in the feud.

While Baird and his men rested in Burnet, Rance Moore, charged by the Hoo Doos as Doell's killer the previous summer, was having difficulties in Kimble County. Moore had made an arrangement with Henry Sharp and James Polk Mason to keep some of his cattle. Sharp and Mason were to mark and brand the calves and attend to them, and Moore would pay the pair on shares. In the fall of 1875 Moore made a settlement with them and took possession of the herd. During the agreement Mason "became angry over some of the camp equipment and cursed one of the cow hands."[31] The matter rested until December 12, when Mason, accompanied by Wes Johnson, rode to the Moore ranch to discuss Mason's grievance.

Moore invited the men into his home to discuss the problem. Initially Mason appeared satisfied, but as they prepared to leave, the argument recommenced and continued outside. Finally Moore asked Mason how he wanted to settle it. Mason patted his pistol and replied "This way." Moore then said that he would go and get his. As he re-emerged from the house Mason killed him.[32]

Mason's identity is confounded by the presence of two James P. Masons, both involved in the feud. The men are both listed in the *1878 Fugitives From Justice*. Henry M. Holmes described Moore's killer as five-feet, eight inches tall with black hair, black eyes, and a dark swarthy complexion, placing Mason's age at about twenty-eight.[33] A James P. Mason described as "black hair, low stature, 26 or 28 years old, dark skin" was indicted for murder in Madison County, Texas, during August 1874.[34] The description is close to that given by Holmes, and the time frame would have allowed him to have been working for Moore during 1875 if he had fled to Kimble County after the killing in Madison County.

The second James P. Mason was indicted on April 5, 1875, for theft of neat cattle, allegedly on January 15, 1875, in Burnet County. This Mason was described as "25 years old, 5 feet 8 inches high, weighs 170 lbs., light complexion, light hair, grey eyes and light moustache." Following this description, the sheriff of Burnet County appended the statement that "Since this indictment he has murdered Rans Moore, of Kimble county, on the head of the Llano river. $1000 is offered by the widow. He formerly lived in Walker county, Texas, and was in that county when last heard from."[35] The sheriff of Kimble County provided no help in the case, stating only "Mason, Jas. P. . . . Murder of Rance Moore."[36] From this, it is clear that Moore's killer, the dark haired Mason from Madison County, was confused with Jim Mason of Burnet. Records from the time make it difficult, if not impossible, to differentiate between the pair. Yet the differentiation must be made, for within days one of the Masons was riding with John Baird. Shortly after the killing George W. Todd wrote a letter to John B. Jones.

Mason, Texas
Dec. 14, 1875

Majr. J. B. Jones.
Dear Sir:

Times in and around Mason seem to be more dangerous.

Cooley and party were in town last night some estimate the number to be 11. They have been in Loyal Valley a few days ago and in fact they are becoming more bold every day. Lieut. Long is the right man and in the right place, but he has not force sufficient to do what the emergency of the case demands. He has now out 2 scouts and has only a few men in town, not enough to cope with the 11 outlaws which were in town last night.

And in order to put a stop to the matter there ought to be a larger force stationed here. If you could spare them say at least 60 men.

I was sorry I could not have time the few days you spent here on your trip south to talk with you.

I understand that the man Mason who killed Rance Mo[o]re is now with the desperadoes and was in town last night.

Now Major I am in great haste and will have to close. But for God['s] Sake don[']t take the Rangers away. But send more for I know they are needed worse here than any where else.

There is a Liquor dealer in Austin by the name of McDonald who sells to our Mason saloons and seems to be familiar with the parties and I think Cooley and Co. make his place Hdqrs while in Austin.

If you have time drop us a line.

Yours Truly
G. W. Todd[37]

Todd's confusion was natural, for the man with Baird was the same man wanted by the sheriff of Burnet County. More importantly however, the Baird faction continued to operate with impunity. Local lawmen in adjacent counties had turned a blind eye to their presence, but the rumored presence of Rance Moore's killer in their ranks changed this. A popular and respected man, Moore's death would not be ignored. Lawmen in the area would not ignore outlaws who attempted to cloak themselves under Baird's protection. It was this mistaken belief and confusion that contributed to Scott Cooley's undoing.

Following his visit to Mason, Cooley returned to Burnet where, in late December, he and Ringo became involved in an altercation with Sheriff John Clymer and his deputy, J. J. Strickland. The men were arrested on December 27 and charged with threatening Clymer and Strickland's lives.[38] Clymer may have been attempting to serve a warrant on Ringo for the old indictment of "disturbing the peace." The action led to harsh words and threats.

News of their arrest created a furor in Burnet. Descendants of various men involved in the feud recalled that Baird's allies feared being mobbed while under arrest. Considering the lack of indictments against the Hoo Doos, their concern was justified. Armed men demanded the release of the prisoners, and Clymer was forced to put additional guards on the payroll.

WAR IN BURNET — Ex-Policeman Johnson returned from Burnet Friday [December 31, 1875], where he had been to conduct a prisoner, and reports a horrible state of affairs in that town. The notorious desperado Cooley and one of his companions had been arrested and placed in the Burnet jail, and when Mr. Johnson arrived there about twenty men were dashing about the town threatening to break open the jail, which was being guarded by fifty or more men, and liberating the prisoners. There was so much excitement in the place in the morning that the sheriff would not receive the prisoner taken up by Mr. Johnson, as he was in constant expectation of an attack. Later in the day however, the prisoner was received, and Mr. Johnson then started home, meeting many armed men along the road. A feeling of dread and insecurity for life seemed to pervade the entire community, and strangers were anxious to get out of those parts. (39)

With possibly intentional irony the *Austin Daily Statesman* placed the article directly above another headed THE WEEK OF PRAYER.

Clymer and Strickland were capable officers. Newly elected on September 20, 1875, Clymer intended only to fill out the term of his predecessor.[40] His deputy, John J. Strickland, was elected sheriff on February 15, 1876, serving until 1877. Like so many others, Strickland was destroyed by the feud.[41] When civil war erupted over the arrests of Cooley and Ringo, the officers, accompanied by ten or twelve guards, transferred the pair to Austin where they were placed in the Travis County jail on January 2. They were to be held until court convened in Burnet on January 24. Even so there is no indication in any of Burnet's County's records that they were to be transferred to Mason to face charges waiting for them there.

In Austin the posse stopped to eat at "Salge's snack house" where Cooley and Ringo found themselves the center of attention. A large group of sightseers gathered to see the two men "who have in the past few months, with others, been 'on the rampage' in the counties of Mason and Burnet."

> The prisoners were apparently cool and reserved, and chatted as freely as any of the guard, and each recognized a person or two in the crowd. Cooley, who is said to have been a very quiet man until about a year ago, is a short, solid man, about twenty-eight years old, and looks like he might have some Cherokee blood in him. . . . Ringgold, who is taller and perhaps older than Cooley, is said to have taken an active part in the Mason county war. . . . [42]

The arrest of Cooley and Ringo was heralded across Texas. The *Dallas Herald* wrote:

SCOTT COOLY [*sic*] and John Ringgold [*sic*], two
Mason county desperadoes, had to be brought from
the Burnet jail under a strong guard to Travis county
and are there safely incarcerated. In Burnet an armed
body of men were dashing through the streets intent
upon a rescue, and Sheriff Strickland determined to
lodge them where release was impossible. Cool[e]y is
charged with killing and scalping John A. Whorlie, deputy sheriff of Mason county. He has some Cherokee
blood in his veins.[43]

Other stories appeared in Galveston and San Antonio newspapers.[44]
To insure that Cooley remained in custody, Long sent four Rangers
under Corporal Simmons to Burnet with warrants from Mason for the
men. The detachment returned to Mason on January 6. Long wasted
no time in advising Major Jones of Cooley's arrest.

Mason Tex
Jan 6th / 76

Maj. Jno B. Jones
Comdg Front. Bat.

Dear Sir

The detachment sent to Burnet returned to-day
with the intelligence that the officials of Burnet had
sent Cool[e]y & Ringgold [*sic*] to Austin for safe
keeping which relieves this country of much trouble.
Gladden & Baird are still at large and are publicly seen
on the streets of Burnet. I have sent warrants for the
arrest of them and will write to-night to the officers
there offering them any assistance necessary to make
the arrest.

Obtly Yours
Ira Long
Lt. Comd; Co. "A" Front. Bat.[45]

Long's letter further illustrates that public feeling was with Baird in the county. The fact that Baird and Gladden roamed the streets of Burnet unmolested provides ample evidence of the support they enjoyed. An obvious question remains as to why the detachment sent to Burnet made no attempt to arrest them. Jones had anticipated that Company A would prove neutral in the feud. Yet, with the exception of the exchange of gunfire the previous fall and the capture of Williams, Company A proved as ineffective as Company D had been. Contrary to folklore and the contentions of their publicists, Company A's presence in Mason had not deterred the violence significantly. Beyond the county's boundaries Baird and his followers operated without hindrance, as Long and the Rangers were about to learn.

Long's action in sending troops to Burnet created a furor. Charges were made to Adjutant General Steele that Long had sent his men to Burnet for the purpose of seizing Cooley and Ringo from the authorities there. An angry Long replied to Steele that:

> I find on my arrival at Mason a letter from you in which I am accused of sending a party of men to Burnet to take charge of Cool[e]y after he was in the hands of the civil authorities. I deny the charge. The object of sending men to Burnett was to take warrants that I had in my posession [sic] for the arrest of Scott Cool[e]y and Jno Ringgold [sic] so that if they were released there, they could be held to answer charges against them here.
>
> If the statement in regard to this matter was in writing, I would like to have a copy of it. If it was a verbal statement I would be glad to know who your informant is.
>
> It has been stated to me that Major Jones has resigned. If such is the case, I would like to be apprised of it.[46]

By January 1876 the focus of Baird and his allies was running Peter Bader to ground. Both Cheyney and Hoerster were dead, and John Clark was beyond their reach. This left only Bader, the man credited with killing both Baird and Williamson, as a target. It was not a fact that was lost on either the Mason or Llano Hoo Doos. Bader was abandoned to his fate by his allies.

According to Max Krueger, Peter Bader had been hiding out in Fredericksburg with his family and planned to flee to Florida. Krueger had taken no part in the feud to this point and had became acquainted with Bader during his stay in Fredericksburg. Bader planned to return to Llano to make a final settlement with Karl Lehmberg and asked Krueger to accompany him, obviously feeling that there was safety in numbers. That he turned to Krueger, an outsider, illustrates his isolation. Krueger recalled in later years that Bader begged him to make the trip with him. "Just to tease him I held out with my right hand an old watch, saying, if you can hit the center of the watch, I shall go with you. Like lightning he turned his horse, pulled his Winchester, and shot the dead center out of my watch."[47] In late December or early January the men began the dangerous trip to Llano County. Along the way they ran into five men led by Baird and Gladden. Recognizing their quarry, Baird and his men opened fire. In a running gun battle, Bader's saddle horn was shattered by a bullet. The men made it safely to the home of Wilhelm Marschall in Llano County, but the incident convinced Krueger that he wanted no more of the feud. The following day he returned unmolested to Fredericksburg. Bader remained in the relative safety of Marschall's home.[48]

For Peter Bader there was no sanctuary. On January 13 Bader left Marschall's in the company of three other men. Perhaps he felt that his pursuers had abandoned the hunt. If so, he sadly misjudged their determination. Baird, Gladden, and another man, possibly Ed Cavin, were waiting for him, concealed in some rocks on the north side of the road at San Fernando Creek. As Bader and the others approached, Baird stepped from the cover of the rocks with his shotgun and said, "Hello Bader." The "words had not died on Beard's [sic] lips until he shot Border [sic]. Border's [sic] horse wheeled and ran about fifty yards, and he fell from the horse, dead."[49]

According to local folklore, Baird retrieved his brother's ring from Bader by severing the finger he had worn it on. Krueger lends some credence to the mutilation of Bader's body, although by the time the story reached him it had grown in the telling: "Poor Bader fared worse. . . . he was killed four miles from von Bieberstein's home. His body was cut into pieces and ruthlessly suspended from the branches of a nearby live oak tree."[50] Had Bader's body been quartered, the papers most certainly would have reported it as news of the latest killing rippled across Texas. They did not. One account noted:

> The Cooley party in the great vendetta in this county are charged with another murder. Report says that one day last week a foreigner by the name of Bourbon [sic: Bader] was riding along the public road when he was attacked by a party of men and shot. The party then seeing some men approaching and supposed them to be friends of their victim, told them to take up the man and take care of his valuables, as they (the assassins) did not want money but his life. Bourbon had $400 and a gold watch when shot. It is said that a general warfare is being waged in the county between what is known as the Dutch population and the Americans. At last accounts the murderers had not been captured.[51]

Newspaper accounts mistakenly reported that the killing had occurred in Mason rather than Llano.[52] Gamel identified the shooter as John Baird, an assertion that has never been questioned. Gladden confirmed that Baird was the killer, but stated there was a third man who participated in the shooting while Gladden held the horses, whom he refused to identify. Evidence strongly suggests that the third man was Ed Cavin.[53] Cavin is known to have participated actively in the feud. By year's end the mob would make an attempt on his life.

Long reported Bader's death to Jones, noting in his letter of January 15 that he had heard "from the Stage driver this morning, that Peter Border [sic] was killed two days ago on Llano River four miles below Limhburg's [sic: Lehmberg's]."[54] Another newspaper provided a garbled account of the killing: "A private letter from Mason county announces that another of the Scott Cooley party, one Peter Porder, has recently been killed."[55]

It was the ultimate bitter irony. Not only had the papers not reported Bader's name correctly, they had mistakenly ascribed his role in the feud as an ally of Scott Cooley.

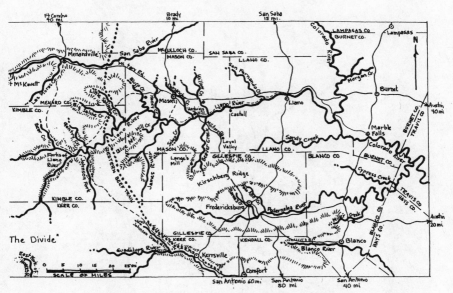

Map of Central Texas at the time of the Hoo Doo War, 1874–76.
Courtesy Peter R. Rose.

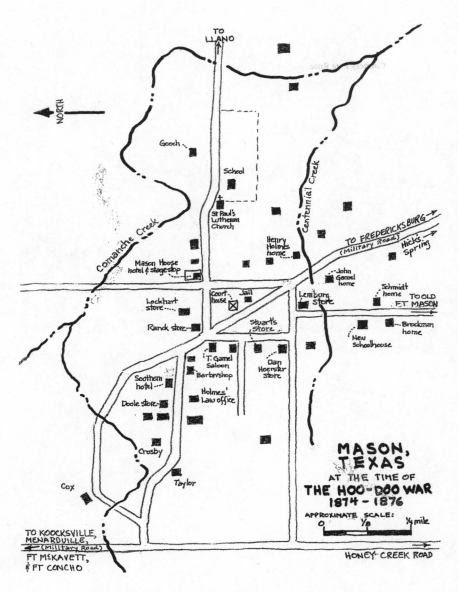

Map of Mason, Texas, at the time of the Hoo Doo War, 1874–76.
Courtesy Peter R. Rose.

William Z. Redding.
Courtesy Michael Redding.

Abraham Teal Taylor.
Courtesy LaFon Commander.

Ann A. Olney Taylor.
Courtesy LaFon Commander.

George W. Gladden.
Author's collection.

(above) Timothy P. and Mary E. Williamson. Author's collection.

(left) Ernst Jordan. Courtesy Mason County Historical Commission.

Dietrich Kothmann.
Courtesy Mason County
Historical Commission.

Charles Walker and Laurinda
Reaves Johnson. Author's
collection.

Thomas and Mary
Cavness Gamel. Courtesy
Mason County Historical
Commission.

Daniel Hoerster. Courtesy Mason
County Historical Commission.

Henry M. Holmes.
Courtesy Mason County
Historical Commission.

Lucia Holmes with
unidentified girl.
Courtesy Mason County
Historical Commission.

Karl and Henriette Leifeste
Lehmberg. Courtesy Mason
County Historical Commission.

John Wohrle. Courtesy
Mason County Historical
Commission.

Heinrich Doell. Courtesy
Mason County Historical
Commission.

Photograph of three
unidentified Texas
Rangers. The author
believes that the man
seated on the left is Scott
Cooley. Courtesy Chuck
Parsons.

(above) Original headstone of Moses B. Baird in Burnet, Texas. The stone was replaced by descendants of the Olneys during the late 1980s. Author's collection.

(right) Joseph Graves Olney. Author's collection.

John Peters Ringo.
Author's collection.

Champion N. and
Virginia Faris.
Author's collection.

William W. and Melissa
Olney. Author's collection.

The Southern Hotel. Courtesy Mason County Historical Commission.

Peter Jordan. Courtesy Mason County Historical Commission.

Roll and Dell Dublin.
Courtesy Frederica Wyatt.

"I Think There Is Some Trouble at Hand"

With the death of Peter Bader, John Baird and Scott Cooley had effectively completed their quest for revenge. Satisfied that justice had been meted out to those responsible for his brother's murder, Baird began to withdraw from the feud. With him went the allies who had rallied to his cause. The Mason mob was broken, and John Clark had fled to parts unknown. Baird had a new daughter, Edna, at home and realized that it was time to stop the conflict.[1] Satisfied with the results, Baird began preparations to leave Texas.

Even as Baird withdrew from the conflict, fate closed in on Ernst Jordan. Since the beginning of the conflict he had gone armed. Sometime during 1876 when the "troubles had hardly subsided" Jordan was removing a pistol from his carriage when it slipped from his hand. The pistol dropped to the ground and discharged, the bullet shattering his knee. The accident left him bedridden during the remainder of 1876 and throughout 1877. A surgeon from San Antonio operated on the leg, but it never healed properly and required treatments for the rest of his life.[2]

Mason County residents were quick to disown the Bader killing. On January 27, a meeting was held in Mason by "the citizens of Mason County" chaired by James M. Hunter. The purpose of the meeting was to condemn an editorial entitled "More Blood" in the *Fredericksburg Sentinel*. The paper had attributed Bader's death to Mason County.

Resolved that we view with regret the course pursued by the Fredericksburg Sentinel as set forth in its editorial headed "More Blood" of the issue of the 22nd inst, in attributing the murder of Peter Bader to our County as such reports tend to produce a false and erroneous impression upon people outside the County, and more than anything else prevent emigration and the development of our natural resources.

Resolved that in that portion of the Sentinel's editorial headed "More Blood" we perceive a desire to stir up more trouble in our County, by means of the false statements contained therein, whereby the out side world would be led to believe that the citizens of Mason County are responsible for a murder which took place in Llano County.[3]

The meeting further praised Long and his troops and credited him with the peace that existed in Mason at the time.

Long's Rangers were reportedly in pursuit of Baird and Gladden in mid-January, but once again the pair vanished into friendly territory.[4] At the end of the month, Steele ordered Long to Burnet "as some trouble is anticipated there during Court." Long did not know how long he would need to remain there, but the necessity was clear. Cooley was conveyed to Burnet by the end of January to answer charges of threatening Clymer and Strickland.[5] The *Austin Daily Statesman* reported:

DEPUTY SHERIFFS Henry Stokes and Fred Peck arrived yesterday morning from Burnet, where they had been with the posse of ten men that conveyed Scott Cooley to Burnet from the jail in this city. They report that they saw no signs of resistance or of an attempt being made to release the prisoner on the road. They state, however, that Deputy Sheriff Johnson, of Burnet, and a man with him were fired upon and pursued several miles while out serving capiases last Tuesday [January 25]. The speed of their horses saved their lives. A minute company has been organized in the town of Burnet, and recently quite an extensive purchase of firearms has been made in this city by citizens of Burnet, whose lives are said to be endangered because they are determined to enforce law and order.[6]

On February 1, 1876, Cooley and Ringo were indicted for "Seriously threatening to take the life of a human being." The indictments of Cooley and Ringo, combined with the unilateral withdrawal of Baird from the fighting, came as a welcome reprieve to Mason County. One paper reported that, "Perfect peace and quiet reign in Mason county, at present. One or two lawless acts last fall were exaggerated to such an extent as greatly to injure the character of our country, but order is well established at present."[7]

There was validity in this self-serving statement from Mason, at least as far as the current state of affairs stood. There were several reasons for this, not the least of which was the fact that many of the forces supporting Baird were in Burnet answering charges in a number of court cases not related to the feud. Some of them failed to make their court appearances, however.

John Olney lost a lawsuit against A. G. Roberts on January 31 and paid the costs of the suit.[8] The following day Ed Cavin failed to appear in court on the murder charge against him and his bondsmen, brothers Nathan and Ham Cavin, were informed that their bond of $2500 would be forfeited unless they could show good cause why he was not present. The case was continued. John Olney and A. T. Taylor were brought to trial charged with assault with intent to murder in Cause 749. Olney was found not guilty by a jury. Taylor entered a guilty plea and was fined $12.50. Charges against John C. Carson and J. B. Liggett for selling drinks without a license were dismissed. Both Sam and Al Tanner failed to appear in court to answer on charges of disturbing the peace.[9]

Baird, Gladden, and T. W. Whittington were also indicted on February 4, 1876, for allegedly stealing a mule from W. Gooden. Neither Baird nor Gladden was in court, but Whittington was tried and found not guilty. The others were never brought to trial.[10] Ringo was also in court and was fined $75 on the charge of disturbing the peace during 1874.[11]

After a year of fighting and the deaths of more than a dozen men, things gave the appearance of cooling down in the feud. Burnet held a municipal election during early February and one paper noted that quite a change was perceptible from what it had been in late December.

> Instead of every man being armed to the teeth, and six-shooters being visible on every man's hips, none but the officers of the law go armed. The people are determined to maintain the laws of the land . . . . Deputy Sheriff J. J. Strickland has acquired some notoriety for his courageous conduct in arresting the celebrated desperadoes, Scott Cooley and one Ringo, alias "Long John," both of whom are now in jail at this place.[12]

Long and his men remained in Burnet through February 8. Following his return to Mason, he reported nothing relevant to the feud as of mid-February.[13] Others had a different view, and shortly after Long penned his report to Jones, David Doole sent a letter of his own. It is enlightening on both his character and role in the feud. After discussing the cost of supplies, Doole related:

> Things are rather gloomy. Ringold [*sic*] & Cooley are in Burnett Jail. Gladden & Beard [*sic*] are still at large in the country. Ranck & his party have been successful in the Election. Hey has been elected Co[unty]. & D[istrict]. Clerk. Holland has beaten Todd for Co. Judge this is the fellow that wrote that Lying letter to Senator Westfall in regard to Roberts men stealing his millett. Lieut. Long is encamped about 5 miles from town. I think that State troops are very necessary here & will be until after the new officers are qualified. Beard & Gladden are still using threats. Huoters [Hoerster's ?] Barn was fired last Sunday while the famly [*sic*] was at Church[.] during Election there was a larger nigger & Mexican vote polled. I do not know where the[y] all came from imported I suppose by

the Radicals. Todd & the Germans about 17 are at
Llano Court tho have not been heard from. The Dutch
has gone back on the Democratic party. I could not
get one of them to vote a ticket with the word on
it. I got over this by trimming the bottom & top of
the ticket as a sampole [sic] I enclose you one. I am
happy to say that the State ticket & the new constitution carried by a big majority. Lieut. Long & his men
have behaved nobly & are highly Respected by both
Parties. . . . Ranck made a speech a few days ago &
stated that if Mr. Hey was not elected that the troubles
heretofore existing in Mason would be but as a drop
in the bucket to what the[y] would be.[14]

From Doole's letter it is clear that Ranck and the Germans blamed the
feud on the Democratic party, undoubtedly due to John Clark's affilia-
tion. Doole resorted to ballot tampering to maintain Democratic control of the county, a not uncommon practice in the years following the
Civil War. Notable is the animosity, similar to that exhibited by Dreux,
against the Republican officials who had preceded Clark. In the end,
however, the Hoo Doos were swept from political power. Jesse Leslie
was elected sheriff to succeed James Baird in the election.

While the war in Mason was over, the underlying causes that had
started it remained unchanged. On February 28 Ira Long reported that
Mason was returning to normal and expressed his opinion that troops
would not be necessary in Mason "now that the newly elected officers of the County qualified."[15] It was a logical conclusion based upon
the activities reported by the Rangers during January and February.
Company A's activities had largely been confined to garrison duties.
Company D captured Porter Lancaster and "delivered him to civil authorities of Mason county," but Lancaster played no role in the feud.
None of the other companies made any mention of the Mason troubles. Along the Rio Grande border, things were also relatively quiet for
McNelly.[16] On the surface it appeared that the feud was over.

Unnoticed by legal officials fresh warriors were entering the feud's
bloody arena. The *Dallas Weekly Herald* reported succinctly that "A
vigilance committee in Burnett [sic] county are hunting down outlaws
and desperadoes."[17] In this the *Herald* erred, for the vigilante commit-

tee was from Llano County, not Burnet. The battleground had shifted east, and the Llano mob, untouched, undaunted, and unrepentant was on the rise.

Writing of the Hoo Doo War, Miles Barler stated of the Llano mob's origins:

> The honest people saw they would have to leave the country at once or take the law into their own hands. So the people all met one night and came to the conclusion that we were here first and had fought the Indians for 15 long years to get what we had and when it came to giving it up and leaving the country, we said no. . . . We formed a vigilance committee and elected a captain.[18]

Like the Mason mob, the Llano Hoo Doos had been compromised from the beginning by members of the Dublin family. Gillett knew the Dublins well, recalling in his memoirs that:

> On the South Llano lived old Jimmie Dublin. He had a large family of children, most of them grown. The eldest of his boys, Dick, or Richard as he was known, and a friend, Ace Lankford, killed two men at a country store in Lankford's Cove, Coryell County, Texas. The state offered $500 for the arrest of Dublin and the county of Coryell an additional $200.[19]

Dick Dublin had been involved in several killings. The fact that these pillars of the community were associated with the "law and order" faction of any county is as surprising as Caleb Hall's association with the mob in Mason. There can be little doubt how the mobs' attention was diverted from the real cattle thieves in the area toward what proved an irresistible target, A. G. Roberts and his associates.

Barler's belief that Roberts and his men were cattle thieves is a common theme with both mobs. The Llano mob had been active during early 1875, but their activities were obscured during the murderous onslaughts in Mason. Never as large as their allies in Mason, there is no doubt that they kept busy forcing men to leave their homes and killing those who refused. Certainly they had had a hand in killing Kelly and Wages in 1875.

On February 16, 1876, John Calvert, one of Ringo's bondsmen, was returning to his home less than a block from the courthouse when he was shot to death on his front porch. The *Burnet Bulletin* for this period is missing, but family recollections recount that he was killed under "mysterious circumstances."[20] Calvert, who had no known enemies, left a widow and four young children. It is highly probable that he was killed as an example of what would happen to anyone supporting the Baird faction. The *Galveston Daily News* hinted broadly that things were about to change.

> The same paper [*Burnet Bulletin*] reports the advent of the era of law and order in the town of Burnet. The shouts of drunken revelry, the blasphemy, ribald sound and laughter, the crack of the six-shooter and Winchester, which only a few months ago made night hideous, and startled and terrified the good people of the town are no longer heard. The *Bulletin* says this mighty change in the condition of affairs in that town is due to the prompt and fearless execution of the law by our officers *and the support and assistance given to them by the citizens of the county*. [emphasis added] A good example for some other counties.[21]

In Mason County, violence flared again when Sheriff Jessie Leslie was shot on March 3.

> MAN SHOT IN MASON COUNTY.—The particulars of the wounding of Jessie Leslie in Mason county are to the effect, that he and Ben Gooch were encamped on Red Creek, and while sitting side by side discussing matters and things, several men appeared on the bluff opposite. As men are so often on the bluff in Mason county possibly their appearance was not unusual. These men on the bluff fired at Leslie and Gooch, one of the bullets passing through the wrist of Leslie, and wounding him also in the leg.

This is all very well as far as it goes, but are our Mason county friends aware that during the last two months while one solitary man only has been crippled in Mason county, no less than four or five men have been sent to their long homes in DeWitt County, and one or two of them officers of the law?

Which is the banner county, any how?[22]

The perpetrators were never identified.[23] Doole wrote:

The Sheriff Elect Jesse Leslie was shot on the 4th inst. on Red Creek, in this county, a large party was with him on a cow hunt. Ben F. Gooch & Rufus Holland were sitting around their camp fire and [?] the shot hit Leslie through the wrist & penetrated the thigh near the groin. Its to be hoped he will recover he is a good man[.] its not known who done the shooting[.] It was not supposed that Leslie had an Enemy in the world.[24]

No one was ever charged with the shooting, and no motive for it was established. Leslie represented citizens opposed to the Hoo Doos, and it is equally possible that he was shot by one of the mob. In Llano, the mob was hampered by the lack of control of the sheriff's office. In due course they moved to place a man more favorable to their activities in power. Possibly the men who shot Leslie had the same thought in mind. Equally possible is that the shooting of Leslie was either a personal quarrel or an attempt to kill Ben Gooch. The shooting remains a mystery.

Ira Long made no mention of Leslie's shooting in his report of March 19. Writing to Jones he noted in part, "I think there is some trouble at hand among the cattlemen on the Llano River. I'll make a scout up in their country and see if I can not quell it for a time."[25] Long did not elaborate on the trouble that he anticipated, but it clearly involved cattle as it had two years earlier. He was apparently successful, but the incident serves to underscore the underlying causes of the feud. For the moment, things remained relatively quiet. Writing from Llano on February 20, citizen J. W. Davis made no mention of any feud activity.

> According to promise I will jot down a few items
> from the frontier. Our court has just adjourned. A
> good deal of business done considering we did not
> begin until Wednesday. Three convictions for misde-
> meanors, two or three important land suits decided—
> one the Houston & Texas Central R. R. against your
> old countryman, Thos. G. McGehee, was decided and
> won by McGehee. They wanted his silver and copper
> mines, but they will never get them that way. . . . All
> quiet on the Llano.[26]

Cooley and Ringo were in the news again in mid-March, having been transferred to Lampasas County on a change of venue from Burnet.[27] Baird and Gladden had dropped from sight. Everything was calm. Deceptively calm.

For Sheriff Albertus Sweet of Lampasas, receiving two of the men who had turned Mason County upside down came during a lull in the Horrell-Higgins feud that erupted into a full-scale shooting war during 1877. Sweet had problems with the Horrell brothers dating back to 1874. Adding Cooley and Ringo into the mix was like pouring gasoline on a fire. It was anything but a routine receipt.[28]

Sweet had served as a deputy under Shadrick T. Denson in 1873 before being elected sheriff on December 3 of the same year. By 1876 he was serving in the dual capacity of sheriff and city marshal. Undoubtedly a tough man, he had faced the Horrells and knew full well how to handle feudists. Sweet put a round-the-clock guard on his new charges, secure in the knowledge that he had them well confined.

What Sweet did not realize was that the allies of Cooley and Ringo had already breached the jail's security. According to family descendants, Bud Faris had deliberately allowed himself to be arrested in Lampasas on a minor charge in order to learn about the jail's security. Fearing the men would be lynched, their allies were determined not to trust Cooley and Ringo's lives to mob rule.[29]

While Cooley and Ringo's friends in Burnet and Llano plotted their release, David Doole was having troubles of his own. On the night of April 5, 1876, his store burned to the ground.[30] DeVos speculates that the burning of the store may have been an act of revenge on the part of the Cooley faction.[31] No hint of this is found in the *San Antonio Herald:* "We are just informed that the Store of D. Doole, at Mason, was destroyed by fire. In less than two hours, nothing but the naked walls was left. One of Hall's Fire Proof Safes, for which Messrs. Norton & Dents are Agents here, was in the hottest part of the fire and came out O. K."[32]

Nor do Long's reports from the time reflect a concern that the burning of Doole's store was arson. This is further confirmed in a letter from Jones to Adjutant General Steele. Jones reported that sixteen Springfield carbines had been lost in the fire at Doole's store, then added, "The fire was the result of accident, or rather carelessness, on the part of Mr. D's clerk. . . . I found everything quiet and peaceable in Mason county and a better feeling among the people than has existed there for more than a year past."[33]

After six months of service in Mason County, Long was preparing to leave the turbulent county, writing to Jones on April 3 that his wagons and pack saddles were ready for moving.[34] On April 12 John Gibson was killed by Joe Woods in Mason.[35] This was the result of a personal feud, however, and the killing was not mentioned by Jones in his correspondence to Steele. The Rangers moved out of Mason on April 16. Less than two weeks later Mason was back in the news.

The following is an extract from a letter from Fort Mason, of April, 1876:

"For the last week or ten days we have had exciting times. This county has been beset by horse thieves and other outlaws, until forbearance had ceased to be a virtue. These 'wolves,' as the boys call them, began to raid upon us in bands of ten to twenty, defying officers and the country generally, until it began to appear that no man's life or property was safe. Last week a host of the best men in the country turned out, and at the first dash they captured four of the worst desperadoes, or 'wolves,' but by the aid of hemp *they got away*. Three others have been captured, one of whom is badly wounded. The people are determined to make this section a terror to evil-doers.[36]

Further details on this incident are obscure, and the report may have been false. One of the Mason County residents who read it was Henry M. Holmes. Holmes penned an angry response.

> From Mason County
> Correction—Peace and Quiet—Faithful Officers
> *Eds. News.*—In your WEEKLY of May 1st, I notice a communication purporting to be an extract from Fort Mason, dated April 25, 1876, which is evidently a case of "mistaken identity," to say the least, and so far as the county of Mason is concerned does not contain one word of truth.
>
> PEACE AND QUIET
>
> The county of Mason is in a state of profound peace, has no bands of organized horse thieves, the law is in full force, and there is no need, neither has there been any use, of hemp in the county for over a year. The old disturbances have entirely died out, and the ring-leaders of them were either killed some months ago, or have run away, and at the present time the moral status of Mason county will compare favorably with any other county in the State.
>
> FAITHFUL OFFICIALS
>
> We are happy in having a faithful and energetic Sheriff, an honest County Judge, and a set of Justices and County Commissioners who are earnest in the discharge of their duty, and though our record in the past, as that of every other frontier county, has not been what it should be, we ask that in the present and future no more obloquy should be cast upon us unless the facts justify it, and in this case, unless the heading of the article is a mistake—which I believe it to be—so far as Mason county is concerned, it is a groundless tissue of falsehood, calculated, unless checked, to inspire the interests of our country beyond repair.
>
> HENRY M. HOLMES
> County Attorney, Mason County[37]

Holmes proved correct in his statements. None of the feudists in either faction were involved in any violence in Mason. The county had had its fill of mob law and murder. While the motivation for the letter remains unclear, it appears that someone was attempting to resurrect the feud. Nor was it the only report of lawlessness in the area. In a letter from Llano dated April 25, J. W. Davis reported in part that "Cattle stealing on a large scale is quite common; the sheriff has gone for a drove to-day that was illegally taken out of the county, and there seems to be a general disposition to put a stop to it."[38]

From subsequent newspaper articles it appears that the Ake brothers, Jeff and Bill, and others were responsible for the raids. Scarcely two months later papers noted the arrests of Silas Berry and Bill Bybee for horse theft. The paper stated that they were "associated with the valorious Bill and Jeff Ake."[39]

In Llano County, John Baird continued to gather forces. From subsequent reports, the main conspirators appear to have been Bill and Tom Redding, the Farris brothers, and the Olney brothers. Baird felt an obligation to those who had supported him. On April 30 they made the next move in the feud. Sometime after midnight, four of the Baird faction seized the jail guard at Lampasas and tied him to a fence. Two of the men attempted to cut a hole in the jail "where by the prisoners (Cooley and John Ringo) might escape." The attempt failed, and as dawn approached the men took the guard down the road toward San Saba about two miles and released him unharmed.[40]

The failure to release the prisoners alerted Sweet. The sheriff prudently added additional guards and had the prisoners hobbled. His concern and the countermeasures taken were the actions of a proven officer. Even then it was unthinkable that a second attempt would be made to free the prisoners hard on the heels of the first with the heightened security at the jail. Both Sweet and the residents of Lampasas underestimated the determination of men involved. The unthinkable was about to happen.

Undeterred by the failure of their first attempt, four days later the Baird faction returned in force. The men first went to Sweet's home where they demanded the jail keys. Sweet reluctantly produced the keys after the men told him that they would kill both him and his family and have the keys anyway if he did not cooperate.[41] After securing the sheriff and his family, they moved on toward the jail.

Deputy Sheriff J. T. Walker later testified that he and another guard, possibly William Gilliam, were walking near the jail when they saw thirteen or fifteen men. The party told the guards "not to shoot that they had the keys & that if we hurt any of them that they would burn up the town." Walker realized that it was futile to attempt a fight. "They told me that they had gotten the keys from Mr. Sweet & that they only wanted Cooley & Ringo & would not take any others out. We were poorly armed and had not sufficient numbers of Guards to give them a fight & I told them I reckoned they would have to have them."[42]

Released from the jail, Cooley and Ringo were soon free of their hobbles. Their rescuers laid the hobbles over a log and cut them with an ax. Walker stated further that he counted fifteen men in the party but recognized none of them. He was able to describe one of the men. "I took especial notice of one of them. He was a tall man 25 or 30 years old light complection with sandy whiskers was about six feet high & would weigh about 175 or 180 pounds."[43]

Walker further testified that some of the men had their faces blackened and others were masked. The description of the man Walker observed matches that given of John Baird who was described as "about 30 years old, about 6 feet high, slender build, weighs about 150 pounds, has light, wavy hair, light beard, blue eyes . . . ."[44]

The fugitives headed for Joe Olney's ranch in Llano County. Located just south of the present Burnet-Llano road, the ranch was close to a ford. A number of travelers were startled to find Cooley and Ringo at liberty in the area. One of them was James Newton Randle.

> I know the time that I heard the Lampasas Jail
> was broken open it was the 5th day of May 1876.
> I heard it at Joe Olney's in Llano County. The day
> I heard it was broke Jack Carson, Bill Wills, Charly
> Furgguson, Ed Cavin, Scott Cooley & John Ringo were
> there. They did not all come there together. Joe Olney
> came for his breakfast, and I think Mr. Ringo came
> next & alone. I do not remember who came next.
> Jack Carson and Jim Mason came together. They all
> came before noon—Cooley came in after Mason &
> Carson.[45]

Sheriff William P. Hoskins of Llano County also encountered the men at Olney's on the evening of May 5. Hoskins stated that he had arrived at Olney's and found Joe Olney, Jack Carson, Andy Murchison, Bud Faris, Jim Mason, Bill Wills, Charley Ferguson, and "some three or four others" there in company with Ringo and Cooley. Hoskins' sudden appearance created a furor among the men.

> I went to see Joe Olney on official business & got within 25 yards of the house before they saw me. There appeared to be considerable excitement among them when they saw me, some got on their horses and others picked up their guns. I continued to ride up to them and spoke to Joe Olney and he asked me to get down. When I got down Scott Cooley threw a cartridge in his gun & step[p]ed behind his horse.[46]

Hoskins remained at Olney's for about twenty minutes. During this time, John Ringo spoke to the sheriff and shook his hand.

From Olney's ranch the fugitives headed west into Mason. By May 8 they were back in Mason, and Lucia Holmes noted in her diary, "Scott Cooley and a crowd here —No one knows what they are after. . . . Eve — . . . Some shooting up town. Feel so frightened. —How I wish Hal was here."[47] Cooley and his "crowd" remained in Mason throughout the following day. Tension was high, and Lucia Holmes noted, "Scott Cooley not gone yet—Eve—Scott Cooley back in town with Tom Gamel—lots of shooting in town."[48]

Why Cooley returned to Mason is unknown. Despite fears that the war would continue, there was no violence beyond what seems to have been a celebration. This may well have been the occasion when a final settlement was reached between the Germans and the Baird faction. Jeff Ake recalled in his memoirs that both gangs "held a meeting with the sheriffs and rangers, and the Beard-Gladden outfit agreed to move out of the country if they was left alone. That was the understanding. They gathered up their cattle, about 1,400 head, and started west."[49] Some credibility is given to Ake's story by an article that appeared in late May.

A gentleman recently arrived from Loyal valley,
reports that Scott Cooley and Ringgold, who were recently released from the jail at Lampasas by armed
men, went to the hotel at Loyal Valley, in broad daylight, armed to the teeth and ate with perfect compo-
sure, and rode off unmolested.[50]

The problem with Ake's account is that no Ranger company was
present at Mason at the time to enter into such an agreement. Nor
would they have. Any compromise in the feud would have come between the leaders of the factions, and there is no evidence supporting
Ake's allegation. No charges were dropped against anyone, and the
Rangers continued to hunt Baird's faction well into 1878. Nor did
most of the men involved leave the area. One exception was Scott
Cooley.

For Scott Cooley, the feud was over. Cooley separated from Baird
and his men and headed for Blanco County. He had friends there, and
may have reasoned that he could retire peacefully. It proved a fatal
error.

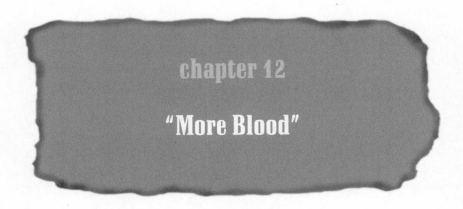

chapter 12

"More Blood"

After reaching Loyal Valley, Ringo and Cooley separated. Ringo returned to Long Mountain in Llano County where the Farris family hid him for some time. Cooley went on to Fredericksburg where he stopped to eat at the Nimitz Hotel. Accounts from this point differ. Gamel relates in his memoirs that Cooley was heading for Blanco County where he had friends. After he finished eating at the hotel,

> he purchased a bottle of whiskey. When he got twelve miles out of Fredericksburg, he rode up to a fellow's house by the name of Moore and got down off his horse and laid down and said, "Moore, I am an awful sick man," and in a few minutes he was dead. It was supposed that there was poison in the whiskey he purchased . . . [1]

Newspapers made no mention of poison. The *Dallas Daily Herald* reported simply that Cooley "died of congestion of the brain" near Fredericksburg.[2] The *Houston Daily Telegraph* provided additional details.

Blanco, June 10, 1876.

> The notorious Scott Cooley died this morning about one o'clock, at the house of Esquire D. Maddox, nine miles north of Blanco, of brain fever.[3]

In later years, rancher Max Gipson would recall that "Wid" Felps, who considered Cooley a likable man, found him raving in a tree. He brought him to the home of Dan Maddox where Cooley died in considerable agony. The symptoms described by the family story are symptomatic of a metallic poisoning.[4]

Cooley's death on June 10, 1876, marks the traditional end of the Hoo Doo War. Cooley's death closed a chapter in the feud, but it was not the end of hostilities. He had succeeded in his aims, however. Cooley had brought terror to Mason and helped destroy the organized Hoo Doos in the county. Those he held most responsible for the death of Tim Williamson were either dead or had fled the state. With Cooley's death, the fire and unrelenting hatred he brought to the feud were gone. This, combined with the withdrawal of Baird and his forces, left only the mob and the cattle thieves as organized forces in the area.

On the same day Cooley died, an anonymous writer signing himself STOCK RAISER penned a letter to the *San Antonio Herald*. The letter provides clear evidence that despite the exit of Baird and his allies from the feud, trouble was still anticipated in the region over the cattle.

> Two-thirds and perhaps three-fourths of the killing and hanging done in Western Texas during the last two or three years grew out of the illegal handling of cattle, and we cannot reasonably hope for permanent peace and prosperity in our stock raising sections, to anything like the degree we would have, if the law were sustained until the people of these sections open their eyes to their own interest and first put their own houses in order and fit themselves to assist in arranging their neighbors premises.
>
> For thieves to undertake to make honest men of others is not practicable, and there is no doubt but that nine tenths of the men are violating the law in some way either by branding calves not their own, killing meat not their own, selling cattle without the Power of Attorney the law requires them to have from the owner, changing ear marks and brands,

road branding cattle not tallied and inspected, and driving them out of the country, deliberately stealing whole herds of cattle irrespective of law or ownership, or blotching out brands or counter branding and branding cattle not their own without authority, or in some way violating the law in regard to cattle.

Stock Raiser further complained that branding calves, killing beef, and selling cattle without the knowledge and consent of the owner were "almost utterly overlooked." The letter went on to state that men committing these crimes "are received and toasted in society as honest men."

There are men in the country who never bought a cow in their lives who now have large stocks, and they get them by branding other peoples stock entirely, and if you will show me a man who cow hunts or lives in the country away from a butcher shop who does not brand calves or eat meat not his own and contrary to law, I will show you nine men to one that does do it. . . . Justice must be dealt out to all alike whether he be a preacher, a preacher's son, a professed christian or a six shooter and bowie knife desperado, before we can have peace and order in our otherwise glorious Western Texas.[5]

There was good reason for concern. Rumors of more violence had already reached the press. The *Galveston Daily News* reported:

I hear of some mobbing above and fighting below; overheard two men talking at church last Sunday; they said sixteen men were killed in a fight at Llano. From the conversation I inferred it was between stock men and desperadoes, some of Scott Cooley's party, who you remember were taken out of jail here not long since by an armed crowd.[6]

While no such fight had occurred, and Cooley himself was dead, rumors continued to circulate that his allies were engaged in cattle and horse theft. None of these charges was ever verified, but the source was likely with mob partisans still feeling the humiliation of the fiasco of 1875. Baird continued to enjoy strong grassroots support in the area, a fact that was not lost on the mob. The newspapers, safely distant from the scene of carnage, expounded on the situation, and men who may or may not have been fighters for his faction began using Cooley's name to throw the law off their trail.

One such case occurred in San Saba County when Frank Gray, who lived along the San Saba-Llano line, observed two men driving Gray's own horses. Gray stopped the pair and asked them what they intended to do with the horses. The men drew their pistols, began to curse and abuse Gray, and told him that they were tempted to kill him but would not do it since he was a "gentlemanly clever fellow." The accidental arrival of two other men caused the pair to leave, but not before they informed Gray "they were of the number that released Ringgold [sic] and Scott Cooley, and that there were quite a number of them, enough, in fact, to take horses when they pleased, and they intended to do so."[7]

Gray recognized neither man. While it is tempting to lay the blame at the feet of Cooley sympathizers, it is far more plausible that the pair were part of Jeff Ake's gang. During the next few weeks, Silas Berry and Bill Bybee Jr. were arrested for horse theft in Kimble County. The men were said to have been partners with Bill and Jeff Ake.[8] The men who had liberated Cooley and Ringo had every reason to keep silent over their involvement. Most, if not all of them, were ranchers, although their identities were unknown at the time.

The Bader brothers' father, Gottfried, made a brief appearance in the papers during July. While traveling near Austin he was held up and robbed of $500. The Burnet Bulletin noted:

> Mr. Bader, the old German of Llano who was robbed
> of $500 near this city Wednesday [July 12], seems to
> be especially unfortunate of late. A few months ago he
> had two sons killed in the Mason county difficulties.
> Soon after that he came down here with some sheep

and while taking them to Galveston got one of his legs broken; and now he has been robbed of $500.[9]

There is no indication that the robbery was related to the feud. The men who had fought with Baird had made names for themselves, and an incident during the summer of 1876 heralded a new theme that would become common over the next few months.

The summer of 1876 saw the arrest of a man named John Redding in Llano County. Redding was charged with robbing the H. R. Martin bank in Comanche, Texas, on January 10, 1876, and for breaking Cooley and Ringo out of the Lampasas jail. There is a great deal of confusion on the part of the *Austin Statesman* with this account. The bank was held up by three men: Joe Horner, George Horner, and a Bill Redding alias Tom Wagman. There is no mention of a John Redding being involved. From the information available, it appears that the man arrested was W. Z. Redding, one of those targeted by the Hoo Doos. In the court case for the trio, it appears that the confusion was caused after Redding (or Redden) made bond and skipped town. Authorities then wrote to Burnet and Llano Counties and the sheriffs there, confusing the men, responded that he had been arrested and taken to Austin charged with murder in Llano County.[10] Further evidence of this was provided in July 1876 when he was taken to Austin. In July, Redding was transferred to Austin by Joe Leverett, a deputy sheriff from Llano County. At Burnet, Leverett reported that:

thirteen of Reddin[g]'s friends were seen ambushed in the cedar brake this side of Austin waiting for him to pass, so as to liberate the prisoners and kill the guard. But, luckily, Leverett and Sheriff Strickland went by Round Rock, and thereby avoiding an attack. It is reported that some one of the waylaying party remarked that they would never get as good an opportunity to kill Strickland and Leverett. The notorious Ringo, who seems to have been the leader, is certainly a very desperate and daring man. All but three of the party finally dispersed, leaving them to waylay Leverett on his return. But the news reached him, and, with the aid of the Sheriff of Travis county and about thirty men, he made a search for but failed to find them. Leverett says that he was assured of the co-operation of the citizens of Williamson and Travis counties in pursuing and hunting down such officers while attempting to do their duty.[11]

Who interviewed the "waylaying party" to learn that the men planned to kill Strickland and Leverett is unknown and probably an indulgence in yellow journalism by the paper. More importantly, the incident provides evidence that Ringo was now the acknowledged leader, or at least one of them, in the feud. By this time the feud had cooled considerably. Gladden had fled to Medina County, and John Baird is believed to have been living west of San Antonio. Ringo was still in the area but, aside from attempting to liberate John Redding, he remained well hidden. He need not have bothered. In September Redding's brother Tom and Andy Murchison posted bond for Redding.[12]

In Mason, things remained quiet. Ernst Jordan was effectively removed from the feud with a shattered leg. Both of the Bader brothers were dead, and Heinrich Hoerster had lost both a son and a son-in-law. The Kothmanns were shorn of their political power. Their allies in Llano remained reasonably quiet following Long's scout earlier in the year. The feud might have ended during the summer of 1876 except that the root cause, cattle theft, continued unchecked. As the summer progressed, events unfolded quickly that fanned the feud's dying embers. The first hint came from a letter dated August 17 from Fredericksburg: "Trouble has started again in Mason county, John Ringo and Bill Randall have been driving cattle off from Gooch, Hogan, Neighbors, and others. Citizens are after them, and a call has been made on Gillespie county for the Mounted Rifles to help capture them."[13] Ringo was not with Randall, however. Abe Taylor reported that R. K. Tucker was believed to have charge of the herd. At the same time he denied that Ringo was with the stolen cattle, stating that he was "certain that it is a mistake about John Ringo being connected with the cattle stealing."[14] Taylor was certainly in a position to know Ringo's whereabouts since he and the Olneys were hiding him in Llano County.

Jesse Leslie led a posse in pursuit of the cattle thieves into Kimble County. The *Burnet Bulletin* reported that "It is thought there will be much trouble and probably bloodshed. Ringo is in charge of the stolen cattle."[15] Taylor's statement was confirmed when the posse overtook Randall and the stolen herd. Randall was killed in the resulting gunfight. John Ringo had not been involved.

In Burnet, Sheriff J. J. Strickland was proving himself a good officer. On August 9, 1876, he arrived in Burnet with three prisoners in hand. Swift Ogle, who had taken over the *Burnet Bulletin* from Charles M. Harris on July 21, 1876, wrote:

> We give a communication from our young and gallant Sheriff J. J. Strickland in this issue. From the reputation given us of the great number of outlaws living in the section, where he arrested these men, we consider this one of the most daring expeditions we have any knowledge of during our abode on the frontier.[16]

Strickland had left Burnet on July 25 in pursuit of the Sneed brothers, Bob and Berry, both charged with killing John Pennell in Burnet County during 1875, and John Smart. Acting on intelligence that the men were hiding in Medina County, Strickland heard on the way that "there was a band of some forty men commanded by George Gladden" ready to attack any officer who ventured into the fugitive's hideout. Undeterred and with the assistance of the sheriff of Kendall County, Strickland was able to capture Bob Sneed and Smart without resistance. Following these arrests he learned that another fugitive, H. H. Hall, wanted for stealing corn, was also in the area and arrested him as well. Berry Sneed was not at home, being "absent with Gladden's company after Indians." With these three men in tow, Strickland returned to Burnet. It was, as Ogle stated, a daring trip.[17] Ogle's support of Strickland began with this incident. Harris had tried to keep the *Bulletin* neutral during the feud. Under Ogle the paper soon changed this position.

On August 21 an anonymous writer signing himself Bennette Novvis reported from Mason that peace was the order of the day.

> Since Mason got rid of its turbulent characters, it has nestled down amid the sweet smiles of peace.

> Its serenity is almost proverbial -- so calm, so quiet,
> so cheerful. Business has resumed its wonted tenor;
> the little birds, unmolested, chirp their daily carols;
> the farmer or ranchero, in his purchase, leans over
> the counter with an air of composure that precludes
> any token of an innate fear of a volcanic explosion of
> firearms in his ear.[18]

Novvis also reported that ranchers in Mason were beginning to fence their ranches. Peace remained tenuous despite Novvis' glowing picture. On September 2, George W. Todd shot a man named Foley. The *Statesman* quipped: "It was in Mason. The weather was warm, and Foley was directing harsh, unchristian language at Col. Todd, when the latter directed a six-shooter at the former and started him on a trip beyond the river Styx."[19] Foley had been an opponent of Sheriff John Clark, and the argument may well have stemmed from this. Lucia Holmes recorded in her diary for September 2 that Todd was "wild about it." Foley survived, but three days later she had further reason for concern. "Hal started to Bluff Creek and came back on account of Ringold [*sic*] being out there. . . . Heard that Ringold had threatened Hal so Hal got his arms ready if he should come to the house."[20]

These were the dying embers of the feud in Mason. The battleground had shifted to neighboring Llano County where the mob remained unscathed and undaunted. On August 23 a man named Burts was killed in Llano. Burts was apparently an anti-mob man, although not necessarily one of the fighters. The *Bulletin* reported Burts was drinking and began making "remarks derogatory to the character of Dept. Sheriff Joseph Leverett." Henry Leverett made some sort of reply at which Burts expanded his abuse, telling Leverett "that he was as much of a rascal and scoundrel as his brother." Leverett then left the saloon, followed closely by Burts who drew his pistol and "was in the act of shooting" when Leverett fired a shotgun at Burts, killing him instantly.[21]

What Burts had against Leverett, whose known actions to this time were creditable, is uncertain. One account stated that the argument was "in regard to tallying a herd of cattle."[22] Possibly it was aggravated by Leverett's involvement in the Llano mob. Like the Cavins, Burts had ties to Neal Cain. The *Galveston Daily News* reported in part: "The

Statesman says: Mr. Frank Beason [*sic*: Beeson], of Llano, reports the killing of a man whose name he could not remember, in that place one day last week. The man was in company with a stockman named Neal Cane [*sic*: Cain]. . . ."[23]

Neal Cain was a cattleman who bore a mixed reputation. One source states that Cain was a "pleasant traveling companion" but that he kept a gang of cattle thieves. The son of Joel Y. and Philadelphis Cain from an old Arkansas family, Cornelius "Neal" Cain was noted in Kansas and Texas as a trail driver. His entry on the scene of the fighting at this time was no coincidence. Whatever the rights or wrongs of the charges against him, Cain did harbor men who were on the dodge as long as they caused him no trouble. It was a situation that could not last.[24]

Burts' killing was followed by another brutal murder, characterized by one writer as "one of the most cowardly murders ever committed along the Burnet-Llano County borderlands." W. H. Sims, a small rancher, was sleeping in camp with his wife, four children, and an employee when masked and painted men seized him in the middle of the night. His body was found hanging the following morning.[25] No motive for the murder was discovered at the time, but recent research indicates that Sims was killed by the mob due to his son-in-law T. J. Faught. Faught was a close friend of Tim Williamson and had acted as a bondsman for A. G. Roberts and William Cavin on charges in Llano County along with John R. Baird.[26]

During August and September 1876, mob activity was on the rise in Llano County. No one could be considered safe, and it was in this situation that Joe Olney found himself on the morning of September 7 when two men rode up to his home along the Colorado River and asked him where the ford was.

At the time, Joe Olney was charged with theft of hogs in Burnet County, a charge he denied. In light of the increased mob activity and his involvement in the escape of Ringo and Cooley, the arrival of two strangers was a matter of concern though not necessarily of alarm. The ford was a convenient place to cross the river, and these strangers were not the only ones who either asked about its location or used it. As the pair rode off, Olney followed them to insure that they really moved on. Within minutes violence erupted along the river. The *Burnet Bulletin* reported under the heading "MORE BLOOD" that Deputy Sheriff Samuel B. Martin and Wilson Rowntree were shot by Olney while they were attempting to arrest him. Unlike other men involved in the feud, Martin and Rowntree provided a statement of what had happened.

> Martin and Rowntree went to Olney's house to arrest him, but being unacquainted with him, talked with him awhile and passed on, intending to cross the Colorado river and return to Burnet. Olney suspecting something was wrong, picked up his gun, buckled on his six-shooter, and remarked that he would see whether they crossed the river or not. Martin and Rowntree noticed him following, and at once concluded he was Olney. They rode back, met him, and ordered him to surrender. Olney quickly drew his pistol and fired, missing his aim. Martin and Rowntree then fired, when Olney, who was on foot, jumped behind a tree and shot Martin, breaking his left arm above the elbow. Martin then spoke to Rowntree and told him to shoot Olney. Rowntree ran up, put his gun very close to Olney and pulled the trigger, but the gun snapped. Rowntree then attempted to draw his pistol, when Olney shot him. Martin's horse had turned around, and was attempting to run away, when Olney shot him again. The fight then ceased.

The men were able to cross the Colorado river. Medical attention was obtained for the men in the form of Dr. J. G. McFarland. Rountree had been shot in the left side "just below the stomach," the bullet penetrating one of his lungs and exiting the body. Martin had one bullet extracted that had "entered near the left side of the backbone, ranging upward, passing under the shoulder blade, and lodging under the main artery of the neck."[27]

Olney responded to the version given by the deputies in a letter dated September 9 signed by "A Relative." The *Bulletin* published the letter with the note that they wished to be impartial.

> Olney was at his house, confined there on account of his wife's delicate condition, when two strangers rode

up and inquired the way to the ford; he directed them, and, learning from parties that he would likely be mobbed and to keep a sharp look out, and expecting that there was more men, he gathered his arms, thinking he would watch them. After going about 150 yards, he met them returning, and made this remark to them, "Could you not find the ford?" They replied "No." He then said, "Go to the house, and there is a man there that will show you the ford." During this conversation, they got the advantage of him. Martin threw his gun down on him, and remarked, "Throw down your gun, G-d d--n you." In an instant Olney presented his gun and Martin fired at him and missed his aim. Olney fired and broke his arm; Martin fell off his horse and called out to Rowntree to shoot the d--n rascal. He rode up to less than ten feet and shot and missed and Olney returned the fire and wounded him. They then left.

Olney's kinsman stated that the men were strangers and did not identify themselves. "Had they have done so, there would have been no fight." Contrary to its claims of impartiality, above the letter the paper noted in part that everyone "who is unprejudiced will observe its lameness."[28]

The accounts of the gunfight differ in the specifics provided by the participants. Both sides assuredly gave the version reflecting most favorably on their own actions, and the central factor in determining the truth is the weapon that Joe Olney used. The deputies admitted that Olney was carrying a rifle: "Olney suspecting something was wrong, picked up his gun, buckled on his six-shooter . . . .". Yet when the shooting occurred, both men testified that he drew his pistol, clearly indicating that the rifle was not available to him. This can only have been the case if, as Olney testified, "they got the advantage of him." The fact that one, if not both, of the deputies had their rifles out lends credence to this. If Joe Olney had attacked them first, logic dictates that the men would have drawn their pistols, not their saddle guns.

This was a determining factor that would not have been lost on a jury, particularly one familiar with weapons in that day and time. That

Olney would feel compelled to draw on two men with their weapons pointed at him can only be explained if, as he stated, one of them had fired at him after he dropped his rifle.

The facts of the case were immediately clear following the shootings. William Haynie of Llano testified that Rowntree was shot the second time when he attempted to draw his pistol.[29] The *Houston Telegraph* reprinted the story published in the *Bulletin*.[30] In Austin the *Statesman* carried Olney's account of the shooting.[31] These inconsistencies were not lost on Strickland or the Rowntrees. In the days that followed, the account provided by Martin and Rowntree was changed to address this. Quoting Burnet resident Norton Moses, the *Austin Daily Statesman* later reported a modified version of the shooting, stating that Olney had shot the men with his Winchester.[32]

While Swift Ogle was attempting to incite the citizens of Burnet County, another incident insured Olney would never surrender to the authorities. On July 26 Jim Williams, a brother-in-law of Bill Redding, was released on bail from the Burnet jail where he was charged with assault and attempt to murder.[33] Williams, who may or may not have been the man accompanying Ringo when Jim Cheyney was killed, was a stockman.[34]

On September 10 Williams was in Llano where he stopped to buy a bottle of whiskey before moving on toward Cat Mountain. At daybreak the following morning a band of men approached the camp and unceremoniously killed him. The *Bulletin* reported the facts from the jury's inquest, noting that on the early morning of September 11 a citizen heard shooting near Cat Mountain. When daylight arrived he went to the spot where he had heard the firing and found Williams dead. His horse was staked a short distance away.

> It appeared that Stewart [*sic*: Cavin] had discovered the approach of the party in time to saddle his horse and escape. Apparently Williams had attempted to unfasten his horse, but failing, had run to a thicket which he passed through, and ran through a glade and got to another thicket, on the far side of which he was found lying on his face, seven bullets having entered his body. The trail of Stewart was followed some distance, and a saddle and a pair of gloves was

found, both girths of the saddle being broken. As yet no one knows who are the murderers of Williams.[35]

The man with Williams was feudist Ed Cavin. In the same issue, the paper also reported:

Mr. John Haynes, a merchant of Backbone Valley, tells us that he learned that news had reached the Lacy's that Jim Williams, a son-in-law of Mr. Jake Lacy, was killed by a party of men who rode up to his camp about daylight and shot him several times, killing him.

Ed. Cavin who was with Williams, ran as soon as he saw the men approaching. He says, shortly after leaving the camp he heard several shots and heard Williams hollow. It is not known who did the killing, but supposed to be some of the Mason county men who were probably trying to catch Cavin. This occurred Monday morning the 11th, six miles this side of Llano town.[36]

Williams' killing created a furor within the county. Llano officials were determined to get the killers. Correspondent J. W. Davis wrote on September 11, 1876, that:

Another man was killed last night in this county, about nine miles below town. He is supposed to be a man by the name of Williams. It is not known who did the deed. A jury of inquest is just starting out to the place, and the particulars will not be known until their return. I am fully convinced this thing will not be stopped until some means are adopted for the protection of the people in their rights.[37]

Mob member Miles Barler recalled in his memoirs that Joe Leverett, Bob Rountree, William Jones, William Clark, and Barler himself were charged with the murder. Barler claimed that the allies of A. G. Roberts "found one of their party dead one day, and they picked out five of our leaders and made comp[l]aint against them for murder."[38] There is some truth to this statement, for on September 26 Davis again wrote to the *West Texas Free Press* in San Marcos: "I should look forward to an early day when this county will begin to develop were it not from the fact that there is almost war going on between two different parties. Four of our best citizens were charged with the murder of a man by the name of Williams . . . ."[39]

The discrepancy in the number of arrests made provides some insight into Barler's recollections of events. Contemporary evidence suggests that Barler often assigned himself lead roles in some of the exciting events of the time when his involvement, if any, was minor. This was one such case.

Intriguingly, Barler does not identify either the man killed or the killer or killers although by the time he wrote both were well known in the Hill Country. Certainly they were remembered in Llano where the murder occurred. The reasons are obvious. It remained for Texas Ranger James B. Gillett to identify the killer, naming the trigger man as Dell Dublin.[40] Linking the Dublin brothers to the Llano mob was undoubtedly embarrassing. As with Caleb Hall, the presence of outlaws within the mob's ranks casts doubts on both the objectiveness and integrity of the Llano Hoo Doos. Certainly it provided cattle thieves in the area with a distinct advantage. While Barler denied his involvement in the killing, he did not deny that Williams was killed by the mob. O. C. Fisher states that Dublin killed Williams "over a beef." Fisher's account of the killing is substantially different from that reported in the newspapers of the time. According to him Williams was killed in a cowlot at the ranch of Bill DeLong on the South Llano.[41] The source of Fisher's information is unknown.

· Williams' murder touched off the next wave of violence. While ostensibly pursuing cattle thieves, the mob was actully targeting men who had allied themselves with John Baird. It was a continuation of the bloodletting that had begun in Mason.

Having been given warrants, Sheriff William T. Hoskins of Llano had no choice but to serve them. Hoskins wasted no time in rounding up a posse to bring in those charged with the murder. Who brought the charges against them and what evidence there was to justify the arrests is unknown. According to Barler he received word from a friend that Hoskins was summoning about two hundred men. I didn't know what it meant at first. He gave me a little hint what it was for. He knew all about it. I laughed and said that I had heard those thieves were going to lay that on some of our party. I told Wilkes that was all foolishness, if he would come with the papers himself not a man would resist arrest. If we were guilty that would be another thing, and I suppose he thought we were.[42]

Barler notwithstanding, he was not nearly as confident as he appeared. In his memoirs Barler recalled that he notified the others who were wanted, then fortified himself in his home and waited for the posse's arrival. Barler recalled that the posse passed his home without stopping although two men did drop out and hide near the house.

They dropped out when they passed by and the sheriff didn't know it. They came up to the haystack where my horse was tied close by, and untied him and led him behind the stack, so when I came out to get him they could kill me right there—there would be no witnesses but themselves. They would claim that they tried to arrest me and I resisted and they were justified in killing me. But didn't I wish I had known they were there. I have been told the two men were Bill Reden [sic: Redding] and Joe Ollany [sic: Olney].[43]

Barler's account is seriously flawed. If the sheriff had truly wanted Barler, he would not have ridden past his home, particularly when he had a force of 200 men at his disposal as Barler claimed. Barler no doubt inflated the number of men. No contemporary evidence has been found concerning a 200-man posse, something contemporary newpapers would certainly have commented on.

Moreover, Joe Olney was not riding with any posse at that time, having just shot two deputy sheriffs. Likewise Bill Redding was in custody in the confusion caused by the Comanche bank robbery.

Barler claimed that he rode into Llano later and surrendered himself together with Bob Rountree. The men refused to surrender their weapons for fear of being mobbed. None of the story is true.

The story that arrests created so much trouble in Llano that the sheriff was forced to resign has some credence according to Davis.[44] The *Galveston Daily News* reported that at the examining trial: "there was not one particle of evidence against them, and they were discharged. Our sheriff resigned, and there is general excitement. The court will appoint a new sheriff tomorrow, when I hope times will get better."[45] Hoskins' resignation in September 1876 is confirmed by contemporary records. If Barler can be believed, the mob had pressured him to resign earlier for obvious reasons. Hoskins actively pursued and arrested mob members and anyone else he had a warrant for. Uncowed by the mob, Hoskins stubbornly hung onto the job, a fact that undoubtedly prevented a great deal of additional violence during 1875. The arrests of four mob leaders created an intolerable situation. This time the mob successfully forced his resignation. John J. Bozarth was appointed sheriff. He immediately appointed R. A. McInnis, Ben Beeson, and Barler as his deputies. According to Barler, their first action was to reactivate the mob.

> Then we formed a junction with Burnet, Mason and San Saba counties. We would have a certain place to meet and sometimes there would be as many as one hundred and fifty men there. Then we would scatter out all over the country; sometimes we would go to the head of the river and we would either arrest or run out nearly every outlaw that was in the country.[46]

An idea of the mob's activities can be found in the *Galveston Daily News* quoting the San Saba paper.

> The San Saba *News*: "It is reported that two young men were hung on the upper Llano recently, charged with unlawfully using their cattle. In justice to their memory, however, it is but right to say the murdered men are said to have had authority to use the cattle. Whether the parties were thieves or not, it is now high

time that the law be recognized a supreme authority. When a man is found guilty of theft he should be punished commensurate with the crime, and not be slain like a brute. The time is near at hand when every man will carry his life in his hand, unless the murderer who stalks about among us is brought soon to realize that his crime is punishable by death.[47]

Barler states candidly that the mob was after John Ringo, George Gladden, and other allies of John Baird.[48] Not unnaturally, the men charged by the mob as "outlaws," whether they were or not, took precautions as the feud shifted eastward. The Llano mob had been successful in seizing power, and if Barler can be believed, Bozarth was Llano's version of John Clark. Unlike their allies in Mason, they were far less successful in keeping the high integrity that had characterized the Mason Hoo Doos.

Barler's accusation that Bozarth was favorable to the mob cannot be verified. Bozarth served with distinction during the troubles. The mob never gained the same degree of power in Llano County that it had held in Mason. Bozarth began his tenure with an energetic move to crush the real cattle thieves.

Prof. R. A. Landrum, just in from San Saba county, informs the *Head Light* that the sheriffs of Llano, San Saba and Lampasas counties are in Llano county with some two or three hundred men making arrests. Some fifteen men have been arrested, and the county is being cleared of all desperate characters who have been depredating for some time past.[49]

In the weeks to come Bozarth would prove himself a capable officer who played no favorites. At the same time, the mob's attention began to focus on the Olney family. The feud was far from over.

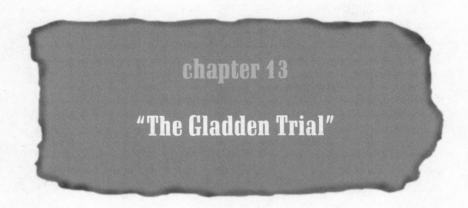

"The Gladden Trial"

As the mob's attention turned to the Olneys and their family, they were aided, inadvertently or not, by the editor of the *Burnet Bulletin*. Dean Swift Ogle made little attempt at remaining impartial. Having the opportunity to sway public opinion, Ogle used it. From the beginning Ogle was a staunch supporter of families who had ties to the mob, such as the Rountrees. When John J. Strickland, sheriff of Burnet County, appointed another brother-in-law James Martin as deputy to replace his brother, the *Bulletin* reported: "Mr. James Martin, brother of the deceased S. B. Martin, will take the place of his brother as Deputy Sheriff. He is a quiet man, sober and discreet, but is cool and brave, which is a characteristic of the family."[1]

Martin may have been an excellent choice, but the appointment can hardly have been viewed with any degree of warmth by Olney supporters. Also on Strickland's payroll was Joseph T. Bozarth, John J. Bozarth's brother. The Bozarth brothers had served under L. H. McNelly in the State Police during 1872 but were dismissed with three other state policemen during August of that year.[2] His presence should have insured that J. J. Bozarth and Strickland worked closely together. It did not. Evidence of this was provided on September 13 when he arrested Sheriff John Bozarth in Burnet.

> Mr. John Bozart[h] was arrested Wednesday for carrying a six-shooter by Sheriff J. J. Strickland. A bond of one hundred dollars was given by Mr. Bozart[h] for

his appearance next term of court. He was on his way to Llano county, and, having been told that his life was threatened, he belted on a pistol for self protection. He is confident that he will come clean, so he says.[3]

Residents of Burnet County were well aware that the feud threatened to expand into their community. The *Bulletin* reported under a column called "Every-Day Locals" that on September 9,

Town livelier than it has been for many days. . . . We were called upon by many of the old and substantial citizens of our county. They all express deep regret that a tragedy should have occurred like the one recorded in our last issue, and hope the friends of Martin and Rowntree will act with prudence and judgment, and only seek to aid the law in its vindication of justice.[4]

Martin died on September 11, 1876, at around four o'clock in the afternoon. The *Bulletin* published a memorial to him on September 15 noting the death of their "young and much beloved friend." Martin's funeral was well attended and at the time was the largest funeral that had ever taken place in Burnet.

Ogle's partiality became more evident with the publication of another letter dealing with the killing on September 22. In what appears to have been a blatant attempt to rally Burnet citizens to form a mob, a correspondent signing himself F. S. angrily replied to the letter supporting Joe Olney's actions.

TOO THIN! TOO THIN!

What is it that is too thin? That letter from Olney's relative. He gives "another version," he says, as gathered from Olney himself. *Olney himself!* Ah! Indeed! He seems to regard the first version as a smattering of facts gathered from flying reports, and not to be credited at all. Mr. Editor, let us examine the two versions, and see which is stamped with the most credibility. In the examination of all cases, the character of the witnesses has great bearing. The first version of this tragedy has for its authors W. B. Rountree and S. B. Martin, young men of good standing and well known integrity. The other version has. for its author Joe Olney—an outlaw. 1st, Olney states that Martin shot first; this is untrue according to Martin and Rountree. 2d, he says Martin fell from his horse; this is false according to Martin and Rountree. Again we don't believe Mr. Martin used the oaths which Olney said he did, as he was a strict member of the Baptist church, and not in the habit of swearing. And again, he says Martin and Rountree were perfect strangers to him. This is too thin; outlaws generally know the officers— besides, Olney has betrayed himself in this by saying that Martin received two wounds and Rountree one. *If* they were such strangers, how did he know which was Martin and which Rountree? Mr. Editor, we have both versions before us, and it is with all honest, unbiased minds to judge which is true.

We would be glad could we credit the statement that Mr. Olney and his friends are in favor of law and justice, but their actions prove the contrary. If Mr. Olney is such a law abiding man, let him come forward and stand his trial like a man. Let them rest assured that all good law-abiding men will do all in their power to drag every thief to justice, and see that every murderer feels the power of the strong arm of the law. For this we will work whether we get the assistance of Mr. Olney's friends or not.

Let us all rally to support the Sheriff in his ardent labor to vindicate the law an to bring evil-doers to justice. Fellow citizens, it is time to awake from our lethargy when we see the good men of our country shot down by villains and outlaws.

F. S. [5]

In the days following Martin's death, a number of attempts were made to capture Olney. Family tradition has it that the posse came to a log cabin where Olney had sought refuge. Confident of taking the man, J. J. Bozarth rode up to the cabin and demanded Olney come out and surrender. From inside Joe cheerfully replied that he would be out in a minute. Moments later he stepped onto the porch as eight or nine rifles presented themselves from the gun ports in the cabin. It was a moment of cold fear for the posse. Posseman Clint Breazeale recalled in later years that "it was the stupidest thing they could have done. If one cap had been fired we would all have been killed."[6] Olney stood on the porch and told them to come and take him. Finding discretion the better part of valor, the posse left without him. Among those said to have been involved in the incident were John Ringo, George Gladden, and some of the Akes.[7] Miles Barler's animosity toward Joe Olney may well stem from this incident even though it is not mentioned in his memoirs. At the same time almost no effort was made in Llano to locate the killers of Jim Williams.

As posses continued the manhunt, J. W. Davis of Llano County wrote a telling letter to the San Marcos *Free Press*, noting in part that

> We are looking for a part of Maj. Jones company to be quartered among us to keep peace, but I do not know that they will come, as our Gov. may countermand the order as *"there is no crime in the State, all mere sensational reports."* I hope they may come and keep the grasshoppers company.[8]

Why the citizens of Llano were anxious to have a company of Texas Rangers at hand requires little speculation. Considering the number of men allegedly riding for "law and order" in the county, there should have been no need for any state assistance. This was precisely the problem that had plagued Mason County during 1875 as the mob rose to power, and the citizens of Llano County requested the Rangers for the same reasons. The citizens believed that the mob's power was on the rise and out of control. That the Rangers were again being called to the troubled Hill Country indicates a clear lack of confidence in the ability of the local law to maintain peace. One such event was the incident of September 15 when two men from Llano arrived with urgent news from Llano.

THE SHERIFF'S POSSE

On Friday night, the 15th inst., two men from Llano town informed our Sheriff, J. J. Strickland, that a band of outlaws, some sixty in number, had assembled themselves at Neal Cain's ranche, seven miles above Llano town, with the sworn intention of making a raid on the place and kill all men who had ever dared to assist in making arrests, and afterwards give Burnet a call and slay some of her law-abiding citizens. This, of course, aroused our impetuous and gallant Sheriff, who, presuming that these messengers came with the sanction of the Llano Sheriff, at once summoned a posse of thirty or forty men, and on Saturday evening, the 16th, started for Llano town. He arrived there on the 17th, and was surprised that the Sheriff was not with the Llano citizens who had assembled, and, in fact, was not to be found. A party of three or four men were sent as spies to the Cain ranch, who returned and reported that no armed outlaws were to be found, and the citizens had been sold. Sheriff Strickland at once gathered his posse and returned to Burnet.[9]

Violence was again on the rise. On September 29, J. W. Davis reported that there was "little" news "as there have only been two men shot, one killed and the other seriously wounded."[10] Unlike the citizens of Mason, Llano would not wait long for a peacekeeping force. Stung by the events of 1875, John B. Jones was quickly in the area. One paper reported, "Major Jones, who commands the frontier battalion, was in town with a part of Capt. Sparks' company of rangers. He has encamped at the Miller spring, four miles west of Burnet, on the Bluffton road."[11]

In Burnet County, the situation was rapidly deteriorating as well. Angered at the letter Strickland had published in the *Bulletin* with the account of Martin's shooting, A. T. Taylor sent word to the sheriff that he was a liar. Strickland came down to the public square and the two men quarreled, "having their guns ready for use." Violence was narrowly averted by Judge W. A. Blackburn who had both men disarmed and placed under a peace bond.[12]

With Joe Olney seemingly beyond their reach, the mob turned its attention to other members of the family. First to be targeted was Ben Erwin, a cousin of the Olneys.[13] On October 13, 1876, Erwin was killed.

> From Sam Olney the Burnet *Bulletin* learns that one Mackey quarreled with Ben Erwin in Llano town last Friday evening. It seems that Erwin had been advised to not have any difficulty with Mackey, and, finally, a Mr. McNutt, Mackey and Erwin left town on their way home. Several times Mackey attempted to raise a row with Erwin, who being unarmed, avoided it. Finally Erwin told Mackey that they would all take a drink, and settle the matter, which was agreed to. McNutt and Erwin then rode off and shortly after Mackey came running up and struck Erwin's horse, and, yelling, frightened him so that he ran, and Mackey followed six-shooter in hand. McNutt, who was riding a mule, followed them, thinking they would come back soon. Some one living near Wright's creek, heard Erwin and Mackey talking, and when they had gone some time, three shots were heard, and a search was afterwards made but Erwin was not found until Sunday morning. He was shot several times, and had the appearance of having been beaten over the head with a pistol. Erwin had three dollars and fifty cents in his pocket, which was missing. The corpse arrived in Burnet Monday morning, 16th inst. The Rangers are in pursuit of Mackey.[14]

J. W. Davis noted the killing of Erwin as well.

> I have still less to report this week than when I wrote last, there only having been one man killed.

Mr. Irvine was killed by a man named McKie, a half Cherokee who has made his escape though pursued and hunted by the officers of the law and the Rangers, a company of which we have stationed here, and I am very much in hope we will have peace for the future.[15]

Erwin was killed three miles from Llano. Jiles Mackey, the killer, was described by one sources as "a transient." Family members recalled that the murder was directly related to mob activity in the region.[16] A daughter of John Olney recorded in her memoirs that Erwin was murdered "at the young age of 18 by one of the secret mobs who infiltrated the south after the civil war. Members of the Mob thought the boy overheard a conversation between members of the mob and he was dragged by horse to his death by a man named Giles, who made his escape to the Indian Territory."[17]

Ben Erwin was twenty at the time of his death. Mackey was described as six feet tall, 155 pounds, with dark complexion, black hair, and hazel eyes. Far from being a transient, Mackey gave his residence as Llano County. Little is known about Mackey's early life, but in later years distinguishing marks on him were described as:

Scar on forehead over left eye; scars right wrist & right thigh; shot through muscle right arm; little finger right hand broken at 1st joint; 3rd finger right hand broke at nuckle [sic]; shot through muscle right arm bullet shows under skin near shoulder; shot in thigh; small scar right rump; scar calf right leg; burn scar small of back, burn scar center of breast.[18]

Following the killing, Mackey made his escape to Oklahoma, hiding in the Indian Territory. Erwin's murder was quickly forgotten, at least by the Bulletin, when a series of arrests by the Texas Rangers made headlines across the state.

On October 26, Eb Stewart and Billy Thompson were arrested about twelve miles northeast of Austin by ten Rangers under the command of Captain Sparks while they were driving cattle toward Rockdale. In an interview with the press the Rangers stated that a drove of cattle had been stolen in the counties of Llano, Mason and Gillespie, and that they had followed the drove from those counties. They did not say who had stolen the cattle, but that they had received a warrant from this county for Stewart, who was known to be one of the principal men in charge of the drove. . . . The rangers also stated that the drove of cattle had been separated somewhere near this city, one part out of which had been regularly inspected, having passed near this city, and the other, which had all been stolen, around the city. Stewart and Thompson were found with the latter drove. The rangers came upon the men at Cain's just as they were penning the cattle for the night. . . . [19]

Cain escaped from the Rangers although they did catch sight of him. Stewart attempted to flee as well, but surrendered after a few shots were fired. Neither he nor Thompson were armed. According to the Rangers' own account, Thompson was arrested "with the hope of getting rewards" for two killings he had been involved in. The arrests were important, and evidence provided by the Rangers sheds additional light on the feud. The Rangers had expected to find George Gladden and Frank Enox, both considered "notorious desperadoes."[20]

The best known man of this group was Billy Thompson, brother of gunfighter Ben Thompson. Thompson had been born in Knottingley, York, England, to William and Mary Ann Baker Thompson on August 28, 1845.[21] On August 15, 1873, Thompson had killed Sheriff Chauncey Belden Whitney in Ellsworth, Kansas. Papers of the time indicate that he had also killed several other men. Frank Enox was a partner of Caleb Hall.

Neither Gladden nor Cain eluded the law for long. On November 2, Neil Cain was arrested by J. J. Strickland at Palestine, Texas, while he was on his way to Kentucky. Strickland had passed through Austin, and Ranger Captain Sparks had informed him to be on watch for the fugitive. Strickland accidentally ran into Cain at the railroad station. Bob Rowntree was dispatched to bring in the prisoner. [22]

Gladden and John Ringo were arrested on October 31 at Moseley's ranch in western Llano County. Ringo was described as "one of the most desperate men in the frontier counties."

These men were arrested last Tuesday at Moseley's ranch, in the western portion of Llano county, by Sergeant Robinson, commanding a detachment of seven men of Company C, Texas rangers, assisted by Sheriff Bozarth, of Llano, and six men. The rangers and the sheriff and his party left camp Monday night, rode to within a short distance of Moseley's ranch and put up for the night. In the morning they surrounded the house and closed in on it, but did not find their men. They then retired a few hundred yards and put out pickets. Later in the morning Gladden and Ringo arrived and were arrested. One of the men attempted to escape arrest by flight, but chase was given and he was soon captured, one of the rangers firing one shot. All three of these prisoners are to be held in the Austin jail until the courts convene in the respective counties where they are to be tried for the crimes committed.[23]

Ringo and Gladden were taken to Austin by a squad of Rangers accompanied by J. J. Bozarth. On November 5 the men passed through Burnet. Four days later Bozarth and Bob Rowntree were back in Burnet where they reported that the men had been lodged safely in the Travis County jail. Rowntree also reported that Cain had been released on bond.[24]

The arrests of Gladden and Ringo gave rise to rumors about a possible attempt to liberate the men.[25] No such attempt was made. Joe Olney, one of the leaders in the Lampasas break, was on the run, and over the ensuing weeks charges were leveled at his other relatives. On November 2, 1876, Dan Olney and Ben Erwin's brother, Alex, were arrested in Burnet

by deputy sheriffs Martin and Howard, on a writ sworn out against them for stealing cattle. Olney gave bond for his appearance before Justice Crews on Saturday, and Erwin was confined in the county jail until Friday afternoon, when he gave bond. On Saturday their trial came off, and they were bound over to appear

at the next term of District Court, Olney in the sum
of $500 and Erwin $200. If they are guilty, they will
not stand much showing to get off without suffering
the full penalty of the law, as they will have to face
the new jury system and the firm determination of
the good citizens of our county to put a check upon
lawlessness of every description. And, if they are not
guilty, it would be hard to find a more just people to
deal with than those of our county.[26]

Early in December, Will Olney was also arrested, this time in
Llano County, again on charges of cattle theft. On December 7 he was
brought back to Burnet.[27] None of these charges were proven in court.
Family descendants maintain that the charges against Joe's brothers
and kinsmen were trumped up in order to pressure him to surrender.
If so, the tactic proved unsuccessful.[28]

In Llano, George Gladden was quickly brought to trial for his role
in Peter Bader's killing. At the end of November Bozarth and a strong
guard went to Austin to provide an escort to bring him to Llano. The
men passed through Burnet on November 25 and returned three
days later, reaching Llano on November 30. At the same time, John
Baird's brother-in-law, J. C. Carson, announced that he was considering moving his family to McCulloch County during the spring of
1877.[29] Carson had good reason to want Burnet behind him, as did
others.

Sergeant Joseph Leverett, with a squad of Rangers,
has arrived from Austin [in Llano], and will remain
until a chance presents itself to make more arrests.
Leverett learned that Reddin [sic: Bill Redding] and
several of his friends have left for a more remote location in the west. He is under heavy bond, which, of
course, he will forfeit. It is said that he defied any set
of men to follow him.[30]

Gladden's arrest gave rise to further controversy. Writing to the
Bulletin, an anonymous correspondent reported that:

Having seen a notice going the rounds of some of the papers of the State, to the effect that "The RANGERS in Llano county had arrested the notorious John Ringo and Geo. Gladden," we, as a citizen of that county, beg leave to say, that the SHERIFF of Llano county, with a posse of citizens assisted by a small squad of Rangers made the arrest spoken of. The whole thing was planned and carried into effect by our Sheriff. While we don't pretend to depreciate the value of the assistance rendered the civil authorities of our county by the Rangers, nor deny but their assistance was really needed, nor do we think the Sheriff cares any thing about newspaper reports, still we think, as a matter of justice, credit should be rendered to those to whom credit is due. Our Sheriff and the citizens of the county are disposed to execute the laws, and doubtless will do it in all possible cases.[31]

Gladden was brought to trial on December 6 for Peter Bader's killing. The *Bulletin* provided full coverage as the trial unfolded. Under the banner "THE GLADDEN TRIAL," the paper reported that the trial was of an importance "not surpassed by any that has even taken place in Western Texas." It had been anticipated that it would take several days for the jury selection. Instead a full jury had been selected by noon, and the trial began at one in the afternoon. By six o'clock in the evening all of the evidence in the killing had been heard. Gladden rested his case primarily on "threats made by the deceased against the defendant."[32]

Closing arguments in the Gladden trial were heard on the morning of December 7.

On Thursday morning the argument of counsel was heard, Mr. Oatman opening upon the part of the State, making a very candid, earnest and forcible talk to the jury, notifying them of the solemnity and seriousness of the duty they were called upon to discharge; while his effort was not characterized by rhetorical display, it left an impression upon the jury that was not overcome. He was answered by Messrs. Fisher and Makemson for the defense, and certainly their client has no cause to complain of the effort made in his behalf. Mr. Wilkes with his usual ability closed the argument about 2 o'clock, when His Honor Judge Blackburn delivered the charge to the jury. Every point of law arising in the case was so clearly given in the charge that neither party had any objections to make or new charges to add.[33]

The jury deliberated until dark, returning then for an explanation of one of the charges. Fifteen minutes later they brought in a verdict of guilty of murder in the first degree and assessed his punishment at "close confinement in the penitentiary for life." Gladden accepted the verdict calmly. Gladden was returned to the jail by "a heavy posse, assisted by Capt. Spark's company" where "a heavy guard was placed and every precaution taken to secure his person." The following day a motion for a new trial was given and overruled. A notice of appeal was then filed.

The trial of this case, considering the momentous question it involved, is certainly a model of brevity and dispatch. Thirty-six hours after the first juror was accepted the jury brought in their verdict, and after two hours consideration by the court of the motions, the case was settled so far as this court and a jury of this county could settle it. It is worthy of remark that the jury were of the quiet unobtrusive class of men, mostly young men, and so far as we have been able to learn, not connected with any of the unfortunate difficulties existing in this county for the past year or two.[34]

On December 9, Gladden was taken from Llano by fourteen Rangers from Sparks' company for transport to Austin. The guard paused in Burnet for the evening, then moved on to Austin on December 10. Gladden was kept in chains the entire trip. Following the Rangers' departure from Burnet, a small amount of excitement occurred when the prisoners at the jail revealed they had cut Gladden's chains during the night. Gladden intended to make a break while on the road, but the opportunity never arose. He was safely delivered to Austin on December 11.[35]

Gladden's conviction ended his role in the feud. With John Ringo in jail awaiting trial and Gladden bound for the penitentiary at Huntsville, the remaining leaders of Baird's faction were out of the fighting. Baird's whereabouts remain uncertain, but it is likely that he was still living west of San Antonio in Bexar County.

Other members of the Baird faction were also having troubles with the law as the year closed. On December 11 Deputy Sheriff R. R. Howard of Burnet arrested Bud Faris at a dance at the home of William Weeks in Llano County. Faris was arrested for disturbing the peace but soon faced more serious charges in Burnet.[36] Will Olney was brought into Burnet by Deputy Sheriff J. T. Bozarth on December 14. Olney made an attempt to escape but was recaptured. On December 16, he was released on bond.[37] As the year closed the Rangers turned their attention to the pursuit of Joe Olney. Olney eluded capture, and the following year moved his family to New Mexico.

With the leaders of Baird's party gone, the mob had every reason to celebrate as 1877 was ushered in. They had effectively achieved their goal. If the mob's advertised contention that these men were the primary cattle thieves in the area are correct, their removal from the scene should have radically reduced cattle theft in the area. It did not. The new year brought new revelations and murders. Even as the original antagonists withdrew from the battleground, other men stood willing to take their place. The Llano mob remained unbroken, as did the cattle thieves themselves.

chapter 14

"A Thiefs Paradise"

By 1877 the Llano mob remained the only organized force of the original factions. While a number of Baird's allies remained in the area, he had long since departed. Cooley was dead. Both Gladden and Ringo had remained behind to salvage what they could of their property. Gladden had a wife and daughter in Mason but was unable to get them away from the area before he was captured and imprisoned. Ringo had three younger sisters to support in California, and abandoning the Hill Country meant starting over. Their determination had cost them their freedom. Only Joe Olney remained at large, and the frustration of the mob was echoed by the *Burnet Bulletin*: "Several unsuccessful attempts have been made lately to catch Joe Olney, who has been hanging around his father's in this county. The supposition now is that he has left the country."[1]

The Rangers remained in Llano County, and on January 8, Henry Hoy, charged with theft of cattle, was arrested by Private Maltimore and five other Rangers.[2] To this point the Hoy family had been only peripherally involved in the feud. John Kelly was killed in 1875 while attempting to reach safety at the Hoy household. Hoy's arrest was followed by the burning of the Mason courthouse by arsonists on January 21. One paper reported that

> Mr. Nimitz, of Fredericksburg, brings the news that
> the court house at Mason was burned on last Sunday
> night. It is due to the better class of citizens of that

county to say that they have recently made a noble
effort to redeem themselves from the rule of bloody
cut throats, who have so long tyrannized over them
with a perfect reign of terror. At the last term of the
District Court of Mason county, the Grand Jury, en-
couraged by the resolute and strict charges of Judge
Blackburn, and assisted by the excellent new Jury
law, have indicted for every violation of the law in
that county, including the series of murders that have
been committed during the past two years. This is
doubtless the cause of the burning of the court house,
but we learn that there has been no destruction of
the criminal records, as they were kept by the Clerk
in another house.[3]

Writing from Llano, J. W. Davis also noted that Mason's courthouse had burned, but made no mention of arson. The postscript for
his January 22 letter states simply, "Have just heard the Court House
and records of Mason County were burnt last night."[4]

The identities of the arsonists have never been determined. There
were a number of men on both sides of the feud who would have ben-
efited from the crime, and it appears probable that the courthouse was
burned to eliminate records pertaining to the feud. However, Baird's
allies gained no benefit from the courthouse's destruction. While the
original indictments were lost for their cases, others were substituted,
including indictments for Ringo, Baird, and A. G. Roberts. No indictments were substituted for any mob member.

Contrary to Miles Barler's claims, Ranger records for the month of
January indicate that cattle thieves continued to find Llano County hos-
pitable to their operations. In addition to Hoy's arrest, Sheriff Bozarth
requested assistance from the Rangers to arrest Green Ferguson and
James Martin, both charged with cattle theft.[5]

Another former mob member was back in the news during
February. In a letter from Brackett, Texas, a correspondent signing
himself Wanderer reported that unknown parties had made off with
the cattle of James Gordon and Celeste Pingenot. A posse pursued
them, overtaking the raiders on February 5. The three thieves made
a run for cover, but one of them, Frank Enoch, was captured. Enoch

was the same Enox whom the Rangers had hoped to capture months earlier. While the stolen property, some ninety-five cattle and eight head of horses, were being driven back to their range, Enoch made an attempt to escape. He was shot in the leg, the bullet passing through his right thigh and coming out the lower part of his abdomen. Enoch died a little after midnight on February 7.

Enoch's testimony while under arrest indicated that Caleb Hall and a man identified only as Brunsen were the others involved in the crime. A fourth man, Sam Evans, was arrested on February 7 as an accomplice. The outlaws' haste in abandoning the herd was evident from the evidence found at the scene.

> Among the effects captured by Lieut. Bullis were a book, power of attorneys, memorandums and letters all in the name of Caleb Hall, also some blank forms of acknowledgements usually used by Clerks of the District and County Courts, impressed with the Seal of the District Court of McCollough [sic] County.
>
> This man Caleb Hall seemed to have every-thing so arranged that he could manufacture his own power-of-attorneys, bills of sale, or any other legal document that he might need, all that was necessary being the insertion of the man's name he wished the document from, and the name of the Clerk to the blank, and he had the thing just as he wanted it.[6]

Nor was Hall the only feudist making news during the early months of 1877. In Austin, William Steele wrote to F. T. Nicholls, governor of Louisiana, that the Ake brothers had been seen in a county adjacent to Louisiana, noting in part that "I do not know in what parish they were indicted & give you this information so that if you have any central Bureau [?] where their names may appear as criminals or any other way of identifying that a Requisition on Gov. Hubbard may be sent which will be promptly executed."[7]

On January 26, Captain John Sparks sent a detachment to Coleman County in search of Joe Olney, Abe Taylor, and Bill Redding. The Rangers checked at Redding's ranch, but found none of the men they wanted.[8] Sparks' report also sheds light on affairs in Llano County. On February 12 he wrote:

> By inspection of Monthly Report you will see what I have done and endeavored to do in the way of arresting Criminals but I must say that it is a fearful undertaking in this Country, where they have so many friends acting as Couriers when I start a scout with Pack Mules. I think every criminal in this country that has a friend is informed at once.

Sparks went on to report that serious trouble was brewing in Lampasas County.

> The trouble grows out of killing of Marich Harle [sic: Merritt Horrell] by Pink Hig[g]ins and from what I can learn, that County is in about the same condition this one was when Camp was first established here so far as Llano County is concerned and those adjoining it. Criminals have gone North and North West and are following the Cattle Range . . .[9]

The trouble that Sparks referred to was the Horrell-Higgins feud that would soon set Lampasas County ablaze. Sparks' company being stationed in the Llano area had helped hold the fighting in check. Rumors were also circulating of thieves in neighboring San Saba County: "It is rumored, and apparently with good ground, that a set of horse-thieves had gone up among the buffalo hunters, and stole their horses; the hunters followed them to Lone Canon, in McCulloch or San Saba county, surrounded and killed eight of the thieves and recovered their horses."[10]

Major John B. Jones had good cause to be worried about the troubled region. None of the mob violence had done anything to stop cattle theft, and in Kimble County, adjacent to Mason on the western side, stock thieves continued their activities unhindered, threatening to reignite the feud in that area.

Kimble County Texas
February 22nd 1877

Maj. John B. Jones

I hear it rumored through the country that you contemplate removing the Ranger Camp from Bear Creek to Copperas or Some other point west of this. If so I hope you will consider the matter and let the company remain where it is, or let it go on the Llano near the junction, where it would be still more convenient to Suppress Crime and Arrest thieves both of which our county is full and running over with as I hope to see and talk with you early this Spring when I can make you more fully comprehend the magnitude of lawlessness and crime that is going on in this county much easier than I can by writing. Our Horses Cattle & Hogs are being stolen almost daily. Cattle from other counties by tens thi[r]tys and fifties are stolen and drove to this. The owners following the trail find their Stock Remarked Rebranded and the Original Brand defaced beyond recognition and are not permitted by the thieves to take their property without the presence of Lt. Moore and his company.

This Maj is a very Short Sketch of lawlessness and crime that is going on in this county, in Short every thing from Murder down to the lowest grade of thef[t] that you can think of—This County Seems to be the great head quarters for men loaded with crime from all parts of the State.

Now if Lt. Moore and his Command Should be taken from this immediate vicinity I am or feel sure the worst has not yet come nor been told.

am Maj most Respectfully
your fellow Citizen
Felix Burton[11]

Jones clearly understood from Burton's letter that the feud, dormant for months in Mason, would rear its head again. Any doubts he may have entertained were shattered quickly by another letter from Mason County dated February 27, 1877. Private H. B. Waddell wrote in part that Kimble County was "a thiefs [sic] stronghold." Waddell went on to report that:

> Old man Dublins may well be called the thiefs house, Black Burt the head man of the thieves. . . . A heavy set dark comp. [man] wants to kill every stranger that comes into the neighborhood fearing that he is a detective. Rich Doublin, Dell Doublin, Black Burt, Thos. Doran, Frank Burk, John Burleson[,] Cale Hall $400 reward for him, Bill Deal, McGrue Allison, John McKiever and numerous others that I could name are in the county, the sheriff of the Co. is in full concert with them. Mr. Burton and several others are afraid to go in the woods for fear of being killed. Burt and party sware [sic] that they will kill them . . . I thought it was useless to arrest parties on charges in Kimble as Sheriff Reynolds will accept anyone as bonds man.[12]

Waddell concluded his report stating that the citizens hoped a company of Texas Rangers would be placed at the junction of the Llano Rivers.

These letters are significant in understanding the Hoo Doo War. The feud had begun largely due to the frustration of ranchers with cattle theft and the law's failure to curb the problem. Before the dawdling authorities reacted, the anger had escalated into a vicious war that had taken months to suppress. Numerous men were killed on both sides. If the mob had been effective, cattle theft should have ceased, or at least declined, in the region. In contrast the situation had worsened. Worse still was the fact that outlaws were now clearly identified as mob infiltrators. Viewed in retrospect, it is quite possible that John Clark was in league with the outlaws who preyed on Mason's cattlemen. This is only theory, however. What is certain is that two years later John B. Jones was desperately attempting to maintain order in the Hill Country. Cattle theft had risen steadily, and mob violence had made no inroads in curbing the problem.

Adding to Jones' difficulties were the remnants of Baird's faction remaining at large. On February 17 Lieutenant Pat Dolan of Company F advised Jones that "I am informed by a truthfull man that Baird has sold out and left but can not Positively say that it is so—he is very wild since McNelleys men went to his house and arrested the wrong man."

After discussing other affairs, Dolan concluded, "I believe I can trace the theft of 17 head of cattle to J. B. Johnson who lives at Camp Wood. The cattle should have been stolen from a man named Dublin on the Llano if you know any one of that name it would be well to refer him to me."[13]

Aggravated by the cattle thieves, other counties were forming their own protection agencies as noted in a letter to Jones from a Kerr County judge.

> I have information this morning which impels me to write to you direct to Frio. Having been busy in Dist. Court last week I could not be informed earlier.
>
> It seems that citizens of the western section of our county have had several "meetings" recently and it is resolved that the proposed cattle stealings should be stopped. I have reason to believe that parties on both sides—the honest men versus the thieves—are combining and moving. I am constrained to believe further that the crisis cannot be long deferred. Therefore I would suggest that very speedy action should be had if it is desired to prevent a conflict such as good citizens should deplore. Our working farmers and stock raisers are desperate and will resort to extreme measures—soon.[14]

It was the bitterest of ironies. While the law and mob targeted non-resident cattlemen who were not involved in cattle theft, the thieves, having infiltrated the mob's ranks, remained relatively unscathed. Two years of violence had only seen the problem escalate. Now, however, Jones' attention was being drawn to the source. On March 31 he wrote to Henry M. Holmes asking him to send particulars of the cattle theft to the town of Junction where he would pick them up.[15]

A parsimonious legislature had left Jones with too few men covering too great a territory. Fearing violence in Lampasas, Jones sent Sparks to the area where he arrived on March 19. Sparks' conduct during this time was exceptional, and Judge W. A. Blackburn reported to Jones, "I believe that the most violent and bloody scenes would have been enacted here during this week, but for the presence of Capt. Sparks & his company. How long this state of affairs may exist I do not now venture a prediction."[16] Blackburn concluded that he would like Sparks to accompany him to the troubled Kimble County region. Jones could not comply with Blackburn's request. The troubles in Lampasas County necessitated Sparks' continued presence, and on April 2 Jones ordered Sparks to remain at Lampasas with his company until further orders. His instructions clearly indicate his intention to strike a crushing blow at the root of the Hill Country troubles. He concluded:

> I wish you to send Sergt. Leverett and one man to Lt. Moores camp on Bear Creek, Kimble County, to remain there on duty with that company until I arrive. They will go via Mason, then up the Llano River and Bear creek. You may recruit two other men for your company, at once, as these two will be absent probably two months.[17]

Jones' letter to Blackburn provided more than a hint of his plans.

> I am pretty well informed of the condition of affairs in Kimble Co. Have late advices from there. Will have three companies in that county by the 15th of this month and will scour it thoroughly before the time for your court.
>
> I hope you will not fail to hold the court there. Unless something is done in the interest of law & order the few good people that are there will have to abandon the Co to the thieves & murderers.[18]

Blackburn reassured Jones by return post that he intended to hold court in Kimble starting on April 30.[19]

Jones planned the assault on Kimble County perfectly. Moving to Frio City, he joined Neal Coldwell's Company A. On April 11 he sent word to Pat Dolan, commander of Company F, that he would reach his camp on April 16. Dolan was to be ready to move immediately.[20] The same day he sent word to F. M. Moore of Company D. Moore was to move the company to Junction City on the evening of the 20th. Two men from Moore's company were to be stationed at Paint Rock on the South Llano on the 18th "who know where everybody lives on both Llanos and Johnsons Fork." In his letter Jones concluded, "I will bring Coldwells and Dolans Companies with me and will make a general 'round up' of Kimble county but want it kept secret until we are ready to make the break."[21] He also ordered supplies from Kerrville to be delivered to a Dr. Kountz in Junction City on April 20 or 21. The teamsters were not to know where they were going until they left Kerrville.[22]

Company A left camp on Elm Creek on April 13 and reached Uvalde County on the 15th, camping along the Nueces. Dolan was unable to leave Frio County but sent thirteen men to the Llano on the 16th.[23] The first arrest in connection with the Kimble County raid was actually made in Uvalde County when W. H. Davis was captured and charged with a theft committed in Blanco County. He was jailed at Uvalde. On the 19th the troops swept into Kimble County. Jones divided his forces into four detachments, sending them down Johnson Fork, Cedar Creek, the South Llano and Maynard's Creek.[24]

The effectiveness of Jones' raid is evidenced from the monthly returns of Companies A and D. On the 19th, Coldwell's men arrested John Walton and Jim Thomas, both sentenced to prison from Lavacca County. In the ensuing days a number of men involved in the feud were also rounded up. In a separate list Coldwell provided information on the arrests his company made in April.

> 19th Jim Thomas alias James Pouton in Kimble Co. under sentence to Penitentiary from Lavacca Co.
> 19th John Walton in Kimble Co. under sentence to Penitentiary from Lavacca Co.
> 20th John Gorman in Kimble Co. charged with murder in Bastrop Co.

"   Jas. Potter in Kimble Co. charged with Theft in Kaufmann Co.

" Bill Allison in Kimble Co. charged with Theft and being accessory to murder of Jim Williams, also theft of horses in Bosque Co.

"   Jas. Graves in Kimble Co. charged with murder in Ellis Co.

"   A. Sanders in Kimble Co. charged with murder in Fayette Co.

"   Frank Potter in Kimble Co. charged with Theft in Menard Co.

"   Jas. Deaton in Kimble Co. charged with Theft in Hamilton, Gillespie and Menard Co's.

21st Al. Roberts in Kimble Co. charged with Theft in Mason, San Saba & Llano Co's.

" Brack Thomas in Kimble Co. charged with Theft in Mason and perjury in Burnet Co's.

"   W. L. Bannister found with Roberts & Thomas arrested on suspicion.

"   Richard Griffin charged with forgery in Lamar County.

"   J. C. McGrew in Kimble Co. charged with murder in Mason Co. and resisting arrest in Brown Co.

" Lou Walton in Kimble Co. charged with Theft in Lavacca Co.

" George Harper in Kimble Co. charged with assault to murder in Palo Pinto Co.

22nd J. Ruff in Kimble Co. charged with Theft in Blanco Co.

" Sam Monroe in Kimble Co. charged with Theft in Menard Co.

"   ----- Hensley in Kimble Co. an escaped convict sent from Burleson Co.

23rd Rol Dublin in Kimble Co. charged with being accessory to murder of Jim Williams.

25th Wm. Collins. Theft of money in Fayette Co.

"   Jack Hall. Theft in Fayette Co.

"   Jos. Gilmore arrested for Jos. Wilmore charged

with attempt to murder in Brown Co.

"   ----- Hunnicutt charged with theft in Mason and Llano counties.

"   Jack Haup Murder in Dallas & Theft in Llano Co.

[Columbus] Rowley Theft in Blanco

C. McMickle Theft in Gonzales Co.

25th John Goodlow charged with murder near Sabine Texas.

J. B. McKiever. Theft of cattle in Burnet Co.

May 1st J. Reynolds.   Theft in Kimble Co.

"   Rol. Dublin.   "   "   "   "

"   Jas. Deaton.   "   "   "   "

"   2nd J. H. Hamilton.   "   "   "   "

"   Sheriff J. M. Reynolds.   "   "   "   "

"   Lou. Walton.   "   "   "   "

"   Chas. Edmunds.   "   "   "   "

Apl 30th. W. A. McFadden. Theft in DeWitt Co.

"   30th M. J. Denman. Theft and Forgery in Lampasas Co.[25]

Coldwell's monthly return added additional names of feudists not located during the month. Among them were Bill Cavin and Richard and Dell Dublin.[26] Moore's Company was also successful during the raid. As April turned to May, Coldwell sent scouts out after Caleb Hall who was believed to be in San Saba County. On May 1 Rol Dublin was captured. On May 10 Pete Casner, wanted for breaking jail in Burnet, was arrested by N. O. Reynolds of Company A. Abe Taylor was taken in on "suspicion" a week later.[27] At the same time Company D narrowly missed capturing the remaining two Dublin brothers on May 20.[28] Following the raid in Kimble County, Moore's men arrested Sheriff J. M. Reynolds on May 3, charged with willfully letting prisoners escape. R. M. Johnson was netted in McCulloch County, and on May 7 William Gentry and Alf Gamel were arrested in Mason on charges of handling stolen cattle. Black Burk was captured by Corporal C. L. Nevill.

Jones had every reason to celebrate the success of the mission, telegraphing Steele on May 6.

Have finished in Kimble. Arrested forty-one law breakers. Court passed off quietly. Good grand jury. Twenty-five indictments. No trials for want of qualified jurors. All quiet there now. Indians passed through Southern part of Kimble three days ago. My scouts followed them into Gillespie. Trail destroyed by rain. Have three detachments scouting for them now.

Will start above tomorrow. Send my mail to Ft. Griffin.[29]

The Lampasas difficulties had also settled down. The *Lampasas Dispatch* reported, "Captain Sparks, with a squad of his Rangers, is off in pursuit of badmen in another county, and we hope he will be successful. He has thinned them out to a considerable extent in this locality. Some who have not yet been picked up have sought other pastures upon which to roam."[30]

Things were also quiet in Mason: "Lawlessness at Mason is being superseded by order and morality. A Methodist revival is progressing up there, and the late evil-doers are doffing the six-shooter and getting themselves checked for a blessed immortality."[31]

It was a well-deserved victory for Jones, and with the suppression of the outlaws in Kimble, the feud finally began to wind down. Winding down, but still not finished. Jones' celebration was cut short by a telegram from Brownwood: "A rescuing party of 12 men took out of our Jail 6 out of 11 prisoners and made their way west today."[32]

The feudists were on the move. This time the law would draw no distinction between the factions.

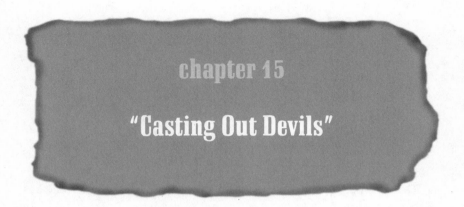

chapter 15

"Casting Out Devils"

As the Reddings and Olneys fled Texas for the safety of New Mexico, the sheriff of Coleman County arrested some of their party. Details of the arrest are lacking, but the sheriff lodged them in the jail at Brownwood due to its greater security. It was a futile effort. On May 11, 1877, a number of men rode into Brownwood and calmly ate lunch. One paper reported that "immediately after dinner" a number of horses were hitched outside the front of the jail and others on the west side. Around three thirty in the afternoon four men entered the sheriff's office and asked if the County Clerk was present. "They then asked to see the 'record of Marks and Brands,' which Mr. Ford very politely placed before them for their inspection."[1]

Having gained access to the sheriff's office, one of the men suddenly drew two pistols and demanded the keys to the jail. At the same time two sentinels posted on the outside of the jail told their comrades to "Hurry up, boys, we are in danger." The sheriff was forced to release the prisoners they had come for. The men immediately armed themselves, then fled the jail.

Outside, chaos reigned in Brownwood. Realizing what was happening, citizens scrambled to locate weapons. The jail breakers quickly mounted and fled Brownwood with an exchange of gunfire that resulted only in one horse being wounded in the neck. A posse abandoned pursuit when they learned that the fleeing men numbered fifteen or twenty, all well armed. About an hour later a rainstorm obliterated the trail.

The bold release of the prisoners at Brownwood created a sensation across Texas. Not only had the release been during broad daylight, but some of the men tentatively indentified appeared to link the Mason County feudists and fighters from the Sutton-Taylor War in DeWitt County.

> The following are the names of those who were identified as being with the crowd who released the prisoners: John Wesley Hardin, for whom there is $5000 [*sic*: $4000] reward; —Olney, murderer of the deputy sheriff of Burnet county; —Caldwell, who had been acting the spy, and one of the Waldrop boys.
> There is a formidable party organized in Coleman county, who make their headquarters near the Santa Anna mountains, composed of the following parties: The Taylor and Hardin party of DeWitt county, and the desperadoes of Mason, Llano and Burnet counties, making in all about 100 to 150 men strong.[2]

Citizens of the county wasted no time in requesting Governor R. B. Hubbard to offer a reward for the jail breakers. On May 15 T. R. Fleming wrote that twelve or fifteen men had ridden into Brownwood and liberated five prisoners. "The Sheriff of Coleman County had arrested four or five of the Redden [*sic*: Redding] gang and one of the Hardin or Clements gang . . . ." Fleming believed that the men had stationed themselves west of Coleman and was in hopes that Rangers would be dispatched to assist the local authorities.

> I wish you would offer a reward of $1000.00 for their capture. I dislike very much to trouble you because I know you have a great many applications of this kind, but if some desperate effort is not made to capture those fellows then the people in my district will hang them as fast as they catch them. The Brownwood Jail is a good secure Jail one of the best in the state. It is impossible to get out of it except in the way these prisoners escaped. If Gen. Steele will send twenty five men up there I am certain he will get them.

> I have instructed the Sheriff of Coleman County
> to summon 50 or 100 men and to act in conjunction
> with the Sheriff of Brown County in making the ar-
> rests, but the difficulty will be in holding the citizens
> together long enough. I will take it as a personal favor
> of you if you will give this matter your immediate at-
> tention.[3]

Fleming added as a postscript a note that the "names of the parties breaking the Jail are unknown." This was apparently not the case,
for several of the party were identified in the newspapers of the time,
some doubtless erroneously. The *Austin Daily Statesman* reported that
Bill Redding had led the party that freed the prisoners.[4]

The *Galveston Daily News* also identified Bill Clements, alias
Robertson, as one of the prisoners.[5] Some of these identifications
were incorrect, however. John Wesley Hardin was not in Texas at the
time, having fled to Alabama where he was living under the alias of J.
H. Swain. On May 3, 1877, the *Mobile Register* reported that he and
Gus Kennedy had been arrested for disorderly conduct.[6]

The Bill Clements noted in the account has not been identified.
Possibly he was one of the Clements family, the most noted of which
was gunfighter Emanuel "Mannen" Clements. Mannen Clements, a
cousin of John Wesley Hardin, ranched in San Saba County and knew
John Ringo and other men involved in the feud.[7] If one of the Clements
brothers were present, it explains the identification of Hardin as a
member of the group. There may have been another Hardin with
the men however, for on March 23, 1879, Billy the Kid related to
Governor Lew Wallace that "A great many of what are known as the
'Gist Hardin' gang are there. Among them Joe Olney . . . ."[8]

Whatever the case, shortly after the jail break reports of a gun battle between the Rangers and the feudists reached the papers.[9] They
were apparently only rumors, and the final chapter of this episode
was not written until the following year. In a letter to June Peak, commander of Company B, then stationed in Coleman County, John B.
Jones noted in part, "If the Reddings are on the Pecos one hundred
miles above Seven rivers, they are in New Mexico and as we have no
right to go beyond the limits of our state with an armed force, they are
beyond our reach."[10]

Other men involved in the feud were not beyond the reach of the law, however. In Georgetown, Texas, the papers reported that Bill and Jeff Ake were in custody.

> To-day [June 8, 1877] two celebrated outlaws, Bill and Jeff Ake, who for years after the war were the boss thieves of this and adjoining counties, against whom numerous indictments are now pending here, arrived by the International Railroad from Arkansas, from which State they have been brought by a requisition. They are said to have stolen as many horses as any two men in Texas, and have been in jail often and been tried but seldom, having usually broken jail.[11]

While the Ake brothers were only peripheral players in the feud, others more directly involved were also netted by the law around this time. In Coleman County the elusive Caleb Hall was run to ground by Company D and placed in the Brownwood jail.[12] In Burnet County, June of 1877 proved equally trying for some of the Baird faction when they were arrested and hauled into court. Champ Faris, Bud Faris, Jim Mason, Andrew Murchisson, Ed Brown, Bill Cavin, and John Carson were all arrested by Sheriff J. J. Strickland charged as being "several of the crowd who broke open the Lampasas jail in May, 1876, and released Scott Cooley and John Ringo."[13]

Brown had been taken at Lampasas. Strickland, acting in conjunction with John Bozarth, arrested the remaining men in Burnet and Llano Counties. The prisoners were bound over for the District Court, then turned over to the Rangers. Jones sent them to Austin for safe keeping, a move that prompted quick action against him.[14]

On July 11, Judge W. A. Blackburn issued a writ of habeas corpus to Jones commanding him to produce the prisoners at Lampasas on July 16 to "show cause, if any you can, why you so restrain them in their liberty."[15] Jones responded to Blackburn immediately after receiving the writ on July 12.

> In regard to the prisoners who are charged with breaking the jail of this county, viz. Farris and others, I deem it proper to make the following statement:

They were held in custody by the sheriffs of Llano and Burnet counties until about 2 o'clock P.M. yesterday when they were turned over to me by the county Judge with verbal orders to deliver them to the sheriff of Travis county. I immediately started them to Austin guarded by a strong detachment commanded by Sergt. Reynolds by whose hands these witnesses were sent to the Sheriff of Travis County.

This morning the writ of Habeas Corpus was served on me, too late for me to overtake the prisoners before they would reach Austin and be delivered to the Sheriff. Consequently they are now beyond my control.

I have however forwarded the writ to the Adjutant General and asked for instruction from him and advice from the Attorney General as to how I shall proceed in the matter or what response make to the writ. This communication is, of course, personal and I shall take the liberty of requesting you to ask Mr. Cook to come up with you or be here on Monday to attend the case as the County Atty. here does not seem to be well informed in regard to it.[16]

Jones took the opportunity to write Neal Coldwell the same day advising him that he had to appear in court "and answer for sending some prisoners to Austin yesterday."[17] To Steele alone Jones confided his personal view of the writ.

My opinion is that the object of the parties applying for the writ is to give the friends of prisoners an opportunity to rescue them, en route, or have them committed to the jail of this county so that they can take them out as they did Cooley and Ringo last year.

The Reddings, Olneys and Farrises who are implicated in this affair and were in fact the leaders in the jail delivery, both here and at Brownwood recently, are the most desperate characters in the state and

210

have a large family connection in this, Burnet, Llano and Mason Counties and will resort to any and all means possible for the release of these prisoners. I have hope that we will catch another of the Farrises and one of the Olneys in a few days as from information which I have just received I think they are still in the country.[18]

With the excitement of the Brownwood jail delivery and the capture of seven of the men wanted in connection with freeing Ringo and Cooley from jail, a small item from San Saba County may well have been overlooked in mid-June.

The District Court adjourned Wednesday last, and everything is quiet. We are informed that there were thirty-nine indictments found. Some ten or twelve of the parties have been arrested and all given bail except George Hoy, against whom there are several indictments, and in default of giving bond in all has been sent to Austin for safe keeping. A change of venue has been taken in all of his cases to Burnet county.[19]

George Riddle Hoy was a brother of Henry Hoy, and was born September 12, 1853. Perhaps suspicion had fallen on the Hoys when Kelly attempted to reach safety at their home in 1875, but indictments against the two brothers made them likely targets for mob action. Emboldened by the departure of the Rangers, the Llano mob struck in August 1877.

The earliest dated newspaper account of the killings was an editorial in the *Austin Daily Statesman* headlined "Casting Out Of Devils—How Texas Does It." The editorial reads in part:

Murders and thieves have suffered fearfully of late in Texas. Two notorious scoundrels, Ringgold [sic] and Gladden, are imprisoned or dead. King Fisher is incarcerated or has been released on bail remaining under the surveillance of the State troops. Scott Cooley was arrested and died in a spasm of rage and chagrin. Bill Longley sweats and swears in the Giddings jail. Ham White, the famous stage coach robber, makes cigars for life in the West Virginia penitentiary. Jim Taylor, of the Taylor gang of desperadoes, was killed when resisting arrest, at San Saba last Thursday. His pal Hoy was killed, under like circumstances, the day before. Both fell before the guns of the State troops. Bill Taylor, brother of Jim, breathes hard and is nervous to the last degree, with three of the Sutton gang, here in the Travis county jail. Wadsworth, a cattle thief, was shot in the Llano jail August 19. He was a terrible boy, the people said, but his murder was an outrage. . . .[20]

This catalog of mayhem referred in part to events of August 1877 that took place over several days. The newspaper account notwithstanding, Jim Taylor was not killed in San Saba. Sheriff J. J. Bozarth of Llano, Sheriff Jesse Leslie of Mason, and H. T. Eubank, sheriff of McCulloch County, gathered a posse to run down a herd of stolen cattle being gathered near Brady, county seat of McCulloch County. Among the posse was Miles Barler, who recalled both Taylor and Hoy in his memoirs but omitted mention of Wadsworth. The posse captured Walter Wadsworth on August 18 and placed him in the Llano jail.[21]

Barler's account of the circumstances surrounding the death of Henry Hoy agrees in part with the contemporary records. According to Barler, the posse gathered in San Saba County. They were met by W. R. Doran, sheriff of San Saba. Among those with Barler were Ben Beeson, Bob Rowntree, Dan Trent, and Francis Taylor.[22] Barler recalled that they separated into two parties, he, Beeson, Trent, and two other men in one of the squads. As they moved forward they saw a rider approach them. Hoy was within one hundred yards of the group when he spotted the Barler party. According to Barler, Hoy dismounted and tied his horse to a tree. "With Winchester in hand, six-shooter buckled around him he stood as straight as a general. He appeared to be perfectly cool." Barler and Ben Beeson advanced on him.[23] This was the same story that initially reached the press: "One Henry Hoy, a bad character, was then pursued by the sheriffs. He had sworn he would never run and never surrender, and when the posse hove in sight of where he was, he took up his arms, sat down behind a tree, and, resting his gun, opened a fusil[l]ade upon his pursuers."[24]

According to Barler, Hoy fired first, his bullet grazing Ben Beeson. Barler and Beeson fired one round each. Beeson's bullet hit Hoy in the face while Barler's took him in the heart. Contemporary accounts indicate that Hoy was actually shot four times.[25] Immediately following Hoy's killing, another man was spotted and run down. Barler identified the man only as one Scott. According to his account, the Rangers killed Taylor the following day.[26]

There are numerous discrepancies in Barler's account when compared with contemporary accounts. The details were far uglier than Barler had portrayed them. One of the details Barler left out was the death of Walter Wadsworth. On August 18, Wadsworth was captured and placed in the Llano jail. He lived less than a day. The *San Antonio Daily Express* reported:

> The night after his capture, a party of men went to the jail, threw in a lighted turpentine ball through the gratings where Wadsworth slept, and then riddled him with bullets. . . . It is said that 300 citizens of Llano, who were confident of Wadsworth's innocence, have sworn to find out and kill the men who murdered him while in jail. Notifications to leave the country are already being passed around. There is a likelihood of another cattle war, or feud between cattle men, in Llano and McCulloch counties.[27]

Indeed, McCulloch County was in a furor. On September 1 it was reported that the citizens of McCulloch County were trying to organize a Ranger company and were attempting to get weapons from the state government.[28] This appears to have been in direct response to the killing of F. W. Taylor on August 21, 1877, not James Taylor, as reported. Not only was Taylor mistakenly identified, but the identity of his killers proved controversial at the time. Initial reports indicated that he was not killed by the Rangers, but by the same posse that ran down Hoy: "Mr. A. L. Patton writes us from Fredericksburg that a report is in circulation up that way to the effect that the posse of men which killed Hoy have since made away with one other cattle thief, Tailor [*sic*], by name, and wounded one Scott."[29]

This agrees with the general account given by Barler, but another newspaper article casts further doubt as to who Taylor's killers were. The coroner's inquest reported on August 25 that:

> F. W. Taylor came to his death by a gunshot wound; said gunshot was discharged from a gun or pistol in the hand or hands of one of four State troopers, belonging to Company C, Frontier Battalion, in trying to arrest the deceased. Said deceased we identify as F. W. Taylor, from evidence and from letters found upon his person. And we further find that said troops were in discharge of their official duty.[30]

The Monthly Return for August 1877, filed by T. M. Sparks from Coleman City on August 31, contains no mention of the Taylor killing or of any other action taken by the company during the month.[31] This may have been an oversight on Sparks' part, but it was more likely due to the circumstances under which Taylor died.

According to a report published in the influential *Galveston Daily News*, Taylor was hailed by the state troops who only intended "to ask him the way to a certain ranch." He ignored them and rode on, and the troops "supposed from this action he was some one fearing arrest; that they pursued and fired their guns over his head to scare him so he would stop." Taylor's response was not unexpected. Possibly believing that he was being pursued by members of the mob or outlaws, he dismounted and returned fire. The three Rangers surrounded him. Taylor was killed with a bullet in his back. As it turned out, there were no charges against Taylor. The report noted ominously that people believed that the killings "will create a deadly feud."[32]

The Monthly Return for September notes in part that on September 1, Private J. F. Collins with seven men left their camp for Brady "for the purpose of attending Court . . . ," obviously to attend the coroner's inquest for Taylor.[33] An interesting sidelight is that the Rangers split their party, one of the groups heading for Concho County "in search of Cale Hall" now on the loose again.[34]

The following day, August 22, 1877, Hoy was killed by Barler and Beeson. The *Austin Daily Statesman* of September 5 reported the truth about what happened to Hoy.

> The STATESMAN's account of the killing of Taylor and Hoy, which was received from a gentleman from the up country, brings the following from the San Saba *News*: "Taylor was killed in McCulloch county, as stated elsewhere, and was shot in the back; and all the evidence received at this office goes to show that Hoy received four shots, three in the body and one in the head entered the back part and came out in the face, as the hair near the bullet on the back of the head was driven into the hole where the ball entered—the three shots in the back also were fired from the rear, as the testimony of those who examined the wounds will disclose. It is also stated that Hoy's gun was of the Winchester pattern, and upon examination of it after his death it was found that the chamber was full of cartridges, and that the barrel was not loaded, neither was there a cartridge ball in it, and his six-shooter was full of cartridges also, and had not been discharged. We understand further that Sheriff Bozarth, of Llano county, and his main body of men were not present at the time Hoy was killed, but that only five or six men, we believe, were there with a deputy. There are many here and in McCulloch county who believe that both Hoy and Taylor were murdered. We have no evidence of any kind, *pro* or *con*, in regard to either case, and we, therefore, submit such as come to us for what it is worth, and hope the courts will reveal the facts.

The reaction to the killings was not what the mob had intended.

> A sheriff's posse from Llano county shot and killed Henry Hoy in San Saba county a week ago. It was also reported that two other men, Scott and Woody, were

shot at, and one of their horses killed. The *News* says there were no writs for the last named men. Matters between San Saba and Llano begin to look ugly, and it is about time for the rangers to spy around a little.[35]

The *West Texas Free Press* reported:

> A mob at Llano the other day shot and killed Walter Wadsworth while a prisoner in jail. He had been arrested on a charge of unlawfully handling cattle. Wadsworth, it is said, was asleep when he was murdered, and it is further stated that the charge against him could not have been sustained. The San Saba News properly denounces the act as a high handed outrage.[36]

The killings of Hoy and Wadsworth outraged the region. Barler and Beeson were arrested and charged with Hoy's murder. The main witness against them was one of the men they had shot, A. K. Scott. Ultimately the pair received a change of venue to Lampasas County where they were both acquitted. Barler boasted, "When court came on and our case was called there was no Scott or any one else to witness against us."[37] Barler admitted that the witnesses were intimidated although he was accusing his enemies of the practice. "The people would indict them but they would swear for each other and get out of it every time. Maybe they would threaten a man's life if he was a witness against them, so that would intimidate some of them."[38]

Allie Keener Scott, born in Goliad, Texas, on October 23, 1855, was the son of Charles Pinkney and Susannah Rouse Scott. Scott married Mary Elizabeth Owens on May 16, 1877, at Goliad before moving to Llano County. At the time he was wounded by the posse he was not a resident of Llano County and was probably on a visit to his parents who were. Scott did settle in Llano County permanently in 1879.[39] He had good cause to remember the posse who had shot him, and it is likely that he was threatened if he made an appearance in court. The mob had not heard the last of him. The other man may have been William Woodie. When the Rangers divided to search for Hall, part of the other party had gone in search of Woodie and Nat Johnson.[40]

Major Jones was not idle during this time, but his attention was focused on the men who had liberated Cooley and Ringo. Jones had received word that an attempt to liberate the prisoners held in Burnet was planned. On August 27, Jones and N. O. Reynolds rode to Burnet to examine the jail and form a plan to prevent the jail from being broken open. Jones had word from Sheriff Strickland that a bribe had been offered him totaling $1,000 to permit the prisoners to escape. On August 30 Jones took thirty-four men from Companies A and E to Burnet where fifteen of them hid in the jail. At midnight, three or four men rode into Burnet and approached.

> Three of one party rode into town, tied their horses, and, finding the door open, were received by Jones—his men being concealed—invited in and arrested. These men, supposing Jones to be the other party, admitted what they had come for. Their names are Bob Sneed, brother of one of the prisoners, Wm. Van Winkle and Andrew Murchison.[41]

The newspaper report was slightly in error. According to the company return Jones succeeded in capturing Tom Sneed and Van Winkle, both of whom were charged with bribery, on August 30. The following day six Rangers pursued Andy and William Murchison toward the Colorado River. Andy Murchison was captured. William Kinneth Murchison, Andy's oldest brother, escaped.[42]

The killings of Hoy and Wadsworth and the subsequent arrest of Andy Murchison did not slow the violence that plagued the area. The mob had no intention of disbanding, and as 1877 moved toward 1878, it was apparent that only the continued presence of the Texas Rangers would suppress them. Local law had once again proven ineffective, Bozarth having been unable to arrest a single member of the mob. Lynch law continued, although no more prisoners were killed in their cells.

The feud was now entering its fifth year. It had gone far too long, and the wounds were deep and festering. Those who felt that they had been wronged had neither forgiven nor forgotten. Opportunities for peace had been squandered. The fighters bided their time, nursing their hatred in silence and waited only for the right moment to avenge themselves.

chapter 16

"A Shocking and Lamentable Sequel"

As 1877 drew to a close, those involved in the feud continued to make news. Caleb Hall, having liberated himself from the jail at Menard, was seen in Mason County in early September.[1] A. G. Roberts, accused by Barler of starting the feud, was now serving as a deputy sheriff in Burnet County. In late September, he and J. J. Strickland were in San Antonio "bearing papers for the conveyance of Isbell, charged with murder in Arkansas, to the authorities of that State."[2]

In Burnet, the men who had helped free Ringo and Cooley proved equally capable of liberating themselves. On September 23 James Polk Mason and Ed Brown escaped from the Burnet jail. Some believed that the guard allowed the men to escape.[3] John Baird was also in the news, having reportedly been arrested in Shackelford County by the Rangers.[4] The man proved to be one Crusoe Beard who was wanted in another county.[5] John C. Sparks reported in October:

> On Oct. 11th Sergt. T. M. Sparks with 17 Privates
> 1 Teamster and 1 guide left Camp for Signal Peak
> for the purpose of arresting Joe Olney, John Baird,
> Bill & Sam Redding[,] — Caldwill[,] — Robinson[,]
> Mike Gardner[,] Wm. Stafford[,] Pete Casner[,] Dave
> George[,] W. F. McMahon and Mart. Lacy charged with
> Jail Delivery and supposed to be Camped on Deer
> Creek at or near Signal Peak. Arrived at Signal Peak
> on the 18th and sent 8 men in different directions in

search of their Camp. The men were gone two days without making any discoveries. On the 20th started back to Camp. . . . [6]

In early November, Wes Johnson was brought to trial in Kimble County for his role in the killing of Rance Moore.[7] Johnson was convicted on May 12, 1880, and sentenced to five years in the penitentiary. He entered Huntsville prison as convict 8804 on June 17. His imprisonment proved brief. Leased out to the work force of John King within weeks of his conviction, Johnson escaped on August 21. He was never recaptured.[8]

Also in November, Dell Dublin was captured by the Rangers in Kimble County. Gillett reported Dublin's arrest simply.

> Arriving in Kimble County, the detail arrested Role and Dell Dublin, Mack Potter, and Rube Boyce. In the running fight that resulted in the capture Role received a bad wound in the hip. The two Dublin brothers and Mack Potter when arraigned in federal court pleaded guilty to stage robbery and were sentenced to fifteen years at hard labor.[9]

Dell Dublin was captured separately from his brother.

> Mason News-Item: On the 19th ult. a squad of Rangers, commanded by Corporal Gillet [sic], of Company E, succeeded in rounding up and capturing Dell Dublin, a daring cutthroat and renegade, who had headed Indian raids into Kimble and Menard counties for the past seven years. Dell Dublin has a brother named Dick, and the pair have committed more murders and robberies than any two men who have ever terrorized the Texas frontiers. When captured, Dublin was at a cow pen in Kimble, about four miles from Junction City. He made desperate resistance against the five Rangers, but fortunately was unarmed and easily taken. After the capture of Dell, Dick, unaware of the situation, rode up to the pen, but retreated in

hot haste upon receiving the following warning from his brother: "Get out, you d----d fool, don't you see the Rangers have got me?" He was closely pursued by two of the Rangers, who emptied their carbines at him, but finally succeeded in making good his escape. Dell Dublin is now in jail at Llano from which place he will probably be taken to Austin.[10]

Ringo and Gladden were also in the news during this time. Gladden appealed his conviction in the murder of Peter Bader but lost. On December 8 he was taken through Austin on his way to the penitentiary at Huntsville.[11] Ringo was still being shuttled back and forth between Austin and Mason, his trial still not having been held.[12] It was apparent that Ringo, unlike Gladden, could not be convicted. In late December he was tried in Mason "by virtue of a writ of habeas corpus." Ringo was placed under bond for $2,500 and released.[13]

As the year closed, an intriguing letter was written to Jones by one G. H. Johnson who was then in the county jail at Austin.

> Having in former days acted concidrable [sic] in the Capacity [sic] of Detective and Since my incarceration here have found this a very rich field from which to gather information. I have in the past two years come in contact with men charged with all kinds of crime and have gained the confidence of many and have given the Matter Some attention. I have recently gained some information which I believe will aid in bringing quite a number of noted desperadoes & fugitives to Justice. I believe I have found out the wherabouts of the principal in the Peg Leg Stage Robery not yet under arrest, as well as nearly all of the Brownwood & Mason Jail deliverers, also nearly all the principals in the Burnett & Llano Mob that has operated so extencively for the past few years, the murderers of Simms and other.
>
> Can give whereabouts of Matt Wolf the Lampasas Cattle thief. Can have Hall the Coreyell Cattle thief under arrest in three days. I can give whereabouts

of Beard, Redding & Olneys also Luke Cathey an accomplice of the Dublin Boys and a number of other
fugitives.

Should you deem this of sufficient importance to
grant me an interview Please get Mr. Corwin or one of
his deputies in whom you have perfect Confidence to
quietly take me to your office when I can fully explain
all.

My reasons for asking for Mr. Corwin or one of his
Deputies is that no suspision may be arroused in the
minds of any of the parties in Jail which might be the
Case if any of the Rangers was to Call for me.[14]

No indication has been found that Jones ever responded to the letter, but in early 1878 partisans in the feud clashed with the Texas
Rangers. The Rangers drew first blood.

According to James B. Gillett, N. O. Reynolds, commanding
Company E, ordered him and five other Rangers on a scout for Dick
Dublin, a fact verified by official records. In his scout were John
and Will Banister, Tom Gillespie, Dave Ligon, and Ben Carter.[15] The
six Rangers rode across country to the Potter ranch where "no one
was at home, so we passed on into the cedar brake without having
been seen."[16] The men headed for a cattle pen built for handling
wild cattle, but, finding no one there, returned to the Potter ranch
to keep watch. Leaving Ligon and John Banister to guard the camp,
the remaining Rangers approached the ranch on foot. As they did, a
rider arrived.

Gillett and the others were concealed from view in a creek bed, but
any movement toward the house would have put them in full view of
the occupants. The Rangers resolved to rush the house on foot, but as
they broke from cover one of the Potters yelled, "Run, Dick, run! Here
come the rangers!" Dublin had no time to get to his horse and ran
for the brush with Gillett in close pursuit. Gillett spotted Dublin running up a ravine and yelled for him to stop. Dublin kept running and
reached under his coat. Believing that he was attempting to draw a
pistol, Gillett fired a single shot from his Winchester. The bullet caught
Dublin in the small of the back, ranging upward and coming out near
his left collarbone. Dublin was killed instantly.[17]

Mob member Jiles Mackey surfaced during February 1878. Mackey had fled to Oklahoma following the killing of Ben Erwin, and a requisition was issued for him in the Choctaw Nation.[18] He eluded the law and was back in Texas by early 1878 when he and two other men were engaged in a pitched battle near Hazel Dell in Comanche County. A news account reported that Mackey, John Holly, and George Latham were surprised at the home of James Mackey on January 25 by a posse from Somervell and Erath Counties who wanted the trio for horse theft. After a sharp gunfight, the posse was driven off. The paper also noted that Nat Mackey was wanted for "the murder of Jones at Hazle [sic] Dell, in 1874."[19] On February 7, vengeance of a sort was meted out to James Mackey, Nat Mackey's father.

> Our readers will remember last week we gave an account of the shooting match at Hazel Dell, and the subsequent escape of three reputed horse thieves at the house of old man Mackey. A shocking and lamentable sequel to this affair occurred Thursday, of which we cannot gain the particulars with any certainty. The substance is that about thirty men came to Mackey's last Thursday night and taking the old man out murdered him by hanging him to a tree. There is no known cause for the deed, excepting the fact that he was the father of Nat Mackey, and on such gave him shelter when he came to his father's house.[20]

James Mackey's killers are still unknown.

Remnants of John Baird's allies were still being run down in 1878. In February, J. J. Strickland, who had resigned as sheriff of Burnet County in January, arrested William S. Gilliam, a former deputy of his, near Waco. Gilliam was charged with aiding Ed Brown and James Polk Mason to escape.[21] Shortly after this, George Gamel, charged in the jailbreak of Cooley and Ringo, was arrested in Mason County.[22] Gamel, like the others charged in the jailbreak, was not convicted.[23] Only one man charged in the jail break was ever sent to prison, having entered a guilty plea in Lampasas County. During the summer of 1878, Ed Stedman was conveyed to prison:

> A. S. Mackay, of Hall's State troops, arrived in town
> [Austin] with E. D. Steadman [sic], one of the ring
> leaders of the mob that broke open the Lampasas jail
> some time ago and turned the prisoners out. He is
> considered one of the worst men that has been on
> the dodge. He says the prisoner has been on the run
> for fourteen years and that he is charged with mur-
> der in Milam county and theft and robberies without
> number. A. S. Mackay, assisted by B. Cavin, on leav-
> ing Gonzales, took a dog button, or nux vomica, out
> of the prisoners mouth, he being bent on poisoning
> himself. He is temporarily lodged in Travis county
> jail, but will be taken by Mackay to his resting place
> shortly.[24]

What brought Stedman into the feud is unknown, and little has been determined concerning his background. Stedman entered a plea of guilty in the case against him in Lampasas on July 15, 1878. On October 10, 1878, he entered the Huntsville penitentiary as convict 7115. He was described as six feet three inches, blond-haired and green-eyed, with a scar on his left knee. A resident of Hill County, he was married and gave his age as twenty-nine, born in Texas.[25] Stedman provides a concrete link between gunfighter John Wesley Hardin and John Ringo. Writing to his wife on April 13, 1879, Hardin commented that "ed [sic] Steadman who come here for Breaking John Ringo and Sco Cooley out of the Lampasas Jail is Dead died of Sickness on the 11th."[26] Prison records indicate that Stedman died at Huntsville of scurvy on April 12, 1879.[27]

The mob struck again on June 5 when a party of six men raided the home of a man named Wyatt in Burnet County six miles north of Burnet. The men accused him of harboring horse thieves and ordered him to leave the county no later than June 9. On the evening of June 8 Wyatt left home to locate one of his horses. He never returned. The press reported, "It is the opinion of the community that Wyatt has been mobbed. Wyatt was a hard working man and had the reputation among his neighbors of being an honest man. He was a man of family, and his wife mourns for him as one dead. The above facts we learn from a citizens living in the community where the missing man lived."[28]

Wyatt's murder cooled mob activity for some time due to the outrage in the community. Throughout the balance of 1878, no mob violence occurred although one mob target came to a violent end in Kansas. George Hoy was in Dodge City on July 26 on a cattle drive. A local paper reported:

> It seems that three or four herders were paying their respects to the city and its institutions, and as is usually their custom, remained until about 3 o'clock in the morning, when they prepared to return to their camps. They buckled on their revolvers, which they were not allowed to wear around town, and mounted their horses, when all at once one of them conceived the idea that to finish the night's revelry and give the natives due warning of his departure, he must do some shooting . . . . [29]

Who the drover was that conceived opening fire is unknown, but the sound of gunfire brought policemen Wyatt Earp and James Masterson on the run. The herder fired two or three rounds at the officers, who returned fire. The men then fled for the bridge out of town. A few yards from the bridge Hoy fell from his horse. His wound was cared for by Dr. T. L. McCarty. Hoy stated that he had done none of the shooting, a statement undisputed by the press.[30]

Although Hoy was thought to have a chance for survival, he died on August 21. The *Ford County Globe* reported:

> DIED. — On Wednesday last, George Hoy, the young Texan who was wounded some weeks since in the midnight scrimmage, died from the effects of his wound. George was apparently rather a good young man, having those chivalrous qualities, so common to frontiersmen, well developed. He was, at the time of his death, under a bond of $1,500 for his appearance in Texas on account of some cattle scrape, wherein he was charged with aiding and assisting some other men in "rounding up" about 1,000 head of cattle which were claimed by other parties.

He had many friends and no enemies among Texas men who knew him. George was nothing but a poor cow boy, but his brother cow-boys permitted him to want for nothing during his illness, and buried him in grand style when dead, which was very creditable to them. We have been informed by those who pretend to know, that the deceased, although under bond for a misdemeanor in Texas, was in no wise a criminal, and would have been released at the next setting of the court if he had not been removed by death from its jurisdiction. "Let his faults, if he had any, be hidden in the grave."[31]

In Mason, another alleged mob member was also in trouble. Along Upper Willow Creek, Fritz Thumm cast lustful eyes at his sister-in-law, Wilhelmina (Nina) Donop, the wife of Otto Donop. Nina, described as "large and obese," was thirteen years older than her sister. Rumor began to spread that Thumm and Nina were "rather too intimate."[32] Nina Donop then began circulating charges of her own against her sister. On August 6, 1878, Thumm and his wife drove to the home of Otto Donop to discuss the matter. Nina met them with a Winchester and fired at the couple. Thumm hastily exited his buggy as a Donop employee, Theodore Wohlberg, grabbed the rifle from Nina Donop, levered a cartridge into the chamber, and pointed it at Thumm. Thumm drew and fired, the bullet taking Wohlberg in the chest, killing him instantly. Thumm was brought to trial and acquitted.[33]

Another man linked to the feud as a mob sympathizer was Joseph T. Bozarth, former deputy sheriff of Burnet County. On August 24, 1878, he died at his father's farm in Lee County, Texas, of consumption. The *Burnet Bulletin* eulogized that Bozarth was "an efficient officer, braving the winter's storms of summer's heat in the discharge of his official duties, ever faithful, ever zealous in the cause of his country's good."[34] Bozarth was twenty-three years old.

By 1879, things looked hopeful that the feud was finally over. Ed Brown, who had escaped with James P. Mason from the Burnet jail, was captured in Menard County during late February or early March, but the jailbreak was old news, and Brown did not receive much attention: "Ed Brown, one of the parties charged with rescuing Scott

Cooley from the Lampasas jail in 1876, was arrested in Menard county and taken to Lampasas, where he is now in durance vile."[35]

In April 1879, two more men were killed, this time in Lampasas County. Historian Frederick Nolan relates both of the killings to the Horrell-Higgins feud then raging there, but there are indications that the killings were mob-related.[36]

On April 7 a dozen riders came to the home of James Collier around midnight. Collier was a close neighbor and friend of Mart Horrell and came out of the house armed. The men persuaded Collier to put down the weapon. According to Nolan one of the men told Collier, "Jim, don't call no names. I don't want to be known in this country." Collier was taken away by the men and found hanging the following morning.[37] That one of the men would not want to be known locally is intriguing, indicating that the speaker was known to Collier but the riders were not from the immediate area. Collier was murdered for allegedly harboring thieves and murderers.

Also on April 7, William van Winkle came to a violent end. He and two of his brothers were camped north of Lampasas when four men rode up and told them that William was wanted by the sheriff. Van Winkle, who had been captured by Major Jones attempting to free some of the men who broke Cooley and Ringo out of jail, went peacefully. His body was found two miles away shot to death. One paper stated:

> The Dispatch contains an account of the hanging of James Collier, which we find in substance about the same as given by us in our last issue. It also gives an account of another killing some four miles of Lampasas on Monday night last. Wm. Vanwinkle, about 21 years of age, was taken from a camp and carried by the mob almost two miles, where they shot him and left him lying dead. No clue to his murderers.[38]

While the killings of Collier and Van Winkle left many questions concerning the identity of the killers, the incident on April 11 in Llano County left no doubt that the feud was ongoing. Two men appeared at the home of Wyatt Perry in Llano County. After determining that it was indeed Perry's residence, the men informed him that they wanted to buy some corn. Perry got the corn, but while he was handing it to them one of them drew a pistol and fired at him. Perry bolted for his house while the pair continued to fire. Grabbing his own weapon he returned fire and the attackers fled. The following day a man by the name of Norman was driving some horses to Perry's when he was fired upon by an unknown attacker. Norman drew his pistol and "snapped at the man a couple of times." No one was injured, and the shooter remains unidentified.

> These parties from all accounts have been prowling around Perry's house every night since. He was a witness against some men who were accused of stealing cattle, and supposing these men were trying to kill him, got nine or ten men to accompany him to this place for the trial which commenced Monday morning. We regret very much that our sister counties are having so much excitement.[39]

Yet another man peripherally linked to the feud was killed at Taylorville, Texas, on April 21. The *Austin Daily Statesman* reported that Neal Cain was shot while sleeping in his bed. Cain had "furnished some information which led to the arrest of two robbers in Bastrop, now in jail here, and the killing of the third, and the breaking up of the thieving gang that robbed the Circleville store, old man Jordan, and Major Lorraine of this city." It was believed that he was killed in revenge.[40]

The attempt to kill Perry was the last act in the feud for some time. No longer were organized bands of men riding at night hunting down their enemies. The year 1880 came and went, the only matter of significance being the death of Sheriff J. J. Bozarth on November 20. Bozarth had proven a competent and successful sheriff, and his death was mourned by many. The next year proved as calm as the previous, passing without mob activity in the region. People began to rely more on the law.

As 1882 broke, the feud had been abandoned by most of the participants, and it appeared to many that the days of violence were over. In this they were mistaken. The feud was only in a lull, gathering force for the next violent confrontation as the pattern came full circle. Cattle thieves were no longer a major problem in the area. The seeds of hatred had been sown and cultivated. New warriors had entered the arena, men who had not been in the area when the original violence began in 1875. Some of them had not even been old enough to carry a gun during that time. They were old enough now, however. This year would witness the most violent confrontation of the feud.

On June 14, 1882, while District Court was in session, the final pitched battle of the feud began. Barler recalls in his memoirs that "A feud was worked up between two parties here. One was called the Carter party and the other the Coggins party. I leaned toward the Carter party because I thought they were right and because I saw they were nearly all good men, while the other side were my bitter enemies."[41]

Barler's account is confirmed by contemporary newspapers, one of which noted the "old feud between the Coggins and Carter-McNutt parties."[42] The *Burnet Bulletin* made it clear that cattle theft lay at the heart of the matter. "The cause of the difficulty was an old feud growing out of charges of theft, one against the other."[43] The Coggin family also had ties by marriage to the Olneys. It was natural that Barler and the mob would side against them.

The Carter-McNutt party was led by Benjamin Franklin Carter and Parish Sims "Doc" Carter.[44] Ben Carter had seen action in the Hill Country during the Hoo Doo War, serving in Company C of the Texas Rangers from November 1876 through August 1877. Doc Carter, the younger of the brothers, also saw Ranger service, joining Company E on September 1, 1878, and serving into 1879. Carter reenlisted during 1880 and served between April 15 and August 31.[45]

The McNutt brothers had not accompanied the Carters to Llano.[46] Others did, however, all of them armed to the teeth. Among them were Jack Herridge and his son John.[47] Two of the Perry brothers, James and William, also accompanied the Carters into Llano. James Perry had had one close encounter with nightriders during 1879.[48] Early reports also stated that John Hughes had accompanied the men as well. All of these men were connected by ties of marriage.

Barler's "bitter enemies" were also in town, although it is likely that neither party knew of the others' presence. Led by John R. "Jack" Coggin,[49] they arrived the same day. The Coggin family, staunch opponents of mob rule, were living in northeastern Llano County. Barler's implication that they were outlaws is not confirmed by contemporary records.

John Coggin and his brother Andrew had arrived in Lampasas County by 1860.[50] The families apparently missed the 1860 census although other records confirm their presence.[51] Following the war, Andrew Coggin settled in Llano County. John Coggin is thought to have first moved to Williamson County where he married Louisiana A. Perkins on January 28, 1877, his first wife having died earlier.[52] By 1876 he had joined his brother in Llano County and was appointed postmaster at the newly formed Lone Grove post office on May 8, 1876, serving until September 28, 1877. He was reappointed on September 19, 1879, a function he served in until September 8, 1884.[53] The 1880 census listed him as a wagoner. Living in his household were his wife, two daughters and son, John Robinson Coggin born October 36, 1863.

Newspapers of the time contain limited information on the Coggin family. The *Burnet Bulletin* reported in 1879 that a daughter of Jack Coggin had been bitten by a rattlesnake, but this was probably one of John's daughters.[54] The Commissioner's Court records in Llano indicate minor incidents in these men's lives. On October 26, 1881, A. J. Coggin sold a cow for slaughter. J. R. Coggin was paid two dollars for his service as an election officer on September 6, 1881.[55] On June 14, 1882, John R. Coggin, son John, and his nephew Tom Coggin[56] rode into Llano accompanied by John Cook, Henry Hatley,[57] and Jim Connor. Both Tom Coggin and Henry Hatley had had some minor legal problems the previous December of 1881.[58]

According to Barler, he and Sam Stoudenmire, brother of El Paso gunfighter Dallas Stoudenmire, were serving as a deputy sheriffs in Llano County at the time. On the morning of June 14 the Coggin party gathered at the rear of Barler's store. While they were talking, Jack Herridge suddenly stepped into view and told them, "if they wanted anything just to open up." Sheriff R. A. McInnis, Bozarth's successor, saw that a fight was brewing and sent the deputies to separate the parties. The men approached the Coggin faction and tried to get them to put down their weapons. "About that time they leveled their guns to shoot. Stoudenmier [sic] and myself gave a spring to one side to get from between them. We did get away in time to escape a volley from both parties."[59]

Newspaper accounts make no mention of Barler's presence at the action.

> On Tuesday morning pretty early, it was discovered that the old feud between the Coggins and Carter-McNutt parties, had reached a dangerous point. Officer Stoudenmire at once began efforts to restore quiet, Sheriff McInnis being at the court house. The immediate cause of the difficulty is very hard to get at, every one seeing and hearing things differently. Both parties came to town armed to the teeth. They came in contact at or in Barler's store, but Deputy Sheriff Stoudenmire managed to to [sic] get them separated, but seeing that assistance would be necessary, sent a runner to Sheriff McInnis, who came at once. At this time the Coggins party had gone out at the back door of Barler's store, and Sheriff McInis [sic] was trying to dissuade them from opening fire while deputy Sheriff Stoudenmire was using every effort to hold the Carter McNutt party on the inside. The parties swayed back and forth two or three times— while both officers were doing their utmost to prevent the collision—each one seemingly intent on getting a good position from which to do battle if need be.[60]

As the lawmen struggled to keep the two parties apart, someone fired a rifle. The Coggin party retreated behind an old restaurant, taking cover behind trees, horses, and wagons as the Carters sailed out of Barler's store into a fusillade of gunfire. In the next few minutes, an estimated fifty or sixty shots were fired as people scrambled for cover. R. L. Harwell, one of the bystanders, was hit in the left arm. In addition, one newspaper noted that "one or two horses and hogs" were killed. Henry Hatley was shot through the throat and body and died at the scene. John Coggin was shot through the chest, dying near midnight the following day. No one was killed on the Carter side, but both Jack Herridge and Ben Carter were wounded. The fight ended abruptly, and those who could run, did.[61] The paper initially identified John Hughes as one of the Carter party. Hughes later denied that he had taken any part in the fight. "We have been reliably informed that Mr. John Hughes took a part in the fight last week. In our hurried report, we so stated, and now offer Mr. Hughes our apology for the wrong statement."[62]

The Llano Battle, as the papers termed it, was the last major confrontation of the feud. With the exception of the Carter brothers, there is no evidence that any of the men involved in this confrontation had any involvement in the early stages of the feud. The Coggin family was tied to the Olneys by marriage and were anti-mob while the Carters favored some of the mob members. It was the most violent confrontation of the feud and proved a pivotal point. The exasperated citizens of Llano had taken all of the bloodletting that they intended to. All of the participants in the fight were indicted. None of them were ever brought to trial, however, and in time most of them left Llano County. Before they did, however, Tom Coggin and one of his children were ambushed while riding into Llano. Both were wounded but survived. Their assailant was never identified.[63]

An intriguing sidelight to the Hoo Doo War is found in neighboring San Saba County. Even as Llano was settling into an aspect of peace, San Saba's troubles, referred to by Sonnichsen as the "Feud of the Pious Assassins," was on the rise.[64] The county was a cattleman's land having the same problems that had plagued both Mason and Llano. Evidence suggests that the feuds were tied to one another, but this cannot be confirmed with certainty at this time. What is known is that in the mid-1880s the violence began in earnest, spreading into neighboring Mills and Brown Counties. Once again the Texas Rangers were called upon to restore order. This feud was finally put down in 1903.

conclusion

"A Bitter Cup of Suffering"

In his biography of Texas Ranger Ira Aten, historian Harold Preece wrote of the feud, "Corpses had dangled from pecan trees. Men were called to their doors at night and gunned to death before their families. Ranchers and cowboys were butchered on rocky roads, then dumped like the carcasses of wild goats into mountain gulches and creek bottoms."[1]

Aten recalled that in 1884 the feud again threatened to erupt, this time in McCulloch County "right next door to Mason County—scarcely an omen of peace."[2] The Rangers hustled to the area, all too familiar with the passions that governed the Hill Country. Another upsurge in the feud was avoided, and in time the violent passions of the region began to cool. Age was overtaking the fighters, and death came for them all in time.

Among the Germans charged with organizing the mob, Ernst Jordan was the first to die. Crippled for life from the gunshot wound to his leg, Jordan was unable to enjoy the active life that he once had. Descendants recalled that "our father had a bitter cup of suffering to drink the last sixteen years."[3] During 1891 Ernst Jordan developed a heart problem. For over a year he battled the disease before death claimed him on December 23, 1892. Ernst Jordan had provided for all of his children at the time of his death, and was considered one of the best citizens of Mason County. At the time of his death the *Mason County News* eulogized:

Mr. Ernst Jordan, Sr. died on the 23rd day of December at his home 6 miles east of Mason, leaving a wife, 3 sons and 3 daughters.

Mankind ever stands appalled before the impenetrable mystery of death. No voice has ever broken the sombre [sic] silence of the grave, but God in the wisdom of His Revelation has responded to the yearnings of the soul and faith gives us a vision of the "city not made with hands, eternal in the heavens."

No man more truly realized these sentiments than Mr. Jordan, and the many christian [sic: Christian] virtues which were exemplified in his life gives assurance that he was ever ready.[4]

For Heinrich Hoerster death came on June 20, 1900. Like Jordan, he was considered one of the pioneers of Mason County. Heinrich Hoerster never forgot either the son or son-in-law that the feud cost him. Unlike the Jordans and Kothmanns, the Hoersters refused to discuss the past and never left memoirs concerning his role in the feud.

The Kothmann brothers all lived into the twentieth century. Dietrich Kothmann was the first to die on August 14, 1914. Descendants recalled that he was "a strict disciplinarian, resorting to drastic measures when he deemed it necessary."[5] Little more than a year later, his brother Fritz followed him to the grave on September 1, 1915. Fritz Kothmann had dedicated his life to the accumulation of wealth and was known as a fine businessman.[6] The feud left him with lasting scars. Following the reprisals of 1875 he was never again elected to the public offices that he had coveted in his youth. On his death the *Mason County News* reported simply: "Mr. H. F. Kothmann of Loyal Valley died at his home Wednesday, Sept. 1, at noon. The funeral will be held at his late home Friday afternoon at 3 o'clock."[7]

A more fitting epitaph appearing in the next edition of the paper recalled that he "supported the church and God's cause most liberally with his material wealth, ever ready to help those in need and all worthy objects."[8] Wilhelm Kothmann, the last of the brothers to die, went peacefully on April 19, 1935.[9] To a man they died believing that they had done the right thing in the early 1870s. All of the families remain prominent in the community to this day.

233

While the German mob members successfully lived down their violent past, Baird's allies were not as fortunate. Some acquired reputations that would remain with them throughout their lives. The most famous of the feudists on either side was John Ringo. Following the dismissal of the charges against him in Mason County, Ringo remained in the area throughout 1878. During 1879 he left Texas for Arizona where enduring fame awaited him in connection with Wyatt Earp. Evidence suggests that Ringo never recovered from the trauma of the feud. In Arizona he began to drink heavily at times and was subject to frequent bouts of depression.[10] On July 13, 1882, Ringo committed suicide by shooting himself in the head. In more recent years numerous writers have made claims that Ringo was killed by diverse individuals, the most popular being Wyatt Earp. None of these claims is supported by contemporary evidence.

At the time of his death, Ringo was highly regarded by his contemporaries, and news of his death was carried in the newspapers of several states. One paper wrote in part:

> It is with much regret that we chronicle the demise of one of the most illustrious men of the southwest. Had the much lamented deceased lived in antiquity his fame might have surpassed that of Hector or Ulysses, but alas, republics are ungrateful, and no public honor was ever shown to the king of the cowboys. . . . Gentleman like and pleasant in his manner, even easy going in many ways, he was a rigid observer of the old fashioned frontier code of honor that unfortunately is fast disappearing.[11]

Another paper eulogized:

> There were few men in Cochise county, or Southeastern Arizona better known. He was recognized by friends and foes, as a recklessly brave man, who would go any distance, or undergo any hardship to serve a friend or punish an enemy. While undoubtedly reckless, he was far from being a desperado and we know of no murder being laid to his charge. Friends and foes are

unanimous in the opinion that he was a strictly honorable man in all his dealings and that his word was
as good as his bond.[12]

John Baird's ending remains obscure. Having fled to New Mexico,
he reportedly became a lawman. According to Gamel, while attempting to make an arrest he was shot in the back.[13] Gamel places Baird's
killing near Santa Fe around 1877 or 1878. Jeff Ake reported simply
that Baird was killed at Socorro.[14]

George W. Gladden lost his appeal and entered the penitentiary at
Huntsville on December 12, 1877.[15] After the feud had burned itself
out, citizens of Llano County petitioned for him to be pardoned. A
conditional pardon was issued on December 30, 1884, on "the rec-
ommendation of the District Judge[,] District Atty.[,] County Judge
and most of the other County officials and many citizens."[16] Gladden
was released from the penitentiary on January 1, 1885. Following
his release he moved to Arizona, settling briefly in Apache County
where he became involved in the early stages of the Pleasant Valley
Feud, siding with the Blevins family whom he had known in Texas.
Gladden prudently left the area and returned to Texas. His last known
whereabouts were in El Paso during 1895. His ultimate fate remains
unknown.[17]

Joseph Olney was never apprehended by the authorities. Olney
settled first in New Mexico, then moved to Arizona where he associated with John Ringo under the alias of Joe Hill. On December 3,
1884, he was killed when he was thrown from a horse into a tree.

Joe Hill, one of the most widely known cattlemen
in this section, met with an accident on Wednesday
last which cost him his life. He was engaged in driving cattle into a corral at Bowie Station, and while
riding at full gallop his horse stumbled and fell, throw-
ing Mr. Hill with great force to the ground. The unfortunate man received internal injuries which resulted
fatally within an hour. As before stated, he was well-
known throughout southern Arizona, and had a host
of friends who will mourn his untimely fate.[18]

Of the Olney brothers, only John remained in Texas. Sam, George, and Dan joined their brother in Arizona. Ed and Oscar moved to Montana, and Will Olney ended up in Idaho. Others moving to the Arizona-New Mexico area included the Redding brothers. Tom Redding was killed by Apaches while acting as a guard on an ore train in 1882. Bill Redding died in Glendale, California, on September 27, 1923.

With the exception of John, the Faris brothers remained in Texas. John Faris went to New Mexico where he ended up at Fort Sumner. On December 29, 1879, he opened fire on Barney Mason, a local gunfighter, for no apparent reason. Mason killed him.[19] Bud Faris eventually moved to Oklahoma where he died peacefully. Both Champ and Bill Faris died in Llano County during the 1900s.

Another feudist who did not fare well was M. B. Thomas. Following the dismissal of the charges against him in Mason County, Thomas also left the state, ending up in Montana. On December 11, 1888, he was killed in a dispute over a card game by William Austin at Alzada, Montana.[20]

Bill and Ed Cavin's fates were far different. Ed Cavin finally left Texas for South America and reportedly never returned to the United States. Bill Cavin became a Texas Ranger, working with Lee Hall. He died peacefully in Texas during the 1900s. A. G. Roberts apparently remained in Texas working as a lawman. Like Gladden, his fate remains unknown.

Violent death also claimed most of Llano's mob leaders. William Clark, one of the leaders, met a violent death in New Mexico. Clark's granddaughter would write:

> My Gran father William Barney Clark . . . was sheriff when they had the herd [?] war the Vigilantes come to put down the out laws but got so bad the rangers had to come in to put down the Vigilantes. My gran father Mother Father went to New Mexico after 2 men that killed a whole family in Mason Co. he was shot down & is buried in Roswell, New Mexico.[21]

Ben Beeson survived the feud and went on to be a lawman in Llano. In 1889 Beeson met M. C. Roberts, a former sheriff of Llano County, in the public square at Llano. The two men had "a misunderstanding of several years standing."[22] The *Statesman* reported:

This morning at about the hour of 9 your reporter was startled by a rapid succession of several pistol shots on the north side of the square. On going to the scene of action the following particulars were gathered: M. C. Roberts was sitting in front of Roberts & Phillips' saloon. Ben F. Beeson came up. Some words passed between Beeson and Roberts relative to some trouble they had yesterday. Beeson remarked that he was not fixed, but that he would fix himself, and went to his hotel and returned with a pistol in his hand. Roberts drew his pistol. Both parties commenced firing and advancing towards each other.

Roberts fell first. Beeson approached with his pistol in hand, when Roberts fired a shot which struck Beeson in the head. Beeson fell lifeless. Roberts was shot in the face, the ball lodging in the jaw. His wound is serious but thought not fatal.

They were brothers-in-law and had had trouble before.[23]

A second account in the same paper indicated that seven shots were fired during the fight. Beeson was struck in the side of the head and killed instantly.

Perhaps the cruelest fate overtook former sheriff John E. Clark. Clark had fled for the safety of Ripley County, Missouri. Even here he feared that the relentless Cooley would track him down and kill him. He purchased a farm in the remotest, ruggedest part of the county, living almost as a recluse for the rest of his life. Clark died on May 4, 1888, still terrified of the specters of his enemies.

By the 1890s there was peace in Llano and Mason. The philosophy of an eye for an eye had given way to live and let live. Men returned to their lives and dreams for the future. Yet not everyone had forgotten the wrongs they suffered during the feud. There remained one last act of revenge. Ironically it would fall on mob leader Bob Rowntree.

On July 20, 1893, Rowntree was hauling supplies from Llano and stopped at the home of James Byfield, an acquaintance, for the night. The following morning Rowntree was ambushed and killed a short distance from his pasture gate. One historian wrote that "he sought to protect himself, his family and cattle interests without 'the law.' This may have led to his untimely death."[24]

The killing of Bob Rowntree created as much furor in Texas as the murder of Moses Baird had. The *San Antonio Express* reported:

MURDERED IN HIS WAGON.

WEALTHY RANCHMAN OF LLANO COUNTY RIDDLED WITH BULLETS.

Robert F. Rowntree's Faithful Team
Come Home, bringing Their Mas-
ter's Corpse—Great Excitement
To Trace the Murderers.

Llano, Tex., July 20. — (Special) — Robert F. Rountree, the wealthiest man in Llano county, was found murdered about fourteen miles west of here at 10 o'clock by unknown parties. Mr. Rountree was in the city yesterday and stayed all night at Jim Byfield's, about five miles from town last night.

This morning Mr. James Jackson saw him on his way from town to the Rowntree ranch and drove up and found his team stopped in front of the gate to his pasture. He was sitting in his wagon dead with about ten buckshot in his body and the back of the seat riddled with shot.

Bloodhounds have been telegraphed for and will arrive to-night at 8 o'clock. Officers have gone to the scene to hold an inquest. Great excitement prevails in the city over the horrible affair.[25]

Rowntree's death, termed a "cold-blooded assassination" was investigated by Chris Dorbandt, sheriff of Burnet County, as well as by local lawmen. On July 21 the posse followed the trail of the killer to the home of Whale and A. K. Scott. The men were arrested and brought to Llano. The bloodhounds had failed to find a scent, but "some men who were good trailers took the trail."[26] From the beginning, the motive for Rowntree's killing was ascribed to the feud.

> Mr. Rountree was one of Llano county's oldest and best known citizens. Years ago, when the county was infested by a gang of outlaws who terrorized the county and defied the law he was one of the leaders of a few honest men who put them down, and it may be that his murder is the result of an old grudge dating back to those days.[27]

If the citizens of Llano County believed the case against the Scotts was strong, they were doomed to disillusionment. On July 25 both men were released due to a lack of sufficient evidence to bind them over for the grand jury.[28] The same day Deputy Sheriff T. O. Phillips arrested a man named Mon Turner for the killing, but the papers noted that "the state has no very strong evidence against him."[29] The case remained unsolved for some time and citizens of Llano petitioned the governor so that "a suitable reward should be offered" for evidence that would lead to a conviction.[30] It was not until 1902 that Miles Barler wrote to his son Lee, "Lee they have got a man in jail for killing Mr. Roundtree and there are several that are implicated in the killing that will be arrested that are concerned in it."[31]

The man in question was none other than A. K. Scott, the same man whom Rowntree had shot at during 1877. Scott was indicted for first degree murder and assault with intent to commit murder on December 29, 1902.[32] In May of 1903 the case was dismissed. It remains unsolved to this day. Nor is there any degree of certainty that Scott killed him. Among the Hoy family of Llano County is a tradition that Rowntree was killed by one of Henry Hoy's brothers.[33] Rowntree's was the last killing of the feud. Although tradition holds that Scott lived in fear of his life for what remained of it, no vengeance was taken or attempted for Rowntree.

The feud was over.

Appendix I

The Factions

Literally dozens of men and their families were involved in the Hoo Doo War as active participants. The following list is a tentative effort to identify the primary participants on either side. The list makes no claim to be definitive, and in the case of the Hoo Doos, who closely disguised their identities, some of the names are based upon strong circumstantial evidence. The list is divided into three sections: Baird-Cooley faction, the Hoo Doos, the Citizenry who attempted to put the feud down or who, as outlaws, preyed upon both sides. In some cases, such as Caleb Hall, they are included with the faction that they were aligned with. Known outlaws of that time period are indicated with an asterisk (*).

Baird–Cooley Faction

William Scott Cooley	John R. Baird
John Peters Ringo	Moses B. Baird
Joseph Graves Olney	John C. Carson
George Gamel	Thomas W. Gamel
Marshal B. Thomas	A. G. Roberts
William Z. "Bill" Redding	Thomas S. Redding
Champion N. Faris	Robert Elihu Faris
John Tanner Olney	Samuel Young Olney
Daniel Stirling Olney	William Wallace Olney
Andes Murchison	Charles Walker Johnson
James Williams	John Edward Cavin
William Thomas Cavin	John Byram Faris
George W. Gladden	The Coggin Family
The Francis "Frank" Johnson family	The James Bolt Family

The Erwin Family

The Tanner Family

Andy Murchison

The Hoo Doos

John E. Clark

Fritz Kothmann

Dietrich Kothmann

Johann Heinrich Hoerster

Pete Bader

August Leifeste Sr.

Melchoir Bauer

Fritz Thumm

Wilhelm Kothmann

Caleb Hall

Peter Jordan

Daniel Hoerster

The Dublin brothers, Dick, Roll and Dell*

Robert F. Rowntree and family

William Clark

Ernst Jordan

Christian Oestrich

Conrad Pluenneke

Ernst Dannheim

Karl Bader

August Leifeste Jr.

Otto von Donop

Friedrich Schmidt

Barnard Durst

Jacob Durst

J. G. Durst

Caleb Hall*

Miles Barler

Ben Beeson

The Citizenry

John O. Meusebach

William Gamel

Tim Williamson

Henry M. Holmes

George W. Todd

Karl Lehmberg

James M. Riley (Doc Middleton)*

Martin J. "Mart" Blevins

Jeff Ake*

Wilhelm Kothmann

Daniel Roberts

Major John B. Jones

Heinrich Doell

------- Morrison

Cicero R. Perry

Johann Keller

William James Bolt

John W. Gamel

George W. Tdd

David Doole

Johann A. Wohrle

Rube Boyce

Frank Eastwood*

William Ake*

Wilson Hey

James Trainer

Ira Long

Rance Moore

Ike Pryor

James A. Baird

Appendix II

A key event of the Mason County War was what correspondent David Doole termed the "Big Raid" in a letter that was published in the *San Antonio Herald* of August 14, 1874. This is referred to in the response published in the *Burnet Bulletin* of September 5, 1874 by A. G. Roberts. Doole's letter has not been located to date, but on August 29, 1874, the *San Antonio Daily Express* published the following article. From the existing references to Doole's correspondence, the article appears to have been drawn, with some editorial changes, from that letter. Its significance is demonstrated by the fact that both newspapers considered it important enough to publish the lengthy correspondence.

STOCK WAR!

—

Mason County Under Arms—A Promised Revenge and Partial Execution

—

[Correspondence Fredericksburg Sentinel]

MASON, TEXAS, Aug. 18, 1874

On the ninth of August, 1874, John Clark, Sheriff of Mason county, with a *posse* of 18 men, went after a set of cow hands of Al. Roberts, who had made a raid into Mason county and driven off 200 head of cattle.

Mr. Clark overtook the cow-raiders, eleven men, at Castell, Llano county, they having the 200 head in possession. When Mr. Clark informed them that he had come to arrest them they showed fight, but seeing the sheriff's *posse* was too large for them, they gave up, and were brought back to Mason and lodged in jail.

The cattle taken in charge by a part of the *posse* were penned at Mr. Bower's [*sic*: Bauer's]. During the night a party of the said Roberts commenced to shoot into the pen, and stampeded the cattle, thereby, as they thought, destroying the proof of their guilt.

Thursday, August 13, 1874, two of the defendants were tried upon the charge of driving out of Mason 200 head of cattle without having them inspected. The evidence not sustaining the charges, they were discharged, and the time for trying the other nine was set for 9 o'clock Friday morning. Just as the court adjourned, there appeared a party of forty armed hands of the said Roberts from Llano and Burnet counties. John Baird, the leader, informed Wilson Hey, presiding justice of Mason county, trying the case, that they wanted to bail out the men in jail, and if they could not bail them out they intended to take them out. Judge Hey informed them that he would fix the bail at $5000 for the nine persons, and would be at the courthouse in half an hour and approve the bond if the sureties were worth the amount required. In the mean time Mr. Clark, the sheriff, rushed around summoning a *posse*, and by the time the court was opened, the sheriff had fifty well-armed men to see that the prisoners were not turned loose.

Judge Hey proceeded to examine as to the sufficiency of the bond offered, which not appearing to his satisfaction, it was not approved, and the court adjourned until Friday morning at 9 o'clock.

Friday morning [the news having spread like fire that A. Roberts had a mob from Llano county to take prisoners out of jail] there were 100 men armed with Winchester rifles, and were ready to make it hot for the cowraiders should they attempt to do anything; but seeing that the company meant business, they mounted their horses and left, and like brave men, killed cows and shot into the schoolhouse, on their way home.

At 9 o'clock the defendants were brought into court for trial, Mr. Todd representing the State, and Mr. J. C. Mathews the defendant. Mr. Todd moved to dismiss as to three of the defendants for the purpose of making witnesses of them. The other parties announced themselves ready for the trial, and plead not guilty, and after a trial of six hours, the jury brought in a verdict of guilty of driving 100 head of cattle out of Mason county, and assessed a fine of $25 for each head, against all of the defendants, making the sum of $2500, whereupon Mr. Mathews moved for a new trial, which being over-ruled by the court took an appeal to the District Court. On Saturday the prisoners gave the required bond and were turned loose.

Since then J. W. Gamel and Henry W. Morris have received threatening letters from Al. Roberts, saying if he did not get even with Mason county he would not charge them anything, and he is carrying his threat into execution, as a party of 20 men are in the country driving cattle again. Major Jones, of the frontier force, (who is now on his way to Fredericksburg) with forty men and a posse of citizens of Mason county, started this morning after them.

THANK
BECOMING

YOUR SAVINGS ADD UP FAST WITH

40% off list price on

20% off list

YOUR

NEW MEMBER CARD

IS READY TO USE.

Appendix III

The following card appeared in the *Burnet Bulletin* on September 5, 1874, in response to the letter from David Doole published in the *San Antonio Herald*. Unlike Doole, the men involved in the incident from Burnet and Llano Counties were more concerned about their reputations at home than in spreading the news to the general population of Texas. The letter was published under the banner "A Card."

EDITOR BULLETIN: --— In the San Antonio Herald of the 14th ult., there is a communication purporting to be from one D. Doole, which for cool deliberate misrepresentations, and uncalled for malicious slander, is unparalleled by any villifying [*sic*] article that ever crept into a newspaper. For studied misrepresentations in that letter of the unfortunate differences that have heretofore existed between the stockraisers of Burnet and Llano counties and some of the citizens of Mason county, and the slanderous and libelous attack that is made upon ourselves and others, calls for a reply from us, and we respectfully solicit space in your columns to vindicate ourselves by giving our versions of the matter.

"The organized gang of cow thieves in Llano county," which gives this D. Doole "a great deal of sorrow to report," are nothing more than peaceable stockraisers of Burnet and Llano counties, who have been in the stock business, some of them for years, and a large proportion of their stock ranges and have for many years ranged throughout the counties of Llano, Gillespie, Mason, San Saba and McCullough [*sic*]; and besides, these stock men (the undersigned and others), have at different times bought out small stocks of cattle in those counties, and paid for them, but have never removed them. For some time past many of the people of Mason county, led on and instigated by some of the stock men there, who desire to monopolize the cattle business and use the stock themselves, have opposed and in many cases prevented persons living out of the county from driving, using or controlling their stock in Mason county, and in many cases persons milking the cows of non-residents, have absolutely refused to surrender them when demanded, and most of those people which have been so active in persecuting and attempting to drive us out of that county, have been in the habit of milking, selling and eating our stock with perfect impunity, and in open defiance to our right of property.

The "big raid," referred to by Doole, was nothing more than a peaceable company of cow-drivers under the management of M. B. Thomas, of Burnet, who went up on the line of Llano and Mason counties for the legitimate purpose of marking and branding their stock and the stock of parties for which they were agents, and collecting a drove of cattle for market. Knowing the animosity that some of the people of that county have towards non-resident stock men, and wishing to have no misunderstanding or trouble, Thomas hired two men of Mason Co., to stay continually with the herd that he was collecting and cut out every animal that might get into the herd belonging to any one in that county. A large proportion of this herd were gathered first in Llano county near the line and driven across the line into Mason. After collecting a while in Mason, Thomas started with the cattle to Roberts' ranch, which was only a short distance from the line in Llano county, with no intention whatever of evading the provisions of the stock law, but intending to return and fill out the drove, and have them inspected as the law directs. It was while the drove was still in Mason county, and according to Doole's own statement, before they were attempted to be removed beyond the limits of the Co., "our sheriff, Col. John Clark, raised his posse of good citizens," to arrest Thomas and his men, against whom at that time, there seems to have been no complaint or charge whatever, except that they were on what Doole chooses to call a "raid." That they were collecting their own cattle, as they had a right to do, contrary to the desire of "our sheriff," and the men whose tool he is. The sheriff and his posse followed Thomas and his men into Llano county, and without the least shadow or show of authority; without warrant of complaint, arrested him and his men and illegally and unlawfully took the cattle from their possession and drove them back into Mason county, turned them loose and scattered them. There were only two head of cattle in the herd when captured by the sheriff that belonged in Mason county, according to the testimony of the men in the sheriff's posse, given at the trial. And it was shown that these two head got into the herd in Llano county, for the testimony of the two citizens employed by Thomas to cut-out showed a clean herd when they left Mason county, and not withstanding this, the "Hon. Hey," in that "fair trial" referred to by Doole, fined them $2500 for driving these two head of cattle from their range, when Sec. 37 of the stock law of 1874 limits the fine to one hundred dollars for each animal thus driven. In this "fair trial" the men were fined by a jury composed of parties who were taking the lead in the prosecution, and although their verdict was oppressive, unjust, against the law and the evidence, and for an amount beyond the jurisdiction of the justice's court, still the Hon. Hey refused to set aside the verdict and grant a new trial.

Thomas and his men surrendered without resistance, Doole's libel to the contrary notwithstanding. There was no attempt made to rescue them on the way to Mason. The cattle were not recaptured, but were turned loose.

Thomas and his men were carried to Fort Mason, and all of them eleven in number, were thrown into a foul dungeon, which was reeking with filth and stench, where they sweltered four days and nights with nothing to eat but bread and water. The sheriff refused to allow them to purchase other provisions although they were anxious to do so and had the money. Several of the men fainted from the terrible heat and suffocation in the close hot nauseous jail, but were still detained there, which was unnecessary except to gratify the malignant spite of those who took the lead in the matter, as all of the witnesses were present and Thomas and his men demanded their trial forthwith.

A more uncalled for and highhanded outrage than this has never been perpetrated on free white men in the State of Texas since it has been from under the Mexican rule, and that too by persons in the position of civil officers.

There were about forty men from Llano and Burnet counties present at the trial, but they did not create any disturbance or attempt the release of the prisoners. They were not desperadoes but were among the most peaceable and law abiding citizens of Burnet and Llano counties. They had not come for the purpose of liberating the prisoners, but for the purpose of protecting them from being mobbed, as some of the sheriff's gang had made indiscriminate threats against Roberts and his men. These citizens were not driven out of Mason, but quietly left when they saw that there was no likelihood of the prisoners being mobbed. They did not return and fire into the town, nor was there any threats or demonstrations made by them what ever.

After Thomas and his men were released, which they were after giving a good and sufficient appeal bond, the chivalrous sheriff "Col. John Clark," instructed his gang to follow Thomas and his men beyond the limits of the town, and if they did not leave the town immediately his gang were instructed to rearrest them and "put them in a worse place than that from which they had recently been taken."

The statement of Doole that these men fired into churches and school houses on their way out of the county is as false as absurd. Followed by a mob, weak and faint from their ill-treatment while in jail, they were in no condition to commit such acts of violence.

To conclude, the whole statement of Doole, is an unblushing series of palpable falsehoods; made partly from a natural propensity to pervert the truth and partly through gratitude to the people of Mason county, for not hanging him when he murdered a poor drunken soldier some time since. It is true that his statement under oath would not be credited where he is known, but being published in a respectable paper, will mislead the minds of many.

Some of the citizens of Mason county, instigated by such men as those civil officers and Doole, have forbid and interfered with citizens of the State of Texas in their right to control and own property in Mason county, and have in the most highhanded arbitrary manner, defied that law of the State which guarantees protection to every citizen to the enjoyment of his lawful property; have made the machinery and officers of the law instruments of oppression, tyranny and wrong; have acted in such a manner that we are justified as peaceable, law-abiding citizens of the State and United States, in appealing to our government to protect us in our rights, and prevent an unlawful invasion of them whether by a whole county, or a faction led on by county officers. It is true the sheriff and his posse have each of them been indicted by the grand jury of Llano county, for robbing us of our cattle in this manner, but this will not afford us protection in the future in the management of our stock in Mason county. We would have no protection there from any unlawful violence, for the sheriff instead of affording us protection, only encourages and leads on a class of robbers who are desirous of taking our stock from us by force. We and those we represent own many thousand dollars worth of stock in Mason county, to which we have a just and equitable right, but if the cow thieves of Mason can only use their county officers a little while longer in persecuting the lawful owners of stock and keep them from the county, the cow thieves will soon own all the [stock] we have there.

It becomes our unpleasant duty to denounce D. Doole, the correspondent of the San Antonio Herald, as an unqualified, shameless and wanton liar; as one who is attempting to wipe out the stain of a cold-blooded cowardly murder by acting the lying, fawning, lick-spittle to the officers of Mason county. It is well known that this D. Doole has always shown a low meddlesome disposition, as is evident from the misrepresentations and lies made to the Secretary of State, under Davis's administration against officers whom he disliked.

> A. G. ROBERTS,
> M. B. THOMAS,
> W. Z. REDDING,
> J. R. BAIRD,
> A. T. TAYLOR,
> M. B. BAIRD

Appendix IV

The following list was developed by Glenn Hadeler based upon the assumption that men who band together have other affiliations in common. The list presents a scientific approach to determining some of the mob members during the Hoo Doo War but should not be interpreted as a definitive fact. It was first presented at the Second Hoo Doo War Symposium held at Mason, Texas, during 2003.

Llano Leather Jackets	Methodist Church	August 1874 Clark Posse	Germans Mentioned In the Hoo Doo War
	Carl Bader		Carl Bader
			Peter Bader
Mathew Bast	Mathew Bast		
Jacob Bauer	Jacob Bauer		
Wilhelm Bickenbach	Wilhelm Bickenbach		
Peter Bickenbach	Peter Bickenbach		
Fred Brandenberger	Fred Brandenberger		
Otto Donop	Otto Donop		
		Henry Doell	Henry Doell
Jacob Durst	Jacob Durst	Jacob Durst	
George Durst		George Durst	
	Bernard Durst	Bernard Durst	
Heinrich Hasse	Heinrich Hasse		
Frederick Hoerster	Frederick Hoerster		
William Hoerster	William Hoerster		
	Daniel Hoerster	Daniel Hoerster	Daniel Hoerster
Ernst Jordan	Ernst Jordan		Ernst Jordan
	Peter Jordan		Peter Jordan
			John Keller
			Carl Keller
			August Keller
Dietrich Kothmann	Dietrich Kothmann		
Fritz Kothmann	Fritz Kothmann	Fritz Kothmann	Fritz Kothmann
William Kothmann	William Kothmann		William Kothmann
Carl Lehmberg	Carl Lehmberg		Carl Lehmberg

Llano Leather Jackets	Methodist Church	August 1874 Clark Posse	Germans Mentioned In the Hoo Doo War
Frederick Lehmberg	Frederick Lehmberg		
	August Leifeste Sr.	August Leifeste Sr.	
August Leifeste Jr.	August Leifeste Jr.	August Leifeste Jr.	
	August H. Leifeste	August H. Leifeste	
	Christian Oestreich	Christian Oestreich	
	Henry Pluenneke		Henry Pluenneke
John Werner	John Werner		
Christian Winkel	Christian Winkel		
Frederick Winkel	Frederick Winkel		
			John Wohrle

Notes

Introduction

1. Noah Smithwick, *The Evolution of a State* (Austin, TX: Stack-Vaughn Company, 1968), 308.

2. There are any number of books dealing with the Lincoln County War. Among the best are Frederick Nolan's *Lincoln County War* and the works of Phil Rasch such as *Warriors of Lincoln County.*

3. The best account of McNelly's raid into Mexico is contained in Parsons and Little's biography of McNelly, *Captain L. H. McNelly—Texas Ranger* published by State House Press in 2001.

4. To the author's knowledge no definitive work on the Sutton-Taylor War has been published although historian Chuck Parsons has authored numerous biographies that touch on the subject. Leon Metz has also written a biography of John Wesley Hardin. See Leon Metz, *John Wesley Hardin: Dark Angel of Texas* (El Paso, TX: Mangan Books, 1996).

5. The terms "German" and "American" are used throughout the text to designate the factions involved in the feud from a cultural standpoint. Many of the German faction had obtained American citizenship prior to the outbreak of violence. Others were born in the United States. The term "Dutch" was applied to immigrants from Germany, not Holland, and was not originally a term of contempt. Emil Friedrich Wurzbach, whose family had come to Texas in 1846, was nicknamed Dutch by both his friends and family.

John Ringo was known by one contemporary as Dutch Ringo, a nickname more accurate in his case due to his Walloon Dutch ancestry. Douglas V. Meed, *Texas Wanderlust* (College Station: Texas A & M University Press, 1997), 20, 177; J. B. Collins to B. M. Jacobs, July 17, 1880, University of Arizona Special Collections, Tucson, Arizona.

6. Gilbert J. Jordan, *Yesterday in the Texas Hill Country* (College Station: Texas A & M University Press, 1979), 34.

7. C. L. Sonnichsen, *I'll Die Before I'll Run* (Lincoln: University of Nebraska

Press, 1988), 5–7.

8. C. L. Douglas, *Famous Texas Feuds* (Austin, TX: State House Press, 1988), 152 *et seq*.

9. C. L. Sonnichsen, *Ten Texas Feuds* (Albuquerque: University of New Mexico Press, 1971), 91.

10. A primary example of this occurred during the troubles at Fort Griffin, Texas, in 1878. At the time, the vigilante committee held sway in the area and included most, if not all of the county officers. When Lieutenant George W. Campbell and Company B of the Rangers began investigating the troubles with the intention of breaking up the vigilante committee, the mob sent strong protests to Coke. Coke responded by having the company disbanded based strictly upon the protests. Major John B. Jones failed to go to the region to investigate independently and the murders continued. Robert K. DeArment, *Bravo of the Brazos* (Norman: University of Oklahoma Press, 2002), 97–124.

11. Sonnichsen, *Ten Texas Feuds*, 89.

12. *Galveston News*, January 23, 1879.

13. *Austin Daily Democratic Statesman*, May 21, 1876.

Chapter 1

1. Joe H. Kirchberger, *The French Revolution: An Eyewitness History* (New York: Facts on File, Inc., 1989), 238.

2. Glen Ernest Lich, "Balthasar Lich, German Rancher in the Texas Hills," *Texana* 12 (1974): 102; Gilbert J. Jordan, *A Biographical Sketch of Ernst and Lizette Jordan* (Dallas, TX: Privately published, 1931), 3. Hereafter cited as *Ernst Jordan*.

3. Glen E. Lich, *The German Texans* (San Antonio: University of Texas Institute of Texas Cultures at San Antonio, 1981), 7–11. Hereafter cited as *German Texans*.

4. Also called the *Mainzer Adelsverein* or simply the *Verein*, the organization was founded by five princes and sixteen nobles. The stated purposes of the *Adelsverein* were to improve the conditions of the unemployed and reduce their poverty; to unite the emigrants by giving them protection to ease their burden by mutual assistance; to maintain contact between Germany and the settlers and develop maritime trade by establishing business connections and to find markets for German crafts in the settlements and Texas products in Germany. Ibid., 24.

5. Ibid., 24.

6. The Fisher-Miller Grant was given to Henry Francis Fisher and Burchard Miller by the Republic of Texas on June 7, 1842. It was renewed several times until the final date of expiration was fixed for August 1847. Fisher sold an

interest in the grant to the *Adelsverein* for $9,000. The group apparently did not realize that they had not purchased any land, but rather the right to put settlers on the land. There were also disadvantages to the grant itself. In addition to being too far from the coast for a first settlement, the northwest part was the hunting grounds of the Comanches. Don H. Biggers, *German Pioneers in Texas* (1925; repr., Fredericksburg, TX: Fredericksburg Publishing Co., Inc., 1983), 26; Irene Marschall King, *John O. Meusebach: German Colonizer in Texas* (Austin: University of Texas Press, 1987), 36.

7. John Meusebach was born Baron Ottfried Hans von Meusebach on May 26, 1812, in Dillenburg, Germany, to Baron Karl Hartwig Gregor von Meusebach and Ernestine von Witzleben. A well-educated man, Meusebach accepted the position of commissioner to replace Solms-Braunfels while engaged to Elizabeth von Hardenberg. Upon his arrival in Texas, Meusebach found the affairs of the *Adelsverein* a near disaster. He later stated: "In place of a balance credit I found only debts. Financially I found the affairs of the Company in the greatest confusion and disorder. . . . [T]he camping, moving, transporting, and supplying such a large body with provisions, required more than 10 times the amount of the estimates." It was a hapless situation heightened by the arrival of even more settlers. Meusebach was able to obtain a treaty with the Comanches that opened the way to settlement in the grant. King, *John O. Meusebach*, *passim*.

8. John O. Meusebach, *Answer To Interrogatories In Case No. 396. Mary C. Paschal et al. vs. Theodore Evans*, District Court of McCulloch County, Texas (1894; repr., Austin, TX: Pemberton Press, 1964). The answer was given in the November term of District Court for McCulloch County in 1893. The author's copy of the document was obtained from the Pioneer Memorial Library in Fredericksburg, Texas.

9. Carl Blumberg, edited by A. E. Skinner, "The True Effectiveness of The Mainz Society for Emigration to Texas As Described in a Letter of November 3, 1846," *Texana* 7, no. 4 (1969): 300.

10. Frederick Law Olmsted, *A Journey Through Texas in 1856*. Reprinted in *Frontier Times* 13, no. 9 (June 1936): 437.

11. Although he later celebrated his birthday on July 21, church records show Johann Ernst Heinrich Christian Franz Jordan was born to Johann Heinrich Christian Jordan and his second wife, Johanne Christina Sophia Wilhelmina Grotjahn, at Wehrstedt, Lower Saxony, in the Kingdom of Hannover on July 23, 1821.

Ernst Jordan married Wilhelmine (Minchen) Uflaker on April 19, 1841, a year after his mother's death. Three months later their daughter, Johanne Ernestine Wilhelmine (Mina) was born on July 1, 1841. Due to family disagreements and the lack of future prospects, in the summer of 1845 Jordan and his family contracted with the *Adelsverein* to emigrate to Texas. They left Bremen on September 1, 1845, aboard the *Margaretha* and arrived shortly before Christmas. Jordan, *Ernst Jordan*, 3, 8–9; Gilbert J. Jordan and Terry G. Jordan, *Ernst and Lizette Jordan: German Pioneers in Texas* (Austin, TX: Von Boeckmann-Jones Co., 1971), 5–8, 28. Hereafter cited as *Jordan Pioneers*.

12. Jordan and Jordan, *Jordan Pioneers*, 11; Jordan, *Ernst Jordan*, 7.

13. Jordan, *Ernst Jordan*, 6–8. Gilbert Jordan was the son of Daniel Jordan. From his references it appears that Jordan was citing a *Questionnaire* and *Statements* from two of Ernst's sons, Daniel and Peter, an indication of the bitterness Ernst Jordan transmitted to his descendants. A revised and expanded edition of the book was published in 1971 as *Ernst and Lizette Jordan: German Pioneers in Texas*. In the revised book, co-authored by his son Terry Jordan, the statement was omitted.

14. Selma Metzenthin Raunick and Margaret Schade, *The Kothmanns of Texas 1845–1931* (Austin, TX: Von Boeckmann-Jones Co., 1931), 4.

15. Heinrich Conrad Kothmann was born January 31, 1798, at Wedelheine in the Kingdom of Hannover, the youngest son of Hennig Heinrich Kothmann and his wife Ilse Dorothee Marwede. From 1818 until he received his honorable discharge on April 26, 1824, Kothmann served in the Second Battalion, Fourth Infantry Regiment of the Hannover army. In 1824 he married Johanne Sophie Wolters Kothmann, widow of his oldest brother, and the couple had two children. After Johanne's death he married Ilse Katherine Pahlmann, with whom the couple had six children in Germany. Kothmann's oldest children remained in Germany when he moved to Texas, but later rejoined the family. Heinrich Kothmann arrived in Texas on December 20 and reached Karlshafen on the 31st. A son, Karl, was born there on March 24, 1846. Raunick and Schade, 1–4.

16. Jordan and Jordan, *Jordan Pioneers*, 11.

17. Johann Heinrich Hoerster and his family arrived in Texas during September 1846. Born July 16, 1814, at Piertzenthal, probably to Johann and Johanna Maria Deluse Hoerster, he had served in the Prussian army prior to his marriage to Maria Christina Gelhausen. Arriving with him in Texas were three sons. The name is spelled Hörster in German and pronounced "Hester." The Anglicized spelling, Hoerster, which the family adopted early on, has been used throughout for the sake of consistency. *Mason County Historical Book* (Mason, TX: Mason County Historical Society, 1978), 102.

18. Raunick and Schade, 39.

19. Jane Hoerster, "Henry Julius Behrens," *Mason County Historical Book. Supplement I* (Mason, TX: Mason County Historical Commission, 1986), 9.

20. Jordan, *Ernst Jordan*, 12; Jordan and Jordan, *Jordan Pioneers*, 13; King,

105–7. New Braunfels had been established as a staging area along the road to the grant.

21. *Jordan Pioneers*, 13.

22. King, 98–101.

23. Ibid., 102–3.

24. When he applied for a permit to emigrate to Texas in December 1845, Gottfried Bader gave his birthplace as Ilsfeld in Wurtemberg. Church records indicate that he was the son of Johann Gottfried Bader and Margaretha Jaeger, born May 26, 1817. By 1847 he had married Christine Mueller. The family was not wealthy, and the 1850 census for Gillespie County notes "Gotfrey Bader" as a wood chopper. Bader moved his family to Castell in western Llano County around 1856. 1850 Gillespie County, Texas, Census; 1860 Llano County, Texas, Census; Ella A. Gold translator. *Church Record Book of the Protestant Congregation at Fredericksburg* (Fredericksburg, TX: Junior Historians, Chapter 21, n. d.), 1; Julius DeVos, ed., *One Hundred Years of the Hilda (Bethel) Methodist Church and Parent Organizations, 1856–1955* (Mason, TX: Hilda United Methodist Church, 1973), 7, 8, 10. Hereafter cited as *Fredericksburg Church Records* and *Hilda Church Records* respectively.

25. King, 102–3.

26. Jerry Ponder, *Fort Mason, Texas: Training Ground For Generals* (Mason, TX: Ponder Books, 1997), 17–18; Harold B. Simpson, et al., *Frontier Forts of Texas* (Waco, TX: Texian Press, 1966), 141–43; Margaret Bierschwale, *History of Mason County Texas Through 1964* (Mason, TX: Mason County Historical Commission, 1998), 344–45. Hereafter cited as *History of Mason County*. On May 15, 1851, Fort Mason was established by Order Number 46 of the Eighth Military District. United States troops first occupied the site on July 6, 1851. The town of Mason was established around the fort.

27. In 1851 Franklin L. Paschall obtained a judgment for $2,400 and Henry Huck for $12,500 for debts owed them by the *Adelsverein*. John Giddings would later receive an additional judgment for $7,705.53. The Fisher-Miller grant was eventually sold at a sheriff's sale to I. A. Paschall for $5,800.

28. J. Marvin Hunter, "Brief History of the Early Days in Mason County, Part 1," *Frontier Times*, 6, no. 2 (November 1928): 77–78. Hereafter cited as "History of Mason County, Part 1."

29. Cox was born September 19, 1827, in Wilson County, Tennessee, to James R. and Lucy Cox. On his arrival in Texas he settled in Cherokee County. Between 1846 and 1850 he acted as a hired guard for wagon trains bound from Texas to California. In 1851 he persuaded the rest of his family to move to his home in Mason. Cox died on March 8, 1907.

30. *Mason County Historical Book*, 42–43; Hunter, "History of Mason County, Part 1," 70.

31. Considered an Indian fighter and real pioneer, William Gamel later located on Bluff Creek ten miles west of Mason. Gamel may have been in Mason County when the Germans arrived, but by 1860 the family had returned to Llano County. 1860 Llano County Census.

32. Mathew Alex Doyal (or Doyle) was born in Louisiana on August 26, 1802, probably to John L. Doyal Sr. and his wife Letitia. Doyal arrived in Texas in 1831 under the sponsorship of G. Polliett and settled at Nacogdoches. He, his wife Parmelia, and son John took up farming, but it appears that his wife and son died in the cholera epidemic of 1831–32. Doyal then married Barbara Walker on March 2, 1839. By his second wife, Doyal had six children: George, Thomas, John C., Martha, Jerry W., and Barbara Jane. First Texas Census, 1835–1836; *Mason County Historical Book*, 55; Milton McWilliams to the author, June 23, 1998; Marvin Doyal to the author, March 8, 1998; J. W. Wilbarger, *Indian Depredations in Texas* (1889; repr., Austin, TX: Eakin Press and State House Books, 1985), 91–98.

33. Hunter, "History of Mason County, Part 1," 72.

34. The *Brady Standard and Heart O'Texas News*, November 12, 1954. A. L. Lang, of German descent, was born February 7, 1874, in Llano County. His knowledge of the feud was gained from oral accounts. Several inaccuracies exist in the article.

35. Julius DeVos, "The Mason County or Hoodoo War," in Mason County Historical Commission, *Mason County Historical Book*, Supplement III (Mason, TX: Mason County Historical Commission, 1999), 62. Hereafter cited as *Mason County Historical Book*, Supplement III.

36. Lich, *German Texans*, 49.

37. Ibid., 81.

38. Max Amadeus Paulus Krueger, *Second Fatherland: The Life and Fortunes of a German Immigrant* (College Station: Texas A & M University Press, 1976), 78.

39. Henry B. Dielmann, "Emma Altgelt's Sketches of Life in Texas," *Southwestern Historical Quarterly* 63 (July 1959–January 1960): 373.

40. George Bernard Erath, edited by Lucy A. Erath, "Memoirs of Major George Bernard Erath," *Southwestern Historical Quarterly* 26 (July 1922–April, 1923): 216.

41. Jordan, *Yesterday in the Texas Hill Country*, 14.

42. George W. Todd was born in Grayson County, Virginia, on January 15, 1827, Todd originally settled in Lamar County, Texas, where he married Mrs. Dizenia Peters Smith. In 1853 Todd and his father-in-law, Joshua Peters, came to Mason County with eighty slaves. By 1854 they were harvesting corn on Peters' Creek and had established a successful mill. Todd was designated to organize Mason County.

43. Election Register 1854–1861; Bierschwale, *History of Mason*, 100.

44. Wilhelm Hoerster was born at Fredericksburg, Texas, on April 16, 1850. Following his return to his family, he would be known as "Wild Bill," a designation given him due to unshakable habits he acquired during this period. *San Antonio Daily Herald*, August 13, 1859, December 17, 1859; David Johnson, "'Wild Bill' Hoerster," in Mason County Historical Commission, *Mason County Historical Book*, Supplement II (Mason, TX: Mason County Historical Commission, 1994), 49–53.

45. Jonas Franklin Dancer was the first settler at Hardbutter Springs (later Dancer's Springs) in Llano County. Born in Tennessee on December 11, 1803, Dancer's early life is obscure. He and his wife Jane brought their family from Tennessee to Texas sometime between the birth of their son Jonas Franklin Jr. in 1836 and the birth of their daughter Tennessee Jane around 1839. By 1854 Dancer had moved to the Llano area. Both Dancer and his son signed the petition to Governor E. M. Pease in April of 1854 for protection from Indian depredations. Wilbarger, 630–31; 1850 Travis County, Texas, Tax Records; 1850 Travis County, Texas, Census; 1860 Llano County, Texas, Census; Reeves files; *Texas State Gazette*, February 1 and February 17, 1851; M. Pease Governor's papers; *Petition for relief from Indian depredations* dated April 20, 1854, TSA; Tax Rolls: 1855 Gillespie County, Texas, 1856 Llano County, Texas.

46. *Austin State Gazette*, March 10, 1860.

47. *Austin State Gazette*, September 6, 1860. John Moses Bolt was born in 1817 in either Kentucky or Virginia to Charles Bolt and Lemina Harbour.

48. Confederate Muster Rolls. Texas State Library and Archives, Austin, Texas. Hereafter cited as TSA.

49. Lily Klasner, *My Girlhood Among Outlaws* (Tucson: University of Arizona Press, 1972), 20–21.

50. William Banta was born to Isaac William Banta and Elica Barker in Princeton, Indiana, on June 23, 1827. The family arrived in Texas during 1839. Banta was an old-time Indian fighter, and during the war he was elected first lieutenant of Company A, McCord's Regiment, Walker's Division in the Confederate army. William Banta and J. W. Caldwell, *Twenty-Seven Years on the Texas Frontier* (No date; repr., Council Hill, OK: L. G. Park, No date), 186–87; David Paul Smith, *Frontier Defense in the Civil War* (College Station: Texas A&M University Press, 1992), 158.

51. Biggers, 60.

52. Homer Martin, "Ludewig (Louis) Martin," in Mason County Historical Commision, *Mason County Historical Book*, Supplement 1 (Mason, TX: Mason County Historical Commission, 1986), 64. Born November 20, 1820, to Nicholaus and Hedwig Sinner Martin at Erndtebruck, Germany, Martin

had arrived in Texas on November 23, 1844, aboard the *Johann Dethardt*. Two years later he married Elisabet Arhelger. Martin was a well liked and respected man. When Gillespie County was organized in 1848 he was elected sheriff. He also served with Biberstein in 1861.

53. Douglas Hale, *The Third Texas Cavalry in the Civil War* (Austin: University of Texas Press, 1993), 275.

54. Sonnichsen, *I'll Die Before I'll Run*, 9.

55. Rick Miller, *Bloody Bill Longley* (Wolfe City, TX: Hennington Publishing Company, 1996), 1.

56. Thomas J. Johnson was noted in the 1860 census as a twenty-two-year-old farmer born in Kentucky. In 1870 he was noted as a stone mason. He was then married, his age given as thirty-three. Living with him were his wife, E. A., aged twenty-five and also from Kentucky and their one-year-old son Ben. David Epley was a relative newcomer to Texas. The 1870 census notes him as a forty-five-year-old blacksmith born in Tennessee. All of his children, except the youngest, William, age one, were born in Tennessee. Ulysses Howard does not appear on either the 1860 or 1870 census by that name although there were Howards living in the county. Brack Thomas was Marshal Brackston Thomas, more commonly referred to by his initials, M. B. Thomas played a significant part in the opening stages of the feud. Burnet County, Texas, District Court Records, Cause 311; 1860 Burnet County, Texas, Census; 1870 Burnet County, Texas, Census.

57. Francis "Frank" Johnson, born between 1812 and 1814, was a son of James Johnson. The family was living in Llano County by 1860, and tax records for 1862 indicate that Johnson had a herd of 300 cattle and six horses. The following year he moved to Mason County where, by 1866, his herds had grown to 500 cattle and 150 sheep. 1860 Llano County, Texas, Census; 1862 and 1863 Llano County Poll Tax Records; 1866 Mason County Poll Tax Records; Betty Marglon Henning to the author, March 29, 1986. Hereafter cited as the Henning files.

58. George Reeves, "The Scalping of Matilda Friend," *Frontier Times* 5, no. 2 (November 1927): 49; O. C. Fisher, *It Occurred in Kimble* (San Angelo, TX: The Talley Press, 1984), 122; Wilbarger, 633–37; Henning files; *Tri-Weekly State Gazette*, February 14, 1868; *San Antonio Daily Herald*, February 19, 1868; Johnie Lee Reeves to O. C. Fisher, February 14, 1986. Courtesy Johnie Lee Reeves. Hereafter cited as Reeves files.

59. Born in Baden on October 12, 1826, Kettner had been one of the liberal young thinkers who were driven from Germany. He arrived in Texas during 1848 and settled at New Braunfels. In 1861 Kettner moved to Mason and filled a number of public offices, including sheriff, tax collector, and assessor. During 1872 and 1873 he served as brand inspector. Of this period of

his life one writer would note that "in that capacity probably did more than any other man to see that everyone got his dues." Kettner died on September 9, 1907. *Mason County Historical Book*, 135.

60. Governor's Papers: E. J. Davis, B. F. Gooch et al. to E. J. Davis, January 18, 1872.

61. Ibid., James M. Hunter to E. J. Davis, March 4, 1872.

62. Ibid., A. Liemering to E. J. Davis, March 10, 1872.

63. *Austin Daily Statesman*, November 14, 1875; *Austin Weekly Statesman*, November 18, 1875.

64. Governor's Papers: Richard M. Coke, George W. Todd to Richard M. Coke, February 9, 1874.

65. J. Marvin Hunter, "Brief History of the Early Days in Mason County, Part 2," *Frontier Times* 6, no. 3 (December 1928), 131. Hereafter cited as "History of Mason County, Part 2."

Chapter 2

1. Edward Everett Dale, *The Range Cattle Industry* (Norman: University of Oklahoma Press, 1960), 2.

2. J. Marvin Hunter, ed., *The Trail Drivers of Texas* (1924; repr., Austin: University of Texas Press, 1985), 20.

3. Joseph G. McCoy, *Historic Sketches of the Cattle Trade of the West and Southwest* (Kansas City, MO: Ramsey, Millett & Hudson, 1874), 37–38.

4. *Mason County Historical Book*, 82.

5. Raunick and Schade, *The Kothmanns*, 41–43.

6. Hunter, "History of Mason County, Texas, Part 1," 68.

7. Bierschwale, *History of Mason County, Texas*, 193.

8. McCoy, 8–9.

9. Hunter, "History of Mason County, Texas, Part 2," 128; Sonnichsen, *Ten Texas Feuds*, 90–91.

10. Sonnichsen, *Ten Texas Feuds*, 91; Doell interview. C. L. Sonnichsen files, University of Texas at El Paso. Hereafter cited as Sonnichsen files.

11. Sonnichsen, *Ten Texas Feuds*, 90.

12. J. Frank Dobie, *The Longhorns* (Boston: Little, Brown and Company, 1941), 53. Mavericking inevitably led to trouble. During the 1870s four brothers named Dunn and a man named Ike Hewitt were employed branding mavericks for fifty cents a head. When the men decided to take up mavericking for themselves the cattlemen who had employed them "captured the five, led them into a thicket, strung them up, and said *adios* with a volley of bullets at the swinging forms." This is only one of many such incidents.

13. John Fischer, *From the High Plains* (New York: Harper & Row, 1978), 8.

14. Day book of Daniel Hoerster. Courtesy Jerry Ponder. Hoerster was paying Daniel Hester five dollars per head of cattle. The day book appears to indicate that Hoerster did most of his business with German ranchers, but a thorough analysis of the document has not been possible to date by either Mr. Ponder or the author.

15. Winfred Blevins, *Dictionary of the American West* (New York: Facts On File, 1993), 296–97; B. A. Botkin, ed., *A Treasury of Western Folklore* (Avenel, NJ: Wings Books, 1975), 371. The term rustler was originally applied to "an active enterprising fellow," an apt description for maverickers. In time it became associated with a stock thief, generally of horses or cattle. This meaning was commonly adopted into modern usage very early, perhaps by the 1890s but certainly by the early 1900s.

16. Sonnichsen, *Ten Texas Feuds*, 90.

17. Riley was the illegitimate son of Nancy Cherry and an unknown father born February 9, 1851, in Bastrop County, Texas. Family members later informed his biographer that Riley's middle name was Middleton, possibly significant in determining his paternal roots. While his father has not been determined with certainty, around the time of his birth a man named Middleton was hung in Bastrop County. Riley established "questionable relationships with horses" at an early age. He was charged or indicted on numerous charges of horse theft, until he and a cousin were sentenced to the penitentiary in Huntsville. Riley entered prison on July 22, 1875, and escaped on April 1, 1876. He established himself in Nebraska under the alias Doc Middleton and was the most noted horse thief in that state. Riley died on December 27, 1913. Harold Hutton, *Doc Middleton* (Chicago: The Swallow Press, 1974), 9–15; Cause 254, Gillespie County, Texas, District Court Records; William Steele, Adjutant General, *A List of Fugitives From Justice* (1878; repr., Austin, TX: State House Press, 1997), 15, 56. Hereafter cited as *1878 Fugitives From Justice*; Convict Record Ledger. Convict Number 4643. TSA.

18. Dee Harkey, *Mean As Hell* (Santa Fe, NM: Ancient City Press, 1989), 7.

19. Harold Preece, *Lone Star Man: Ira Aten, Last of the Old Texas Rangers* (New York: Hastings House Publishers, 1960), 92.

20. Reuben Hornsby "Rube" Boyce, was born January 8, 1853, to Isaac Ely and Caroline Wilkins Boyce in Williamson County, Texas. By 1855 the family had moved to Burnet County. One of the earliest records concerning him is that on August 8, 1874, he served as a petit juror with A. T. Taylor who was later involved in the feud. Boyce received two dollars for his work. Over the ensuing years he would spend more time before a jury than sitting on one. During his lifetime he is said to have killed three men. He died on May 23, 1927, and is buried at Coahoma, Texas. Darrell Debo, ed., *Burnet County*

History, Volume II (Burnet, TX: Burnet County Commissioners Court, 1979), 28; Burnet County District Court Records, Volume A.

21. Martin Blevins was the son of Armstead and Delilah Blevins born in Arkansas around 1840. He and wife Mary Atkison had seven children: Andy, Charles, Hamp, John, Delila, Sam, and Meesy. By 1860, the family had moved to Texas. Wade Hampton "Buck" Blevins was also charged in Llano County for his role in the killing of Wade Smith on January 12, 1882. Cause 952, Llano County District Court Records; Causes 183, 341, 342, 343, 344; Mason County District Court Records; *Semi-Weekly Farm News*, San Marcos, Texas, December, 1937, courtesy John Blevins. The Mason County indictments were dismissed in 1888 due to the death of the defendants.

22. 1870 Kerr County, Texas, Census.

23. Miller, *Bloody Bill*, 67.

24. Causes 6, 49, 50, 51 and 55. Kerr County, Texas, District Clerk records.

25. Miller, 67.

26. *Austin State Journal*, August 15, 1873.

27. Eastwood's gang included John Jamison, alias Pinkney, George DeGraffenreid, James Ratliff, Tom Odum, and William Baker among others and appears to have been a link in what Gamel refers to as the "chain raid system," which was a coalition of outlaws who passed stolen goods along the "chain" to put them out of reach of their rightful owners quickly. At times they disguised themselves as Indians while conducting their raids. Bell's origins have not been determined with certainty. The record of State Police arrests confirms that he was killed by Miller during 1872 although the exact date is not given. It appears to have been sometime during the month of June.

28. *San Antonio Daily Express*, July 29, 1873.

29. *Daily State Journal*, July 23, 1873.

30. Peter R. Rose and Elizabeth E. Sherry, eds. *The Hoo-Doo War: Portraits of a Lawless Time* (Mason, TX: Mason County Historical Commission, 2003), 13.

31. *Brenham Banner*, May 17, 1873; May 24, 1873.

32. Doell interview; Sonnichsen files.

33. C. L. Sonnichsen, *I'll Die Before I'll Run*, 39.

34. Taylor was born in Tennessee on April 10, 1820, the son of Josiah and Hephzibeth Luker Taylor. Josiah Taylor moved to Texas in 1824, ultimately settling near what later became Cuero. Following the burning of Linnville in 1840, Creed Taylor fought at the battle of Plum Creek and later served as a Ranger under Jack Hays. He saw action at both Bandera Pass and Salado where he was wounded. Taylor was a veteran of the war with Mexico, fighting under Captain John J. Tumlinson at the Grass Fight, Mission Concepcion, and the storming of San Antonio. He was also present at the battle of San Jacinto. Marjorie Hyatt, *Fuel for a Feud* (Smiley, TX: Privately published, 1990), 174, F-162.

35. The brothers were children of Creed Taylor and his first wife Nancy Goodbread. While Hays Taylor is credited with being the man who killed Thompson and McDougal, he was charged along with his brother Doboy and brother-in-law W. A. Spencer. Hyatt, *Fuel For A Feud*, F-175; Bierschwale, *History of Mason County, Texas*, 93, 495; Gamel, 11; *Weekly Austin Republican*, November 27, 1867.

36. *Galveston Daily Civilian*, November 29, 1869.

37. *San Antonio Daily Herald*, December 5, 1870.

38. Ibid., October 31, 1871.

39. Ibid., May 12, 1872.

40. Herman Lehmann, *Nine Years Among the Indians 1870–1879* (1927; repr., Albuquerque: University of New Mexico Press, 1996), 92–93.

41. *Brenham Banner*, May 17, 1873.

42. *San Antonio Daily Herald*, May 25, 1875.

43. Sonnichsen, *Ten Texas Feuds*, 92.

44. These views were expressed by Mr. Hadeler during the Hoo Doo War Symposium in Mason, Texas, July 27, 2003. Using common links he established a list of suspects in the feud. This is detailed further in Appendix IV.

45. Jordan, *Yesterday in the Texas Hill Country*, 100.

46. Max Amadeus Paulus Krueger, *Second Fatherland* (College Station: A&M University Press, 1976), 99.

47. Telephone interview with Peter R. Rose, June 1, 1989.

48. At a talk given during the Second Hoo Doo War Symposium in Mason on July 27, 2003, Hadeler advanced the theory that the mob had links prior to the feud. Comparing the roster of the Llano "Leather Jackets," an organization for frontier defense, against the membership in the Willow Creek Methodist Church and Clark's 1874 posse, he named a number of probable mob members including Ernst Jordan, the Kothmann brothers, the Bader brothers, Lehmberg, August Leifested Senior and Junior, George Durst, Frederick Brandenberger, Otto Donop, and others. The list is reprinted as Appendix IV.

49. Richard Maxwell Brown, *Strain of Violence: Historical Studies of American Violence and Vigilantism* (New York: Oxford University Press, 1975), 23.

50. Jordan had served in von Bieberstein's company of Minute Men in 1861. In 1867 he was elected as a county commissioner, and in 1869 was elected justice of the peace in Precinct 2 but failed to quality. On May 10, 1871, he was one of nine men enlisted in the State Police. Jordan was based in the Fourth District. Kathryn Burford Eilers, "A History of Mason County, Texas," Master's Thesis, University of Texas, 1939, 242; Confederate Muster Rolls; State Police Rosters. TSA.

51. Jordan, *Ernst and Lizette Jordan*, 29.

52. Other catch phrases include joining "the side that belonged to law and order" or joining the "side that was right."

53. Raunick and Schade, *The Kothmanns*, 41; Eilers, 244–45; J. Marvin Hunter, "Brief History of Early Days In Mason County, Part 3," *Frontier Times* 6, no.4 (January 1929): 158–60, hereafter cited as "History of Mason County, Part 3"; Sammy Tise, *Texas County Sheriffs* (Albuquerque, NM: Oakwood Printing, 1989), 357.

54. Raunick and Schade, *The Kothmanns*, 62.

55. Ibid., 90.

56. Eilers, 243–44; Hunter, "History of Mason County, Part 3," 158–60; Tise, 357; *Austin Weekly State Gazette*, June 28, 1873.

57. Doell interview.

58. H. O. Schulze, "Book Report on 'Branded' From the German History 'Gebrandmarkt,'" unpublished manuscript, 1972, 3. Courtesy Mason County Historical Commission, Mason, Texas. Hereafter cited as "Branded." Christopher Hagen published *Gebrandmarkt* after interviewing a number of residents of German descent in the Mason area. H. O. Schulze read the book and, feeling that it might be of value to future historians, prepared a report on it. His son, R. Clinton Schulze, prepared several copies of the report for distribution to local libraries. While the book itself is fiction, Hagen based it upon information provided to him. How much is the author's imagination is unknown, but Schulze's report indicates that much of the local folklore was incorporated in it.

59. District Court Records, Kerr County, Texas, Cause 45.

60. District Court Records, Llano County, Texas, Cause 372.

61. 1870 Llano County, Texas, Census, Llano County Poll Tax records, 1875; Rose and Sherry, *The Hoo-Doo War*, 46.

63. Born to Michael and Christiana Bayha Thumm in Bernhausen, Wurtemburg, Christoph Friederich Thumm was christened on January 28, 1851. Thumm came to Texas around 1868 as Germany was on the brink of war with France. By the mid-1870s he was living in Mason County where he married Caroline Dannheim from the Willow Creek community. Gary P. Fitterer, "F. Thumm, Deer Revolverheld Von Deutschland," NOLA *Quarterly* 14, nos. 3–4 (1990): 24.

63. Ibid., 25–26.

64. His grandmother, Eliza Low, married Charles Bolt in Polk County, Missouri, in 1851. It was Bolt's third marriage, and his family accompanied the Bolts to Texas during the 1850s. Tommy Clark to the author, April 8, 1988; Author's interview with George Mack Taff, June 10, 1988; *Llano County Family Album* (Llano, TX: Llano County Historical Society, 1989), 89; Mason County Tax Rolls, 1874–1876; Llano County Tax Rolls, 1874–1877.

65. Jerry Ponder, "Captain John E. Clark," draft manuscript, courtesy the author. Copy in the author's collection; Rose and Sherry, *The Hoo-Doo War*, 107–21. Clark had petitioned the local Masonic Lodge for membership and was admitted on November 8, 1873. From these records his birth can be placed in 1834.

66. Ibid.

67. Adam R. Johnson, "Daily Journal," Kentucky Historical Society Library, Frankfort, Kentucky. Copy courtesy Jerry Ponder.

68. *Austin Daily Statesman*, October 17, 1875."

69. Dan W. Roberts, *Rangers and Sovereignty* (San Antonio, TX: Wood Printing & Engraving, 1914), 92.

70. Texas Ranger Muster Rolls. TSA.

71. Governor's Papers, Richard M. Coke. TSA.

72. *Austin Daily Statesman*, October 17, 1875.

73. Described as an unmarried native of Mexico, Escobel entered Huntsville penitentiary on July 27, 1874, for a five-year term. He was killed on November 4, 1874, while in prison. *Reports on the Condition of the Texas State Penitentiary, For the Year 1873–1874* (Houston, TX: A. C. Gray, State Printer, 1874), 43; *Reports on the Condition of the Texas State Penitentiary, For the Years 1874–5–6* (Houston, TX: A. C. Gray, State Printer, 1876), 93.

74. *Houston Daily Telegraph*, May 7, 1874.

Chapter 3

1. Petition of Jess Bourland and others, October 14, 1871, Adjutant General's Records, TSA. Hereafter cited as AGR.

2. Petition of J. C. Rogan and other officials, August 1, 1874. Governor's Papers, Richard Coke, TSA.

3. Miles Barler, *Early Days in Llano* (Llano, TX: Privately published, ca. 1898), 31. The articles were first serialized in the *Llano Times* during 1898.

4. Llano County District Court Records, Cause 307. Peter Allen Rainbolt was born at Bridgeport, Alabama, on December 26, 1826. He married Anna Jane Stafford in Burnet County on September 25, 1856. Rainbolt died in San Saba County December 28, 1917.

5. Sugar M. Cain was the son of Joel Yancy and Philadelphia Harrison Cain and was born around 1855 in Texas. He was apparently named for one of his uncles, Sugar Molasses Cain. Cain was a younger brother of Cornelius "Neal" Cain. 1860 and 1870 Travis County, Texas, Census, Gen Web Inquiry, Travis County, Texas: Valri Darling, January 31, 1999.

6. Llano County District Court Records, various causes including Causes 270, 329, 355, 356, 381, 384, 385, 386, 388, 390, 393, 394, 403, 491, 492, 493, 496, 497, 498, 512.

7. Texas Supreme Court Decision Book. TSA; Llano County, Texas, District Court Records, Cause 276.

8. Friedrich Oestreich, born January 4, 1827, arrived in Texas during the 1840s. He married Wilhelmina Hiechen, born November 9, 1832. He died on January 14, 1907. Fritz Grote was the son of Reverend Charles A. Grote born in Detmold, Germany, on September 10, 1839. Grote fought for the Confederacy during the Civil War and later worked as a drover for Karl Lehmberg. He died on November 23, 1931.

9. *1878 Fugitives From Justice*, 77; Llano County, District Court Records. Causes 381, 383, 385, 386, 388, 390 and 394. Joe Olney was indicted on August 24, 1875, on all of these charges. In Cause 381 he was indicted with Charles Hammons, but the charges against Hammons were later dismissed. In Cause 394 he was indicted with Hammons and John Olney. The list of fugitives described Joe Olney as "about 30 years old, 5 feet 8 inches high, slender built, weighs about 130 pounds, red complexion, hair and beard almost white, light blue eyes." Joe Olney was never brought to trial on these charges. No indictment for assault to murder has been located for Joe Olney in Llano County.

10. Llano County District Court Records, Cause 410. John Olney was indicted for aggravated assault on December 24, 1874.

11. Hester was age twenty-four at the time of the census and gave his birthplace as Mississippi. 1870 Burnet County, Texas, Census; Daniel Hoerster day book, courtesy Jerry Ponder.

12. Burnet County, Texas, District Court Records. Cause 390.

13. A summary of the law appeared in various Texas newspapers during the early months of 1874. The summary used is drawn from the *Burnet Bulletin*. *West Texas Free Press* of San Marcos, Texas, April 11, 1874, also contained a summary of the law.

14. *San Antonio Daily Herald*, April 18, 1874.

15. William Zachariah Redding was the son of James M. and Elizabeth Frances Chambliss and was born February 2, 1850, in Forsyth, Georgia. Following the war, the two brothers and their sister Elizabeth left for Texas. Elizabeth remained in Alabama, but the brothers arrived in Burnet County where they became friends of the Lacy family. He married Loveda Ann Lacy. Wilson Hey to Governor Richard Coke, June 25, 1874. AGR. Courtesy Texas State Archives; Michael Redding to the author, September 5, 2003.

16. Hey was the son of James and Catherine Ryan Hey and was born August 24, 1836, near Leighley, West Yorkshire, England. Hey ran away from home and arrived in America in 1854. He was drafted into the Confederate Army, serving in the Ninth Mississippi Infantry. He reached Mason in the latter half of 1869. In 1871 he was elected registrar and married Hannah Korn

on December 3. Hey occupied the dual role of district clerk and justice of the peace for Precinct 1. The remaining justices of the peace were Otto Donop, Precinct 2, John Meusebach, Precinct 3, Robert Zesch, Precinct 4, and Louis Kuhn, Precinct 5. Hey died in Mason on November 3, 1906. Rose and Sherry, *The Hoo Doo War*, 37–44.

17. Confederate Muster Rolls, TSA.

18. 1870 Burnet County, Texas, Census.

19. State Police Muster Rolls, TSA.

20. Trail log of M. L. Hayes, ca. 1873–1875. Courtesy Mason County Historical Commission. Copy in author's files.

21. *Burnet Bulletin*, March 7 and May 23, 1874.

22. Ibid., February 20, 1875.

23. John B. Jones was born in the Fairfield District of South Carolina to Henry and Nancy Robertson Jones on December 22, 1834. The family moved to Texas in 1838. Jones enlisted in the Eighth Texas Cavalry under Benjamin F. Terry. He later became a captain in Joseph W. Speight's Fifteenth Texas Infantry. By the end of the war he had achieved the rank of major. In 1868 he was elected to the state legislature but was denied his seat by radical Republicans. Jones assumed command of the Frontier Battalion of Texas Rangers on May 2, 1874, serving with distinction. In 1879 he was named Adjutant General of Texas. He died in Austin July 19, 1881. *Handbook of Texas Online*, s.v. "Jones, John B.," http://www.tsha.utexas.edu/handbook/online/articles/view/JJ/fjo54.html.

24. David Doole was born in Belfast, Ireland, on November 25, 1832. His parents came to the United States around 1840, settling in New York. Doole served in the Union Army during the war and later saw action against the Apaches. Following his discharge from the army he settled in Mason where he was the post trader for two years. During 1867 he served as district clerk amidst Reconstruction. He later opened a store in Mason where he enjoyed the honorific title of Major. He remained in Mason until his death of natural causes on August 16, 1924. "Major David Doole," *Frontier Times* 2, no. 1 (October 1924): 10.

25. This was probably Johann Melchior Bauer who was born in Dettenhausen, Germany, on October 13, 1808. Bauer and his wife Rosina Durst landed at Galveston on October 22, 1846. The Bauers moved to Fredericksburg and were enumerated there in both the 1850 and 1860 census. By the early 1860s they had moved to Upper Willow Creek, but they later removed to the Upper Llano River near Castell in Mason County. He died on May 7, 1894.

26. *San Antonio Daily Express*, August 29, 1874. The entire article is reproduced as Appendix II.

27. *Burnet Bulletin*, September 5, 1874. The entire article is reproduced as Appendix III.

28. *San Antonio Daily Express*, August 29, 1874.

29. Ibid.

30. *Burnet Bulletin*, September 5, 1874.

31. *San Antonio Daily Express*, August 29, 1874.

32. Jordan, *Ernst Jordan*, 23.

33. *San Antonio Daily Express*, August 29, 1874.

34. *Burnet Bulletin*, September 5, 1874.

35. *San Antonio Daily Express*, August 29, 1874.

36. *Burnet Bulletin*, September 5, 1874.

37. Mason County District Court Records, Cause 10.

38. *Burnet Bulletin*, September 5, 1874.

39. Timothy P. Williamson was born on December 20, 1842, to Cyrus and Hannah Alexander Williamson in Mecklenburg County, North Carolina. Following Hannah's death on February 3, 1855, Cyrus Williamson took his three sons to Texas. Cyrus died on the trip. Fred and Tim Williamson moved to Llano County, where Tim Williamson married Mary Elizabeth Johnson, probably around 1863. O. C. Fisher reports that Williamson was one of the early settlers of the western Mason/eastern Kimble area. "A neighbor to Louis Deats was one Tim Williamson. He was in the cattle business, and, like all Kimble settlers, did a great deal of hunting to provide a livelihood for his family." Mary Elizabeth Johnson was the daughter of William J. Johnson and Clementine "Tiny" Townsend. Following William's death Clementine married Green Moyne (or Marion) Caudle, who was a friend of the Ringo family, and his presence there helped lure John Ringo to the area. Joan Buck de Korte to the author, December 5, 1993; 1850 Mecklenburg County, North Carolina, Census; 1850 Mecklenburg County, North Carolina, Slave Schedule; Fisher, *It Occurred in Kimble*, 64; 1870 Mason County, Texas, Census; Newspaper clipping from an unknown paper, probably ca. 1902, courtesy Public Library of Charlotte and Mecklenburg County.

40. George W. Gladden was the son of James and Letty N. "Gladdin." The earliest record yet located for George Gladden shows him living in Kansas during 1855. Gladden is noted as a minor who had emigrated from Missouri. This is confirmed in part by the 1880 census that places Gladden's birth in Missouri around 1851 although the date is in error. By 1862 Gladden had moved to Llano County where his name appears on the tax records. On December 19, 1871, he married Amanda Susan McFarland in Travis County, Texas. The 1873 tax records for Mason County indicate that he was living at Loyal Valley where he owned two and one-half town lots valued at $1000 and 300 cattle, eight horses and two mules valued at $1,750. 1866 Kansas

Territory Census; 1862 Llano County, Texas, Tax Records; Marriage Records of Travis County, Texas; 1873 Mason County, Texas, Tax Records; Trail log of M. L. Hayes; J. M. Franks, *Seventy Years In Texas* (Gatesville, TX: No publisher, 1924), 111–12; 1880 Walker County, Texas, Census.

41. State Police Arrests Ledger, AGR, 78. TSA.

42. Williamson was working for Lehmberg as his foreman during the early 1870s. Gladden had purchased his town lots for $1200 "to be paid in good steers from 2 years old up to Mr. Charlie Lehmberg." The cattle were to be delivered between March 1 and March 10, 1874. Gladden's brands were noted as P and FL. Civil Case 14, Amanda Gladden vs. August Jones. Mason County Civil Records, Mason, Texas; Doell interview.

43. Information is lacking on most of these men. George Cullen Arnett was the son of Cullen Curlee Arnett and Elizabeth Warren Norred and was born September 21, 1844, in Texas. By 1860 the family had moved to Burnet where, on April 5, 1862, he and his father were mustered into the Seventeenth Texas Infantry, Company G, of Allen's regiment. Following the war, Arnett married Frances Ann Coon on June 11, 1866. He died in Colorado City, Texas, on July 5, 1900. He remained a cattleman his entire life. *Record of Criminals by Co[unty], crime, description*, Mason County, 58–59, AGR, TSA; 1850 Milam County, Texas, Census; 1860 and 1870 Burnet County, Texas, Census; Civil War Muster Rolls; Jerry Watkins to the author May 29, 2000; Texas Ranger Muster Rolls.

44. David Pickering and Judy Falls, *Brush Men and Vigilantes: Civil War Dissent in Texas* (College Station: Texas A&M University Press, 2000), 46.

45. John Preston Thomas was a schoolteacher. Due to his abolitionist sympathies, he moved his family to Burnet County, arriving there in February of 1855. The family first settled at Backbone Valley where they remained until 1857. They then moved to Burnet. Diary of Travel by John Preston Thomas, courtesy Don Watson; Thomas family data, courtesy Don Watson; Don Watson to the author, September 23, 1999; 1860 Burnet County, Texas, Census.

46. 1870 Burnet County, Texas, Census.

47. *Burnet Bulletin*, September 5, 1874.

48. Llano County District Clerk's Records, Causes 366 and 368. The bondsmen for Roberts in this case were John R. Baird and T. J. Faught.

49. Johann Jacob (or Jakob) Durst was the son of Johann and Christina Margarethe Binder Durst and was born December 15, 1838, in Dettenhausen, Germany. The family sailed to Texas in 1846, on board the *Element* and reached Fredericksburg on February 6, 1847. Later he moved to Mason County, settling a few miles west of Castell. He married Sophia Leifeste (born July 20, 1852) on December 8, 1870. Durst continued ranching until the early 1900s when he moved to Mason. He died on November 17, 1920.

50. Johann Bernhardt Durst was another son of Johann and Christina Margarethe Binder Durst and was born June 13, 1841, in Dettenhausen, Germany. He married Maria Finke Kopp and died in 1889.

51. Leo Zesch was the son of Robert and Lina Dangers Zesch and was born December 5, 1859, in Mason, Texas. He married Agnes Elizabeth Meusebach, born January 21, 1862, by whom he had three daughters. Descendants recalled Leo as a fun-loving man. He died in Mason County on April 5, 1921.

52. Frederick Johann George Schmidt was born September 17, 1827, at Goettern, Nassau, Germany. According to family tradition he stowed away on a ship bound for Texas to avoid conscription into the army. He settled in the Simonville community where he married Katherine Simon on January 14, 1859. A descendant recalled the family speaking of Schmidt's involvement in the feud. He died on December 4, 1891.

53. Johann George Durst was another son of Johann and Christina Margarethe Binder Durst. He was born in Dettenhausen, Germany, on June 20, 1831. He later married Charlotte Seagmann.

54. This was probably August Heinrich Leifeste, born October 31, 1856, the son of Johann Heinrich Gottfried and Margrete Rheinhard Leifeste.

55. August Heinrich Leifeste Sr. was born at Broistedt, Grossherzogtum, Braunschweig, on August 1, 1812. He was one of thirteen children of Johann Konrad Leifeste. He and his wife Elizabeth Viedt emigrated to Texas in 1852. The family moved immediately to Mason County. He died on June 24, 1894.

56. August Leifeste Jr. was born Heinrich August Conrad Leifeste to August Leifeste Sr. and his wife Elizabeth Viedt. During the Civil War he was initially a member of Captain Biberstein's Minute Men from September 17, 1861, to February 18, 1862. After his discharge he enlisted in Company E, Thirty-third Regiment, Texas Cavalry on November 1, 1862. During the war he contracted tuberculosis, of which he eventually died on July 20, 1888.

57. Mrs. Meckel was Henriette Luckenbach born October 13, 1829, in Nassau, Germany. She was married to Conrad Meckel, born November 11, 1826, in Nassau, Germany, on June 12, 1853, in Gillespie County, Texas. Meckel was a store keeper and livestock trader in Fredericksburg. He was killed by Indians on October 25, 1866, while driving a herd of cattle toward his ranch on Willow Creek. Henriette Meckel died on February 4, 1892, in Fredericksburg, Texas. Gillespie County, Texas Marriage Records, Book 1, p. 13, Number 84; Luckenbach Family Tree, copy in author's files; Meckel Family Tree, copy in author's files; Email, Scott Zesch to Dave Johnson, July 16, 2002.

58. James A. Baird, no known kinsman of John and Moses Baird, was born in Buncombe County, North Carolina, to Adolphus E. and Loretta Hunter Baird on July 31, 1852. Following the Civil War he lived in Philadelphia for

about four years before moving to Texas. He had worked as a drover prior to his appointment as deputy sheriff under John Clark. Baird later moved to New Mexico where he died on April 9, 1921. State Docket, District Court, Book, Mason County, Causes 1, 2 and 3; John B. Jones to William Steele, October 28, 1875, AGR.

59. Christian Oestreich was born August 2, 1854, to Frederick and Wilhelmina Hiechen Oestreich on the Oestreich ranch near Castell. Local lore claims that he was the first white child born in Llano County. Oestreich served in the Minute Men during 1872. Court records indicate that charges were dropped against him in return for his testimony against John Clark. He died on June 22, 1936. Llano County District Court Records, Cause 395.

60. A critical analysis of possible mob members and their links was conducted by historian Glenn Hadeler for the Hoo Doo War Symposium held in Mason on July 27, 2003. See Appendix IV.

61. *San Antonio Daily Express*, August 29, 1874.

62. S. P. Elkins, "Served as a Texas Ranger," *Frontier Times* 5, no. 11 (August 1928): 447.

63. Jones to Doole, August 25, 1874. AGR, TSA.

64. Doole to Jones, September 4, 1874. AGR, TSA.

65. *Burnet Bulletin*, September 5, 1874.

66. Ibid.

67. *San Antonio Daily Herald*, August 24, 1874. Quihi is located in Medina County, and aside from this account there is no contemporary documentation that the village was ever the scene of any violence associated with the feud. It is significant that the newspaper's editor referred to the incident as one of "many others."

68. *San Antonio Daily Herald*, August 27, 1874.

69. Ibid., August 30, 1874.

70. Ibid., September 5, 1874. The letter giving the details of Shelburn's death was dated August 28, 1874, from Bridges' Camp near the Blue Mountains.

71. Ibid., July 3, 1874.

72. Cicero Rufus Perry, the son of William Marshall and Mary Indiana Shropshire Perry, was born in Montgomery County, Alabama, on August 23, 1822. The family arrived in Texas in 1833. Perry served as an early day Ranger and Indian fighter and was present at the Siege of Bexar. When the Texas Rangers were reorganized in 1874 he was named commander of Company D. Perry left the company at the end of the year and died on October 7, 1898, at Johnson City, Texas.

73. Jones to Perry, August 17, 1874, AGR, TSA. This is the incident referred to by Elkins.

74. Perry to Jones, August 25, 1874, AGR, TSA.

75. *Burnet Bulletin*, September 5, 1874. John Clark and his posse were indicted in Llano County on August 24, 1874, in Causes 395, 397, 398, and 399 with bail set for $300 in each cause.

76. Sergeant N. H. Murray for C. R. Perry to Jones, October 28, 1874. AGR, TSA.

77. *San Antonio Daily Herald*, November 9, 1874.

78. James Martin Trainer was born in Schuyler County, Illinois, in 1833. His parents moved to Texas in 1843 and settled in what would become Lockhart, Texas, about two years later. As Lockhart began to grow, the family moved to what would become Blanco County. Trainer died in 1920.

Chapter 4

1. Roberts, *Rangers and Sovereignty*, 93.

2. *1878 Fugitives from Justice*, 77.

3. Llano County District Court Records, Causes 365, 395, 397, 398, 399.

4. *San Antonio Daily Herald*, August 30, 1875.

5. Jack Burrows, *John Ringo—The Gunfighter Who Never Was* (Tucson: University of Arizona Press, 1987), 132.

6. 1850 Lamar County, Texas, Census; 1860 Collin County, Texas, Census; Baccus family information, courtesy Karylon Russell; Baccus family information, courtesy Janet Baccus. Charles A. Baccus was born around 1848.

7. Denton County, Texas, Marriage Records. Rachel was born July 7, 1830, to Henry and Sarah (Sally) Kincaid Cook in Green County, Illinois. She died on April 19, 1912, in Collin County.

8. 1860 Collin County, Texas, Census; Baccus family information, courtesy Karylon Russell; Baccus family information, courtesy Janet Baccus. The census data indicates that Benjamin had a number of children. Benjamin's occupation was listed as herdsman.

9. 1870 Denton County, Texas, Census.

10. Louisa Baccus was born June 6, 1829, to Enoch C. and Elizabeth Brown Baccus. She married Henry Boren on February 22, 1849. Boren sided with Peacock during the feud, but other Boren family members supported Bob Lee.

11. Interview with Denise Maddox, June 7, 2004.

12. Thomas W. Gamel, *The Life of Thomas W. Gamel* (Mason, TX: Privately published, 1933), 18. Hereafter all endnote references to Gamel are to this edition unless otherwise noted.

13. Turley may have been Thomas Jesse Turley born to Jesse Jones and Lucy Herndon Turley in Missouri c. 1854. Turley married Mattie Whttington. This identification is far from conclusive, however. 1860 Travis County, Texas, Census;

Record of Criminals by County, crime, description. Mason County, 58. TSA.

14. Bierschwale Collection, "Attorney's Business Book—Henry M. Holmes," 11. TSA. Hereafter cited as Holmes Attorney Book; 1870 Mason County, Texas, census; Jo Ann F. Hatch to the author, June 9, 1999.

15. Charles Walker Johnson was born February 17, 1859, to Frank Johnson and his wife Elizabeth "Betsy" Townsend. Johnson was a cousin of Tim Williamson's wife Mary Elizabeth.

16. Interview with Henry Doell, July 12, 1944, by C. L. Sonnichsen. Courtesy University of Texas at El Paso, El Paso, Texas. Hereafter cited as Doell interview.

17. Schulze, "Branded," 2.

18. 1875 Mason County, Texas, Tax Rolls.

19. Hunter, "History of Mason County, Part 3," 162.

20. Holmes Attorney Book, 11.

21. Lucia M. Holmes, *The Lucia Holmes Diary 1875–1876. The Hoo Doo War Years* (Mason, TX: Mason County Historical Commission, 1985), entry for February 15, 1875. Hereafter cited as Holmes diary.

22. Gamel, 18.

23. Ed Bartholomew to David Johnson, undated letter.

24. Roberts to Jones, February 14, 1875. AGR. TSA.

25. Fisher, *It Occurred in Kimble*, 76.

26. Holmes Attorney Book, 10.

27. Holmes diary, February 17, 1875.

28. Ibid.

29. Gamel, 18.

30. Hunter, "History of Mason County, Part 3," 162.

31. Gamel, 19.

32. Phillip J. Rasch, *Warriors of Lincoln County* (Stillwater, OK: The National Association for Outlaw and Lawman History, 1998), 146; 1850 Graves County, Kentucky, Census.

33. *Record of Arrests*, State Police Ledger Book, 234–35, TSA.

34. *Flake's Semi-Weekly Bulletin*, May 3, 1871.

35. Holmes Attorney Book, 1–2.

36. *1878 Fugitives From Justice*, 33.

37. *Galveston Daily News*, September 15, 1877.

38. Gamel, 19.

39. Sonnichsen, *Ten Texas Feuds*, 93.

40. Gamel, 20.

41. C. L. Sonnichsen interview with Ernest Lemburg, July 12, 1944. Sonnichsen files, University of Texas at El Paso. Hereafter cited as Lemburg interview. Ernest J. Lemburg was born February 9, 1871, in Mason, Texas. His

father was from Holstein, Denmark, a Dane of German descent. Mr. Lemburg died on February 1, 1961.

42. John A. Lindsay was born May 22, 1836. The Lindsays were prosperous cattlemen in Mason County during this time. Lindsay died of a sudden heart attack while working in his cow lot on October 1, 1891. Doell's account is the only reference to John Lindsay being involved in the mob.

43. Doell interview; Holmes diary, February 18, 1875; Holmes Attorney Book, 11.

44. Lemburg interview.

45. Roberts, *Rangers and Sovereignty*, 88.

46. Holmes diary, February 18, 1875.

47. Ibid.; Roberts, *Rangers and Sovereignty*, 89; Holmes Attorney Book, 11. Lucia Holmes correctly identified the Baccuses as cousins. Her husband recorded that they were brothers. John Martin was never sent to prison. He died in Texas on February 13, 1897.

48. *Houston Daily Telegraph*, March 3, 1875.

49. Sonnichsen, *Ten Texas Feuds*, 93.

50. *San Antonio Daily Herald*, August 30, 1875.

51. Holmes diary, February 19, 1875.

52. Ibid.

53. John William Gamel, born in 1844, was the oldest son of William and Catherine Gamel. Gamel was raised in the cattle trade and served a stint in the Thirty-third Regiment, Texas Cavalry, during 1862 and 1863. After the war he married Kathleen Crosby in 1864. By 1876 his ranch exceeded 35,000 acres in southwestern Mason County. John Gamel made his fortune in the cattle trade and was one of the influential men of the time. His wife was from a noted Mason family, and one of her siblings was the witness noted in the Holmes papers concerning the Baccuses.

54. Holmes diary, February 19, 1875.

55. *San Antonio Daily Herald*, August 30, 1875.

56. *Austin Daily Statesman*, November 14, 1875; *Austin Weekly Statesman*, November 18, 1875. It appears likely that Dreux was actually David Doole.

57. Holmes diary, February 25, 1875.

58. Gamel, 21; Roberts, *Rangers and Sovereignty*, 89.

59. Gamel, 21.

Chapter 5

1. Roberts to Major John B. Jones, March 1, 1875. AGR. TSA.

2. Holmes Attorney Book, 4. The trial probably took place in late November or early December 1874.

3. Roberts, *Rangers and Sovereignty*, 90.

4. Holmes diary, March 6, 1875.

5. Ibid., March 7, 1875.

6. Newton Harrison Murray was born at Liberty, Missouri, in 1847. During the Civil War Murray fought under Wiliam Clarke Quantrill. Following the war, Murray moved to Blanco County, Texas, where he enlisted in the Texas Rangers on May 25, 1874. He received his discharge in August 1876.

7. Holmes diary, March 13, 1875; N. H. Murray to Jones, March 15, 1875, AGR.

8. *Houston Daily Telegraph*, March 20, 1875.

9. Ibid., March 26, 1875; [Britton, Frank L.], *Report of the Adjutant General of the State of Texas for the year 1872* (Austin, TX: James P. Newcomb and Co., 1873), 213. John W. Kelley is listed in the muster roll for Company Q of the Minute Men as a sergeant, mustered into the company on August 21, 1872.

10. Gamel, 22–23. Dick Roberts was not a relative of either Dan Roberts or A. G. Roberts. Rufus Allen Winn, the main leader of the opposition, was born in Jasper County, Texas, on March 20, 1839. Following the Civil War he moved to Menard County where he married Mary Elizabeth Vaughan on April 1, 1869. A rancher, Winn also raised race horses and was a respected leader of the community.

11. James B. O'Neil, *They Die But Once, the Story of A Tejano* (New York: Knight Publications, 1935), 123.

12. The family listed Robert and Mary "Caviness," both aged thirty-six in the 1860 census. There were eight children ranging in age from ten months to nineteen years, including two older brothers Stephen and William H. By 1870 the older brothers were gone from the census. Jim and Jap Cavaness were still living at their home and their occupation was noted as cattle raising. 1860 Mason County, Texas, Census; 1870 Mason County, Texas, Census.

13. Gamel, 22.

14. Ibid., 23.

15. Holmes diary, March 19, 1875.

16. *San Antonio Daily Herald*, August 30, 1875.

17. Holmes diary, March 20, 1875.

18. *San Antonio Daily Herald*, August 30, 1875.

19. Lucy A. Erath, "Memoirs of Major George Bernard Erath," *Southwestern Historical Quarterly* 26 (July 1922–April 1923): 208.

20. Holmes diary, March 19, 1875; Gamel, 23.

21. Ibid.

22. *San Antonio Daily Herald*, August 30, 1875.

23. Holmes diary, March 23, 1875.

24. Ibid., March 24, 1875.

25. Ibid., March 26, 1875.

26. Monthly Return for March 1875, Company D. AGR. TSA.

27. Holmes diary, April 8, 1875.

28. Roberts to Jones, April 15, 1875. AGR. TSA.

29. *San Antonio Daily Herald*, April 22, 1875; Holmes diary, April 24, 1875.

30. Gamel, 23.

31. 1875 Mason County Tax Records. During 1875 Williamson was assessed for thirty acres of land, valued at $30, seven horses at $245, 220 cattle at $1,100, miscellaneous property valued at $60, and a single town lot valued at $1,200.

32. 1875 Tax Records, Mason County, Texas.

33. Gamel, 23.

34. Ibid.

35. Doell interview.

36. *Austin Daily Statesman*, October 17, 1875.

37. Ibid.

38. Johann Anton Wohrle was born in Weil der Stadt, Wurtemberg, Germany, on November 14, 1845. Emigration records indicate that in July 1847 his family left Germany for the United States. On January 24, 1864, Wohrle enlisted in Troop B, Third Regiment, U. S. Cavalry, at Cleveland, Ohio. During his service he was promoted to corporal prior to his discharge at Fort Craig, New Mexico, on January 27, 1867. When Wohrle arrived in Mason from New Mexico is uncertain, but on October 4, 1871, he was arrested by state policeman M. V. Bridges on a miscellaneous charge. On August 5, 1872, Wohrle married Helene Geistweidt at Willow Creek. When Wohrle became deputy sheriff is unknown, but he appears to have served under J. J. Finney as well as Clark. He also supplemented his income by working as a carpenter. Lucia Holmes noted in her diary for April 24 that "John Wordly [*sic*] commenced to work on our porch." Wohrle was not a wealthy man. The tax rolls for 1873 indicate that he owned a town lot in Mason valued at thirty dollars and miscellaneous merchandise valued at ten dollars. Military record of John Anton Wohrle, courtesy National Archives, Washington, D.C.; State Police Arrests ledger. AGR, TSA; DeVos, *Hilda Church Records*, 46; Nelson Geistweidt, *Geistweidt Family History* (Doss, TX: Privately published, 1971), 7; Mason County, Texas, Tax Rolls. 1873–1874.

39. According to historian Peter R. Rose, Karl Lehmberg was charged by one local historian as being a mob organizer, but the known actions on his part refute this. Karl Friedrich Lehmberg was born in Bodenstadt, Braunschweig, Germany, on August 7, 1833, to Heinrich Conrad Lehmberg and his wife Anna Dorothea Elizabeth Lampe. Lehmberg, along with four brothers and a sister, came to Texas in the early 1850s. He held considerable ranch holdings in the Castell area. Lehmberg was a wealthy merchant and

cattleman as evidenced by an article from the *San Antonio Daily Herald* of June 15, 1875.

> If anyone is laboring under the hallucination that Western Texas is light in the export business the [Austin] Statesman wishes to correct them in the delusion. We yesterday met Mr. Carl Lehmberg, of Castel, Llano county, one of the largest and most enterprising merchants of northwestern Texas. He has this season shipped to Wm. Brueggerhoff, of this city, 30,000 pounds of Texas bacon and oceans of lard, and he will soon ship 60,000 pounds of wool.

40. Rose and Sherry, *The Hoo-Doo War*, 92.
41. *San Antonio Daily Herald*, August 30, 1875.
42. DeVos, *Mason County Historical Book*, Supplement III, 64.
43. *San Antonio Daily Express*, May 22, 1875.
44. Holmes diary, May 14, 1875.
45. Doell interview.
46. James B. Gillett, *Six Years With The Texas Rangers* (1925; repr., Lincoln: University of Nebraska Press, 1976), 47.
47. Gamel, 20.
48. Holmes diary, May 14, 15, 1875.
49. *San Antonio Daily Herald*, August 30, 1875.
50. Holmes diary, May 17, 1875.
51. *San Antonio Daily Herald*, August 30, 1875.
52. Holmes diary, May 18, 1875.
53. Holmes diary, May 24, 1875; Roberts to Jones, May 30, 1875. AGR. TSA.
54. *San Antonio Daily Herald*, May 25, 1875.
55. Letter Press Book. Steele to John B. Berry, May 31, 1875. AGR. TSA.
56. *San Antonio Daily Herald*, August 18, 1875.

Chapter 6

1. Roberts, *Rangers and Sovereignty*, 90.
2. Ibid.
3. Ibid.
4. *Galveston News*, August 4, 1875.
5. *San Antonio Daily Herald*, August 30, 1875.
6. Mathias Cooley was born February 1, 1818, to James and Elizabeth Goode Cooley. James died while Mathias was still young. 1850 Izard County, Arkansas, Census; Cooley family genealogical information, courtesy Vickie Bonner.

7. 1878 Description of Fugitives, AGR; *Austin Daily Statesman*, January 4, 1876.

8. Executive Record Book: Richard M. Coke, TSA.

9. 1860 Jack County, Texas, Census.

10. *Austin Daily Statesman*, October 17, 1875.

11. Charles Goodnight and others, *Pioneer Days in the Southwest from 1850 to 1879* (Guthrie, OK: The State Capital Company, 1909), 278.

12. Hunter, *The Trail Drivers of Texas*, 414.

13. Allen Lee Hamilton, *Sentinel of the Southern Plains* (Fort Worth: Texas Christian University Press, 1988), 240. A facsimile of the petition is reproduced in the appendix. The name of T. Tooley is clearly legible.

14. *Dallas Herald*, February 10, 1872.

15. *Galveston Christian Advocate*, May 29, 1872.

16. Thomas F. Horton, *History of Jack County* (Jacksboro, TX: Gazette Publishing Co., n. d.), 124–25; 1870 Mortality Schedule, Jack County, Texas; M. K. Kellogg, Llerena Friend, ed, *M. K. Kellogg's Texas Journal 1872* (Austin: University of Texas Press, 1967), 86.

17. Gillett, *Six Years With The Texas Rangers,* 47.

18. Hotel register of the Grand Central, Ellsworth, Kansas, courtesy Chuck Parsons.

19. Considering the distance involved, Cooley had obviously come to the Hill Country for a distinct reason, probably to be close to Tim Williamson. Ranger life offered him a chance at immediate employment. Texas Ranger Muster Rolls. AGR. TSA.

20. This is disputed by historian Robert W. Stephens who places Cooley's birth around 1852, stating further that the entry for the Cooleys on the 1860 census "is so inaccurate that it is of only limited historical value." No rationale for this assertion is provided. "Muster and Pay Rolls of Company D," AGR, TSA; Robert W. Stephens, *Bullets and Buckshot in Texas* (Dallas, TX: Privately published, 2002), 19, 25.

21. C. R. Perry, Kenneth Kesselus, ed., *Memoir of Capt'n C. R. Perry of Johnson City, Texas—A Texas Veteran* (Austin, TX: Jenkins Publishing Company, 1990), 29. C. R. Perry was not a literate man and his memoirs, recorded in his later years, are at times disjointed. Perry notes in part that "Cooley and all of my Company that was with [Jones'] escort quit them and join[e]d thair one Companey and was in the fight."

22. *Houston Daily Telegraph*, July 23, 1874.

23. "Muster and Pay Rolls of Company D," AGR, TSA.

24. Elkins, "Served as a Texas Ranger," 447.

25. *Austin Daily Statesman*, November 28, 1874. William Burrell Trayweek was born August 30, 1853, at Round Rock, Texas. The 1870 census for Blanco

County notes his family living in Precinct 1. His father, Robert "Trawick," was noted as a forty-three-year-old farmer born in Alabama. His mother, Margaret, was from South Carolina. Trayweek served in Company D from May 25, 1874, through December 9, 1874. He died at Slaton, Texas, on July 27, 1942.

26. Ibid.

27. "Recollections of Nannie Moore Kinser," *Burnet Bulletin*, June 6, 1974.

28. Adjutant General's Records, Texas Ranger Muster Rolls.

29. Gillett, *Six Years with the Texas Rangers,* 47.

30. *San Antonio Daily Herald*, August 30, 1875.

31. *Austin Daily Statesman*, August 24, 1875.

32. *Galveston News*, August 4, 1875. Despite using the Germanic name Otho, the writer appears to have been an American due to his spelling of Doell's name.

33. DeVos, *Mason County Historical Book*, Supplement III, 64.

34. Sonnichsen, *Ten Texas Feuds*, 96–97.

35. Holmes diary, July 21, 1875.

36. Gamel, 16. Streeter is a small community roughly nine miles west of Mason. The community was first settled around 1855 by William Gamel and the Caveness brothers between Little and Big Bluff Creeks near Honey Creek. The settlement was originally called both the Bluff Creek and Honey Creek community. When the first post office was established on September 5, 1890, the community was named Streeter by the postmaster after early settler Samuel T. Streeter.

37. *Galveston News*, August 4, 1875.

38. *San Antonio Daily Herald*, August 30, 1875.

39. Gamel, 15.

40. Johann Heinrich Doell was born on January 22, 1842, in Prussia, possibly at Rassdorf, to Johann Adam Doell and his wife Anna Margaretha Craemer. In 1845, the Doells arrived in Texas aboard the *Geronne*. His father was described as age twenty-seven, and a farmer. Anna was a year older. Two sons were noted on the manifest: Georg and Henry, ages eight and two. Doell's father died during the winter of 1845–1846, and his mother later married Georg Anschutz. During the Civil War, Doell enlisted in Captain Alf Hunter's company from Mason County on November 18, 1861. The earliest tax records for Doell in Mason County are during 1862 when he had cattle valued at $39 and personal property valued at $200. Doell married Christiane Eckert on August 7, 1864, in Gillespie County, and they had three children. Christiane Doell died on March 2, 1869, and Doell then married Mina Kensing, who had three children after the marriage. 1850 and 1860 Gillespie County, Texas, Census; 1862 Poll Tax Records, 1870 Mason County,

Texas; Census; Gold, *Church Record Book*, 14, 120, 122, 131, 144; Doell family. data, courtesy Thomas and Susan Doell; DeVos, *Hilda Church Records*, 25, 30; Statement of Emigrants from Bremen per Brig *Geronne*; Confederate Muster Rolls. TSA.

41. *Austin Daily Statesman*, July 31, 1875.

42. Jones to William Steele, July 1, 1875. AGR. TSA.

43. Ransom Moore, categorized by one historian as a cattle raiser, Indian fighter, and frontiersman, was born in Independence County, Arkansas, on March 13, 1823. His father, William Moore, brought the family to Texas in 1834, and two of his brothers fought in the Texas Revolution. Like others involved in the feud, Moore was a member of Bieberstein's company during the Civil War. Toward the end of the war he moved to Kimble County and was highly regarded in the region. Evidence suggests that the Rangers briefly investigated the assertion and discarded Moore as a suspect on any charge. Moore enjoyed a good reputation in the area, the only exception being charges made by the mob faction during the feud. Fisher, *It Occurred In Kimble*, 47.

44. Doell interview. Sleepering was a method of stealing cattle by using the same ear marks as the owner. Cattle thieves would ear mark calves when they were young with the owner's mark but not brand them. During a drive, the owner would normally check the ear marks, it being easier than checking the brands when the herd was on the move. When the cattle were old enough to leave their mothers, the cattle thieves would return and place their own brand on the unbranded beef. This was particularly effective when brand laws and ear marks were controlled at the county level.

45. Ibid.

46. Records of Marks and Brands, Mason County, Texas.

47. *San Antonio Daily Herald*, August 30, 1875.

48. Hunter, "History of Mason County, Part 2," 124.

49. Jones to William Steele, July 9, 1875. AGR. TSA.

50. Holmes diary, July 25, 1875.

Chapter 7

1. Gamel, 24.

2. Ibid.

3. Charles Harcourt was born in Devonshire, England, on July 18, 1833. In 1857 he was a member of the Twelfth Royal Dragoons and fought in the Sepoy Rebellion. Following his service in the British Army, Harcourt moved to the United States in December 1861. It appears possible that Harcourt had come to the States for the opportunity to fight, for scarcely a month after his arrival in Massachusetts he enlisted in the army, serving from January

22, 1862, through April 23, 1864. Two years later he reenlisted in Troop B, Third U. S. Cavalry, and served from 1866 through 1872. Harcourt arrived in Mason sometime during 1873, possibly at the behest of Wohrle.

4. Holmes diary, August 14, 1875.

5. Gillett, *Six Years with the Texas Rangers,* 48.

6. Gamel, 24.

7. *San Antonio Daily Herald*, August 18, 1875.

8. *Galveston News*, September 7, 1875.

9. *Jacksboro Frontier Echo*, August 25, 1875.

10. *Austin Daily Statesman*, August 22, 1875.

11. *San Antonio Daily Herald*, August 30, 1875.

12. Gamel, 24.

13. DeVos, *Mason County Historical Book*, Supplement III, 65.

14. Sonnichsen, *Ten Texas Feuds*, 104.

15. DeVos, *Hilda Church Records*, 47.

16. Gillett, *Six Years with the Texas Rangers,* 48.

17. Gamel, 30.

18. *Austin Daily Statesman*, October 17, 1875.

19. Schulze, "Branded," 9.

20. DeVos, *Mason County Historical Book*, Supplement III, 65.

21. John B. Jones to Dan Roberts, October 11, 1875. AGR.

22. While Hagen's account of the feud is fictional, it was written after he interviewed a number of Mason residents. Unfortunately his notes have not been located, and it is impossible at this point to determine what he based on local testimony and what was invented from whole cloth.

23. Gillett, *Six Years with the Texas Rangers,* 48.

24. *Austin Daily Statesman*, October 17, 1875.

25. Raunick and Schade, *The Kothmanns*, 90–91.

26. Ibid.; 1870 Burnet County, Texas, census.

27. Miller's death is noted in the Masonic meeting minutes. Miller was buried on September 3, 1875. The most likely theory developed to date is that he was one of the men involved in the murder of Tim Williamson. This remains speculation, however.

28. Gamel, 26.

29. Executive Record Book: Richard M. Coke. Governor's Papers, TSA.

30. Llano County District Court Records, Cause 365.

31. Gamel, 25.

32. Roberts, *Rangers and Sovereignty*, 91–92.

33. Gamel, 25.

34. Holmes to Coke, September 8, 1875. Coke papers.

35. Dennis McCown to the author, October 17, 1999.

36. Gamel, 25.

37. Doell interview. The mutilation of Baird's body was a trademark of the Hoo Doo War. In the feud's early phases scalping and mutilation were common. This mutilation and theft of Baird's ring was also confirmed during various interviews with Foster Casner and Todd Faris whose grandfathers were among those who recovered the body.

38. *San Antonio Daily Herald*, September 14, 1875.

39. Holmes diary, September 8, 1875.

40. Governor's Papers: Holmes to Coke, September 8, 1875.

41. *Austin Weekly Statesman*, November 18, 1875.

42. *Galveston Daily News*, October 2, 1875.

43. Eilers, 247.

44. Personal interview, H. V. "Todd" Faris, June 24, 1983.

45. Personal interviews, Foster Casner, September 14, 1982, and H. V. "Todd" Faris, June 24, 1983. Mr. Casner heard the story from both his grandfather, John Olney, and from Sam Tanner.

46. Personal interview, Sarah Lockwood, March 27, 1989.

47. Holmes diary, September 9, 1875; Gamel, 26. This Williams may or may not have been the same man later involved in the shooting of Jim Chaney. See Chapter 8.

48. Gamel, 26.

49. Ibid., 26–27.

50. Nina Legge to the author, May 3, 1986.

51. Conversation with Glenn Hadeler, July 25, 2003. Mr. Hadeler was quoting Della Moneyhan, a sister of Jane Hoerster.

52. Personal interview with Jane Hoerster, March 8, 1994. Otto Ernest Hofmann was her father.

Chapter 8

1. Holmes to Coke, September 8, 1875. Governor's Papers.

2. Madison County, Missouri, Marriage Records, Book B.

3. 1850 Madison County, Missouri, Census. The Baird family was living in district 54. Moses B. Baird, according to his headstone, was born on September 25, 1850. His brother John is consistently listed as having been born in 1847.

4. The location of Hartshorn Baird's death has not been determined with certainty. The only Baird noted in Burleson County with similar holdings is James M. Beard who was on the tax rolls as early as 1857. In 1860 Beard owned a total of $570 in taxable property roughly equivalent to the figures noted in the census. 1860 Burleson County, Texas, Census; 1860 Burleson County, Texas, Poll Tax Records; Beard family information, courtesy Richard White.

5. Burnet County, Texas, District Court Records.

6. Burnet County, Texas, Deed Records. Volume G, 155.

7. 1870 Burnet County, Texas, Census.

8. Pay vouchers for Baird indicate that he was on active service during the period from September 8 through September 15, 1872, and was paid sixteen dollars for the eight-day period. An additional nine days of service were recorded between November 9 and November 17. In 1873, he served ten days from January 7 through 16, and between February 1 and 12 served an additional nine days, a total of forty-nine days of service during his enlistment. Texas Ranger Muster Rolls: J. R. Baird. TSA.

9. Burnet County Marriage Records, Volume C, 215.

10. 1880 Burnet County, Texas, Census.

11. Burnet County, Texas, Deed Records, Volume I, 717, 146 and 724.

12. DeVos, *Mason County Historical Book*, Supplement III, 62.

13. John and Moses Baird were indicted on June 3, 1869, on separate charges of assault and battery. On April 19, 1870, Moses Baird was again indicted for assault and battery along with Samuel McKee and William Stokes. Moses Baird entered a guilty plea on April 20 in the 1869 indictment and was fined one dollar and costs. John Baird's charge was reduced from assault and battery to assault, and he waived a jury trial and pleaded guilty. He too was fined one dollar plus costs. The remaining charge was quashed on motion of the defense council on November 30, 1870. On April 5, 1871, John Baird was charged with two counts of aggravated assault in cases 392 and 397. Burnet County, Texas, District Court Records, Cases 340, 342, 346, 392 and 397.

14. William B. McFarland was born to Samuel McFarland and Jane Pricilla Morrow around 1843 in Centerview, Missouri. His father had been a friend of Sam Houston in Tennessee. The family moved to Texas around 1849 and settled in Williamson County. By 1860 the family had moved to Burnet County where William was now living in the household of his brother, James Gillis. By 1870 William was operating a hotel in Burnet, the census noting his occupation as "hotel keeper." The McFarlands were considered among the pillars of the Burnet community. It is possible that they were related to Gladden's wife, Susan Amanda McFarland, but this has not been determined with certainty. Darrell Debo, ed., *Burnet County History*, Volume II (Burnet, TX: Burnet County Commissioners Court, 1979), 222–25; 1850 Williamson County, Texas, Census; 1860 Burnet County, Texas, Census; 1870 Burnet County, Texas, Census.

15. Martin Jasper Bolt, son of Charles Bolt and Martha Slaughter, was a half-brother of William James Bolt. Born in Polk County, Missouri, on October 7, 1841, Bolt listed his occupation as "stock raising" in the 1870 census. Living with him were his wife Mary Jane Brooks, age twenty-four, and their

one-year-old daughter Josie. The Bolt families remained in contact with each other, and the killing of Allen Bolt can hardly have set well with them. The Bolts would have shared information on events in Mason County with the Bairds. 1870 Burnet County, Texas, Census.

16. Byron Hamilton "Ham" Cavin, born ca. 1847 in Alabama, was one of the sons of William Cavin and Harriet Lamar, part of an extensive family of cattlemen. The family arrived in Burnet County between 1863 and 1866, probably after the close of the Civil War. After briefly living near Camp San Saba, the Cavins returned to Burnet County due to Indian raids and settled three miles north of Marble Falls. Ham Cavin married Amanda A. Howard on December 22, 1867. (Mrs. J. C.) Foster to the author, May 9, 1983; Debo, *Burnet County History*, Volume II, 45–47; 1870 Burnet County, Texas, Census.

17. Nathan Cavin was indicted on August 16, 1871, for theft of a beef. Bail was set at $250, but four months later, on December 13, 1871, the district attorney dropped the case. Wiley Cavin was found guilty the following year for "altering the mark and a brand of cattle," fined fifteen dollars and sentenced to one hour in jail. Bill Cavin, similarly charged on December 3, 1872, had his case dropped by the district attorney. Burnet County District Court Records, Cases 449, 557, and 558.

18. *Burnet Bulletin*, June 19 and 26, 1878.

19. More serious charges were leveled against both John Edward "Ed" and William Thomas "Bill" Cavin and one Clay Stinnett during 1874 when the men were indicted for murder in Burnet County for the killing of a man named Johnson. The same day Stinnett and Bill Cavin were also indicted for assault with intent to murder. Details concerning the murder charge indicate that Johnson had been killed on September 1, 1873. None of the men was convicted. Bill Cavin and Peter Casner were also indicted on separate counts of aggravated assault. Burnet County District Court Records, Cases 445, 765, 775, 776, and 779; 1880 Burnet County, Texas, Census; R. L. Faith to the author, August 15, 1983. Little is known of Clay Stinnett.

Ed Cavin was described as "about 24 years of age, 5 feet 11 inches high, slender form, weighs about 160 pounds, brown hair, blue eyes and regular features, wears a brown moustache, and travels from Burnet county to the Rio Grande, frequently in Kimble, Mason, and Gillespie counties." Bill Cavin was "about 22 years of age, near 6 feet high, weighs some 200 pounds, dark complexion, black hair, brown eyes, no beard, has youthful but homely features; ranges through the counties of San Saba, Mason, Gillespie, and to the Rio Grande." *1878 Fugitives From Justice*, 36.

20. Samuel Young Olney was born on September 9, 1845, in Burleson County, one of ten children. It was in Burleson County that the family first

met the Bairds. Around 1860, the family moved to Burnet County where their last two children were born. It appears probable that the Bairds accompanied them in this move. Unlike the Bairds, the Olneys were considerably well off. By 1850 their land alone was valued at $2,881.

Sam Olney and his brother John had both served in the war. The brothers had enlisted in a joint company for frontier defense from Burnet, Llano, Mason, and San Saba Counties along with A. G. Roberts. John Olney later enlisted in Company A, Morgan's Texas Cavalry, on March 26, 1862. Sam remained with the Rangers until they were mustered into J. E. McCord's Company K, Mounted Volunteers, on July 2, 1863. Like the Bairds, the Olneys were hot-tempered men. Samuel Olney had been in court in Burnet as early as April 17, 1867, charged in an unspecified cause 119. The district attorney dropped the case on that day, but over the ensuing years, particularly during the Reconstruction period, the Olneys were frequently in court. 1840 Yalobusha County, Mississippi, Census; James H. Olney, *A Genealogy of the Descendants of Thomas Olney* (Providence, RI: E. L. Freeman & Son, 1889), 92; Sophie Olney Haynes manuscript, courtesy Iru Zeller; Burleson County Deed Records, Volume AP, 96; 1850 Burleson County, Texas, Census; "Ranger of the Sixties," *Frontier Times* (October 1923): 27; John T. Olney, Soldier's Application for Pension, Number 40122; Samuel Olney War Record, TSA; Burnet County District Court Records, Cases 119, 288, 293, and 307.

21. John Peters Ringo was born to Martin and Mary Ringo on May 3, 1850, in Wayne County, Indiana. The family moved to Missouri in 1856 where Martin engaged in the mercantile business. In 1864 Martin Ringo was accidentally killed while en route to California. John Peters Ringo supported his family, remaining in California through 1870 and working as a ranch and farm hand. In 1871 he returned briefly to Missouri leaving his family provided for with a boarding house. There he informally continued his education while working in family members' mercantile business. By 1872 his brother, Martin Albert, had contracted tuberculosis and was unable to work. His mother was forced to sell the boarding house, and John Ringo headed for Texas in hopes of making enough money in the blossoming cattle trade to provide financial support for his family. Ringo may be the "John Ringer" who appears in the San Saba County tax rolls for 1872 and 1873. The rolls note him as having 102 acres of land valued at $500, five horses valued at $300, twenty-five cattle valued at $125, $575 in personal estate and $150 of "miscellaneous" property. He was drawn to the area by the presence of family friends, such as Green Caudle, and kinsmen such as Isaac Jones. 1850 Wayne County, Indiana, Census; *Liberty Tribune*, September 12, 1856; 1860 Davies County, Missouri, Census; Mary Ringo, *The Journal of Mrs. Mary Ringo* (Santa Ana, CA: Privately printed, 1956), *passim*; *Liberty Tribune*,

September 16, 1864; Mary Enna Ringo to David Leer Ringo, January 4, 1935, copy in author's files; 1870 Santa Clara County, California, Census; San Jose City Directory 1871–1872, 299; David Johnson, *John Ringo* (Stillwater, OK: Barbed Wire Press, 1996), 12–44, 47–48; Era Fay Huff, "Ringo Genealogy," letter to the editor, *True West* (July 1988): 6; 1872, 1873 San Saba County, Texas, Tax Records.

22. Tombstone *Daily Epitaph*, July 18, 1882; Tombstone *Weekly Epitaph*, July 22, 1882. These articles detailed John Ringo's suicide.

23. Burnet County District Court Records, Case 854.

24. Debo, *Burnet County History*, Volume II, 41; 1870 Burnet County, Texas, Census. John Wardlow Calvert was born September 17, 1848, to Hugh Hudson Calvert and Louisa Pearson. Calvert married Mary Jane Carruth on January 17, 1866, in Burnet.

25. The Tanners were one of the wealthiest families in Burnet. John Allen Tanner, scion of the clan, was born in Virginia in 1799 to Jonathon Tanner and Mary Young in Mecklenburg County. Tanner married Ann Kirkpatrick around 1818 and had a daughter, Mary Katherine, who married Joseph Olney. By 1840 Tanner was living in Yalobusha County, Mississippi. Tanner owned thirty-four slaves at the time. In 1843 he is known to have loaned Joseph Olney $1,414.32, a clear indication of the family's wealth. By 1850 Tanner had moved to Burleson County where he was also engaged in farming. The family was there for the 1860 census when Tanner's real estate was valued at $1636 and personal estate at $1040. His wife owned personal estate valued at $12,000. The family moved to Burnet after selling all of their slaves.

The Tanners' friendship with the Bairds is evidenced by the burial of Moses Baird in the Tanner cemetery plot. Lucy "Mackie" Tanner, one of John Tanner's daughters, married Dr. John Luther Hansford on January 8, 1874. Hansford had served with the Olney brothers during the Civil War. Hansford's sympathies were with the Bairds, and he rendered medical attention to the men when necessary. The Tanners also had legal problems in Burnet County. Mecklenberg County, Virginia, marriage records; Brunswick County, Virginia, Marriage Records; Tanner family Bible records, courtesy Edward Tatum; Nina L. Olney to the author, June 7, 2000; Descendants of John A. Tanner, genealogy report, courtesy Nina L. Olney; Yalobusha County, Mississippi, Deed Records, Book I, 10; 1840 Yalobusha County, Mississippi, Census; 1850 and 1860 Burleson County, Texas, Census; undated interview, H. V. "Todd" Faris; Personal interview, H. V. "Todd" Faris, June 24, 1983; Burnet County District Court Records, Causes 254, 288, 336, and 464.

26. Ann Olney had married Abraham Teal Taylor. Taylor, born in Cherokee County, Alabama, in 1849 to David and Jemima Stanford Taylor, came from a wealthy family. By 1860 the Taylors were well established in Burnet. The

census identified him as a farmer with real estate valued at $6,000 and personal property valued at $2,000. His oldest son, Charles B., was noted as "stockraising." All of the older Taylor sons saw service during the war. Abe Taylor served under John Alexander in Company O of the Minute Men as a corporal along with Joe Olney. The pair enlisted on August 11, 1872. During the first month of service a detached portion of the men with some citizens successfully attacked a party of Indians and captured all of their equipment. Taylor received his discharge on August 13, 1873. At various times the Taylor brothers served as jurors in Burnet County. A. T. Taylor is recalled as a hot tempered man, a fact confirmed by court records. 1840 Cherokee County, Alabama, Census; 1850 Cherokee County, Alabama, Census; 1860 Burnet County, Texas, Census; Military records: David Taylor, Israel Taylor, C. B. Taylor and James W. Taylor; Texas Ranger Muster Rolls. TSA; Personal interview, LaVoy Taylor, July 18, 1983; Burnet County District Court Records, Causes 747, 749, 757, and 758.

27. The Faris (or Farris) brothers were the sons of Solomon Boone Faris and his wife Laurinda Hinds. Their oldest son, John B., was born in Mississippi around 1845. By 1847 the family moved to Sevier County, Arkansas, where twins, William Jasper and Champion Newton, were born on February 16, 1847. The following year they were in Texas where Benjamin A. was born on May 15, 1852. Another brother, Robert Elihu "Bud" Faris was born in Texas around 1856. There were also two daughters in the Faris family, Mary E. born around 1843 in Alabama, and Laura. The spelling of the Faris family name is often given as Farris in legal documents and newspapers of the time. Following their father's death on May 12, 1857, the family was raised in part by their uncles of whom gunfighter gambler Benjamin J. Hinds is the best known. Hinds' influence on the Faris boys was profound. Marshall County, Alabama, Marriage Records; Ina Davis to the author, February 26, 1984; Bowden, Gail H., *The Hinds Family Heritage* (Mooreville, MS: privately published, 1988), 13; 1850 Williamson County, Texas, Census; 1860 Llano County, Texas, Census; Personal interview, H. V. "Todd" Faris, June 24, 1983; *Burnet Bulletin*, July 19, 1881.

28. *Burnet Bulletin*, February 20, 1875. An identical notice appeared in the issue of February 27.

29. Burnet County District Court Records, Case 879.

30. Steele to Jones, September 23, 1875. Letter Press Book 401-622. AGR.

31. Holmes to Coke, September 24, 1875. Governor's papers. AGR.

32. Gamel, 23; Holmes diary, September 25, 1875.

33. Andes Henry Murchison was the son of Daniel Alexander Murchison and Wilheminna Adolphena Holzgreve and was born March 9, 1855, in New

Braunfels. His father was a land agent and surveyor. Like others in the Baird faction, Murchison was a cattleman. He had started driving cattle at an early age and is credited with making twelve drives to Kansas while a young man in addition to being one of the builders of Menard, Texas. In 1870 the Murchison family was living in Llano County where the census indicates combined personal and real estate valued at $12,000. Martha Gilliland Long, ed., *Llano County Family Album* (Llano, TX: Llano County Historical Society. 1989), 217; "Builders of Menard," *Frontier Times* 4, no. 11 (August 1927): 3; 1870 Llano County, Texas, Census.

34. Mason County, Texas, District Clerk Records, Case 21.

35. Gamel, 27.

36. Krueger, 108.

37. Glenn Hadeler to the author, summer 2000; *Mason County Historical Book*, 213. Adolph Albert Reichenau, born November 16, 1824, at Frankfurt am Main, Germany, had come to New York in the late 1830s. Reichenau headed for Texas during the mid-1840s and fought in the Third Company, Fourth Regiment, of the Louisiana Militia during the war with Mexico. Later he joined the Texas Mounted Volunteers and served under Jack Hays. Following the war, Reichenau stayed on as a Ranger based at Castell. On October 16, 1848, he married Katherine Arhelger at Fredericksburg. He had known Tim Williamson from when the family lived in Kimble County. In 1868 the family was forced by increasing Indian depredations to return to Hedwig's Hill.

38. Jones to Steele, September 28, 1875. AGR.

39. Mrs. D. W. "Lou" Roberts. *A Woman's Reminiscences of Six Years in Camp with the Texas Rangers* (Austin, TX: Von Boeckmann-Jones Co, ca. 1928), 7.

40. Jones to Steele, September 28, 1875. AGR.

41. Holmes diary, September 28, 1875.

42. Interview with Jane Hoerster, March 5, 1984.

43. Gamel, 29.

44. 1870 Mason County, Texas, Census.

45. Gamel, 27–28.

46. Mrs. D. W. Roberts, 8.

47. Undated personal interview with Jane Hoerster.

48. Della Hofmann Moneyhon, "August Wilhelm Hofmann," in Mason County Historical Commission, *Mason County Historical Book*, Supplement I (Mason, TX: Mason County Historical Commission), 69.

49. Gamel, 28.

50. Personal interview with Walker Jordan, July 7, 1989.

51. Gamel, 29.

52. Ibid.

53. Little is known of Bill Coke. The 1870 census describes him as age twenty-five which places his birth around 1845. At the time of the census he gave his occupation as "laborer." He was living in John Gamel's household. On September 12, 1870, he had enlisted as a private in Company 1 of the Frontier Forces under James M. Hunter. Coke served until January 24, 1871. 1870 Mason County, Texas, Census; Ranger Muster Rolls.

54. Holmes diary, September 18, 1875.

55. Jones to Steele, September 30, 1875, AGR.

56. Holmes diary, September 30, 1875.

57. Gamel, 29. Isaac A. Beam was the son of Jacob Beam and was born May 28, 1850, in Shelby, North Carolina. Beam came to Texas around 1870 and married Louise Hays, born August 20, 1854. He died in Mason County on August 2, 1938.

58. Roberts, 91; Holmes diary, October 3, 1875.

59. Doell interview.

60. Ischar had come to Texas with the Eckert family. He married Elisabetha Eckert on May 1, 1853, at Fredericksburg. The couple later settled in Simonsville where ten children were born. *Mason County Historical Book*, 114; *Church Record Book*, 19, 104.

61. *San Antonio Express*, October 6, 1875.

62. *Galveston Daily News*, October 12, 1875.

63. *San Antonio Daily Herald*, October 11, 1875.

Chapter 9

1. Holmes diary, October 4, 1875.

2. King, *John O. Meusebach*, 169.

3. Petition, citizens of Loyal Valley to Jones, October 4, 1875, AGR.

4. DeVos, *Mason County Historical Book*, Supplement III, 66.

5. Monthly Return, Record of Scouts. Company D. September, 1875, AGR.

6. Gillett, *Six Years with the Texas Rangers,* 49–50.

7. Special Order No. 47, October 7, 1875. AGR.

8. Special Order No. 48, October 11, 1875. AGR.

9. Holmes diary, October 14, 1875; Holmes Attorney Book.

10. Ralph Emerson Twitchell, ed., *The Leading Facts of New Mexican History*, Vol. 3 (Cedar Rapids, IA: The Torch Press, 1917), 451.

11. Holmes diary, October 5, 1875.

12. Jones to Roberts, October 16, 1875, AGR.

13. Roberts to Jones, October 17, 1875, AGR.

14. Jones to Roberts, October 18, 1875, AGR.

15. Steele to Jones, October 14, 1875, AGR.

16. Jones to Steele, October 20, 1875, AGR.

17. Steele to Jones, October 22, 1875, AGR.

18. Jones to Roberts, October 11, 1875, AGR.

19. Jones to Steele, October 12, 1875, AGR.

20. Jones to Steele, October 28, 1875, AGR.

21. Jones to Steele, October 20, 1875, AGR.

22. Gamel, 32.

23. Jones to Steele, October 28, 1875, AGR.

24. *San Antonio Daily Herald*, October 11, 1875.

25. Long, *Llano County Family Album*, 211–15; 1870 Llano County, Texas, Census; Odie Minatre, "Sole Survivor of Packsaddle Mountain Fight," *Frontier Times* 15, no. 5 (February 1938): 197; James R. Moss, "James R. Moss," unpublished manuscript, courtesy Llano County Historical Society, copy in author's collection. In 1819, Moss moved from Tennessee to Texas. During the Texas Revolution he fought at San Jacinto. In 1838 he married Mary Ann Boyce. In 1857 the family moved to Llano County where they ranched. Moss had a number of children, mainly sons, and the census indicates that all of them were engaged in stock raising. Three of them participated in the Packsaddle Mountain fight on August 5, 1873, in Llano County.

26. O'Neil, *They Die,* 92–96.

27. Jones to Coldwell, October 25, 1875. Devil's River, where Ake claimed to have been, is an intermittent stream that rises in southwestern Sutton County. In close proximity is the headwater of the North Llano River, which rises in west central Sutton County and runs generally east where it joins the South Llano just east of Junction in Kimble County.

28. *Galveston Daily News,* June 15, 1877.

29. Ibid., October 12, 1875.

30. Barler, *Early Days,* 31.

31. Jones to Roberts, October 21, 1875, AGR.

32. Jones to Steele, October 23, 1875, AGR.

33. Cora Melton Cross, "Ira Long, Cowboy And Texas Ranger," *Frontier Times* 8, no. 1, 22. Born May 27, 1842, in Indiana, Ira Long was raised in northwest Missouri. Long had served as a lieutenant in the Confederate Army. Following the war he settled in Wise County where he married Julia Adams.

34. Texas Ranger Muster Rolls, TSA.

35. Holmes diary, October 23, 1875; October 25, 1875.

36. Ibid., October 26, 1875.

37. *San Antonio Daily Express*, October 23, 1875.

38. Steele to Long, November 6, 1875.

Chapter 10

1. Holmes diary, October 29, 1875.

2. *San Antonio Herald*, November 6, 1875. The letter was also quoted in the *Galveston Daily News* of November 10, 1875.

3. Ibid., November 12, 1875.

4. Holmes diary, 111; Masonic Lodge Records.

5. Gamel, 21–22.

6. *San Antonio Daily Express*, November 23, 1875.

7. Roberts to Jones, November 15, 1875, AGR.

8. *Galveston Daily News*, December 3, 1875.

9. *San Antonio Daily Herald*, November 3, 1875; the *Dallas Weekly Herald*, November 13, 1875.

10. Holmes diary, November 8, 1875; Holmes Attorney Book, 23.

11. *Austin Daily Democratic Statesman*, November 18, 1875.

12. *San Antonio Daily Express*, November 10, 1875.

13. Ibid., November 23, 1875.

14. Gamel, 30; Holmes Attorney Book, 24.

15. *San Antonio Daily Express*, November 25, 1875.

16. Company A, Record of Scouts, November, 1875. AGR.

17 *Galveston Daily News*, November 23, 1875.

18. *Galveston Daily News*, December 3, 1875.

19. *San Antonio Daily Express*, November 23, 1875.

20. Company A, Record of Scouts, November, 1875. AGR.

21. Holmes diary, November 20, 1875.

22. *San Antonio Daily Express*, November 30, 1875.

23. Parsons and Little, *Captain L. H. McNelly*, 227–46; Chuck Parsons, *"Pidge" A Texas Ranger From Virginia* (Wolfe City, TX: Hennington Publishing Company, 1985), 87–91.

24. *Galveston Daily News*, December 3, 1875.

25. *The Story of A Century: St. Paul's Lutheran Church, Mason, Texas* (Mason, TX: Privately published, 1972), 33–34.

26. *Galveston Daily News*, December 3, 1875.

27. Long, *Llano County Family Album*, 172.

28. *Galveston Daily News*, December 3, 1875.

29. *Austin Daily Statesman*, December 4, 1875.

30. Burnet County District Court Records, Causes 669, 672, 673, 676, 681, 682, and 683.

31. Fisher, *It Occurred in Kimble*, 51–52.

32. Ibid., 52.

33. Holmes Letter Press Book, Bierschwale Collection, TSA.

34. Records for Madison County indicate that James P. Mason, a farmer, was living in the county during 1870. Mason was listed as age twenty-three with an estate valued at $2000. His birthplace is given as Mississippi. From the

census data it appears that the family arrived in Texas around 1852 or 1853. *1878 Fugitives From Justice*, 97; 1860 Madison County, Texas, Census; 1870 Madison County, Texas, Census; 1850 Lauderdale County, Mississippi, Census.

35. Records for Walker County show a James Mason, aged sixty-four, living there. Mason had an estate valued at $2500. Living with Mason were Ann, age thirty-two, either his wife or daughter, noted as keeping house and son James, nineteen, listed as a farmer. The Masons were all born in Kentucky. The older Mason died in Walker County on October 18, 1873. 1870 Walker County, Texas, Census; Montgomery County, Kentucky, Marriage Records; *1878 Fugitives From Justice*, 37–38.

36. Further complicating the situation is the belief of historian Ed Bartholomew that Mason had also operated in the Sutton-Taylor War and was one of the men who killed Wiley W. Pridgen in 1873 in company with Bill Sutton and three other men. *1878 Fugitives From Justice*, 162; Chuck Parsons to the author, August 25, 1994.

37. Todd to Jones, December 14, 1875. AGR.

38. Burnet County District Court Records, Causes 925 and 926.

39. *Austin Daily Statesman*, January 2, 1876; *San Antonio Daily Express*, January 5, 1876.

40. Long, *Llano County Family Album*, 94–95; Tise, 76; 1850 Jackson County, Missouri Census. John Clymer was the son of Simon and Jane McAfee Clymer and was born December 17, 1841, in Marshall County, Tennessee.

41. John J. Strickland was the son of Joseph Strickland who was then living in Bell County. Strickland was born in Indiana around 1855. The 1880 Travis County census noted that he was twenty-five and married to Kate Martin.

42. *Austin Daily Statesman*, January 4, 1876; *Austin Weekly Statesman*, January 6, 1876.

43. *Dallas Daily Herald*, January 6, 1876; *Dallas Weekly Herald*, January 8, 1876.

44. *Galveston Daily News*, January 6, 1876; *San Antonio Daily Express*, January 7, 1876.

45. Long to Jones, January 6, 1876, AGR.

46. Long to Steele, January 28, 1876, AGR.

47. Krueger, 108.

48. Ibid., 108–9.

49. Gamel, 31.

50. Krueger, 108–9.

51. *Galveston Daily News*, January 28, 1876.

52. *Austin Daily Statesman*, January 21, 1876; *San Antonio Daily Herald*, January 21, 1876.

53. *Cases Argued and Adjudged in the Court of Appeals of the State of Texas* II (St. Louis, MO: The Gilbert Book Co., 1878), 510.

54. Long to Jones, January 15, 1876, AGR.

55. *Austin Daily Statesman*, January 21, 1876.

Chapter 11

1. Jordan and Jordan, *Jordan Pioneers*, 37–38.

2. 1880 Burnet County, Texas, Census.

3. Resolutions of January 26, 1876, Hunter to Steele, AGR.

4. *Galveston Daily News*, January 22, 1876.

5. Long to Jones, January 31, 1876, AGR.

6. *Austin Daily Statesman*, February 1, 1876.

7. *Galveston Daily News*, February 3, 1876.

8. Burnet County District Court Records, Cause 409.

9. Ibid., Causes 775, 749, 906, 873, 923, and 924. The murder charge against Cavin was unrelated to the Hoo Doo War. He, his brother Bill, and Clay Stinnett had been charged with killing a man named Johnson. Details on this incident have not been located to date.

10. Ibid. The cause is also noted in the *1878 Fugitives From Justice*, page 38, which notes only Baird and Whittington. For Baird the entry notes in part that "When last heard from he was living in Bexar county, west of San Antonio."

11. Ibid., Cause 854.

12. *Galveston Daily News*, February 9, 1876.

13. Long to Jones, February 13, 1876, AGR.

14. Doole to Jones, February 17, 1876, AGR.

15. Long to Jones, February 28, 1876, AGR.

16. *Report of the Adjutant-General of the State of Texas for the Year Ending August 31st, 1876* (Galveston, TX: Shaw & Blaylock, State Printers, 1876), 7–9.

17. *Dallas Weekly Herald*, January 29, 1876.

18. Miles Barler was born on January 29, 1833, at Johnstown, Ohio, to John Barler and his second wife, Catherine Lee. He moved to Texas in 1849 and to Llano County during 1857, and on February 28, 1858, he married Jane Buttery. During the Civil War Barler enlisted in the Llano State Guards on September 14, 1861, for a term of one year and later joined the Confederate army. The final entry in his military record indicates that he deserted at Piedmont Springs on April 13, 1865. By 1870, Barler was noted as a cattle raiser with four children. His concern over stock theft was understandable, and by his own admission he willingly joined the Llano mob whose membership included Peter Bader. Barler, *Early Days, passim*; Long, *Llano County*

Family Album, 58; Miles Barler Papers, University of Texas, Austin, Texas, hereafter cited as Barler Papers. J. P. Blessington, *The Campaigns of Walker's Texas Division* (Austin, TX: The Pemberton Press, 1968), 173–74; Confederate Muster Rolls; Military Record: Miles Barler, National Archives, Washington, D. C.; 1870 Llano County, Texas, Census; Indian Depredations Claim Number 6608, U. S. Court of Claims.

19. The Dublin brothers have been more associated with Kimble County than Llano. Closely associated with Dick Dublin were his brothers, James Roland "Roll," born April 7, 1856, and Dell, born March 17, 1857. Gillett, *Six Years with the Texas Rangers*, 87–88; *1878 Fugitives From Justice*, 15, 162.

20. Debo, *Burnet County History* Vol. II, 41.

21. *Galveston Daily News*, March 11, 1876.

22. *San Antonio Daily Herald*, March 9, 1876.

23. *Houston Daily Telegraph*, March 11, 1876.

24. Doole to Jones, March 6, 1876, AGR.

25. Long to Jones, March 19, 1876, AGR.

26. San Marcos *West Texas Free Press*, February 26, 1876.

27. *Houston Daily Telegraph*, March 15, 1876.

28. Jeff Jackson, "Victim of Circumstance: Albertus Sweet Sheriff of Lampasas County, Texas, 1874–1878," NOLA *Quarterly* 20, no. 3 (July–September 1996): 14; 1870 Lampasas County, Texas, Census.

29. H. V. "Todd" Faris interview with author, June 24, 1983.

30. Holmes diary, April 5, 1876.

31. DeVos, *Mason County Historical Book*, Supplement III, 67–68.

32. *San Antonio Daily Herald*, April 8, 1876.

33. Jones to Steele, April 15, 1876, AGR.

34. Ibid., April 3, 1876. AGR.

35. Holmes diary, April 12, 1876.

36. *Galveston Daily News*, April 28, 1876. The letter was dated from Austin on April 25, 1876.

37. Ibid., May 10, 1876.

38. San Marcos *West Texas Free Press*, May 6, 1876.

39. *Galveston Daily News*, June 28, 1876.

40. LaGrange *Fayette County New Era*, May 12, 1876.

41. *San Antonio Daily Express*, May 19, 1876.

42. Lampasas District Court Records, loose papers. Testimony of J. T. Walker. The actual cause that Walker was testifying in is unknown. Over the years the papers in the courthouse became disorganized. A number of men were brought to trial for the jail delivery in succeeding years, but only one man was actually sent to prison. From the papers located to date it ap-

pears that the witnesses may have been testifying at the trial of John Carson. Hereafter referred to as Lampasas District Court Records, loose papers.

43. Ibid.

44. *1878 Fugitives From Justice*, 78.

45. Lampasas District Court Records, loose papers. Testimony of James Newton Randle.

46. Ibid., Testimony of W. P. Hoskins.

47. Holmes diary, May 8, 1876.

48. Ibid., May 9, 1876.

49. O'Neil, *They Die*, 135–36.

50. *Galveston Daily News*, May 23, 1876.

Chapter 12

1. Gamel, 30–31.

2. *Dallas Daily Herald*, June 11, 1876.

3. *Houston Daily Telegraph*, June 14, 1876.

4. Interview with Max Gipson, February 15, 1989.

5. *San Antonio Daily Herald*, June 16, 1876.

6. *Galveston Daily News*, June 14, 1876.

7. *Houston Daily Telegraph*, June 17, 1876; *Galveston Daily News*, June 18, 1876. Both papers were quoting from the *San Saba News*.

8. *Galveston Daily News*, June 28, 1876.

9. *Burnet Bulletin*, July 14, 1876.

10. Comanche County, Texas, District Court Records, Cause 384; Robert K. DeArment, *Alias Frank Canton* (Norman: University of Oklahoma Press, 1996), 33–42. Redding was probably charged in the killing of Peter Bader although this is uncertain. Both Joe and George Horner eventually ended up in Oklahoma where Joe Horner changed his name to Frank Canton. He died on September 27, 1927.

11. *Burnet Bulletin*, July 14, 1876.

12. Comanche County, Texas, District Court Records, Cause 384.

13. *Galveston Daily News*, August 18, 1876; *Burnet Bulletin*, August 25, 1876.

14. *Burnet Bulletin*, September 1, 1876.

15. Ibid., August 25, 1876.

16. Ibid., August 11, 1876.

17. Ibid.

18. *Austin Daily Statesman*, August 26, 1876.

19. Ibid., September 13, 1876.

20. Holmes diary, September 5, 1876.

21. *Burnet Bulletin*, September 1, 1876.

22. *Galveston Daily News*, September 6, 1876.

23. Ibid., September 2, 1876.

24. M. Jourdan Atkinson and Eugene V. Giles, *Kingdom Come! Kingdom Go!* (Burnet, TX: Eakin Press, 1980), 56–57.

25. Sims had served as first sergeant in Company O of the Minute Men from Burnet County commanded by John Alexander. Between September 11, 1872, and August 13, 1873, he served sixty-seven days. C. L. Yarbrough, *Canyon of the Eagles* (no date or place), 30; Ranger Muster Rolls, AGR, TSA.

26. Thomas Jefferson Faught was born in Missouri on April 22, 1847. The 1870 Burnet County, Texas, Census shows him living with Tim Williamson and his family. There are two historical markers mentioning him at Snyder, Texas, the county seat. Faught died on August 2, 1912. 1870 and 1880 Burnet County, Texas, Census; Llano County District Court Records, Causes 366 and 368; Burnet County Marriage Records, Book D; historical markers at Snyder, Texas.

27. *Burnet Bulletin*, September 8, 1876.

28. Ibid., September 15, 1876.

29. *Galveston Daily News*, September 16, 1876.

30. *Houston Daily Telegraph*, September 16, 1876.

31. *Austin Daily Statesman*, September 17, 1876.

32. *Austin Daily Statesman*, September 15, 1876.

33. *Burnet Bulletin*, July 28, 1876.

34. James Williams, born around 1852, married Arabelle Lacy in Burnet on December 7, 1873. The Lacy family were old pioneers of Burnet County. Burnet County Marriage Records, Books A and C; 1870 Burnet County, Texas, Census.

35. *Burnet Bulletin*, September 15, 1876.

36. Ibid.

37. *West Texas Free Press*, September 16, 1876.

38. Barler, *Early Days,* 33.

39. *West Texas Free Press*, September 30, 1876.

40. Gillett, *Six Years with the Texas Rangers,* 88.

41. Fisher, *It Occurred in Kimble,* 216.

42. Barler, *Early Days,* 34.

43. Ibid., 35–36.

44. Ibid., 40–42.

45. *Galveston Daily News*, October 5, 1876.

46. Barler, *Early Days,* 42.

47. *Galveston Daily News*, September 27, 1876.

48. Barler, *Early Days,* 42.

49. *Galveston Daily News*, September 28, 1876.

Chapter 13

1. *Burnet Bulletin*, September 15, 1876.

2. Parsons and Little, *Captain L. H. McNelly*, 109–12.

3. *Burnet Bulletin*, September 15, 1876.

4. Ibid.

5. The identity of F. S. is a matter of speculation. The Burnet Census for 1870 notes several possibilities. One was F. M. Slaughter, a farmer born in Alabama, noted as age thirty-six. Another was F. R. Smith, also a farmer, whose age was given as forty-one. A more likely candidate is Felix Smith. Bob Rowntree would later marry Smith's daughter, Betty. Alternatively the author could have been Felix Smith Rowntree, another brother of Wilson Rowntree, born to James Lewis and Martha Ann in 1852. The matter remains unresolved. *Burnet Bulletin*, September 22, 1876; 1870 Burnet County, Texas, 1870.

6. Interview with Foster Casner, August 1982.

7. Ibid.; interview with Jim McFarland, August 1982.

8. *West Texas Free Press*, October 7, 1876; *Galveston Daily News*, October 11, 1876.

9. *Burnet Bulletin*, September 22, 1876.

10. *West Texas Free Press*, October 7, 1876.

11. *Galveston Daily News*, October 14, 1876.

12. Ibid.

13. Ann Tanner, a sister of Mary K. Tanner Olney, married William Erwin, possibly the son of Samuel A. Erwin and Mercy Tilson, who was born at Unicoi, Tennessee. Erwin is believed to have been a Masonic organizer. Like the Olneys and Tanners, the Erwins had settled in Burleson County on their arrival in Texas, and the census notes "William Ervin" aged twenty-seven, born in Tennessee with a value on his holdings fixed at $2600. By 1860 the family had moved to Smith County where Erwin's personal and real estate were now valued at $5200. The Erwins joined the Olneys and Tanners by 1870. William Erwin was dead by this time, but Ann was noted living in Precinct 1 with her four youngest children. Haynes manuscript; 1850 Burleson County, Texas, Census; 1860 Smith County, Texas, Census; 1860 Smith County Mortality Schedule; 1870 Burnet County, Texas, Census.

14. *Galveston Daily News*, October 21, 1876.

15. *West Texas Free Press*, October 28, 1876.

16. *Galveston Daily News*, October 26, 1876.

17. Haynes manuscript.

18. Convict Record Ledger, Huntsville Penitentiary, Walker County, Texas. TSA.

19. *Austin Daily Statesman*, October 28, 1876.

20. Ibid.

21. John Thorpe, "Ben and Billy Thompson: Their Documented Origins," *Brand Book* (of the English Westerners' Society) 23, no. 1 (Winter 1984): 9–10.

22. *Austin Daily Statesman*, November 7, 1876; *Burnet Bulletin*, November 14, 1876.

23. Ibid.; *Houston Daily Telegraph*, November 9, 1876.

24. *Burnet Bulletin*, November 14, 1876.

25. *Austin Daily Statesman*, November 7, 1876.

26. *Burnet Bulletin*, November 14, 1876.

27. Ibid., December 15, 1876.

28. Interviews with John Olney, June 1, 1983, and January 10, 1985.

29. *Burnet Bulletin*, December 1, 1876.

30. *Galveston Daily News*, December 3, 1876.

31. *Burnet Bulletin*, December 8, 1876. The paper reported that "Mr. Gladden is a man of about thirty years of age, dark hair inclined to curl, large dark eyes, a large roman nose, and wears a heavy black moustache, the only beard upon his face, a little over the medium height, rather corpulent, and we presume would weigh about one hundred and seventy or eighty pounds."

32. Ibid.

33. Ibid.

34. Ibid., December 15, 1876.

35. Ibid.; Monthly return, Company C, December, 1876.

36. *Burnet Bulletin*, December 22, 1876.

37. Ibid.

Chapter 14

1. *Burnet Bulletin*, January 12, 1877.

2. James Henry Hoy was one of twelve children of James Kindred and Sarah Brown Hoy and was born October 5, 1857. Hoy's family hailed from Tennessee, but by 1860 the family was living in Llano County. The 1870 census indicates that the elder Hoy was a stockraiser. *Austin Daily Statesman*, August 19, 1877; Monthly Return, Company C, January 1877, AGR; 1870 Llano County, Texas, Census.

3. *Burnet Bulletin*, January 26, 1876.

4. *West Texas Free Press*, January 27, 1877.

5. Monthly Return, Company C, January 1877, AGR.

6. *San Antonio Daily Express*, February 13, 1877.

7. Steele to F. T. Nicholls, January 25, 1877, AGR.

8. Monthly Return, Company C, January 1877, AGR.

9. Sparks to Jones, February 12, 1877, AGR.

10. *West Texas Free Press*, March 3, 1877.

11. Burton to Jones, February 22, 1877, AGR.

12. Waddell to Jones, February 27, 1877, AGR.

13. Dolan to Jones, February 17, 1877, AGR.

14. Judge A. M. McFarland to Jones, March 27, 1877, AGR.

15. Jones to Holmes, March 31, 1877, AGR.

16. Judge W. A. Blackburn to Jones, March 31, 1877, AGR.

17. Jones to Sparks, April 2, 1877, AGR.

18. Jones to Blackburn, April 2, 1877, AGR.

19. Blackburn to Jones, April 6, 1877, AGR.

20. Jones to Dolan, April 11, 1877, AGR.

21. Jones to Moore, April 11, 1877, AGR.

22. Jones to Fattin and Schreiner, April 11, 1877, AGR.

23. Monthly Return, Company A, April 30, 1877; Monthly Return, Company F, April 30, 1877, AGR.

24. Jones to Steele, May 6, 1877, AGR.

25. List of arrests made during the month of April 1877, Company A, AGR.

26. Monthly Return, Company A, April 30, 1877, AGR.

27. Monthly Return, Company A, May 31, 1877, AGR.

28. Monthly Return, Company D, May 31, 1877, AGR.

29. Telegram, Jones to Steele, May 6, 1877, AGR.

30. *Lampasas Dispatch*, May 3, 1877.

31. *Austin Weekly Statesman*, May 3, 1877.

32. Telegram, Sheriff M. B. Wilson to Jones, May 11, 1877, AGR.

Chapter 15

1. *Galveston Daily News*, May 19, 1877.

2. The Sutton-Taylor War began during Reconstruction, although there is, not surprisingly, disagreement as to the main cause. The violence pitted the forces of the Taylor family against the forces of Reconstruction government as represented by the Texas State Police led by William E. Sutton. Sonnichsen's account of the feud in *I'll Die Before I'll Run* provides one of the best general accounts of the trouble. There are a number of books that touch on the feud and various men involved in it including the works of Chuck Parsons, Leon Metz, and Richard Marohn.

3. *Galveston Daily News*, May 19, 1877.

4. T. R. Fleming to Governor R. B. Hubbard, May 15, 1877, AGR; John Hancock Lacy, narrator, "Life of John Hancock Lacy," unpublished manuscript courtesy Helen C. Marschall. In his recollections, Lacy recalled that he checked out the jail's security before the break took place. Lacy identi-

fied three of the prisoners as Mike Blakely, John Robson, and Tom Redding. Among those participating in the break were Mart Lacy, Bill Redding, and Joe Olney.

5. *Austin Daily Statesman*, May 19, 1877.

6. *Galveston Daily News*, May 22, 1877.

7. Metz, *John Wesley Hardin*, 163.

8. Robert W. Stephens, *Mannen Clements: Texas Gunfighter* (Dallas, TX: Privately published, 1996), 9–11. The son of Emanuel Clements and Martha Balch Hardin, Mannen Clements was born on February 26, 1845. Clements did have a brother named William Barnett, born September 21, 1839, but he died during the Civil War on June 22, 1862. His mother was an aunt of John Wesley Hardin.

9. "Statements made by the Kid," March 23, 1879, Wallace Collection, courtesy Indiana State Library, Indianapolis, Indiana.

10. *San Antonio Daily Express*, June 27, 1877; *Austin Daily Statesman*, July 4, 1877.

11. Jones to Peak, October 7, 1878, AGR.

12. *Galveston Daily News*, June 15, 1877.

13. Monthly Return, Company D, June 30, 1877, AGR.

14. *Austin Daily Statesman*, July 15, 1877.

15. *Galveston Daily News*, August 1, 1877.

16. Writ of Habeas Corpus, Blackburn to Jones, July 11, 1877, AGR.

17. Jones to Blackburn, July 12, 1877, AGR.

18. Jones to Coldwell, July 12, 1877, AGR.

19. Jones to Steele, July 12, 1877, AGR.

20. *Galveston Daily News*, June 29, 1877.

21. *Austin Daily Statesman*, August 29, 1877.

22. Walter Lavega Wadsworth was the son of Martin Harvick and Frances C. D. Henderson Wadsworth and was born in Texas on August 20, 1854. The family originated in North Carolina where Martin Wadsworth was born on August 13, 1804. In 1870, the family was living in San Saba County. The *San Antonio Daily Express*, August 30, 1877; 1850 Rusk County, Texas, Census; 1870 San Saba County, Texas, Census; Wadsworth Family Bible.

23. Barler, *Early Days*, 45–49.

24. Ibid., 46–47.

25. *San Antonio Daily Express*, August 30, 1877.

26. Ibid.; Barler, *Early Days*, 47.

27. Barler, *Early Days*, 48.

28. *San Antonio Daily Express*, August 30, 1877.

29. Ibid., September 1, 1877.

30. Taylor was the son of William J. and Mary Cooper Taylor and was

born in Kentucky. The *Galveston Daily News*, August 30, 1877, September 15, 1877; the *San Antonio Daily Express*, September 2, 1877; B. B. Paddock, *History and Biographical Record of North and West Texas* Volume 2 (Chicago: Lewis Publishing Co., 1906), 36–37.

31. *Galveston Daily News*, September 22, 1877.
32. Company C Monthly Return, August 1877, AGR.
33. *Galveston Weekly News*, September 10, 1877.
34. Company C Monthly Return, September 1877, AGR.
35. Ibid.
36. *Austin Daily Statesman*, September 5, 1877.
37. *West Texas Free Press*, September 8, 1877.
38. Barler, *Early Days*, 49.
39. Ibid., 31.
40. *Llano County History*, 264, 266.
41. Company C Monthly Return, September 1877, AGR.
42. *San Antonio Daily Express*, September 6, 1877.
43. Report of Operations, Companies A and E, August 1877; Record of Scouts, Companies A and E, August 1877. William Murchison was born in 1852.

Chapter 16

1. *Galveston Daily News*, September 15, 1877.
2. *San Antonio Daily Express*, September 20, 1877.
3. *Lampasas Dispatch*, September 27, 1877; *Austin Daily Statesman*, October 3, 1877. The *Statesman* reported that the escape occurred in Lampasas County.
4. *Austin Daily Statesman*, September 12, 1877; *Dallas Weekly Herald*, September 15, 1877.
5. Company B Fifteen Day Report, Lt. G. W. Campbell to Jones, September 15, 1877, AGR.
6. Company C Monthly Return, October, 1877, AGR.
7. *Galveston Daily News*, November 10, 1877.
8. Convict Record Ledger, Huntsville Penitentiary, TSA. Prison records describe Johnson as age thirty-two, five feet nine inches tall, with blonde hair and blue eyes. He weighed 145 pounds and had three scars on his right arm and another on his upper lip.
9. Gillett, *Six Years with the Texas Rangers*, 103–4.
10. *San Antonio Daily Express*, November 19, 1877.
11. *Texas Capital*, December 10, 1877.
12. Company E Monthly Return, November, 1877; *Texas Capital*, November 25, 1877; *Galveston Daily News*, December 7, 1877.

13. *Galveston Daily News*, January 17, 1878; *Galveston Weekly News*, January 21, 1878.

14. G. H. Johnson to Jones, December 31, 1877, AGR.

15. Gillett, *Six Years with the Texas Rangers*, 92; Company E Monthly Return, January 1878, AGR.

16. Ibid., 93.

17. Ibid., 94–95.

18. Requisition on Choctaw Nation for A. J. alias Nat Mackey, November 27, 1877, AGR.

19. *Lampasas Dispatch*, February 7, 1878.

20. Ibid., February 14, 1878.

21. Ibid.

22. *Galveston Weekly News*, February 18, 1878.

23. George Gamel, the least known of Tom Gamel's brothers, is not mentioned by either Tom Gamel or Miles Barler in connection with the feud. George Gamel was born around 1847. Biographical information of Kate Rutledge Gamel, courtesy Norma Karter.

24. *Austin Daily Statesman*, June 5, 1878.

25. Convict Record Ledger, Huntsville penitentiary, TSA. Stedman appears to have been the son of William Stedman and Clara Harvey White. Stedman was the second of five children.

26. John Wesley Hardin to Jane Bowen Hardin, April 13, 1879. Courtesy Chuck Parsons.

27. Convict Record Ledger, Huntsville penitentiary, TSA.

28. *Lampasas Daily Times*, June 12, 1878.

29. *Dodge City Times*, July 27, 1878.

30. Ibid.; *Ford County Globe*, July 30, 1878.

31. *Ford County Globe*, August 27, 1878.

32. *San Antonio Daily Express*, August 10, 1878.

33. Ibid.; *Galveston Daily News*, January 29, 1888; Gary P. Fitterer, "F. Thumm, Der Revolverheld Von Deutschland Part 1," NOLA *Quarterly* 14, no. 3–4, 24.

34. *Burnet Bulletin*, September 11, 1878.

35. *Brenham Weekly Banner*, March 7, 1879.

36. Frederick Nolan, *Bad Blood: The Life and Times of the Horrell Brothers* (Stillwater, OK: Barbed Wire Press, 1994), 150–51.

37. Ibid., 150.

38. *Burnet Bulletin*, April 16, 1879.

39. Ibid.

40. *Austin Daily Statesman*, April 23, 1879.

41. Barler, *Early Days*, 52.

42. *Burnet Bulletin*, June 22, 1882.

43. Ibid.

44. The Carter brothers were sons of Jesse and Mary Sims Carter. Following the Civil War the family moved to Bell County, Texas. The family settled in Llano County around 1872.

45. Benjamin Franklin Carter's death certificate indicates that he was born June 11, 1849, in Kentucky. Ben Carter also served in Company E from October 29, 1877, until February 28, 1878. Parish Sims "Doc" Carter was born in Jackson County, Tennessee, on June 24, 1854. Pay vouchers, Company E, TSA; pension application, B. F. Carter; Texas Ranger Muster Rolls, TSA; Death Certificate, Benjamin Franklin Carter, TSA; Marriage Certificate, B. F. Carter and L. F. Perry, TSA; 1880 Llano County, Texas, Census.

46. Like the Carters, the McNutts were latecomers to Llano County. Census records indicate that the McNutt family arrived in Llano sometime between 1870 and 1880. 1880 Llano County, Texas, Census; Wilburn Oatman, *Llano, Gem of the Hill Country* (Hereford, TX: Pioneer Book Publishers, Inc., 1970), 23.

47. Jackson J. Herridge hailed from Kentucky where he was born on August 12, 1820. Herridge had come to Texas in 1840 and settled in Llano County where he married Susanna Coggin Johnson, sister of the Coggin brothers. Herridge had found himself siding against his brothers-in-law, but the reason appears obvious. Both he and his son, John, born October 11, 1861, worked for the Carters until they had enough money to start their own ranch. Karylon Russell to the author, August 29, 2000; *Llano County History*, 144–45.

48. James Wyatt Perry was born December 8, 1853, to William and Mary Kuykendall. Perry became head of their ranch in 1869 following the death of his father. The Perry family were noted on the 1850 Travis County Census and by 1857 had settled in Llano County. The 1880 Census indicates James Wyatt Perry as the head of the household living with his wife and other family members. Also in the household was William D. Perry, his brother, born March 29, 1859. *Llano County History*, 236–37; 1850 Travis County, Texas, Census; 1880 Llano County, Texas, Census.

49. John R. Coggin was born on August 13, 1832, to James Frank Coggin and Margaret Tate in Alabama. By 1850 the family had moved to Texas, settling in Kaufman County. That year the census noted that Coggin was working as a laborer for James and Sarah Esters. Elsewhere in the county his father James Coggin was living with three of his children. During the Civil War, John Coggin enlisted in Company L, Carter's Regiment of the Twenty-First Texas Cavalry for a period of nine months. Following this service he enlisted in the Texas State Troops, Second Frontier District, under Captain W. B. Pace.

John Coggin is noted in the company serving with the rank of private. 1850 Kaufman County, Texas, Census; Van Zandt County, Texas, Marriage Records; Civil War Pension of John R. Coggin; Military Rolls, Texas State Troops, TSA.

50. Andrew Coggin married Margaret Null, a sister of John's wife Polly Ann, sometime prior to 1860. No record of the marriage date has yet been located.

51. Coggin family data. Courtesy Karylon Russell.

52. Williamson County Marriage Records.

53. Oatman, *Llano,* 35.

54. *Burnet Bulletin,* July 3, 1879.

55. Llano County Commissioner's Court Minutes. Many of the early records from Llano County were destroyed in a courthouse fire.

56. Thomas Jefferson Coggin, son of Andrew J. Coggin and Margaret Null, was born January 16, 1859, in Lampasas County. Early records on Tom Coggin are scarce. In February 1881 he spent some time as a road hand.

57. Henry Hatley was a son of William Ellison Hatley by his first wife. The Hatleys had come to Texas prior to 1870.

58. Both Tom and Andrew Coggin were jailed in Llano County during December, Tom Coggin for three days at a cost of ninety cents. Andrew Coggin spent two days behind bars at a cost of sixty cents. Henry Hatley and his father, William E. Hatley, were also incarcerated in Llano at the same time. Henry spent nine days in jail and William six. Llano County Commissioner's Court Minutes.

59. Barler, *Early Days,* 52–53.

60. *Burnet Bulletin,* June 22, 1882.

61. Ibid.

62. Ibid., June 29, 1882.

63. Yarbrough, *Canyon of the Eagles,* 32.

64. Sonnichsen, *I'll Die Before I'll Run,* 206.

Conclusion

1. Preece, *Lone Star Man,* 57–58.

2. Ibid., 59.

3. Jordan and Jordan, *Jordan Pioneers,* 40.

4. *Mason County News,* January 6, 1893.

5. *Mason County News,* August 21, 1914; Raunick and Schade, *The Kothmanns,* 63.

6. Ibid., 48.

7. *Mason County News,* September 3, 1915.

8. Ibid., September 10, 1915.

9. Ibid., April 25, 1935.

10. *Tombstone Epitaph*, July 22, 1882.

11. *New Southwest and Grant County Herald*, July 22, 1882.

12. *Tombstone Epitaph*, July 22, 1882.

13. Gamel, 31.

14. O'Neil, *They Die,* 136.

15. Convict Record Ledger, Huntsville Penitentiary Records, TSA.

16. Executive Clemency Documents, TSA.

17. Dave Johnson, "George W. Gladden: Hard Luck Warrior," NOLA *Quarterly* 15, no. 3 (September 1991): 1, 3–6.

18. *Arizona Weekly Citizen*, December 13, 1884.

19. *Santa Fe New Mexican*, January 19, 1880.

20. *Daily Yellowstone Journal*, December 15 and 16, 1888.

21. Mrs. Lou Metcalfe to the author, undated letter. Author's files.

22. "A Duel To The Death," *Frontier Times* 10, no. 4 (January 1933): 160.

23. *Austin Statesman*, October 3, 1889. Matthew Caldwell Roberts was the son of Abraham and Cinthia Jeffery Roberts born November 23, 1848, in Caldwell County, Texas. He had married Lenora Beeson, Ben Beeson's sister, in Caldwell County December 13, 1866.

24. Oatman, 48.

25. *San Antonio Express*, July 21, 1893.

24. Ibid., July 22, 1893.

26. *Austin Daily Statesman*, July 24, 1893.

27. Ibid.

28. *San Antonio Express*, July 26, 1893.

29. *Austin Daily Statesman*, July 27, 1893. Turner had been convicted of rape years earlier in Burnet County.

30. Petition to Charles A Culberson, Governor's papers, TSA.

31. Miles Barler to Lee Barler, January 12, 1902. Barler Papers. University of Texas at Austin. The date is probably an error for 1903, quite common immediately following a year change. Scott was charged with murder on December 29, 1902.

32. Llano County District Court Records, Cause 2203.

33. Interview, Foster Casner with the author, October 11, 1982.

Selected Bibliography

Books and Pamphlets

Anonymous. *The Story of a Century: St. Paul Lutheran, Mason, Texas*. Mason, TX: No publisher, 1972.

Anonymous. *The Communities of Mason County*. Mason, TX: Mason County Sesquicentennial Committee, 1986.

Banta, William, and J. W. Caldwell. *Twenty-Seven Years on the Texas Frontier*. Reprint. Council Hill, OK: L. G. Park, No date.

Barler, Miles. *Early Days In Llano*. Llano, TX: The Llano Times, c. 1898.

Bierschwale, Margaret. *History of Mason County Texas Through 1964*. Mason, TX: Mason County Historical Commission, 1998.

Biggers, Don H. *German Pioneers in Texas*. Fredericksburg, TX: Fredericksburg Publishing Co., 1983.

Blevins, Winfred. *Dictionary of the American West*. New York: Facts On File, 1993.

Botkin, B. A., ed. *A Treasury of Western Folklore*. Avenel, NJ: Wings Books, 1975.

Burrows, Jack. *John Ringo—The Gunfighter Who Never Was*. Tucson: University of Arizona Press, 1987.

Dale, Edward Everett. *The Range Cattle Industry*. Norman: University of Oklahoma Press, 1960.

DeArment, Robert K. *Alias Frank Canton*. Norman: University of Oklahoma Press, 1996.

———. *Bravo of the Brazos—John Larn of Fort Griffin, Texas*. Norman: University of Oklahoma Press, 2002.

Debo, Darrell, ed. *Burnet County History*. Volume II. Burnet, TX: Burnet County Commissioners Court, 1979.

DeVos, Julius, ed. *One Hundred Years of the Hilda (Bethel) Methodist Church and Parent Organizations, 1856–1955*. Mason, TX: Hilda United Methodist Church, 1973.

Dobie, J. Frank. *The Longhorns*. Boston: Little, Brown and Company, 1941.

Douglas, C. L. *Famous Texas Feuds*. 1936. Repr. Austin, TX: State House Press, 1988.

Fischer, John. *From the High Plains*. New York: Harper & Row, 1978.

Fisher, O. C. *It Occurred in Kimble*. San Angelo, TX: The Talley Press, 1984.

Franks, J. M. *Seventy Years in Texas*. Gatesville, TX: No publisher, 1924.

Gamel, Thomas W. *The Life of Thomas W. Gamel*. Mason, TX: Privately published, 1932.

———. *The Life of Thomas W. Gamel*. Annotated by Dave Johnson. Mason, TX: Mason County Historical Society, 1994.

———. *The Life of Thomas W. Gamel*. Annotated by Dave Johnson. Second edition. Mason, TX: Mason County Historical Society, 2003.

Geistweidt, Nelson. *Geistweidt Family History*. Doss, TX: Privately published, 1971.

Gillett, James B. *Six Years with the Texas Rangers*. 1925. Reprint, Lincoln: University of Nebraska Press, 1976.

Gillett, James B., and Howard R. Driggs. *The Texas Ranger: A Story of the Southwestern Frontier*. Yonkers-on Hudson, NY: World Book Company, 1927.

Gold, Ella A., trans. *Church Record Book of the Protestant Congregation at Fredericksburg*. Junior Historians, Chapter 21. Fredericksburg, TX: No date.

Goodnight, Charles, and others. *Pioneer Days in the Southwest from 1850 to 1879*. Guthrie, OK: The State Capital Company, 1909.

Hale, Douglas. *The Third Texas Cavalry in the Civil War*. Austin: University of Texas Press, 1993.

Hamilton, Allen Lee. *Sentinel of the Southern Plains*. Fort Worth: Texas Christian University Press, 1988.

Hardin, John Wesley. *The Life of John Wesley Hardin*. Norman: University of Oklahoma Press, 1980.

Harkey, Dee. *Mean As Hell*. Santa Fe, NM: Ancient City Press, 1989.

Holmes, Lucia M. *The Lucia Holmes Diary 1875–1876. The Hoo Doo War Years*. Mason, TX: Mason County Historical Commission, 1985.

Horton, Thomas F. *History of Jack County*. Jacksboro, TX: Gazette Publishing, No date.

Hunter, J. Marvin, ed. *The Trail Drivers of Texas*. 1924. Reprint, Austin: University of Texas Press, 1985.

———. *Doc Middleton*. Chicago: The Swallow Press, 1974.

Hyatt, Marjorie. *Fuel For A Feud*. Smiley, TX: Privately published, 1990.

Johnson, David. *John Ringo*. Stillwater, OK: Barbed Wire Press, 1996.

Jordan, Gilbert J. *A Biographical Sketch of Ernst and Lizette Jordan*. Dallas, TX: Privately published, 1931.

———. *Yesterday in the Texas Hill Country*. College Station: Texas A & M University Press, 1979.

Jordan, Gilbert J., and Terry G. Jordan. *Ernst and Lizette Jordan: German Pioneers in Texas*. Austin, TX: Von Boeckmann–Jones, 1971.

Jordan, Terry G. *German Seed in Texas Soil*. Austin: University of Texas Press, 1985.

Kellogg, M. K. *M. K. Kellogg's Texas Journal 1872*. Edited by Llerena Friend. Austin: University of Texas Press, 1967.

King, Irene Marschall. *John O. Meusebach: German Colonizer in Texas*. Austin: University of Texas Press, 1987.

Kirchberger, Joe H. *The French Revolution: An Eyewitness History*. New York: Facts on File, 1989.

Klasner, Lily. *My Girlhood Among Outlaws*. Tucson: University of Arizona Press, 1972.

Krueger, Max Amadeus Paulus. *Second Fatherland: The Life and Fortunes of a German Immigrant*. College Station: Texas A&M University Press, 1976.

Lehmann, Herman. *Nine Years Among the Indians 1870–1879*. 1927. Reprint, Albuquerque: University of New Mexico Press, 1996.

Lich, Glen E. *The German Texans*. San Antonio: University of Texas Institute of Texas Cultures at San Antonio, 1981.

Linn, John J. *Reminiscences of Fifty Years in Texas*. 1883. Reprint, Austin, TX: State House Press, 1986.

Long, Martha Gilliland, ed. *Llano County Family Album*. Llano, TX: Llano County Historical Society, 1989.

Maltby, William J. *Captain Jeff or Frontier Life In Texas With The Texas Rangers*. Waco, TX: Texian Press, 1967.

Mason County Historical Commission, comp. *Mason County Historical Book*. Supplements I, II, III, and IV. Mason, TX: Mason County Historical Commission and Mason County Historical Society, 1978, 1986, 1994, 1999, 2003.

McCoy, Joseph G. *Historic Sketches of the Cattle Trade of the West and Southwest*. Kansas City, MO: Ramsey, Millett & Hudson, 1874.

Meed, Douglas V. *Texas Wanderlust*. College Station: Texas A&M University Press, 1997.

Metz, Leon. *John Wesley Hardin: Dark Angel of Texas*. El Paso, TX: Mangan Books, 1996.

Meusebach, John O. *Answer to Interrogatories in Case No. 396, Mary C. Paschal et al. vs Theodore Evans*, District Court of McCulloch County, TX, 1894; reprint, Austin: Pemberton Press, 1964.

Miller, Rick. *Bloody Bill Longley*. Wolfe City, TX: Hennington Publishing Company, 1996.

Nolan, Federick. *Bad Blood: The Life and Times of the Horrell Brothers*. Stillwater, OK: Barbed Wire Press, 1994.

Oatman, Wilburn. *Llano, Gem of the Hill Country*. Hereford, TX: Pioneer Book Publishers, 1970.

Olney, James H. *A Genealogy of the Descendants of Thomas Olney*. Providence, RI: E. L. Freeman & Son, 1889.

O'Neil, James B. *They Die But Once*. New York: Knight Publications, 1935.

Paddock, B. B. *History and Biographical Record of North and West Texas*. Chicago: Lewis Publishing Co., 1906.

Parsons, Chuck. *"Pidge": A Texas Ranger From Virginia*. Wolfe City, TX: Hennington, 1985.

Parsons, Chuck, and Marianne E. Hall Little. *Captain L. H. McNelly–Texas Ranger*, Austin, TX: State House Press, 2001.

Perry, C. R. *Memoir of Capt'n C. R. Perry of Johnson City, Texas—A Texas Veteran*. Edited by Kenneth Kesselus. Austin, TX: Jenkins Publishing Company, 1990.

Pickering, David, and Judy Falls. *Brush Men and Vigilantes: Civil War Dissent in Texas*. College Station: Texas A & M University Press, 2004.

Ponder, Jerry. *Fort Mason, Texas: Training Ground For Generals*. Mason, TX: Ponder Books, 1997.

Preece, Harold. *Lone Star Man: Ira Aten, Last of the Old Texas Rangers*. New York: Hastings House Publishers, 1960.

Ramsdell, Charles William. *Reconstruction in Texas*. Austin: University of Texas Press, 1970.

Rasch, Phillip J. *Warriors of Lincoln County*. Stillwater, OK: The National Association for Outlaw and Lawman History, Inc., 1998.

Raunick, Selma Metzenthin, and Margaret Schade. *The Kothmanns of Texas 1845–1931*. Austin, TX: Von Boeckmann-Jones Company, 1931.

Ringo, Mary. *The Journal of Mrs. Mary Ringo*. Santa Ana, CA: Privately printed, 1956.

Roberts, Dan W. *Rangers and Sovereignty*. San Antonio, TX: Wood Printing & Engraving Co., 1914.

Rose, Peter R., and Elizabeth E. Sherry, eds. *The Hoo Doo War: Portraits Of A Lawless Time*. Mason, TX: Mason County Historical Commission, 2003.

Simpson, Harold B., and others. *Frontier Forts Of Texas*. Waco, TX: Texian Press, 1966.

Smith, David Paul. *Frontier Defense in the Civil War*. College Station: Texas A&M University Press, 1992.

Smithwick, Noah. *The Evolution of a State*. Austin, TX: Stack-Vaughn Company, 1968.

Sonnichsen, C. L. *I'll Die Before I'll Run*. Lincoln: University of Nebraska Press, 1988.

———. *Ten Texas Feuds*. Albuquerque: University of New Mexico Press, 1971.

Steele, William, Adjutant General. *A List of Fugitives from Justice, 1878*. Reprint, Austin: State House Press, 1997.

Stephens, Robert W. *Bullets And Buckshot In Texas*. Dallas, TX: Privately published, 2002.

———. *Mannen Clements: Texas Gunfighter*. Dallas, TX: Privately published, 1996.

Tise, Sammy. *Texas County Sheriffs*. Albuquerque, NM: Oakwood Printing, 1989.

Twitchell, Ralph Emerson, ed. *The Leading Facts of New Mexican History*. Vol. 3. Cedar Rapids, IA: The Torch Press, 1917.

Wilbarger, J. W. *Indian Depredations In Texas*. 1889. Reprint, Austin, TX: Eakin Press and State House Books, 1985.

Williams, R. H. *With The Border Ruffians*. 1907. Reprint, Lincoln: University of Nebraska Press, 1982.

Williams, R. H. and John W. Sansom. *The Massacre on the Nueces River*. Grand Prairie, TX: Frontier Times Publishing House, No date.

Yarbrough, C. L. *Canyon of the Eagles*. No date or place.

Zesch, Scott. *The Captured*. New York: St. Martin's Press, 2004.

Articles

"Builders of Menard." *Frontier Times* 4, no. 11 (August 1927): 3.

"Burnet County Pioneers." *Frontier Times* 3, no. 3 (December 1925): 1–2.

"A Duel To The Death." *Frontier Times* 10, no. 4 (January 1933): 160.

"Major David Doole." *Frontier Times* 2, no. 1 (October 1924): 10.

"Ranger of the Sixties." *Frontier Times* 1, no. 1 (October 1923): 27.

"Was a Survivor of the Nueces Battle." *Frontier Times* 2, no. 1 (October 1924): 24–30.

Biesele, Rudolph Leopold. "The First German Settlement in Texas." *Southwestern Historical Quarterly* 34 (April 1930–July 1931): 334–39.

———. "The Relations between the German Settlers and the Indians in Texas, 1844–1860." *Southwestern Historical Quarterly* 21 (July 1927–April 1928): 116–29.

Blumberg, Carl. "The True Effectiveness of The Mainz Society for Emigration to Texas As Described in a Letter of November 3, 1846." Edited by A. E. Skinner. *Texana* 7, no. 4 (1969).

Burrows, Jack. "John Ringo—The Story of a Western Myth." *Montana* (October 1980): 2–15.

Cross, Cora Melton. "Ira Long, Cowboy and Texas Ranger." *Frontier Times* 8, no. 1 (October 1930): 22–31.

DeMattos, Jack. "Johnny Ringo." *Real West* (April 1985): 35–42, 51.

———"Johnny Ringo! The Elusive Man Behind the Myth." NOLA *Quarterly* 3, no. 2 (1977): 1-5, 10.

Dielmann, Henry B. "Emma Altgelt's Sketches of Life in Texas." *Southwestern Historical Quarterly* 63 (July 1959–April 1960): 363–84.

Elkins, S. P. "Served as a Texas Ranger." *Frontier Times* 5, no. 11 (August 1928): 438–39.

Elliott, Claude. "Union Sentiment in Texas, 1861–1865." *Southwestern Historical Quarterly* 50 (July 1946–April 1947): 449–77.

Erath, George Bernard. "Memoirs of Major George Bernard Erath." Edited by Lucy Erath. *Southwestern Historical Quarterly* 26 (July 1922–April 1923): 207–33.

Fitterer, Gary P. "F. Thumm Der Revolver Von Deutschland Part 1." NOLA *Quarterly* 14, no. 3–4 (1990): 23–26.

———"F. Thumm Der Revolver Von Deutschland Part 2." NOLA *Quarterly* 15, no. 1 (1991): 25–29.

———"F. Thumm Der Revolver Von Deutschland Part 3." NOLA *Quarterly* 15, no. 2 (1991): 16–21.

——— "F. Thumm Der Revolver Von Deutschland Part 4." NOLA *Quarterly* 15, no. 3 (1991): 8–11.

Hatley, Allen G. "The Mason County War: Top Texas Feud." *Wild West* (August 2005): 24–30.

Huff, Era Fay. "Ringo Genealogy." *True West* (July 1988): 6

Hunter, J. Marvin. "Brief History of the Early Days in Mason County Part 1." *Frontier Times* 6, no. 2 (November 1928): 65–78.

———. "Brief History of the Early Days in Mason County Part 2." *Frontier Times* 6, no. 3 (December 1928): 113–34.

———. "Brief History of the Early Days in Mason County Part 3." *Frontier Times* 6, no. 4 (January 1929): 153–166.

———. "Brief History of the Early Days in Mason County Part 4." *Frontier Times* 6, no. 5 (February 1929): 185–91.

———. "Brief History of the Early Days in Mason County Part 5." *Frontier Times* 6, no. 6 (March 1929): 225–29.

Jackson, Jeff. "Victim of Circumstance: Albertus Sweet Sheriff of Lampasas County, Texas, 1874–1878." NOLA *Quarterly* (July–September 1996): 20; 3, 14–21.

Johnson, Dave. "Daniel Hoerster and the Mason County War." NOLA *Quarterly* 9, no. 3 (Winter 1985): 15–18.

———. "The Doell Killing: Feudal Vengeance or Private Murder?" NOLA *Quarterly* 11, no. 1 (Summer 1986): 8–10.

———. "G. W. Gladden: Hard Luck Warrior." NOLA *Quarterly* 15, no. 3 (July–September 1991): 1, 3–6.

———. "Revenge in Mason County, Texas." NOLA *Quarterly* 10, no. 1 (Summer 1985): 7–8, 12.

Lich, Glen Ernest. "Balthasar Lich, German Rancher in the Texas Hills." *Texana* 12 (1974): 101–23.

McAlavy, Don. "The Mysterious Death of John Faris." *The Outlaw Gazette* 11, no. 1 (November 1998).

Minatre, Odie. "Sole Survivor of Packsaddle Mountain Fight." *Frontier Times* 15, no. 5 (February 1938): 197–98.

Olmsted, Frederick Law. "A Journey Through Texas in 1856." *Frontier Times* 13, no. 9 (June 1936).

Reeves, George. "The Scalping of Matilda Friend." *Frontier Times* 5, no. 2 (November 1927): 49–52.

Snider, Clarence. "Frontier Days at Camp San Saba." *Frontier Times* 13, no. 6 (May 1936): 380–82.

Thorpe, John. "Ben and Billy Thompson: Their Documented Origins." *The Brand Book* (of the English Westerners' Society) 23, no. 1 (Winter 1984): 9–10.

Newspapers

ARIZONA
    Arizona Weekly Citizen
    Tombstone Daily Epitaph
    Tombstone Weekly Epitaph
KANSAS
    Dodge City Times
    Ford County Globe
MISSOURI
    Liberty Tribune
MONTANA
    Daily Yellowstone Journal
NEW MEXICO
    New Southwest and Grant County Herald
    Santa Fe New Mexican
NEW YORK
    New York Times
TEXAS
    Austin American Statesman
    Austin Daily Democratic Statesman
    Austin Daily Statesman
    Austin State Journal
    Austin Weekly State Gazette

Austin Weekly Statesman
Austin Tri-Weekly State Gazette
Brady Standard and Heart O' Texas News
Brenham Banner
Burnet Bulletin
Clarksville Northern Standard
Dallas Herald
Galveston Flake's Semi-Weekly Bulletin
Galveston Christian Advocate
Galveston Daily Civilian
Galveston Daily News
Galveston Weekly News
Houston Daily Telegraph
Jacksboro Frontier Echo
Lampasas Daily Times
Lampasas Dispatch
Marshall Texas Republican
Mason County News
Semi-Weekly Farm News
San Antonio Daily Express
San Antonio Daily Herald
Texas Capital
Travis County Texas State Gazette
Weekly Austin Republican
West Texas Free Press

Archives Records

Texas State Archives:

"Attorney's Business Book—Henry M. Holmes." Bierschwale Collection.

Confederate Army Muster Rolls.

Confederate Army. Military Record of John T. Olney.

Confederate Army. Military Record of Samuel Olney.

Confederate Army. Military Record of A. G. Roberts.

Confederate Army. Military Record of C. B. Taylor.

Confederate Army. Military Record of David Taylor.

Confederate Army. Military Record of Israel Taylor.

Confederate Army. Military Record of James W. Taylor.

John T. Olney, Soldier's Application for Pension, Number 40122.

Governor's records: R. B. Hubbard.

Governor's records: E. M. Pease.

Governor's records: Richard M. Coke.

Governor's records: Charles A Culberson.

State Docket, District Court, Book.

Texas Election Register 1854–1861.

Texas Supreme Court Decision Book.

Bounty Warrant 298 for service from October 27, 1835, to January 22, 1836, dated June 29, 1847; Donation Warrant No. 81 for the 5–9 December 1835 storming of Bexar, TX, Bounty 221, Title Volume 2, Original Land Grant Collection.

"Certificate of J. C. Neill re: Lewis Johnson," September 30, 1837. Audited Military Claims (Republic), Lewis Johnson folio.

Character Certificate for James Johnson, TX General Land Office.

J. B. Collins to B. M. Jacobs, July 17, 1880. University of Arizona Special Collections, Tucson, AZ.

"Commissioner Charles A. Taylor's Orders for Survey," 1835.

B. F. Carter, Soldier's Application for Pension, Number 14124.

Andrew J. Coggin, Soldier's Application for Pension, Number 21695.

John R. Coggin, Soldier's Application for Pension, Number 100802.

B. Collins to B. F. Jacobs, July 17, 1880, University of Arizona Special Collections.

C. L. Sonnichsen Collection. University of Texas at El Paso.

U. S. Army. Military Record of John Anton Wohrle. National Archives.

U. S. War Department. *The War of the Rebellion: A Compilation of the Official Records of the Union and Confederate Armies*. 128 volumes., Washington, D. C., 1880–1901. These are noted throughout the footnotes as *War of the Rebellion* plus series and volume.

"Weekly return of Col. John H. Moore's Regiment of Texas Volunteers for the week ending Wednesday 21st October 1835." Austin Papers, Series IV.

Widow's Application for Pension, Number 21999, Elizabeth Williamson.

Legal Sources

Convict Record Ledger, Huntsville Penitentiary Records. Texas State Archives.

Executive Clemency Records. Texas State Archives.

Burleson County, TX
    Deed Records
    Poll Tax Records

Burnet County, TX
    Deed Records
    District Court Records
    Marriage Records

Claiborne Parish, Louisiana
        Conversion Records
Gillespie County, TX
        District Court Records
        Marriage Records
        Poll Tax Records
Kerr County, TX
        District Court Records
Llano County, TX
        Commissioner's Records
        District Court Records
        Marriage Records
        Poll Tax Records
Madison County, Missouri
        Marriage Records
Mason County, TX
        Civil Action Records
        District Court Records
        Poll Tax Records
        Records of Marks District Court Records and Brands
Mecklenburg County, North Carolina
        Marriage Bonds
San Augustine County, TX
        Deed Records
San Saba County, TX
        Poll Tax Records
Travis County, TX
        Marriage Records
        Poll Tax Records
Van Zandt County, TX
        Marriage Records
Williamson County, TX
        Marriage Records
First Texas Census, 1835–1836, Sabine District.
Reports on the Condition of the Texas State Penitentiary, For the Year 1873–1874. Houston, TX: A. C. Gray, State Printer, 1874.
Reports on the Condition of the Texas State Penitentiary, For the Years 1874-5-6. Houston, TX: A. C. Gray, State Printer, 1876.

Unpublished Material
Baccus family information, courtesy Karylon Russell.

Baccus family information, courtesy Janet Baccus.

Baccus family information, courtesy Goldie Seay.

Barler papers. University of Texas at Austin, Barker Texas History Center.

Church Records of Flint Hill Baptist Church, 1792–1882. Transcribed by Joyce Little Graham. Author's files.

Diary of Travel by John Preston Thomas. Courtesy Don Watson.

Eilers, Kathryn Burford. "A History of Mason County, TX." Master's Thesis, University of Texas at Austin, 1939.

Clarence Grier to "Dear Relative," February 16, 1918. Author's files.

Haynes, Sophie Olney, unpublished manuscript. Copy in author's collection.

Hotel register of the Grand Central, Ellsworth, Kansas. Microfilm copy.

Lacy, John Hancock narrator, "Life of John Hancock Lacy," unpublished manuscript courtesy Helen C. Marschall.

Moss, James R. "James R. Moss." Unpublished manuscript, courtesy Llano County Historical Society. Copy in author's files.

Rose, Peter, "The Hoo-Doo War." Unpublished manucript. Copy in author's collection.

Schulze, H. O. "Book Report on 'Branded' From the German History 'Gebrandmarkt.'" Mason County Historical Commission.

Ringo, Mary Enna correspondence. Author's files.

San Jose City Directory 1871–1872. Author's files.

Statement of Emigrants from Bremen per Brig *Geronne*.

Trail log of M. L. Hayes, ca. 1873–1875. Mason County Historical Commission.

Interviews, Letters, Research Notes

In compiling this work a number of interviews and significant correspondence has taken place. Those of particular help include, but are not limited to, Bob Alexander, Francis Blake, Vickie Bonner, Joyce Capps, Bob Cash, Foster Casner, Tommy Clark, Ina Davis, Joan Buck de Korte, Julius DeVos, Thomas and Susan Doell, Marvin Doyal, R. L. Faith, H. V. "Todd" Faris, Paralee (Mrs. J. C.) Foster, Jo Ann F. Hatch, Allen G. Hatley, Betty Marglon Henning, Jane Hoerster, Era Fay Huff, Norma Karter, Mrs. Beatrice Langehennig, Nina Legge, Sarah Lockwood, Milton McWilliams, Mrs. Lou Metcalfe, Nina Olney, Jerry Ponder, Michael Redding, David Leer Ringo, Pete Rose, Karylon "Bitsy" Russell, Goldie Seay, George Mack Taff, LaVoy Taylor, Don Watson and Iru Zeller. A special thanks is due to the guru of researchers, Donaly E. Brice.

Rick Miller Archival Collection.

Chuck Parsons Archival Collection.

Johnie Lee Reeves Archival Collection.

Pete Rose Archival Collection.

Karylon Russell Archival Collection.

United States Census

Alabama
> Cherokee County: 1840, 1850
> Tallapoosa County: 1850

Arkansas
> Izard County: 1850

California
> Santa Clara: 1870

Indiana
> Wayne County: 1850

Kansas
> Territorial Census of 1855

Kentucky
> Graves County: 1850

Louisiana
> Bienville Parish: 1850
> Claiborne Parish: 1850
> Natchitoches Parish: 1840, 1850
> Sabine Parish: 1850

Mississippi
> Yalobusha County: 1840

Missouri
> Davies County: 1860
> Madison County 1850
> Polk County: 1840

North Carolina
> Mecklenburg County: 1850
> > 1850 Slave Schedule.

Texas
> Burleson County: 1850, 1860
> Burnet County: 1860, 1870, 1880
> Llano County: 1860, 1870
> Gillespie County: 1850, 1860
> Hopkins County: 1860
> Jack County: 1860
> > 1870 Mortality Schedule
> Kaufman County: 1850
> Kerr County: 1870
> Llano County 1860, 1870, 1880
> Mason County: 1860, 1870
> Rusk County, 1850

San Saba County, 1870
Travis County: 1850, 1860
Walker County: 1880
Williamson County: 1850

Index

A

Abilene, Kansas, 19
Ackse, Charles, 28
Adelsverein, 2, 9, 11, 254 n. 4, 257
   n. 27
Akard, Carl, 110
Ake, Bill, 22–23, 129–130, 160,
   167, 196, 209
Ake, Jeff, 22–23, 67, 129–30, 160,
   162–63, 167, 196, 209, 235,
   291 n. 27
Alazan (correspondent), 117, 134,
   139–40
Alzada, Montana, 236
Allen, Hugh, 106
Allen, J. M., 12
Allison, Bill, 203
Allison, McGrue, 199
Apaches, 25
Arnett, George C., 44, 270 n. 43
Aten, Ira, 232
Austin, Texas, 1, 8, 14, 190, 192–
   93, 196, 210–11, 220
Austin, William, 236
Austria, 7

B

Baccus, Benjamin, 52–53
Baccus, Charles, 52
Baccus, Elijah, 52–57, 59, 66–67,
   125, 275 n. 47
Baccus, Joseph, 52
Baccus, Josie (Bigelow), 52, 60–61
Baccus, L. P. "Pete," 52–56, 59,
   66–67, 125, 275 n. 47
Baccus, Louisa, 53, 272 n. 10
Baccus, Lucinda (Brown), 52
Baccus, Rachel (Cook), 52
Baccus, Roxanne (Stovall), 52
Bader, Carl, 26, 28, 46, 95–96, 98,
   101–3, 169
Bader, Katherine. *See* Hoerster,
   Katherine
Bader, Gottfried, 10–11, 167, 257
   n. 24
Bader, Peter Heinrich, 5, 26, 28–
   29, 46, 74, 95, 99, 111, 124;
   death of, 146–50, 169, 191,
   220, 295 n. 18
Bailey, D. W. H., 81
Baird, Alf, 54, 66, 68, 70
Baird, Areminthy "Lucy" (Eaton),
   105–6
Baird, Edna, 106, 149
Baird, Hartshorn, 105, 384 n. 4
Baird, James A., 46, 54, 102, 109,
   121, 127, 137, 153, 272 n. 58
Baird, John R., 39, 41–43, 45, 95,
   101–3, 105–6, 117, 119, 122,
   125–29, 139–40, 143, 145–49,
   151–52, 155, 157, 160–61,
   163, 165, 167–69, 172, 177,

180, 190, 193–94, 200, 209, 218, 222, 234–35, 270 n. 48, 284 n. 8, 13, 293 n. 10; marries Nannie Robison 106, 108; kills Daniel Hoerster, 111–13
Baird, Laura. *See* Olney, Laura
Baird, Mary (Marietta), 105–6
Baird, Moses B., 5, 29, 39, 45, 95–96, 98–101, 103–6, 108, 128, 146, 238, 283 n. 37, 283–84 n. 3, 284 n.13, 287 n. 25
Baird, Nannie (Robison), marries John Baird, 106
Baird, William, 105
Bandera County, Texas, 110
Bannister, John, 221
Bannister, Will, 221
Bannister, W. L., 203
Banta, William, 14, 259 n. 50
Barler, Lee, 239
Barler, Miles, 34, 154, 176–79, 184, 212–13, 215–16, 218, 228–30, 239, 295 n. 18
Bartholomew, G. W., 135
Bass, Sam, 21
Bastrop County, Texas, 202
Bauer, Johann Melchoir, 11, 41, 46, 268–69 n. 25
Baxter, Robert, 20
Beam, Ike, 116
Beard, Crusoe, 218
Beeson, Benjamin Franklin, 172, 179, 212–13, 215–16, 236–37, 286 n. 23
Behrens, Heinrich Julius, 10
Bell, Bill, 22
Berry, John B., 76
Berry, Silas, 160, 167
Bexar County, Texas, 193
Biberstein, Herman R., 12,14, 147
Billy the Kid, 208
Bird, George, 19, 56
Blackburn, W. A., 186, 192, 201–2, 209

Blanco County, Texas, 163–64, 202–3
Blaylock, ----, 11
Blevins, Andy, 22
Blevins, Hamp, 22
Blevins, Martin J., 22, 264 n. 21
Blue Mountains (Mason County), 49
Bluff Creek, 59
Blumberg, Carl, 8
Bolt, Allen, 56, 64, 78
Bolt, Benjamin Franklin, 134
Bolt, John Moses, 13, 259 n. 47
Bolt, Martin J., 106, 385 n. 15
Bolt, William James, 11, 13
Boren, Henry, 53, 272 n. 10
Bosque County, Texas, 203
Bourland, James G., 79
Boyce, Ruben Hornsby, 21, 219, 262–63 n. 20
Bozarth, John J., 179, 180–81, 184, 189–91, 195, 212, 215, 227
Bozarth, Joseph T., 181, 193, 225
Bradberry, James, 25
Bradford, Adam, 56
Brady Creek, 54
Breazeale, Clint, 184
Bridges, J. D., 25
Bridges, M. V.   , 30
Bridges, S. F. "Lace," 19, 110
Bridges, Mrs. S. F., 110
Brite, John, 56
Brite, Tom, 95
Brown County, Texas, 39, 107, 203, 208
Brown, Ed, 209, 218, 222, 225
Brownwood, Texas, 205–7, 209–11
Burgdorf, L., 12
Burleson, John, 199
Burleson County, Texas, 105, 129, 152–54, 203
Burnet, Texas, 67, 102, 108, 112,

131, 143, 145–46, 150–51,
161, 170, 181, 185, 189–90,
192, 204, 217
Burnet County, Texas, x, 2, 15,
23, 30, 39, 41–42, 45, 47, 97,
100–2, 105–8, 140–41, 143–
44, 157, 168, 172, 175, 179,
182, 203, 207, 209, 211, 220,
222–23, 239
Burk, Black, 199, 204
Burk, Frank, 199
Burton, Felix, 198–99
Burts, -----, 171–72
Bybee, Bill, 160, 167
Byfield, James, 238

C

Cain, Joel Y., 172
Cain, Neal, 171–72, 185, 188, 227
Cain, Philadelphis, 172
Cain, Sugar M., 34, 266–67, n. 5
Caldwell, -----, 207, 218
Calvert, John W., 107, 155, 287
n. 24
Camp Chase, Ohio, 30
Campbell, G. W., 254 n. 10
Carson, John C. "Jack," 102, 151,
161–62, 190, 209, 296 n. 42
Carter, Benjamin Franklin, 221,
228, 230–31, 304 n. 44, 45
Carter, Parish Sims "Doc," 228,
231, 304 n. 44, 45
Casey, Mrs. ----, 14
Casner, E. V. "Pete," 204, 218
Cathey, Luke, 221
Castell, Texas, 40, 73, 110
cattle trade, 2, 18–20, 33–36,
70–71, 75, 103–4, 261 n. 12,
262 n. 15, 281 n.44
Caveness, Ed, 11
Caveness, James N., 67–68
Caveness, Jasper "Jap," 67–68
Caveness, Robert "Bob," 11, 58,
67–68, 276 n. 12

Caveness, Jerry, 11
Cavin, A. H., 39, 107
Cavin, B., 223
Cavin, Byron Hamilton "Ham,"
106–7, 151, 285 n. 16
Cavin, John Edward "Ed," 107,
147–48, 151, 161, 175, 176,
209, 236, 284 n. 9, 285 n. 17,
285–86 n. 19
Cavin, L. Wiley, 39, 45
Cavin, Nathan, 151, 385 n. 17
Cavin, Rusk, 107
Cavin, William Thomas, 107, 172,
204, 236, 284 n. 9, 285 n. 17,
285–86 n. 19
Centennial Springs, 115
Chapman, Joe, 80
Cheyney, Jim, 98, 110, 126, 146,
175
Cheyney, Mrs., 127
Civil War, ix, 2–3, 14–15, 1 –18,
22, 24, 26, 30, 65, 153
Clark, Dave, 54
Clark, Isaiah, 29
Clark, John E. (sheriff), 4–5, 17,
40–41, 43, 45–46, 48, 50,
53–54, 56, 58–62, 65–66,
69–72, 76, 83–84, 89, 94, 108,
112–13, 115, 121–23, 125, 131,
137, 146, 149, 153, 171, 180,
199; controversial election of
as sheriff, 29–32; orchestrates
ambush of Moses Baird and
George Gladden, 96–104;
terrorizes Loyal Valley with mob
119–20; death of, 237, 272 n.
75
Clark, John Rufus, 29–30, 265 n.
64
Clark, Mary E. (Worley), 30
Clark, Sarah E. (Low), 30
Clark, Will, 176, 236
Clark, William   , 30
Clements, Bill, 208

Clements, Mannen, 208, 301 n. 8
Clymer, John, 143–44
Coalson, Nick, 55
Cochise County, Arizona, 107, 234
Coggin, Andrew, 228–29, 305 n.
    49
Coggin, John R. "Jack," 229, 305
    n. 50, 58
Coggin, John Robinson, 229–30
Coggin, Tom, 229, 231, 305 n. 56,
    58
Coke, Bill, 113–16, 122, 134, 139,
    290 n. 53
Coke, Richard (governor), 3, 31,
    37, 75, 84, 94, 97, 99, 108–9,
    123–25, 254 n. 10
Cold Springs. *See* Loyal Valley
Coldwell, Neal, 129, 138, 202,
    204, 210
Coleman County, Texas, 205–8
Collier, Jim, 226
Collin County, Texas, 52
Collins, J. F., 214
Collins, William, 203
Colorado River, 106
Columbus, Ohio, 30
Columbus, Texas, 112
Comal County, Texas, 134
Comanche, Texas, 168, 178
Comanche County, Texas, 222
Comanches (Nauni), 13, 49, 81,
    129
Comanche Creek, 110
Comancheros, 25
Connor, Jim, 229
Conway, Lou. *See* Roberts, Lou
Cook, -----, 210
Cook, John, 229
Cook, William, 139
Cooley, Frank, 79
Cooley, James, 79, 81
Cooley, John, 79
Cooley, Martha, 79
Cooley, Mathias, 79, 81, 279 n. 6

Cooley, Thomas, 79
Cooley, William, 79
Cooley, William Scott, 5, 101–3,
    110–11, 113, 117, 125–31, 134–
    35, 137–38, 142–46, 148–52,
    157–58, 172, 194, 209–11,
    217, 223, 226, 279 n. 19, 20;
    early life of, 79–84; kills Johann
    Wohrle and Carl Bader, 91–97;
    death of, 160–67
Corn, Lee, 81
Covington, S. W., 108
Cowan, Gid, 24
Cox, William S. "Uncle Billy," 11,
    257 n. 29
Cox, Thomas, 13
Crews, Justice -----, 189
Crosby, Chris, 54

D

Dancer, Jonas Franklin, 13, 259
    n. 45
Dannheim, Ernst, 10–11
Davis, E. J. (governor), 15
Davis, J. W., 156, 160, 176, 179,
    184–86, 195
Davis, W. H., 202
Day, James P., 121, 125
Deal, Bill, 199
Deaton, James, 203–4
DeLong, Bill, 177
Denman, M. J., 204
Denson, Shadrick T., 157
Denton County, Texas, 52
Devil's River, 129
Devine, Thomas S., 31
DeWitt County, Texas, x, 137, 140,
    156, 204, 207
Dodge City, Kansas, 224
Doell, Heinrich (Henry) Sr., 46,
    84–89, 95, 140, 28 –81 n. 40
Doell, Henry Jr., 20, 23, 28, 58,
    74, 87, 116
Dolan, Pat, 200, 202

Doniphan, Missouri, 122
Donop, Otto, 11, 13, 101, 225
Donop, Wilhelmina, 225
Doran, Thomas, 199
Doran, W. R., 212
Dorbrandt, Chris, 239
Doole, David, 14, 40–42, 44–48,
    54, 69, 94, 110, 152, 156–57,
    268 n. 24
Doyal, Matthew, 11, 258 n. 32
"Dreux" (correspondent), 16–17,
    61–62, 100
Dublin, Dell, 40, 177, 199, 204,
    219–20, 295 n. 19
Dublin, James, 154
Dublin, James Roland "Rol," 40,
    177, 203–4, 219, 295 n. 19
Dublin, Richard "Dick," 40, 154,
    177, 199, 204, 219, 221, 295
    n. 19
Durham, Paul, 121, 125
Durst, Johann Bernhardt, 46, 271
    n. 50
Durst, Johann Georg, 46, 271 n. 53
Durst, Jacob Johann, 46, 270–71
    n. 49
"Dutch," slang for German, 2–3,
    12, 49, 112, 121, 123–24, 126,
    129, 148, 153, 3 n. 5

E

Earp, Wyatt, 224, 234
Eastwood, Frank, 22, 263 n. 27
Eckert, Rudolph, 19
Edmunds, Charles, 204
Edwards County, Texas, 55
Edwards, George, 81
Edwards Plateau, 23
El Paso Salt War, 19
Elkins, Samuel P., 46, 80
Ellis County, Texas, 203
Ellsworth, Kansas, 28, 81
Enoch (or Enox), Frank, 188,
    195–96

Epley, David, 15, 260 n. 56
Erath, George Bernard, 12, 69
Erwin, Alex, 189–90
Erwin, Ben, 186–87, 222, 298–99
    n. 13
ethnic intolerance, 2, 12, 115, 117
ethnic purity, 3, 12
Eubank, H. T., 212
Evans, Sam, 196
Everett, I. N., 66

F

Faris, Benjamin A., 288 n. 27
Faris, Champion N. "Champ,"
    160, 209, 236, 288 n. 27
Faris, John B., 160, 236, 288 n. 27
Faris, Robert Elihu "Bud," 110,
    157, 160, 162, 193, 209, 236,
    288 n. 27
Faris, William Jasper, 102, 160,
    236, 288 n. 27
Faught, Thomas Jefferson, 172,
    270 n. 48, 297 n. 26
Fayette County, Texas, 203
Felps, "Wid," 165
Ferguson, Charles, 161–62,
feud legacy, 3–4
feud psychology, 2–3
Finney, James J., 16–17, 30–31
Fisher, ----- (attorney for George
    Gladden), 192
Fisher, H. F., 254 n. 5
Fisher, King, 211
Fisher-Miller Grant, 8, 10–11, 254
    n. 5
Fisher, Dr. C. E., 135–38
Fleming, T. R., 207
Foley, -----, 92, 171
Ford, -----, 206
Fort Concho, Texas, 49
Fort Martin Scott, Texas, 10
Fort Mason, Texas, 11, 14, 24, 28,
    59, 73, 158, 257 n. 26
Fort Sill, Oklahoma, 80

Fort Sumner, New Mexico, 236
Fort Union, New Mexico, 19
Foster, Blue, 127–28
Frandzen, Eugene, 15
Fredericksburg, Texas, 10, 26, 41, 46, 59, 99, 111, 133, 139, 147, 164, 169, 194, 213

G

Gamel, Alfred Hunter, 87–88, 204
Gamel, George, 221, 303 n. 23
Gamel, John William, 14, 19, 25, 46, 5 –59, 61, 66, 74, 91, 114, 116, 137, 275 n. 53
Gamel, Thomas Wiley, 14, 22, 53–58, 60, 62–63, 67–70, 72, 74, 78, 85, 88, 91–92, 98, 102, 110, 113, 115–16, 126, 131, 133, 137, 164, 235
Gamel, William, 11, 14, 86, 258 n. 31
Gardner, G. L., 44
Gardner, Joe, 44
Gardner, Mike, 218
Gentry, William, 204
George, Dave, 218
Germans, xi, 2 – 4, 7–8, 11–12, 15, 26, 49, 61, 65, 69–70, 100, 103, 108, 111, 115, 117, 131, 134, 139, 232, 234, 253 n. 5
Germany, 7–9, 5–51
Gibson, John, 158
Gilliam, William, 161, 221
Gillespie County, Texas, 14, 22, 26, 49, 94, 110, 129, 188, 203, 205
Gillespie, Tom, 221
Gillett, James B., 74, 81–82, 95, 121, 154, 177, 221
Gilmore, Joseph, 203
Gladden, George W., 5, 44, 95– 103, 108, 117, 122, 125–26, 129–30, 143–48, 151–52, 157, 162, 170, 180, 184, 211, 220– 21, 235–36, 269–70 n. 40, 270

n. 42, 299 n. 31; ambushes Daniel Hoerster, 112–13; trial of, 188–94
Glass, W. A., 81
Gonzales County, Texas, x, 204
Gooch, Benjamin F., 16, 33, 155–56
Gooden, W., 151
Goodlow, John, 204
Gordon, Joseph, 195
Gorman, John, 202
Graham family, 22
Graves, James, 203
Graves County, Kentucky, 56
Gray, Frank, 167
Great Hanging at Gainesville, 80
Grenwelge, August, 28
Griffin,Richard, 203
Grote, F. A., 35

H

Hall, Caleb, 40, 55–58, 60, 65–66, 154, 188, 194, 196, 199, 204, 209, 214, 218, 220
Hall, Caleb Sr. , 56
Hall, H. H., 170
Hall, Jack, 203
Hall, Lucy, 56
Hall, Lee, 6, 236
Hamilton, B. K., 44
Hamilton, B. P., 44
Hamilton, J. H., 204
Hamilton County, Texas, 203
Hanson, A. F., 44
Harcourt, Charles "Doc," 91–94, 282 n. 3
Hardin, John Wesley, 207–8, 223, 253 n. 4
Harkey, Dee, 21
Harper, George, 203
Harris, Charles, 170
Harris County, Texas, 57
Harwell, R. L., 230
Hatley, Henry, 229–30, 304 n. 57

Haup, Jack, 204
Hayes, M. L., 39
Haynie, James A., 127
Hedwig's Hill, 98, 102, 110–12
Hensley, -----, 203
Herridge, Jack, 228–30, 304 n. 47
Herridge, John, 228
Hester, Daniel, 21, 35, 267 n. 11
Hey, Wilson, 15, 37–38, 41–42,
    50, 68, 70, 101, 125–26, 153,
    267–68 n. 16
Higgins, Pink, 197
Hill Country, 1, 4, 13–15, 21, 23,
    25, 57, 139, 177, 184, 194,
    200–1, 228, 232
Hasse, Heinrich, 11
Haynie, William, 175
Hoerster, Anton, 54, 97, 115
Hoerster, Daniel, 13–14, 17–19,
    21, 30, 33–35, 37, 43–44,
    46, 56, 67, 70, 96, 98, 103,
    110, 126, 129, 132, 146, 262
    n. 14; as bondsman for Tim
    Williamson 72; killed 113–17
Hoerster, Frederick "Fritz," 14
Hoerster, Johann Heinrich, 10–11,
    13, 17, 26, 28, 34–35, 58, 152,
    169, 233, 256 n. 17
Hoerster, Katherine, 28
Hoerster, Wilhelm, 13–14, 19, 259
    n. 44
Hofmann, Otto Ernest, 104
Hofmann, Karl, 114
Hofmann, Wilhelm, 104, 114
Holland, -----, 152
Holland, Rufus, 156
Holly, John, 222
Holmes, Henry M., 52–54, 56, 59,
    65–66, 68, 74–75, 78–79, 86,
    94, 98–100, 105, 108, 110, 121,
    124, 141, 159, 162, 171, 201
Holmes, Lucia, 54, 56, 58–59,
    65, 68–71, 74, 76, 85, 91–92,
    99, 114–15, 121, 131, 133–34,
    138, 162, 171
Holton, Newberry H., 44
Honey Creek, 49
Hoo Doos, 62, 65, 67, 69, 71, 75,
    83, 95–96, 101, 103, 108, 119,
    124, 126–28, 140, 143, 147,
    153–54, 156, 165, 177, 180;
    derivation of term, 5–6
Hoo Doo War, 1, 19, 23, 25, 29,
    33, 45, 51, 74, 76, 82, 84, 107,
    154, 165, 199, 228, 231
Hopkins, Mark, 110
Horner, George, 168, 296 n. 10
Horner, Joe, 168, 296 n. 10
Horrell, Merritt, 197
Horrell-Higgins Feud, 157, 197
Horton, Joe, 81
Hoskins, William P., 162, 177, 179
House Mountain, 140
Howard, R. R., 193
Howard, Ulysses, 15, 260 n. 56
Hoy, George Riddle, 211, 224–25
Hoy, Henry, 194, 211–16, 239
Hoy, James K., 66–67
Hubbard, Richard B., 196, 207
Hughes, John, 228, 230–31
Hunnicutt, -----, 204
Hunter, James M., 14–15, 149
Hunter, Laura, 114

I

Indians, ix, 2, 15, 24, 33, 49–51,
    75–76, 84–86, 89, 130,
    170, 205. See also Apaches,
    Comanches, Kiowa
Ischar, Johann Georg, 116
Iwonski, Rudolph, 10
Izard County, Arkansas, 79

J

Jack County, Texas, 79–80
Jacksboro, Texas, 55
Jackson, James, 238
Johnson, Adam R., 30

Johnson, Betsy, 16
Johnson, Charles W., 53–55, 59,
    62–63, 65, 75, 77, 95–96, 110,
    125, 133–34, 274 n. 15
Johnson, Deputy -----, 150
Johnson, Francis "Frank," 16, 260
    n. 57
Johnson, G. H.   , 220
Johnson, J. B., 200
Johnson, James, 22
Johnson, Nat, 216
Johnson, R. M., 204
Johnson, Thomas J., 15, 260 n. 56
Johnson, Thomas G. "Babe," 14
Johnson, Wes, 62–63, 110, 141,
    219, 303 n. 8
Johnson County War (Wyoming),
    21
Jones, Isaac, 11
Jones, John B., 40, 46–47, 55, 75,
    81–82, 84, 86, 89, 96, 108,
    111–12, 115, 117, 120–22,
    124–27, 129, 131, 142, 146,
    158, 184–85, 197–202, 204–5,
    208, 217, 220, 226, 254 n. 10,
    268 n. 23
Jones, Will, 176
Jordan, Ernst, 9, 11–14, 19, 26,
    42, 46, 150, 169, 232–33,
    254–55 n. 7
Jordan, Johanne E., 9–10, 255 n. 7
Jordan, Peter, 113, 116
Jorndan, Wihelmine, 9, 14
Junction, Texas, 219, 201–2

K

Karl of Solms-Braunfels, 3, 8
Karlshafn, 8–10, 29
Karnes County Uprising, 21
Kaufmann County, Texas, 202–3
Keller, Adam, 16
Keller, August, 84–86
Keller, Carl, 99
Keller, Johann, 10

Keller, Johann Adam, 10
Keller, Karl, 19
Kelly, John, 66, 155, 194, 276 n. 9
Kendall County, Texas, 22
Kennedy, Gus, 208
Kerr County, Texas, 22, 28, 86
Kerrville, Texas, 22, 138. 202
Kettner, Franz, 14, 16–17, 260–61
    n. 59
Keyser, H. F., 13
Kidd, John, 140
Kidd, Matilda Jane (Stone), 139
Kidd, William, 139
Kidd, William Siree, 139
Kimble County, Texas, 67, 110,
    140–41, 167, 169, 197–99,
    201–2, 204–5, 219
Kinney County, Texas, 57
King, -----, 57
King, John, 219
Kinser, Nannie Moore   , 82
Kiowas, 13, 76
Klasner, Lily, 14
Koock, Wilhelm, 113
Koockville, Texas, 58, 113
Kothmann, Caroline, 9
Kothmann, Dietrich, 10, 14, 19,
    26–27, 46, 233
Kothmann, Friedrich "Fritz," 10,
    13, 19, 26–27, 46, 86, 124,
    233
Kothmann, Heinrich Conrad,
    9–11, 13, 15, 19, 256 n. 15
Kothmann, Karl, 19, 28
Kothmann, Wilhelm, 26–27, 46,
    96–97, 233
Kountz, Dr. -----, 202
Krueger, Max, 12, 26, 111,
Ku Klux Klan, 6
Kuchuck, Hannchen, 9
Kuchuck, Johann Heinrich, 9
Kuchuck, Johanne, 9
Kuhn, L., 101

L

Lacy, Jake, 176
Lamar County, Texas, 52, 203
Lampasas, Texas, 160, 163, 189, 201, 205, 209, 223, 226
Lampasas County, Texas, 39, 107, 110, 157, 180, 201, 216, 222, 226, 228–29, 231, 236–38
Lancaster, Porter, 153
Landrum, Professor R. A., 180
Lang, A. L., 11
Lange, Otto, 19, 35
Lankford, Ace, 154
Latham, George, 222
Lavacca County, Texas, 202–3
law and order faction. *See* mob, Hoo Doos
Lee-Peacock Feud, 53
Legion Valley Massacre, 16
Lehmann, Hermann, 25
Lehmberg, Fritz, 19
Lehmberg, Julius, 11
Lehmberg, Karl, 14, 19–20, 29, 33–34, 44, 72–73, 83, 267 n. 8, 277 n. 39, 277–78 n. 40
Leifeste, August Heinrich, 46, 271 n. 54
Leifeste, August Heinrich Sr., 46, 271 n. 55
Leifeste, August Heinrich Jr., 46, 271 n. 56
Leifeste, Christoph, 11
Leifeste, Fritz, 11
Lemberg, Ernest, 58, 275 n. 41
Leslie, Jesse, 153, 155, 169, 212
Leverett, Henry, 171
Leverett, Joseph, 168–69, 171, 176, 190, 201
Lewis, W. C., 13
Liemering, A., 16
Liggett, J. B., 151
Ligon, Dave, 221
Lincoln, Abraham (president), 14
Lincoln County War, 1, 40, 253 n. 2

Lindsay, Al, 86
Lindsay, John, 54, 58, 85–86, 271 n. 42
Llano, Texas, 51, 156, 161, 172, 185, 187, 190, 192, 212–13, 216, 220, 231–32,
Llano County, Texas, xi, 1–2, 5, 11, 13, 16, 21–23, 26, 29, 33–35, 38–43, 45, 50–53, 62, 64, 66, 73, 83, 97, 100, 102, 105–7, 123, 127–29, 139, 147–48, 150, 15 –54, 156–57, 160, 162, 167–69, 171–72, 177, 179, 180, 182, 184, 187–88, 193–95, 197, 203, 207, 209, 211–13, 215–16, 220, 226, 228–29, 231, 236–38
Llano River, 57, 71, 87, 99, 129, 141, 156, 199, 201–2
Lockhart, W. P., 16
Lone Grove, Texas, 229
Long, Ira, 124, 130–32, 137–38, 142, 145, 148, 150, 152–53, 156, 158, 291–92 n. 33
Longley, Bill, 22–23, 212
Loyal Valley, Texas, 71–72, 98, 101, 111–12, 129, 139, 163–64; raided by mob 119–20

M

Mackay, A. S., 223
Mackey, James, 222
Mackey, Jiles "Nat," 186, 222
Maddox, Dan, 164–65
Madison County, Texas, 141
Magill, John, 45
Makemson, -----(attorney for George Gladden), 192
Marschall, Hans, 96
Marschall, Wilhelm, 147
Martin, James, 181
Martin, John, 53–54, 59, 63, 77, 275 n. 47

Martin, Ludwig "Louis," 15, 259–60 n. 51
Martin, Nancy, 53
Martin, Samuel, 172–74, 182–83
Martin, Judge W. W., 135–36
Martin, William W., 53
Mason, Texas, x–xi, 5, 14–15, 19, 24–26, 41–42, 44, 49, 54, 59–60, 65, 70–72, 75–77, 91–92, 98, 109–10, 112–16, 120–22, 125, 127, 131, 134–35, 137, 140, 142, 146, 152, 158, 162, 201. *See also* Fort Mason
Mason County Disturbances, 5
Mason County, Texas, x, 1–2, 5, 11–12, 14–15, 19–23, 25–27, 32–25, 38–44, 49–51, 56–57, 62, 64, 68–69, 71, 75–77, 84, 89, 94, 96, 100–3, 107–8, 110, 119–22, 124, 126–28, 131–32, 134–37, 139, 140, 144–45, 147–50, 151, 156–60, 165, 167, 169–71, 179–80, 184, 188, 194–95, 203, 205, 207, 211–12, 218, 225, 231–33, 236–37
Mason, Barney, 236
Mason, James P. (Baird partisan, confused with James Polk Mason), 141–42, 161–62, 209, 218, 222, 293 n. 35, 36
Mason, James Polk (killer of Rance Moore), 140–42, 293 n. 34
Masterson, James, 224
Matagorda Bay, 8
Matthews, J. C., 42
McCarty, Dr. T. L., 224
McCoy, Joseph G., 19–20
McCulloch County, Texas, 54, 190, 196–97, 204, 212–13, 215, 232
McDonald, -----, 142
McFadden, W. A., 204
McFarland, J. G., 173
William B., 106, 384–85 n. 14

McGehee, Thomas, 157
McGrew, J. C., 203
McInnis, R. A., 179, 229–30
McKiever, John B., 199, 204
McMahon, W. F., 219
McMickle, C., 204
McNelly, Leander H., 1, 57, 138–39, 181, 253 n. 3
McSween, John, 12
Meckel, Mrs. Conrad, 46, 271–72 n. 57
Medina County, Texas, 48, 169, 272 n. 67
Menard County, Texas, 56, 67, 82, 112, 203, 218, 225
Menardville (Menard), Texas, 57, 122, 134
Meusebach, John O., 3, 8, 10, 12–14, 71, 101, 119–20, 139, 255 n. 7
Mexican bandits, ix, 2, 49, 51, 75,
Mexican War, 9
Middleton, Doc. *See* Riley, James M.
Miller, Burchard, 254 n. 5
Miller, J. P., 116, 126, 133–34
Miller, Joseph, 91, 97, 282 n. 27
Miller, Naomi Cox, 53
Miller, Nimrod J., 22, 44
Milligan, Thomas, 13, 27
mob, xi, 2, 9, 26, 40, 46, 48, 62–65, 83–84, 94, 103, 119–21, 124, 127–28, 149, 154, 160, 177, 194, 211, 220, 264–65 n. 49, 272 n. 60. *See also* Hoo Doos
Monroe, Sam, 110, 203
Moore, F. M., 198, 202, 204
Moore, George, 81
Moore, Rance, 24, 86, 140–43, 219, 281 n. 43
Morris, Henry W., 46
Morrison, -----, 32
Moseley, John P., 120
Moses, Norton, 175

Moss, James R., 291 n. 25
Matthew Jr., 127–28
Matthew, Steve, 127
Murchison, Andes Henry, 110, 162, 169, 209, 217, 289 n. 33
Murchison, William K., 34, 217
Murray, Newton H., 66, 276 n. 6
Murray, Thomas, 25

N

Nassau Farm, 8
Nevill, C. L., 204
New Orleans, Louisiana, 19
Nicholls, F. T. (governor of Louisiana), 196
Nueces River Massacre, 15
New Braunfels, Texas, 9–10
NOMAD (correspondent), 131
Nueces River, 129

O

Oatman, Wilburn, 191
O'Brien, William G., 38
Oestrich, Christian, 46, 52, 97, 272 n. 59
Oestrich, Friedrich, 35, 267 n. 8
Ogle, Dean Swift, 170, 175, 181–82
Olkers family, 9
Olney, Daniel S., 189–90, 236
Olney, Edward T., 236
Olney, George A., 236
Olney, John T., 34–35, 102, 151, 187, 236, 267 n. 9, 10, 286 n. 20
Olney, Joseph G., 34–35, 131, 140, 160–62, 173–75, 178, 182–84, 186, 190, 193–94, 196, 206–8, 218, 235, 267 n. 9, 301 n. 4
Olney, Laura Ann (Baird), 103; marries Samuel Y. Olney, 106–7
Olney, Oscar R., 236
Olney, Samuel Tanner, 103

Olney, Samuel Young, 103, 140, 186, 236, 286 n. 20; marries Laura Baird 106–7
Olney, William W., 110, 190, 193, 236
Orsay, Henry, 126
Otho (correspondent), 84–86

P

Palestine, Texas, 188
Palo Pinto County, Texas, 80, 203
Payne, Amanda Melvena, 45
Parker, Cynthia Ann, 22
Parker, L. J., 44
Patton, A. L., 213
Peacock, Lewis, 53
Peak, June, 208
Peck, Fred, 150
Pennell, John, 170
Perkins, Louisiana H., 228
Perry, Cicero Rufus, 46, 49–50, 81, 126, 272 n. 72, 279–80 n. 21
Perry, James, 228, 304–5 n. 48
Perry, William, 228
Perry, Wyatt
Perryman, -----, 126
"Peter" (correspondent), 30–31, 80, 135
Peters, Stephen, 13
Phillips, T. O., 239
Pingenot, Celeste, 195
Pluenneke, Conrad, 10–11, 19
Pluenneke, Heinrich "Henry," 96, 113
Potter, Frank, 203
Potter, James, 202–3
Potter, Mack, 219
Prussia, 7
Pryor, Ike, 34
Pulliam farm (battle), 30
Putman, Madison, 120

Q

Quihi, Texas, 48, 272 n. 67

R

Rainbolt, Peter Allen, 34, 266 n. 4
Ranck, James E., 15, 153
Randall, Bill, 169–70
Randle, James Newton, 161
Reconstruction, ix, 15–17, 33, 68
Redding, Bill, 168
Redding, John, 168
Redding, Sam, 218
Redding, Thomas S., 34, 160,
    169, 206, 236, 301 n. 4
Redding, William Z., 34, 38–39,
    45, 160, 168–69, 175, 178,
    190, 196, 206, 218, 236, 267
    n. 15, 296 n. 10, 301 n. 4
Reichenau, Adolph, 111, 116, 289
    n 37
Reugner, John, 114
Reynolds, J. J. (general), 27
Reynolds, J. M., 199, 204
Reynolds, N. O., 50, 70, 12 –21,
    125, 204, 210, 217, 221
Riley, James M., 21, 262 n. 17
Ringo, John Peters "Long John," x,
    11, 95–96, 102, 107, 129, 137,
    143–46, 151–52, 157, 160–64,
    167–70, 171–72, 175, 180,
    184, 188–89, 191, 193–95,
    199, 209–11, 217, 220, 222–
    23, 234, 253 n. 5, 286–87, n.
    21; kills Jim Cheyney 110
Rio Grande River, ix, 14, 153
Rios, Ramon, 25
Ripley County, Missouri, 30, 122,
    237
Roberts, A. G., 33, 37–46, 48,
    50–52, 56, 64, 68, 94–95, 97,
    101, 107, 126, 130, 154, 172,
    176, 195, 203, 236, 269 n. 48,
    286 n. 20
Roberts, Alexander "Buck," 65
Roberts, Daniel Webster, 30, 51,
    55, 58–59, 64–66, 68, 70–71,
    75–78, 89, 96, 112, 116, 120,

122, 125, 130–31, 134, 139
Roberts, Dick, 67, 70
Roberts, Kate, 39
Roberts, Lou (Conway), 112–13
Roberts, Louisa, 38
Roberts, M. C., 236–37, 306 n. 23
Roberts, William, 39
Robinson, Sgt. -----, 189
Robison, Nannie. *See* Baird, Nannie
Rossberg, Wilhelmina, 29
Rowley, Columbus, 204
Rowntree, Felix S., 183, 298 n. 5
Rowntree, Robert F. "Bob," 176,
    179, 188–89, 212, 237–39
Rowntree, Wilson Baxter, 172–75,
    182–83
Ruff, J. , 203

S

Sampson, E., 67
San Antonio, Texas, 15
Sanders, A., 203
San Antonio, Texas, 218
San Saba County, Texas, 30, 33,
    39, 107, 127, 129, 167, 180,
    197, 201, 203–4, 211–12,
    215–16, 231
San Saba County War, 5
San Saba River, 49
Saunders, George W., 18
Schmidt, Friedrich, 46, 52, 271
    n. 52
Scott, A. K., 214–16, 239–40, 306
    n. 31
Scott, Charles Pinkney, 216
Scott, Mary Elizabeth (Owens),
    216
Scott, Susannah R., 216
Scott, Vanty, 92
Scott, Whale, 239
Sewell, James, 25
Sharer, S. M., 44
Sharp, Henry, 140
Shelbourne, Dr. -----, 57

Shelburn, -----, 49

Shuks, David, 31

Simmons, -----   ,145

Sims, W. H., 172, 297 n. 25

Smart, John, 170

Smith, C. C., 19, 30

Smith, Marion, 24

Sneed, Berry, 170

Sneed, Bob, 170, 217

Sparks, John, 185, 188, 192, 196–
  97, 201, 205, 218

Sparks, T. M., 214, 218

Stedman, Ed, 222–23, 303 n. 25

Steele, William (adjutant general),
  75–76, 84, 108, 122, 124, 130,
  132, 139, 146, 158. 196, 204,
  207, 210

Stevens, G. W., 81

Stewart, Ben, 54, 97

Stewart, Eb, 187–88

Stewart, F. C., 67, 106

Streeter, Texas   , 280 n. 36

Stokes, Henry, 150

Stone, R. G., 120

Stoudenmire, Dallas, 229

Stoudenmire, Samuel, 229–30

Stricker, Rev. Johann G., 139

Strickland, J. J., 143–45, 152, 168,
  170, 175, 181, 185–86, 188,
  217, 222, 293 n 41

Sutton-Taylor War, x, 1, 24, 207,
  253 n. 4, 300–1 n. 2

Sweeney, Booker, 96–97, 113

Sweeney, Mariah, 97

Sweet, Albertus, 157, 160

T

Table Mountain, 129

Tanner, Allen Young, 102, 131, 151

Tanner, John Allen, 287 n. 25

Tanner, Sam, 102, 131, 151

Taylor, Abraham T., 35, 45, 102,
  140, 151, 169–70, 186, 196,
  204, 288 n. 26

Taylor, Ann A. (Olney), 288 n. 26

Taylor, Bill, 212

Taylor, Creed, 23–24, 87, 263–64
  n. 34, 264 n. 35

Taylor, Francis W., 212–15, 302
  n. 30

Taylor, James, 212–13

Taylor, John Hays, 24, 264 n. 35

Taylor, Phillip DuBois "Doboy," 24,
  264 n. 35

Tewksbury family, 22

Texas Rangers, 6, 40, 49–50,
  65–66, 70, 79–81, 94, 111–12,
  120–21, 125, 128–29, 137–39,
  146, 187, 189, 193–94, 196,
  199–202, 204, 207, 213, 231–
  32, 236, 254 n. 10

Theis, Hermann, 88

Thomas, Christine "Lea," 6

Thomas, James, 45

Thomas, Jim (alias James Pouton),
  202

Thomas, John Preston, 45, 270 n.
  45

Thomas, Marshal B. "Brack," 4,
  15, 44, 48, 50, 107, 140, 203,
  236, 260 n. 56

Thomas, Oliver, 45

Thompson, Bill, 187–88

Thompson, John A. (major), 24

Thompson, Mary Ann (Baker), 188

Thompson, William, 188

Thumm, Fritz, 29, 225, 265 n. 63

Todd, George W., 12, 14–15, 17,
  31, 42, 54, 64, 142–43, 152,
  171, 258 n. 42

Tooley, T., 80

Torrey brothers, 9

Trainer, James Martin, 50, 58, 76,
  273 n. 78

Travis County, Texas, 14–45, 168–
  69, 210

Trayweek, William Burrell, 82, 280
  n. 25

Trent, Dan, 212
Tucker, R. K., 169
Turley, Tom, 53, 55, 59, 63, 65–66, 274 n. 13

U

Upper Willow (*Oberwillow*) Creek. *See* Willow Creek
Uvalde County, Texas, 202

V

Valois, Gustave, 49
Van Winkle, William, 217
Vasterling, Henry, 88
Villareal, E., 54
Villareal, Eusrbio, 54

W

Waddell, H. B., 199
Wadsworth, Walter, 212–13, 216, 301–2 n. 22
Wages, William, 64, 155
Wagman, Tom (alias for Bill Redding), 168
Waldrop, -----, 207
Walker, A. S., 31
Walker, J. T., 161, 296 n. 42
Walker County, Texas, 141
Wallace, Lew (governor), 208
Walton, John, 202
Walton, Lou, 203–4
Wayne County, Kentucky, 45
Weatherby, B. T., 13
Weeks, William, 193
West, F. J., 44
Wheeler, William, 19
White, Ham, 212
Whitney, Chauncey Belden, 188
Whittington, T. W., 151
Wiggins, Abe, 53, 55, 59, 61
Wilkes, Frank, 178
Williams, C. A., 79
Williams, James, 34, 102, 126–27, 146, 175–77, 203, 297 n. 34; kills Jim Cheyney(?), 110
Williamson County, Texas, 22, 169, 229
Williamson, Frederick, 44
Williamson, Mary (Johnson), 72
Williamson, Timothy P., 4, 14, 29, 32, 44, 53, , 73, 75, 78, 84–87, 91, 94–95, 101, 111, 121, 128, 165, 172, 269 n. 39, 270 n. 42, 277 n. 31, 279 n. 19, 281 n. 27; trouble with Clark over taxes, 71–72; murder of, 80–82
Wilmore, Joseph, 203
Wills, Bill, 161–62
Willis, D. S., 75
Willow Creek, 11, 13, 27, 46, 73–74, 110, 225
Wilmore, Joseph, 203
Winkel, Christel, 19
Winn, Rufus, 67, 276 n. 10
Wittington, T. W., 294 n. 10
Wohlberg, Theodore, 225
Wohrle, Helena, 58, 62; infant, 62, 71
Wohrle, Johann Anton; 30, 46, 54, 58–59, 68, 78, 83, 91–95, 97, 145, 277 n. 38; role in Tim Williamson murder, 72–76
Wolf, Matt, 220
Woodie, William, 215–16
Woods, Joe, 158
World War I, 4
World War II, 2
Wyatt, -----, 223–24

Z

Zesch, Leo, 46, 271 n. 51
Zesch, Robert, 101